Popular Education and

Democratic Thought

in America

Popular Education and Democratic Thought in America

BY RUSH WELTER

COLUMBIA UNIVERSITY PRESS

New York and London

for Matilda

Preface

LOOKING back on a completed manuscript, every scholar must be conscious of two things: the imperfections that continue to haunt it in spite of all that he could do to overcome them, and the assistance of friends and colleagues, scholars and editors, who have made the book immeasurably stronger than it would have been without their active encouragement and advice. Customarily he thanks these invisible collaborators for their assistance while absolving them of responsibility for his errors. So too do I; but the time-honored formula is inadequate to express my sense of their contributions to this study.

My interest in American attitudes toward education stems from a doctoral dissertation in the History of American Civilization, which I completed at Harvard University in 1951. I was fortunate both in my field of concentration, which permitted me to undertake a cross-disciplinary thesis, and in my advisers, who encouraged me to persevere in it as well as challenged me to improve it. They were Louis Hartz and John M. Gaus, and they have been as generous with their help since the dissertation was completed as they were beforehand.

I have also been fortunate in my friends and colleagues since leaving graduate school. Harry W. Pearson has read and criticized my study in several different versions; both as scholar and as friend he has made the necessity of drafting successive versions easier to live with. Louis P. Carini has also been of great help in that same task. Although not a specialist in any of the fields of scholarship the book draws on he has been an indispensable adviser and ally. My students—especially Patricia Fitzsimmons (now Mrs. Louis Carini)—have also contributed much to the final formulation of my ideas. Their genuine interest in the problem I have posed and their willingness to dispute points of interpretation with me have more than made up for their relative inexperience as scholars. At different times I have also benefited from the kindly but not uncritical advice of William R. Taylor, William C. Fels, and Henry S. Kariel, who have read parts of different versions of the manuscript.

In addition, I am most grateful for the extensive criticisms that scholarly readers and editors leveled against my manuscript in its earlier stages. Some must remain anonymous, but I am pleased to be able to acknowledge the help given me (in order of their appearance) by Charles Frankel, Earl Latham, Richard Hofstadter, and D. Angus Cameron. Now that the work their criticisms made necessary has been accomplished I realize that it was indispensable to whatever success the book may find.

I have incurred a number of other debts I can hardly repay but may at least acknowledge here. I am beholden to the Huber Foundation of Rumson, New Jersey; to Frederick H. Burkhardt and William C. Fels, presidents of Bennington College; and to the Faculty Facilities Fund of Bennington College, donated by the Class of 1936, for grants in aid of research and typing. Clearly, I am indebted to every library I have ever used, and especially to the several libraries of Harvard University, the New York State Library in Albany, the library of the Astor, Lenox & Tilden Foundations in New York City, the Williams College Library, and the Bennington College Library. Although not a research library, the last-named has been exceedingly generous in answering to my needs as a scholar, as has Bennington College as a whole in providing the necessary conditions of scholarship. Nor am I likely to forget the assistance of Mrs. Alice Miller, who has typed my manuscript with loving care and a constant interest in its progress, and of my colleague Lionel Nowak, who has proofread the galleys with great skill.

I also wish to acknowledge the courtesy of The Macmillan Company in granting me permission to quote from *The Promise of American Life* and *Progressive Democracy*, by Herbert Croly, and from *A Preface to Politics*, by Walter Lippmann, and of the Public Affairs Press in granting me permission to quote from *The Deflation of American Ideals*, by Edgar Kemler.

Finally, I can only suggest my abiding gratitude to Matilda Walsh Welter, who too often comes last but is never least, and who has shared fully in every stage of the writing of this work. She has allowed its emergencies to dominate her life; she has patiently assumed the burden of correcting its deficiencies; and she has constantly offered encouragement and technical advice under the most trying circumstances. She has been, in short, a scholar's wife, and she more than deserves to be recognized in the dedication of this book.

Bennington, Vermont   RUSH WELTER
July 4, 1962

Contents

Popular Education and

Democratic Thought

in America

Introduction

IN order to understand the American people one must understand their belief in education. This volume is intended to contribute something toward that understanding. It is an analysis, not of the American commitment to education in its entirety—a task that would stagger the imagination of anyone even superficially familiar with American thought—but of the idea of education in its essentially political applications and functions. Here, indeed, is a sufficiently demanding problem. American democratic theory has often been identical with a theory of education, and even where the Americans have not reduced their theory of politics wholly to educational terms they have blended the two areas of social thought so closely as to make it impossible to understand our political thinking without also understanding its educational elements and assumptions. This volume, then, focuses on the political aspects of the American belief in education.

The topic constitutes both a necessary and a difficult inquiry. Although we have accumulated a good deal of factual information about American educational institutions, and although a few able scholars (chief among them Merle Curti) have explored the social context and significance of our institutional developments, no one has done more than suggest in a rather tentative way the extent to which the idea of education has become one of the major terms in our social thought. One reason, presumably, is the difficulties inherent in proof: there is no easy way to demonstrate that our belief in education has had significant noneducational implications. Yet we hardly need to be reminded that the belief itself has been an extraordinarily powerful American value, nor that Americans have led the world in putting democratic educational ideals into practice. Given such hints we may suppose that the idea of education has been an important practical principle, a functioning part of our democratic theory, and we may pursue its ramifications with an unusual confidence that we perceive thereby a fundamental commitment of the American civilization.

Here, at least, is the working assumption behind the writing of this book. The method of analysis corresponds to my definition of the problem. In order both to clarify the origins of our belief in education and to emphasize the remarkable loyalty different groups gave to it even while disagreeing over the practical issues of their times, I have chosen to trace the evolution of the idea in terms of representative schools of political and social theory, grouping American thinkers substantially as they grouped themselves. Focusing on group rather than individual doctrines, I have also deliberately restricted my evidence to public statements, subordinating personal communications and biographical information so as to avoid the temptation of following out the innermost thoughts and private motives of individual writers at the expense of losing sight of the main trends of more nearly common opinion.

On the other hand, in addition to analyzing overt statements of the idea of education in our political thought, I have also sought to delineate the indirect role it has played in defining the major concerns and techniques of that thought. Perhaps I have found only what I looked for, but I think that its influence is undeniable, and a large part of the book is concerned with seeing successive generations of political commentators in the context of an established American belief in education. In every case the guiding purpose has been to understand more fully the dynamic interrelationships between two of the most characteristic American political commitments, popular rule and public education.

Approaching the belief in education in these terms frees us from commonly accepted misconceptions of its place in American life. Some of our scholars have thought of education primarily as a political invention of conservatives, intended to discipline a democratic people who might grow unruly in the absence of elaborate political authority. Others have linked it mainly to the hope for personal success, and so made it almost exclusively an economic instrument. Hence a few commentators have identified our schools as a calculated conservative sop to popular discontent, intended to misdirect public attention away from basic social issues. While all of these interpretations have some merit as an explanation of the proliferation of our educational institutions, they miss a more basic truth: American democratic thought has very largely visualized the possibilities of popular education irrespective of special interests and transcending special circumstances. It has insisted upon the enlightenment of the people for expansive rather than restrictive reasons.

This is not to say that the American commitment to education has undergone no significant shifts in meaning, or that it has served no distinctive purposes. The principle of universal education at public expense that evolved during the early nineteenth century embraced both political and economic values, which subsequent generations have emphasized in varying proportions to suit varying needs—most of which we may well describe as conservative so long as we know how broadly we use the term. But it is also necessary to understand the commitment as an idea, not only because it has continued to be powerful apart from the motives that originally called it into being, but also because in accounting for any commitment in terms of its putative origins we may well miss its ultimate practical significance. Scholars have gone too far in recent years in treating ideas as the passive accomplices of personal and group interest, whereas it should be clear that an established doctrine or belief may influence cognition itself by defining the terms in which successive generations understand themselves and their problems. It is time, at least so far as the idea of education is concerned, to recognize how powerfully it has affected our social and political judgments as well as reflected our urgent practical needs.

We find, I think, that a belief in popular education has been the archetypal element in our political thinking. For nearly one hundred years after the Jacksonian upheaval, American democratic theorists both systematic and occasional described our society and our politics in terms of the controlling power and effectiveness of popular education. In the first place, they thought of it as a primary instrument of social order and social organization, the means by which overarching social values and social responsibilities would be enforced; they opted for what I describe in Part Two of this volume as anarchy with a schoolmaster. At the same time, they treated popular education as the one sure cure for contemporary social and political evils. Hence, without fully recognizing the larger implications of their commitment, they substituted theories of education for theories of society based upon class order and theories of politics based upon class struggle, and developed the characteristic patterns of American political belief in virtual indifference to the social and political assumptions that shaped most of European political thinking.

Moreover, the basic commitment to popular education was common to almost the whole range of American political thought. Jacksonian democrats originally put the ideal forward during the course of their attempt to dislodge the "aristocratic" residue of early republican institutions; liberal and radical reformers after the Civil War constantly returned to it as the basic element in their politics; the progressive movement made forms of education its primary instrument of reform. But Whigs as well as Democrats adopted education as the vehicle of their liberal hopes; critics as well as supporters of postbellum reform treated it as the preeminent technique of social improvement; even the "higher conservatives" who repudiated progressivism typically offered no more drastic challenges to progressive educational innovations than a literal constitutionalism that depended in the final analysis on formal education. It is not too much to suggest that until the First World War, with rare exceptions, only disgruntled reactionaries quarreled with the Americans' wholehearted commitment to expanding the education of the people. These dissidents included old-guard Federalists who questioned the very idea of public schooling, proslavery theorists to whom universal intelligence was an obvious travesty of the order of nature, right-wing opponents of progressivism who denied that the people could ever learn to be right—all of whom were discredited and ignored as thoroughly as any alien critics of American attitudes. For most Americans it was enough to look to education both to preserve social stability and to secure as-yet unachieved ends.

Not only did the Americans call upon common schools to serve their political ends; they also broadened their original concept of universal education to meet new social and political problems. On the one hand, each generation witnessed a concerted attempt to improve and extend our formal educational institutions; American history is in large measure the history of the expanding education of the people. On the other hand, the idea of "education" understood as a means for achieving democratic ends through the schools evolved into a quite different concept of achieving such ends through informal popular agitation or through innovations in the structure of government to make the processes of politics educate public opinion more effectively. Americans almost universally believed in the promise of a universally enlightened electorate, which they proposed to create by every means that came to hand.

In general, the dividing line between the literal and the more extended application of education to American politics was the Civil War. Before it, education primarily connoted formal training for citizenship and economic independence, which the schools alone might guarantee, although Americans also counted upon the services of press and pulpit, lyceum and library, to continue the process of education. After the war the belief in formal education continued to flourish, but the more important innovations in our theory of politics and society took place elsewhere, in the elaboration of political techniques intended to secure better-informed deliberation of public issues and more effective popular rule. After 1865, indeed, Americans almost universally believed that the success of their democratic experiment depended upon elaborating the informal educational mechanisms of the antebellum period. Understood in these terms, their original belief in popular education as the bulwark of democracy remained not only a paramount American value but also the fundamental perspective with which they approached their politics and their society.

Yet that broad educational commitment has proved vulnerable to twentieth-century hazards. During the progressive era, our belief in education continued to shape our definitions of public issues in such a fashion as to restrict the scope of our political inquiries. During the years since the First World War, however, and especially since the Great Depression, Americans have learned to question educational beliefs they once took for granted. In particular the political education of the people has come to seem a visionary purpose, and because it has been so much a part of our democratic theory, its disappearance threatens democratic theory itself. Nevertheless, the weakening of our faith in political education has been accompanied by a strengthening of our commitment to practical careerist training, which comes more and more to shape our definitions of democracy. As a result, although we have virtually conceded the failure of democratic political education to serve its intended purposes, we have been dissuaded by the strength of our commitment to practical education from recognizing the political impasse we have reached.

In all probability this outcome was implicit in our democratic theory of education from the beginning. Hence this study leads to two disparate conclusions. On the one hand it documents a faith most Americans held and built upon between the Jacksonian revolution and the First World War, a faith that sometimes weakened their political judgment by representing both formal and informal education as sufficient instruments for dealing with pressing social problems. On the other hand it suggests that as the American faith in political education weakens it also threatens our theory of democracy. Both conclusions indicate, however, that our faith in education has been and remains our most characteristic political belief.

Part One

EARLY PRECEDENTS AND

POLICIES

WHEREAS sundry laws and statutes by act of Parliament established, have with great wisdom ordained, for the better education of youth in honest and profitable trades and manufactures, as also to avoid sloth and idleness wherewith such young children are easily corrupted, as also for relief of such parents whose poverty extends not to give them breeding, that the justices of the peace should, at their discretion, bind out children to tradesmen or husbandmen to be brought up in some good and lawful calling.

Virginia Assembly, 1646

THE Court looking upon it as their great duty to establish some course that (through the blessing of God) learning may be promoted in the jurisdiction as a means for the fitting of instruments for public service in church and commonwealth, did order that £40 a year shall be paid by the treasurer for the furtherance of a grammar school for the use of the inhabitants of this jurisdiction.

New Haven General Court, 1659

1. Colonial Precedents for

Democratic Education

THE American ideology that revolves around democratic education was not born with the thirteen colonies. Two centuries were to pass before the democratic educational ideal became a commonplace of American social thought, and decades more before the ideal was put into common practice. Therefore, although Americans tend to believe that their contemporary educational establishment is an accumulation of over three hundred years' experience—an extension, let us say, of the Massachusetts school law of 1647—it is more accurate and also more fruitful to consider colonial institutions as a kind of preamble to democratic innovations.

Indeed, the purposes and practices of colonial education stand historically as a kind of false start from which it was necessary to turn away before education could become a key principle of the American democratic faith. So long as the political, economic, and social assumptions of colonial times governed men's minds there would be little room in them for the characteristic later belief in an educated democratic utopia. Considered in this light colonial achievements are most helpful in defining the democratic ideology of education by indicating what it was not.

THE INSTITUTIONS OF COLONIAL EDUCATION

The fundamental fact about colonial education was that it imitated English precedents except where those precedents were obviously inadequate to serve colonial needs. Hence a major part of colonial education took place in the home, and many children—from prosperous homes as well as poor ones—never attended school. When a man or his wife was literate, their children and their servants would in all likelihood acquire at least a rudimentary education at home before they came of age. Only the parents' illiteracy, or the wish to train the older boys to tasks that the head of the household could not teach, necessitated more formal schooling.[1]

Probably the major vehicle of education outside the home, moreover, was apprenticeship. This was the typical British method of bringing up male children to be useful, and it survived easily in the American colonies where there was more than enough work for any craftsman. (Admittedly, it survived in attenuated form, because the demand for labor made protracted apprenticeships implausible.) Nor was apprenticeship limited to training in a craft; in America as in England a master was expected to see to the literacy of his charges, and frequently he contracted to provide them with training in such skills as casting accounts besides.

Hence formal schooling as we know it was in many respects the last rather than the first resort of a colonial parent or master. Those who could not teach their wards to read usually sent them to a neighborhood dame school, where for a very small sum an elderly widow or childless wife would teach them their letters. Beyond the dame school, children might attend a writing school or a so-called English school (learning not only reading and writing but also arithmetic and sometimes other subjects as well), a Latin grammar school (preparing them for entrance to college), or (in the larger towns) a private-venture school to learn such skills as navigation and surveying. Most of the learned professions rested upon apprenticeship rather than formal training, however, and the only higher education available on a formal basis was that of the handful of colonial colleges, which offered their students the same humanistic disciplines that prevailed in England.

Furthermore, it was quite in keeping with English precedent that schools as well as colleges should depend for their support upon bequests and other charitable gifts and upon the tuition fees of pupils. Generally the colonial governments encouraged the founding of schools and colleges, and frequently they granted them some form of public assistance, but almost never did a colonial government provide fully for the annual expense of any educational institution. (In the case of private-venture schools, of course, the governments provided no assistance at all.) It followed that the education of the poor depended even more than education generally upon private benevolence; but the benevolence existed, and education was widely available.

Clearly, colonial education rested upon perspectives quite different from those of the nineteenth and twentieth centuries. Most of the early settlers were concerned for the education of their children, but they expected to provide it informally, and they were often content to make up its inadequacies privately or to have their children do without. Nevertheless, these very inadequacies sometimes prompted colonial authorities to attempt formal provision for the education of the people. The measures they took, which initiated distinctively American developments in popular education, indicate even more clearly than the accustomed practice of the first inhabitants the characteristic hopes and limitations of colonial educational policy.

We must approach these colonial efforts regionally, for both geography and religious variations conspired to produce quite dissimilar educational developments in New England, the Middle Colonies, and the South.

In New England, religious antagonism to the Anglican Church encouraged an unusual commitment to public education during the seventeenth century. Historians have often exaggerated the extent to which New England owes its educational preeminence to the religious zeal of the founding fathers, and it is clear that Puritan educational legislation drew very heavily on secular precedents. But a religious impulse is also evident, one that made the Massachusetts Bay Colony an example to all the other settlements save Rhode Island. First Connecticut and New Haven, next Plymouth, then New Hampshire upon its separation from Massachusetts, and finally the District of Maine introduced formal educational institutions patterned on those of the Puritan founders.

Not even the Bay Colony established universal elementary schooling during the first decade of settlement, however. The General Court acted first to establish Harvard College in 1636, "dreading to leave an illiterate Ministery to the Churches, when our present Ministers shall lie in the Dust," as *New Englands First Fruits* expressed it.[2] Nevertheless, during the 1640s the same legislature took two major steps to ensure public education at the elementary level. First it directed all parents and masters of apprentices to see to the education of their wards at least to the extent of an "ability to read and understand the principles of religion and the capital laws of the country." Subsequently, and even more strikingly, it required all towns of fifty families to provide common schools, and towns of one hundred families to establish Latin grammar schools.[3]

This educational legislation established neither free nor universal schooling even where the towns conscientiously followed the letter of the law. The primary obligation still lay upon parents, and even the school law did not insist upon public support of the schools it required. But it became a general practice during the seventeenth century for the towns to contribute to the support of schools out of regular rates, and to admit poorer students without charging them tuition, so that formal education was widely available to every class in society that sought to make use of it. Moreover, although grammar schools were far from universal, most of the early towns boasted one, and there may be said to have been an educational establishment that was effective from common school to Harvard College.

As the Massachusetts provision for Latin grammar schools clearly indicates, however, that establishment was geared primarily to the requirements of the ministry and secondarily to the needs of a prospective ruling class. Consequently the system of schools initiated during the 1640s became increasingly less effective. As the first well-educated generation died, as the population spread out in ever greater diffusion, as the original religious impulse waned and was replaced by an urgent quest for prosperity, and as the clergy lost first their political and then their religious monopoly, the common schools fared badly and the Latin schools fared worse. By the time of the American Revolution, therefore, all that was left of the intended Massachusetts system was the college at Cambridge, a handful of Latin schools, and a fairly large number of common schools that were gradually being converted into "moving schools" and district schools teaching little more than the dame schools had been wont to do.[4]

Most of the same destructive forces were at work in the other New England colonies from their founding. All suffered from the scattering of the population and from a growing popular indifference to classical training, and most suffered even more heavily than Massachusetts from the depredations and the financial burdens of Indian wars. Although all except Rhode Island enacted compulsory educational legislation by 1671, and although most also adopted modified versions of the Massachusetts school law, none advanced so far as she during the seventeenth century, and none advanced further during the eighteenth.

Hence the best education to be obtained in New England by the middle of the eighteenth century was usually that of the entirely private schools in the largest towns, which offered their pupils training in a wide variety of commercially useful disciplines such as accounting and modern languages, as well as in many of the traditional skills. There was ample precedent in England for private-venture schools of this sort, but in New England they were an innovation that had not been anticipated in the 1640s. Their curriculum marked the transition from a medieval to a modern economic order, while their facilities were neither so free nor so widely accessible as the academic training available in the Puritan colonies generally in 1700.

None of the colonies outside New England attempted systematic provision for popular education in the same measure or by the same means as Massachusetts Bay and its allies. New Netherlands, for example, was one of the most secular and commercial enterprises among all the seventeenth-century colonies, and the fact permitted an official indifference to public education quite out of keeping with the original New England pattern. The political instability of the colony—twice Dutch, twice English, and divided internally by intense factional rivalries—added difficulties which understandably complicated all provision for education. Yet the Dutch founders were as good Protestants as the New Englanders; they were under instructions from the Dutch West India Company and the Classis of Amsterdam to establish schools; and early records show that from time to time the governments and congregations of Manhattan Island and of a number of outlying towns employed schoolmasters. The schools in which they taught apparently derived their support varyingly from the company itself, from municipal governments (which usually provided buildings), from individual subscriptions, and from tuition charges. Clearly, however, they represented no very systematic provision by the authorities for schooling, and there was no legal compulsion upon parents to educate their children.[5]

Nor did the introduction of English rule particularly improve educational opportunities in the colony. With the change in government, established Dutch schools continued as voluntary enterprises associated with the Dutch Reformed Church, and additional private English-language schools (some of them denominational) came into being in different towns in the colony. The most nearly universal instruction, however, was that encouraged by the Society for the Propagation of the Gospel in Foreign Parts, which began subsidizing schoolmasters after 1706 if they would undertake to teach a specified number of pauper children the three R's and the Church of England catechism in their private schools. But for different reasons Dissenters and well-to-do Anglicans both boycotted these pauper schools, and after 1764 (at least in Manhattan) Dissenters were barred from them. Therefore the education of the people of New York depended almost entirely upon their voluntary efforts, and it appears that New York lagged well behind New England in providing for its children. So did the Jerseys, in which most of the same practices obtained.[6]

Education in Pennsylvania also depended almost exclusively upon voluntary efforts, but it flourished there even while it dwindled in New York. The main impulse to formal schooling came from the Quakers, who saw no need for a learned ministry such as Puritan New England had established, but who were often eager advocates of universal literacy and also of practical training for a career. William Penn's celebrated Frame of Government of 1682 called for the early establishment of "public" schools, and his second Frame of 1683 directed the Pennsylvania Assembly to provide for education. It responded by enacting a requirement "that all persons in this province and territories thereof, having children, and all the guardians or trustees of orphans, shall cause such to be instructed in reading and writing; so that they may be able to read the Scriptures; and to write by that time they attain to twelve years of age; and that then they be taught some useful trade or skill, that the poor may work to live, and the rich, if they become poor, may not want. Of which every county court shall take care. . . ."[7] In other respects, however, the Quaker colony left education to private initiative and the churches. After the first settlements it could hardly do otherwise, given its policy of religious toleration and the religious diversity it encouraged, for effective public education in a devout age demanded some degree of consensus on religious issues. The new Frame of Government of 1701 ignored education entirely, and from this time on legislation affecting it was infrequent and simply permissive.[8]

In 1715 and again in 1731 the Assembly authorized Protestant bodies to hold property in virtual perpetuity for the purpose of supporting eleemosynary institutions. This was the statutory origin of Pennsylvania's many denominational schools and "colleges," which Quakers and German sects, and later Anglicans and Presbyterians, built and maintained during the eighteenth century. They were public in that the customary charity of Quakers and other Pennsylvanians made provision for the free education of poor students; but outside of Philadelphia (where there were also a number of secular private schools like those in New England) they tended to reflect the zeal of the various churches rather than serve directly the needs of the people. Hence it is difficult to say how effective the total educational establishment was. Undoubtedly more effective than the roughly parallel arrangements in New York, Pennsylvania schooling was on the whole probably inferior to that of Massachusetts even in its later years.[9]

In Virginia there was even less reason than in Pennsylvania and New York to introduce innovations in the traditional English provisions for education. In the first place, the early settlers were predominantly Englishmen and Anglicans, neither aliens nor religious dissidents opposed to the established church. Furthermore, the social and political institutions of the English countryside accommodated themselves to the circumstances of plantation agriculture much more readily than to the economic life of New England

and the Middle Colonies. Hence Governor William Berkeley's reply in 1671 to a question put him by the Commissioners of Foreign Plantations, "What course is taken about the instructing the people within your government in the Christian religion?" was substantially true in every realm of education: "The same course that is taken in England out of towns; every man according to his abilities instructing his children." [10]

Almost the only general educational legislation of the Virginia colony dealt with paupers and orphans, applying and extending precedents established in the English poor laws. The earliest law (1631) authorized county officials to take children away from parents who could not support them in order to bind them as apprentices, while a similar act provided in 1646 that orphans whose inheritances were not adequate to ensure their education should likewise be bound out. In the eighteenth century these provisions were amended by a requirement that masters and also parents see to the literacy as well as the vocational skills of their children, but the extended county and parish organization of the colony seems to have made its enforcement less effective than the comparable law affecting the New England townships. [11]

In any event the broad result was to leave the general education of the people a predominantly voluntary affair. At the apex of the colony's official educational establishment was the College of William and Mary, chartered in 1693, and immediately below it were a number of private Latin and English schools. Many of these institutions received a small appropriation from the colony, and some were endowed to teach poor but able students, but others existed solely as private business ventures. Some of them were excellent, some inferior; some offered the equivalent of a secondary education while others produced only a minimum literacy. Good or bad they did not make a system, and there was no authoritative supervision to ensure that they would serve the whole public according to its greatest needs. [12]

The other southern colonies more or less duplicated the patterns that Virginia had set. For the most part parents and masters relied on their own resources for the education of their children, and the nearest equivalent of a general system of education was schools subsidized as in New York by the Society for the Propagation of the Gospel. Both Maryland and South Carolina attempted to establish semipublic corporations for the support of Latin schools, one in each county and free to poor children, but like many of the generous educational aspirations of individual southerners this was an innovation that failed to take hold during the colonial era. Only in the western counties, peopled by members of the dissenting sects, was any great attention paid to schools, and there on the same voluntary basis that prevailed in Pennsylvania, from which so many of the settlers had come.[13]

THE SOCIAL FUNCTIONS OF COLONIAL EDUCATION

Differences in educational practice among the colonies should not blind us to the underlying likenesses. The colonists were products of a European environment; they dreaded the destruction by ignorance of the precarious civilization they had created; and they tried by various means to ensure the education of the people. For our purposes here, their various devices and achievements are less important than the nature of their commitment to popular education. We may best express that commitment by pointing out that all colonial education was instrumental, hierarchical, authority-oriented, and limited in scope.

Above all else, it was an instrument of the Protestant Reformation. Almost every colony's inhabitants had a direct and compelling motive to see to the literacy of their children, not only so that they might better seek their individual salvation through reading of the Bible, but also so that the holy experiment planted in the New World—be it Massachusetts, Pennsylvania, or early Virginia—would survive and prosper. In a frontier society it was very nearly impossible to maintain education, whether Anglican or Dissenting, at the level that had been achieved in Elizabethan England; yet frontier conditions admonished the leaders of the settlements and of the churches to establish what they could. Hence colonial educational institutions, although eroded by the scattering of the population and by other circumstances of colonial life, tended to parallel religious energy, and at least in the early decades there was a close correlation between the degree of religious urgency a colony felt and the comprehensiveness of the educational institutions it established. Thus Puritan New England in the seventeenth century drew ahead of other regions; thus an adamant Massachusetts led all of her sister colonies; thus the pious inhabitants of Pennsylvania, and most notably the Scotch-Irish Presbyterians, overcame both the diffusion of population and the inactivity of government by privately establishing dozens of small isolated schools.

On the other hand, in New York and in the South there were undoubtedly fewer schools per capita during the seventeenth century. One reason probably is that in those colonies the Church of England was dominant and English religious precedents were most readily accepted, and the sense of religious urgency was diminished. Furthermore, the English church was liturgical rather than evangelical, and correspondingly less insistent upon literacy. Yet in the Anglican colonies provision was early made for catechistic instruction of paupers and apprentices, while the dissenting sects in the southern back country generally established such schools as they could afford.

If colonial education was originally an instrument of religious zeal, however, it was almost equally an instrument of social and economic well-being. Puritans and Anglicans alike abhorred the idler and expected every child to become useful in some way, and of course Quakers made diligence in a calling a prime tenet of their faith. Hence Massachusetts, Virginia, and Pennsylvania all sought to ensure that their people would be trained for socially profitable employments, even if the devices they relied upon varied. As the Puritan colonies lost some of their early theological commitment, moreover, their educational institutions came more and more to resemble those of their less dedicated neighbors. While the original educational establishment of New England waned, private schools increasingly catered to a variety of utilitarian demands, just like private schools in the other colonies. As early as the 1670s the ministers of New England foresaw in the decline of the public schools the end of civilization itself, but they were mistaken. It was only their very special theocentric civilization that was endangered, and both society and an education instrumental to it survived and even flourished.

We must also acknowledge that a hierarchical orientation was common to educational institutions throughout the colonies despite the distinctions that may have existed between the substantially free, universal, and public schools of early New England and the charitable, random, and private schools of other regions. In every colony, schools were established to serve the varied requirements of a hierarchically divided society—not a society in which there was no upward mobility but one in which functional stratification was well developed. Consequently colonial education almost invariably made class distinctions of one sort or another.[14]

In Virginia and the South, for example, official attention to the education of paupers and orphans bespoke the concern of legislators that there be a trained artisan class and no unemployed hands subsisting on the bounty of church or state. Meanwhile the law was relatively silent on the education of other classes in the society, either because their status did not warrant education—this was the case with slaves—or because they would as a matter of course acquire a suitable education by private means. Obviously the silence of the law constituted assent to educational distinctions already observed in the society, which public aid to grammar schools and the college at Williamsburg only reinforced.

Given visible political and religious differences, moreover, much the same hierarchical orientation affected the educational institutions of the Middle Colonies as well. In leaving education to voluntary efforts and religious charity, New York clearly left unchallenged the social distinctions its various educational institutions reflected. But Pennsylvania's heavy reliance upon church schools had much the same effect. Religious benevolence supported the education of paupers far more generously in Pennsylvania than in New York, and it generally provided for them in the same schools as their betters, yet church schools inevitably both mirrored and lent their support to the social status quo. As we shall see, during the 1820s and 1830s the undemocratic quality of Pennsylvania schools was to become a major complaint against them.

On the other hand, we often think that New England practiced a full-fledged democracy in its educational institutions. There is some reason for our belief. The town schools were open to all classes without social distinction, and a poor but ambitious boy could usually pursue his education as far as his ability would carry him. Moreover, the same legislative authority had established both Harvard College and the elementary educational institutions of the 1640s; there was no such segmentation of effort as existed in Virginia. Nevertheless, it would be a mistake to think that education in the Puritan colonies transcended their social organization, even where it was most effective. For one thing, even the New England towns generally made free schooling available only to the poor. More important, the very motives that ensured public provision for education also ensured that educational institutions would be functionally differentiated. For his soul's sake, and for the sake of conformity to the laws of the bibliocracy, everyone must know how to read; this was a provision that made no distinctions among persons. But in the seventeenth century only a minority of the population made the laws that everyone was to obey, and then with the guidance of the ministry. The Puritans correspondingly offered the higher reaches of formal education only to those who proposed to enter the ministry, or who were expected to become leaders of the commonwealth.[15]

Puritan attitudes and Puritan arrangements for schooling are epitomized in a decision to establish a Latin grammar school the Northampton town meeting reached in 1668. One school had already failed, but

The town considering of the need of a schoolmaster that should be able to instruct the children and youth in learning, and so be able to instruct such children as their parents desire to bring up to learning to fit them for the college, that so they may be fit for the service of God in the church or otherwise in the public, voted to give 20 pounds out of the town's stock, this to be beside what may be raised on the scholars which shall come to be taught by him, and ordered the selectmen now to be chosen to procure one that may be suitable for the service above expressed for the year ensuing.[16]

The Puritan commonwealth encouraged not social leveling but the harmonious and complementary organization of government, church, and society at large into rulers and ruled, and education was geared to what Perry Miller describes as "leadership by the learned and dutiful subordination of the unlearned." [17]

What was different from the Virginia pattern were the criteria of stratification. True learning and intellectual merit tended to be paramount during the early seventeenth century. By the eighteenth this meritorious aristocracy had dwindled with the voiding of the Massachusetts charter and the widespread rise of a class of commercial magnates who subordinated things of the mind to their practical concerns. Their rise accelerated the development of private schools catering to the utilitarian needs both of their own sons and of others who sought to emulate them. By the same token it extended and intensified the social stratification that devout men had begun.[18]

Colonial education was also authority-oriented, if one phrase may be used to conjure up different but related characteristics. Being instrumental to a hierarchical society it inevitably and often explicitly supported the status quo, as when the ministers of New England preached a strengthening of the schools during the 1670s to restore the polity of the founding fathers, or when most colonial governments required that prospective teachers be licensed by the established clergy. The particular goals that colonial authorities pursued shifted somewhat over the years, and the curriculum and character of the schools they sanctioned changed with them, but the most drastic shifts of this sort could not alter the essentially conservative role education was expected to play in colonial society.[19]

Again, colonial education was authority-oriented in its pedagogy. Especially during the seventeenth century the student learned what his instructor taught simply because it was being taught, and in the manner in which it was presented. In the higher education this meant intensive formal drilling in traditional medieval disciplines, and discussion took the form of elaborate disputation but not genuine inquiry. Otherwise rote memorization was the rule, and even the liberalized curriculum of private "English" schools did not significantly change teaching methods during the eighteenth century.

Finally, colonial education was limited in scope, in that schools occupied only a subordinate place among the instrumentalities to which colonial authorities would turn to achieve their political, economic, and social goals. Many colonies left popular education to private initiative, not simply because traditional vehicles of education seemed adequate, nor because a class bias made the needs of the poor seem different in kind from the needs of the wealthy, but also because education itself appeared to be only one of many ways of shaping public behavior. This was true despite the fact that formal education acquired additional responsibilities as colonial society developed and colonial economies expanded. Even in Massachusetts, schools were never conceived as the engines of social control they were to appear in later years, although Massachusetts had outdistanced all the other colonies in its conscious attention to schooling as an instrument of reformation.

We have traced these four characteristics of colonial education, not because they created precedents for subsequent developments, but because they provide points of contrast with democratic innovations in a later period. Indeed, it is clear that organized popular education developed in the colonies in far from democratic fashion, as an instrument dedicated to the preservation and perpetuation of an established social order. Granted, it was also a remarkably flexible instrument, one that responded constructively to many of the challenges of modern times even while its founders sought to preserve the essential characteristics of the past by the means at hand. But the forms that colonial leaders introduced could not prosper forever in the new environment. They survived temporarily despite the undermining influences of a new society in the making. In the long run, however, fundamental social changes were to cause the disruption and rearrangement of all colonial institutions, and not the least of these was to be education.

11. Republican Innovations in Theory

and Practice

THE American Revolution had a disastrous effect upon colonial
educational institutions. Settlements near the Atlantic coast,
which had done most to establish schools and colleges, were also
most directly touched by the war, which destroyed many school
buildings and put others to military uses. Again, the events of the
1770s and 1780s distracted public attention from educational matters, while constant inflation and the heavy financial demands of
the war inhibited public support even for established schools. Considering the handicaps under which they labored, indeed, it is
surprising that colonial educational institutions survived at all. But
the Americans of the revolutionary generation were only distracted,
not uprooted, by their military exertions. When the war ended and
they assumed the role of founding fathers they would return with
new zeal to the education of the people.

Their success in war made for unexpected shifts in their attitudes toward education, however. Significantly, leading public men
like John Adams and Francis Marion attributed the movement toward independence to the literacy and intelligence of the American
people. More important still, many public figures also urged the
new states and the new nation to adopt educational measures that
would ensure the continued success of the republican experiment.
In order to understand later developments in American beliefs
about popular education we must examine these republicans' views
in some detail. They marked a considerable advance beyond the attitudes of the colonial period; but they also fell far short of the
democratic belief that was to succeed them.[1]

THE FOUNDING FATHERS

The major innovation the founding fathers introduced into American educational theory was an explicit commitment to broadening the dissemination of knowledge. Typically, seven of the fourteen states that drafted new constitutions before 1800 adopted articles or clauses calling for public aid to education. Although their specifications varied widely, the elaborate Massachusetts statement reflected a common view:

Wisdom and knowledge, as well as virtue, diffused generally among the body of the people, being necessary for the preservation of their rights and liberties; and as these depend on spreading the opportunities and advantages of education in the various parts of the country, and among the different orders of the people, it shall be the duty of legislatures and magistrates, in all future periods of this commonwealth, to cherish the interests of literature and the sciences, and all seminaries of them; especially the university at Cambridge, public schools and grammar schools in the towns. . . .[2]

Nor was the republican belief in popular education limited to the solemn occasions when leading men gathered in constituent assemblies. In New York, for example, Governor George Clinton repeatedly urged extension of existing provisions for education. He pointed out to the state legislature in 1802 that the state must gain "advantages to morals, religion, liberty and good government . . . from the general diffusion of knowledge," and he observed hopefully in 1803 that "the diffusion of knowledge is so essential to the promotion of virtue and the preservation of liberty, as to render arguments unnecessary to excite you to a perseverance in this laudable pursuit." His political rival John Jay, addressing the legislature as governor in 1801, also recommended measures to encourage education; it complied by setting up lotteries primarily for the benefit of the common schools.[3]

Similarly, in Virginia Thomas Jefferson began while the Revolution was still in progress to advocate his now-famous plan for a pyramidal system of education reaching from district elementary schools to a state university, and he continued to press for a comprehensive scheme of public instruction throughout his life.[4] Even in North Carolina, which had gained a reputation as a backward state because of the poverty and the penuriousness of its inhabitants, republican governors urged greater attention to public education. James Turner epitomized their exhortations when he observed to the legislature in 1803: "As the most certain way of handing down to our latest posterity, our free republican government, is to enlighten the minds of the people, and to preserve the purity of their morals, too much attention can not be paid to the education of youth, by promoting the establishment of schools in every part of the State. Education is the mortal enemy to arbitrary governments, and the surest basis of liberty and equal rights." [5]

Simultaneously, the new federal government also undertook to further republican education. The land ordinance of 1785 reserved one lot in each township for public schools, and the Northwest Ordinance decreed that "religion, morality, and knowledge being necessary to good government and the happiness of mankind, schools and the means of education shall forever be encouraged." These pious phrases probably echoed a New England lobby in the capital, but the central government's interest in education was not limited to any one group. Thomas Jefferson had drafted the ordinance of 1785, and George Washington's Farewell Address admonished the people to promote "as an object of primary importance, institutions for the general diffusion of knowledge. In proportion as the structure of a government gives force to public opinion, it is essential that public opinion should be enlightened." [6]

Acting, it seems, on Alexander Hamilton's advice, Washington failed to revive in the same address a tentative recommendation he had already made in 1790 that the federal government grant aid to schools throughout the several states. But Benjamin Rush of Pennsylvania and Samuel Knox of Maryland proposed elaborate systems of nationally supervised education culminating in a national university, and other men devised comparable schemes for consolidating American nationality and supporting continued American progress in both the social and the natural sciences. It was indeed an era marked by national plans for a systematic republican education, as Allen Hansen's collection of fugitive tracts from the 1790s, *Liberalism and American Education in the Eighteenth Century,* demonstrates.[7]

The idea of a national university also captured the imagination of the founding fathers. George Washington devoted part of his last annual message to it in 1796, asking Congress rhetorically, "In a republic what species of knowledge can be equally important and what duty more pressing on its legislature than to patronize a plan for communicating it to those who are to be the future guardians of the liberties of the country?"—a sentiment James Madison was to reiterate in 1810 when he argued that a national university would enlighten the opinions, expand the patriotism, and harmonize the principles of those who attended it, and thus "contribute not less to strengthen the foundations than to adorn the structure of our free and happy system of government." But Benjamin Rush had already urged in 1788 that thirty years after the establishment of a national university only those who held degrees from it should be eligible for elective or appointive office. "Should this plan of a federal university or one like it, be adopted," he wrote, "then will begin the golden age of the United States." [8] His educational qualification for officeholders was more rigorous perhaps than what his contemporaries were willing to demand, yet the basic proposition was a commonplace: education is indispensable to governors as well as governed.[9]

But early republican enthusiasm for a national university failed to create such an institution, while even the common school systems urged by public men generally failed to materialize. In most states, the establishment of public school systems waited upon the accumulation of a common school fund or a literary fund, the interest of which might be devoted to school support. Between 1795 and 1825 nearly every state, following the precedent of Connecticut, established such a fund; yet it was clear that at least a generation must pass before it could become effective. Meanwhile the generation of the founding fathers followed colonial precedent in devoting public funds chiefly to education at the two extremes, colleges and academies, and pauper schooling. During the same period in which they initiated literary funds, for example, most southern states also established state universities, and even the funds they set aside were sometimes intended to benefit private academies as well as public schools. Nor was their failure to press for universal education at public expense a peculiarly southern phenomenon: northern states continued to assist private colleges and secondary schools with funds that might instead have been devoted to common schools.[10]

Were it not for the generous hopes expressed by early republican advocates of education, we might account for their limited educational achievements by treating them as simply an extension of colonial precedents. Obviously, precedent was important, and many states sought rather to strengthen established institutions than to develop new ones. Furthermore, the chronic shortage of funds the new states experienced clearly encouraged them to postpone universal public education until funds had accumulated from the sale of lands or from other nontax sources, as both the common school funds and federal land-grants in western townships attest. But in many areas of public life the founding fathers had deliberately broken with colonial precedent, and they had almost unanimously proclaimed the need for new educational institutions to safeguard the republic. Hence the limited nature of their educational achievements also testifies in some measure to the limited nature of their educational commitments. If they imitated colonial precedent, they did so deliberately and not merely as the passive accomplices of history.

Early republican commitments to education were limited in other senses that are particularly striking to anyone who expects to discover a democratic orientation in the founding fathers' demands for a universal dissemination of knowledge. One is their tendency to stress the conservative role of educational institutions in overcoming an excess of popular liberty. Benjamin Rush expressed this conservative ideal bluntly in an "Address to the People of the United States" that he published in 1787: "To conform the principles, morals and manners of our citizens, to our republican forms of government, it is absolutely necessary, that knowledge of every kind should be disseminated through every part of the United States." Alongside a theoretical belief in the right of revolution and in social progress, in fact, many of the national plans for education emphasized the importance of instruction in common obligations to government and to the established institutions of society. Within the areas to which common agreement limited government, an informed obedience on the part of the people was at least as important as their particular freedoms.[11]

For the founding fathers were not anarchists. Monarchy had been overthrown, titles of nobility and interferences with traditional liberties had been prohibited by the Constitution, unwarranted foreign intrusions on American prosperity had been shaken off— the political and social order of the eighteenth century had been unsettled, and Federalists and Republicans battled for preeminence in a republican and a predominantly secular society. But despite their conflicting opinions of the French Revolution, despite their bitter differences on the proper scope of national economic policies, and despite gradations in their republican liberalism, the founding fathers agreed in substance on what a republican education should accomplish. Washington and Madison, Jay and Clinton, Rush and Knox, Adams and Jefferson hoped to acquaint all men with the information that was necessary to preserve their liberties, but they did not anticipate a day when an educated people might wish to extend those liberties. Education, Jefferson wrote home from France, is "the most certain and the most legitimate engine of government. Educate and inform the whole mass of the people, enable them to see that it is their interest to preserve peace and order, and they will preserve it, and it requires no very high degree of education to convince them of this. They are the only sure reliance for the preservation of our liberty." [12] Here were the main grounds for going beyond colonial provisions for elementary schooling.

One other aspect of the early republicans' thought that strikes the modern reader most forcefully is their concern for an informed leadership in the new society. This concern obviously affected all of the proposals for a national university, but it also operated at the state level. There, such innovations as the state university were introduced primarily to improve the work of schools above the elementary level, and no matter how inexpensive they gave advanced training to only a few students. Again, although Jefferson's Bill for the More General Diffusion of Knowledge provided for three years of elementary public education for all children, it sought chiefly to arrange for the selection of potential leaders from the mass of the people—and Jefferson, after all, was a radical for his times. Most of the constitutional provisions for education adopted during this period, with their brief references to public encouragement of seminaries and colleges, had in view a similar purpose, and even the elaborate Massachusetts article did not propose education for a democracy. Cherish education "among the different orders of the people," wrote its draftsman, who was probably John Adams; Jefferson echoed him in 1820 when he wrote to Joseph C. Cabell, his ally in the fight for a state university, that if he sponsored a plan for common education it would reconcile the friends of elementary schools and so "promote in every order of men the degree of instruction proportioned to their condition, and to their views in life." [13]

Indeed, one of few genuinely egalitarian proposals of the age was drafted by an unlettered farmer of North Billerica, Massachusetts. During the late 1790s, William Manning proposed to the *Independent Chronicle* of Boston, a Jeffersonian organ, that knowledge be disseminated to the public at large through common schools and through a monthly magazine devoted to the interests of the productive classes. "Larning," he explained, "is of the gratest importance to the seport of a free government, & to prevent this the few are always crying up the advantages of costly collages, national acadimyes & grammer schooles, in ordir to make places for men to live without work, & so strengthen their party. But are always opposed to cheep schools & woman schools, the ondly or prinsaple means by which larning is spred amongue the Many." But the editors of the *Chronicle* refused to print Manning's letter, and his rebuke to contemporary leaders went unheeded. He was in effect a Jacksonian democrat born at least a generation before his time, and his plea for democracy in politics supported by democratic education was alien even to the Jeffersonian press.[14]

THE LATER REPUBLICANS

As a second generation of republican leaders succeeded the founding fathers near the turn of the century, it became apparent

that many of the institutions the earlier generation had cherished
must either change or perish. Inevitably, geographical expansion
and the rapid diversification of the country's economy, which had
begun by 1800 and which were stimulated by the War of 1812,
threatened extraordinary changes in social structure and politics
and thus in educational thought and practice. But though change in
these realms was imminent, most of the basic elements of the early
republican theory of politics and education survived the first three
decades of the new century. The main difference between the
founding fathers and their republican successors, therefore, was
that the more effectively the latter provided for popular education
the more surely they also provided the grounds on which popular
agitators would ultimately repudiate them. Their educational views
have significance for us precisely because by 1830 they would become the direct targets of widespread democratic criticism.[15]

Perhaps the leading advocate of universal education during
these transitional years was De Witt Clinton, for eight years governor of the state of New York, and mayor of New York City for
twelve. Repeatedly his messages to the state legislature pointed
out that publicly supported common education is an inescapable
obligation of republican government to its people and to itself. "The
first duty of a state," he told the legislature in 1822, "is to render
its citizens virtuous by intellectual instruction and moral discipline,
by enlightening their minds, purifying their hearts, and teaching
them their rights and their obligations." Clinton also recognized
that education might be the most effective social engine against vice
and crime and poverty, yet his central principle remained almost
exclusively political. "The first duty of government, and the surest
evidence of good government," his message of 1826 proclaimed, "is
the encouragement of education. A general diffusion of knowledge
is the precursor and protector of republican institutions; and in it
we must confide as the conservative power that will watch over our
liberties, and guard them against fraud, intrigue, corruption and
violence." [16]

Prominent figures in Pennsylvania also pressed for popular education at public expense. In 1810, for example, Nicholas Biddle urged
the commonwealth's House of Representatives to establish a com-

prehensive system of district schools that children might attend without distinction of wealth or religion or native tongue or sex. (Clearly, his proposal was intended to overcome objections to a state-wide common education that could be anticipated from the German-speaking population, many of whom also belonged to pietistic sects.) The Report of the Committee on Education in which these recommendations appeared hailed the United States as almost the last free nation in the world, and urged that its liberties be guarded by "a general republican system of education" on the model proposed by the founding fathers and sanctioned by the Pennsylvania Constitution of 1790. But it also argued that popular political authority and economic and social equality depended upon an effective system of education; Biddle in some measure anticipated and advocated democratic modifications of Pennsylvania's traditional provision for higher education and pauper schooling. Still, his plan called for no more than inexpensive common schools, which children from the wealthy and middling classes would attend because they were cheap, while paupers would be admitted free. Biddle was sensitive to democratic needs without adopting a fully democratic perspective.[17]

In Massachusetts, which was beginning to feel the impact of textile manufacturing, Governor Caleb Strong recommended as early as 1816 that the legislature require education of children working in the mills in order that they might be trained to judge and protect their rights. Nine years later Levi Lincoln referred to the problem in his annual message. A committee of the legislature held in reply that public opinion would prevent the millowners from degrading factory children, but it agreed that industrialization might necessitate some measures to ensure their adequate intellectual development. In this respect it was less optimistic than a vigorously Republican spokesman in New York, Samuel Young, who acclaimed his state's manufacturers in the constitutional convention of 1821 on the grounds that they voluntarily arranged for the education of their child laborers. That is to say, advocates of manufacturing saw virtues in education; but they did not act forcefully to establish it, nor did they undertake any important revision of its republican categories.[18]

By the same token, even a second-generation republican who welcomed democratic innovations was likely to treat education in measured terms as a way of safeguarding traditional liberties. In one of the classic statements of the late republican attitude, for example, a prominent Maine lawyer described popular education as a corollary of popular sovereignty. "With a view to improve the principles of self-government in a state of society, that subjects everything to its sense," Charles Stewart Daveis told a celebration at Fryeburg, Maine, in 1825,

—in a country, where the whole sovereignty is lodged in the people— and all authority is exercised upon the strictest responsibility, to the end of its universal welfare, *the education of the whole becomes the first interest of all.* . . . The proper system of republican education should *combine* the regular course of useful elementary instruction, with that species of education which naturally "results from the political order of society." In this manner, the moral education of *the prince*, if I may use the expression, becomes of the first importance, and it is a happy circumstance, that there is always a generation of young and fair minds springing up among the people, free from any false impressions, in proper season to assume the real reins of power, and exemplify the true principles and influence of education.[19]

Northern spokesmen were not alone in demanding education that would suit the young republic. During the 1810s and 1820s Hezekiah Niles's *Weekly Register* of Baltimore, a leading organ for business interests everywhere, kept up a drumfire of propaganda in favor of public support for educational innovations that would stabilize American politics.[20] Perhaps the leading southern advocate of popular education, however, was Charles Fenton Mercer of Virginia. A Federalist in politics, Mercer led the fight in the Virginia legislature of 1817–18 in support of state aid to elementary schools and against Joseph C. Cabell's plan, sanctioned by Jefferson, to spend state funds on a university and to leave elementary education to local initiative. Nevertheless, addressing a commencement gathering at Princeton in 1826, Mercer was surprisingly tentative in his view of education. Urging it in the name of the republican values to which Clinton and Biddle also subscribed, he *hoped* that the diffusion of knowledge would reduce the degradation of labor, combat pauperism, augment national strength and prosperity, and help true worth to achieve recognition. He could not be sure.[21]

Other southerners, lacking a tradition of universal public schooling to buttress their recommendations, simply urged the enlargement of existing institutions to secure and encourage republican virtues. The result was an odd kind of anticlimax in their educational pronouncements, as for example in Governor Henry Middleton's message to the South Carolina legislature in 1811:

I cannot suffer the present occasion to pass, without bringing to your view the propriety of establishing *free schools*, in all those parts of the State where such institutions are wanted. . . . A system of general instruction is essential to the preservation of our political institutions. Your liberal support of the South Carolina College, a monument of your veneration for science and learning, testifies your anxious solicitude to secure to our youth the highest advantages of instruction, and doubtless that seminary will yield annually an accession of able and virtuous citizens to the State; but those alone whose affluent circumstances have enabled them to pass through certain preparatory studies, can enjoy the benefit of that institution; it is now hoped that you will employ some portion of your funds in procuring the elements of education for the children of indigent persons.[22]

Clearly, Middleton's recommendation carried forward established perspectives on popular education, and failed to recognize that free pauper schooling was unlikely either to serve the needs or to ensure the education of the lower ranks of society.

In most respects, that is, while the later republican advocates of public education proposed a more generous provision for schools, academies, and colleges than their predecessors had achieved, the underlying political and social assumptions governing popular education had not really changed. The shortcomings of their theory were illustrated in their practical achievements. Confronted by growing illiteracy, for example, the states continued to establish common school funds, while those which had already established funds tended to seek out and appropriate new kinds of revenue to the task of building them up as rapidly as possible. Still, direct legislative appropriations for education were relatively rare, and were as likely to be devoted to colleges and academies as to common schools. (Typically, a university was founded in Virginia but no common school system materialized, and even in Massachusetts the legislature appropriated funds for Harvard College but was slow either to require local school taxation or to establish a common school fund.) In 1813 the Connecticut legislature enacted a law requiring the education of factory children, which other states also adopted or at least considered, but such laws generally went unenforced, and in addition they had the disadvantage of requiring education without providing schools. Almost everywhere the only children who could attend free schools were those whose parents were declared paupers, and while the number of impoverished families increased by leaps and bounds after the War of 1812, the number who were willing to accept education as charity did not. On balance, the educational innovations sponsored by later republican leaders may have been less effective in meeting contemporary needs than the institutions sponsored by the founding fathers.[23]

Perhaps the most striking illustration of their inadequacies was the work of the Free School Society of New York City. This was a private charitable organization, founded in 1805 by such leading men as De Witt Clinton, which offered free elementary education to poor children. Instruction followed the monitorial method, which was used to inculcate a nondenominational Protestantism as well as to teach reading, writing, and arithmetic. After 1813, recognizing the society's services to popular education in the city, the state legislature appropriated public funds in its support, with the result that between 1813 and 1842 the society virtually controlled municipal education. Even though it was reconstituted as the Public School Society, however, its schools were not public institutions, and their religious bias rapidly alienated New York's growing Catholic population. In the end, therefore, New York found itself compelled to substitute genuinely public schools for those of the Public School Society. Neither public spirit nor religious benevolence was adequate to the task of educating the whole people of the city.[24]

In some respects, New York's experiment with universal elementary education under private auspices was unusual, and religious controversy undoubtedly exaggerated its difficulties. But the attempt of a charitable society to educate an increasingly illiterate and im-

poverished population was more or less duplicated in Philadelphia
and other major cities with even less satisfactory results. Indeed,
the general failure of such makeshift schemes of popular education
contributed in the long run to the "Common School Awakening"
of the 1830s and afterward; yet it is important to keep in mind that
the second generation of republican leaders was slow to recognize
the failure of its schemes.

One of the earliest writers to criticize them was James G. Carter of
Massachusetts, whose *Essays upon Popular Education* (1824-25)
stressed the dangers that lay in inadequate provision for public
instruction. The ignorant and degraded members of society do not
voluntarily seek education, he explained, and in the long run they
threaten us with revolution; hence a free government must assume
arbitrary power to eradicate ignorance, even as the Pilgrim fathers
created schools in order to maintain their republic. In the name of
ancestral precedent Carter demanded a revival and an improvement
of the common school system, warning his contemporaries that
without public education "you may preserve and amuse yourselves
with the name of free institutions, and of a republican government,
but you will not be blessed with the reality. You may incorporate
in your constitution, if you like, the articles, 'that all men are born
free and equal,' and 'that all are eligible to the highest offices;' but
this is not freedom, while ninety-nine hundredths of the community
have not the means of fitting themselves or their children, for dis-
charging the duties of those high offices." [25]

In urging schools as a means of protecting republican institutions,
Carter obviously identified himself with men like Nicholas Biddle
and De Witt Clinton who thought of popular education as an indispensable auxiliary of free government. At the same time, in
praising the educational pioneering of the early settlers, he identified
himself with contemporary New England conservatives. In insisting
upon common schools, however, and in stressing the inequalities
that the existing school system permitted even in Massachusetts,
Carter belonged more nearly with the generation to come. Significantly, the main consequence of his agitation was the creation in
1837 of the Massachusetts Board of Education, which subsequently
became the single most important agency of the common school

awakening. Carter's sanctions were traditional and republican but his vision was democratic, and his writings testified to the growing need for drastic reform in educational theories and practices that had been supported by two generations of republican spokesmen.

THE SOCIAL FUNCTIONS OF REPUBLICAN EDUCATION

What its republican advocates expected of education, then, was remarkably the same, early and late, right wing and left. So far as individual human beings were concerned, they hoped that the general diffusion of knowledge would both maximize happiness and help to elevate deserving youths to the highest places in society and government. But even here they had in view at least as much as the individuals' gains the benefits that such a policy would confer on the state as a whole, and for the most part the state or the community was more important in their eyes than the individual. Thus, they hoped for contributions to American scholarship and American technology. They hoped for encouragement of national loyalty, of loyalty to republican institutions, of loyalty to what they identified in a single word as "freedom." During the early years, as their interest in universities suggests, most of them were only moderately concerned over education of the mass of the electorate for participation in politics. As time passed, and with varying degrees of anxiety they saw the suffrage broadened to include propertyless workingmen as well as independent yeomen-farmers, they came to be increasingly interested in elementary education for all. Early and late, however, they sought to employ education to support government by those who were best qualified to govern.

There was a fairly sharp difference between their views and those of the democratic era to come, while the opinions of even the most liberal figures among them betrayed significant links to the past. It would be foolish to maintain that no changes took place in American politics and American social theory during the fifty years that began with the Declaration of Independence, but the argument that there was a radical revolution may also be overworked. Important changes occurred: disestablishment of particular churches and separation of church and state; broadening of the suffrage and reduction of the influence of property in the state legislatures; a tentative liberalizing of the traditional gloomy view of human nature. Possibly this last development was the most important of all innovations for the long run, yet the conception of human nature employed in American political thought remained remarkably constant from 1630 through 1826.[26] On the whole, and allowing for the drastic break with the past that disestablishment of the churches represented, it would seem that the most characteristic elements of federal and republican thought made it more nearly a liberalization of colonial attitudes than an adumbration of democratic beliefs.

The new perspective that (roughly speaking) Jackson's election symbolized has been obscured by the fact that republican terminology was adapted to democratic needs, by the survival of republican political leaders into the succeeding era, and by the deliberate retrospective appeal of Jacksonian democrats to the plastic image of Jefferson. Presumably the clamor of republicans for a general diffusion of knowledge, coming as it did historically just before the common school awakening, has also served to minimize the change. But it need only be pointed out that to the extent republican education departed from disorganized eighteenth-century practice it came close to reviving seventeenth-century precedents in secular terms, or that when Virginia and other states began to adopt democratic educational systems shortly before the Civil War they did not follow Thomas Jefferson's views. Indeed, Jefferson was wiser than many of his recent worshipers have acknowledged when he requested that his tombstone identify him as "author of the Declaration of American Independence, of the Statute of Virginia for religious freedom, & Father of the University of Virginia."[27] National independence, religious liberty, and public support for the most elevated education possible—these were the typical objectives of the American as republican.

How valid this general interpretation is may appear more clearly if we apply to republican attitudes the conceptual framework we used to characterize colonial educational theory and practice. The resemblances are close. Colonial education was thoroughly instrumental, and clearly republican was also. Its novelty lay not in diminishing its utilitarian purposes—certainly Jefferson and other heirs of the Enlightenment, advocates of the education of the people, were in their way even more instrumental in their thinking than their predecessors—but in shifting its uses from religion to politics and economics. Moreover, republican education was unmistakably hierarchical, unless every pronouncement of the radical Jefferson concerning a natural aristocracy and the proper gradations of education be ignored. Even educational plans that described an academic continuum rather than a bipolar scheme like Jefferson's for educating common people and *aristoi* were decidedly selective, as James G. Carter pointed out.

Republican education was by the same token authority-oriented, in the terminology I have already applied to colonial practice. Despite miscellaneous innovations in pedagogy and curriculum (and these are often exaggerated), it was intended to function as an instrument supporting the existing arrangement of society and social authority. Still further, it was limited in scope. Those who believed with Jefferson that education is the "most legitimate engine of government" conceived of it as only one among several engines, and most of them were not so optimistic as to accord it that influence Jefferson proclaimed. More often it seemed a useful auxiliary in an over-all design for the constructive use of the state's powers, rather than the essential definition of the state's role in society. Of course too much may be made of an analytical scheme, but this proposition provides us with an important criterion for distinguishing democratic theories of the role of education from republican theories. We shall find that when Americans fully embraced democracy, education achieved a new status in their thought. At least in the theory of its advocates it was to seem more than a democratic instrument of democratic politics; it was in many ways to absorb politics and political structure, and in effect to be identified with them. In a real sense this identification was precisely what neither colonial nor republican education was capable of achieving.

There is another way of characterizing the republican commitment to popular education, which may be equally helpful in distinguishing it from the democratic commitment that was to succeed it. This is the extent to which republican theory and practice alike imitated or anticipated educational developments in England, which was slow to adopt either democratic suffrage or public education. For example, education under the auspices of the Public School Society in New York was almost identical with that in England immediately after the Great Reform Bill and until the extension of the suffrage in 1867. After 1832 Parliament annually appropriated sums in aid of two private religious societies that undertook to provide an elementary education, by the monitorial method, in all the towns of England. These societies monopolized the parliamentary grants, using them for teaching not only the three R's but also the Protestant religion. What made two societies necessary was the fact that there were both an established church and a large body of dissenters. In New York City, which in other respects adopted the plan the English government was to follow, there was no establishment and hence need for only one society.[28]

More significantly still, the doctrines many republican leaders subscribed to virtually paralleled those of England's Philosophical Radicals, who advocated reform in the British constitution but who cherished the interests of the middle classes rather more than those of factory workers and the urban poor. In his famous review-article on the education of the poor for the *Edinburgh Review,* for example, James Mill justified pauper education at public expense on the grounds of social necessity but not of individual right, and he advocated a plan for state aid to education very much like that proposed by Nicholas Biddle two years before. Other advocates of popular education in Great Britain tended to visualize a hierarchy of schools and voluntary institutes adapted to the needs of a rising middle class rather than the exigencies of the poor. Even Francis Place—"the radical tailor of Charing Cross"—believed that the poor should be expected to contribute something to the cost of their own education, while he particularly urged the proper education of the middle class because it would "necessarily, and at once, elevate the condition of the class below, and raise the standard of knowledge and virtue in the class above." In America his reference to three distinct classes would have seemed strange, but his belief in an education geared to different social roles would not.[29]

Perhaps the most significant difference between British and

American advocates of popular education during our republican era, therefore, rested on the fact that in Britain male suffrage was restricted to householders well past the time at which it became virtually universal in the United States. Consequently, British spokesmen had less reason than their American counterparts to urge the political education of the people. Yet even in this respect their theories were remarkably similar. On the one hand, the British tended to believe that a free press was more important than free schools to good government. While few American writers would have subscribed to this proposition in literal terms, much of their thought clearly suggested that gaps in the formal education of the electorate might be made up by informal means, among which they listed a free press. "Where the press is free, and every man able to read," Thomas Jefferson wrote Colonel Charles Yancey in 1816, "all is safe." On the other hand, when the suffrage was finally extended to most town dwellers in 1867, British leaders pressed the demand for formal education at public expense. "We must educate our masters," Robert Lowe was to insist then, much as Charles Stewart Daveis had insisted at Fryeburg, Maine, in 1825.[30]

In other words, republican advocates of popular education in the United States often shared the perspectives of middle-class reformers in England, who saw themselves exercising social and political authority between an idle and often dissolute aristocracy and an idle and often dissolute working class. We need not press this transatlantic comparison, but it may help to point up the ultimate weakness of our republican schemes for popular education. Not only were they inadequate in fact to meet the demands of the rising generation; they were also inadequate in theory.* In republican thought, the common man was not given enough cause for supporting education with public funds. He ignored exhortations that gave primary emphasis to the social utility of education and skimped on the individual advantages; he resisted a social theory that mani-

---

* Strikingly, British liberals continued to hold up American republican achievements in public education as a model to their countrymen during the 1830s even after American liberals had begun to criticize them for their inadequacy. Even if American advocates of educational reform exaggerated the deficiencies in republican provisions for popular education it is significant that they repudiated what the British hailed.

festly fixed him in a status even while it gave him opportunity to work his way out of it through education. Indeed, he resisted the very conception of a "general diffusion of knowledge," which in most republican writings smacked of *noblesse oblige* and of a suggestion that what mattered most to every man would be trickled down to him from above. Republican education aimed both too high and too low for the democrats whose day was beginning to dawn.

Part Two

THE THRUST OF JACKSONIAN

LIBERALISM

THE "monuments of genuine glory" are the school houses raised by a free people. These humble but mighty institutions, scattered all over our soil, are the fairest ornaments of the land. They are the people's colleges, and the temples of freedom. Within their walls, on this day, are educating four millions of sovereigns, each one to be a citizen king. Our common schools are the sun of the people's mind, daily scattering light and warmth over the nation. They should be the idols of a free people, and around them all should gather to honor and elevate, for they are the sources and guardians of freedom.

J. Orville Taylor, 1839

AND in saying that, I am but saying in other words that we are in an epoch of anarchy. Anarchy *plus* a constable! There is nobody that picks one's pocket without some policeman being ready to take him up. But in every other point, man is becoming more and more the son, not of Cosmos, but of Chaos.

Thomas Carlyle, 1866

III. Preliminary Definitions of Democratic

Education: The Workingmen

THE first significant group of American writers to criticize republican theories of education as undemocratic and to condemn republican educational achievements as inadequate were the self-styled "working men" and "mechanics" of Pennsylvania, New York, and New England. Whereas a handful of early critics like William Manning had fulminated without effect against contemporary educational institutions and assumptions, during the late 1820s and early 1830s these spokesmen for the lower middle and working classes elaborated a theory of democratic education that was to become the most characteristic social theory of the age. Their numbers were few and their direct political influence was slight, but they first spelled out the educational perspective in which several generations of American democrats would see their society and their politics.[1]

THE DOCTRINES OF THE WORKINGMEN'S PARTIES

The causes of the early workingmen's movement were both social and economic: skilled craftsmen and petty entrepreneurs sensed that the comfortable handicraft society in which they had grown up was threatened by such developments as factory production and industrial capitalism. "We are fast approaching those extremes of wealth and extravagance on the one hand, and ignorance, poverty, and wretchedness on the other," said the Philadelphia *Mechanics' Free Press* in 1830, "which will eventually terminate in those unnatural and oppressive distinctions which exist in the corrupt governments of the old world." [2] Acting on this premise they set out to destroy the engines of corporate wealth—banks, chartered monopolies of all kinds, an antiquated legal system—and to protect their own kind against the hazards of debt and bankruptcy. They were conservative republicans, in the sense that they thought of themselves as finding ways to perpetuate the social patterns of an agrarian democracy. But they were also radical democrats. They did not propose to stand idly by and be overwhelmed by what they identified as "aristocratic" economic and social innovations.

Inasmuch as most workingmen already possessed the suffrage, the characteristic vehicle of their early agitation was political parties formed for the purpose. Their willingness to go into politics attracted in turn a miscellaneous group of political adventurers, some of whom were neither workingmen by trade nor democrats by temperament. Yet the confusions that these adventurers introduced into the workingmen's parties should not blind us to the doctrines the parties voiced. Their great target was special privilege, which they thought that state legislatures could abolish simply by refusing to incorporate banks and turnpikes and other economic enterprises. But they also insisted that the same legislatures must establish public schools in order to secure the blessings of education to all who wanted it.

Their belief in public education was as much a product of anti-monopoly sentiment as was their attempt to restrict legislative incorporation. In the fall of 1830, for example, the workingmen of New York City, assembled to nominate candidates for state office, declared that public education was their preeminent political measure, on the grounds that "unless this safeguard of liberty is secured, and by the enlightening of the mass, the axe of knowledge is laid at the root of aristocracy, there is effected, as it were, nothing. The best labours are lost, and the success of the present is ever hazarded in the future." Likewise, Boston workingmen formed a political organization in 1830 which proposed most of the egalitarian reforms that characterized the movement everywhere and which held: "5. That the establishment of a liberal system of education, attainable by all, should be among the first efforts of every lawgiver who desires the continuance of our national independence," and "6. That provision ought to be made by law for the more extensive diffusion of knowledge, particularly in the elements of those sciences which pertain to mechanical employments, and to the politics of our common country." [3]

Nor would the workingmen be content with a mere extension of existing educational institutions. Indeed, their restlessness led them to repudiate as "aristocratic" the very educational innovations that had constituted the outstanding achievements of the republican era. Particularly in Pennsylvania, they mounted an exaggerated attack upon the granting of state funds to "colleges and universities . . . . exclusively for the benefit of the wealthy." "Funds thus expended," a committee of Philadelphia workingmen argued, "may serve to engender an aristocracy of talent, and place knowledge, the chief element of power, in the hands of the privileged few; but can never secure the common prosperity of a nation nor confer intellectual as well as political equality on a people." Because they treated educational privilege as a source of political privilege, moreover, the workingmen demanded identical privileges for all. "The original element of despotism," the committee's statement continued, "is a monopoly of talent, which consigns the multitude to comparative ignorance, and secures the balance of knowledge on the side of the rich and the rulers. If then the healthy existence of a free government be, as the committee believe, rooted in the will of the American people, it follows as a necessary consequence . . . that this monopoly should be broken up, and that the means of equal knowledge, (the only security for equal liberty) should be rendered, by legal provision, the common property of all classes." Workingmen's groups everywhere joined in the demand for equal treatment and the abrogation of a class-oriented education, and in New York as well as Philadelphia they were loud in their criticisms of the educational establishment introduced by the founding fathers.[4]

Thus antimonopoly sentiment and the fear of "aristocratic" innovations led workingmen to demand an effective system of public schools in place of the inadequate institutions of the previous generation. But we cannot understand their educational faith in its full significance if we treat it simply as a logical extension of their opposition to monopoly. The workingmen's belief in public education entered so largely into their diagnosis of contemporary evils that we must also trace the specific responsibilities they assigned to public education as a vehicle of democratic reform.

In the first place, they clearly believed that education would secure the political authority of the people, who might otherwise be led astray from their true objectives. One of the earliest manifestoes of the Philadelphia workingmen's movement articulates this assumption.

It is true [it observed in the spring of 1827] in this favored nation we enjoy the inestimable blessing of "universal suffrage," and constituting as we everywhere do, a very great majority, we *have the power* to choose our own legislators, but . . . this blessing . . . can be of no further benefit to us than as we possess sufficient *knowledge* to make a proper use of it. It will be an instrument of unlimited good to the great mass of the people when they shall possess that degree of intelligence which will enable them to direct it *for their own benefit;* but at present this very blessing is suffered, through our want of information, to be directed against our prosperity and welfare by individuals whose interest is at variance with ours.[5]

In these terms, public education had a twofold political purpose. On the one hand, it would bring about urgent social reforms by alerting the victims of inequality to the machinations of the aristocracy and the misrepresentations of the politicians. On the other hand, it would also protect established democratic principles against political and social evils that had not yet materialized. It seemed, that is, a political engine of extraordinary promise, which would serve both radical and conservative democratic purposes, immediately and in the distant future.[6]

Nevertheless, we must not infer that the workingmen contemplated a truly positive or constructive use for political education. In their eyes political knowledge was useful, not because it supported the exercise of governmental authority, but because it provided an intellectual resource against authority. Although the advocates of democratic education thought that it would inform the suffrage and instruct potential legislators, they hoped that in the long run it would cause state governments to cease tampering with the economy.

By contrast, the workingmen visualized education in its social and economic aspects as a major instrument of public policy. Nor was the role they assigned it in the society and the economy accidental. Skeptical of contemporary governments, and resolved to eliminate "aristocratic" influences from the economy, they proposed to employ education to destroy adventitious social distinctions and to ensure every man an equal opportunity for prosperity. They would educate to abolish class distinctions, to guarantee social and economic equality, to preserve an open society in which merit would find its appropriate reward.

For this reason the early "unions" strove to establish mechanics' institutes and reading rooms and libraries where aspiring young men might both broaden their intellectual horizons and improve their command of their crafts. Even more characteristically, they demanded common schools in which children of every social class might mingle as equals, and where all might acquire the elements of education that would be indispensable to them in later life. From our point of view, elementary schooling could never have been an adequate vehicle for the hopes of the workingmen; but from the point of view of the workingmen, who found themselves deprived of formal education, nothing short of universal common schooling could overcome contemporary evils and redeem contemporary society. Their theory of society led directly to public schools.[7]

In the social and economic realm, therefore, the single compelling reform the workingmen proposed was a reform in education itself, while in the realm of politics education was to be either the chief instrument of reform (the original weapon against aristocracy and despotism) or one of several crucial instruments. In either case, workingmen assumed with remarkable unanimity that once public education had been achieved it would eradicate obstacles to democracy and maintain equality and prosperity. Looking back we may see in their pressure for educational innovations a dawning recognition that in an industrial society talent will not rise without some assistance from the state, but we see too much. Rather, the thought of the early workingmen implied, educational innovation was to be a substitute for other kinds of legislation.

Here, indeed, was the fundamental proposition that gave point to the workingmen's demands for public schools: effective universal education depends upon legislation, but when it has been achieved it will make unnecessary other forms of legislative activity. So far as domestic policy was concerned, the workingmen were advocates of laissez-faire liberalism who proposed to support and extend liberty by means of popular education. Hence their attack on "monopoly" was both destructive and constructive. Attacking existing legislation, they repudiated the traditional authority of government to shape economic development through selective incorporation and other forms of public encouragement to private enterprise. But in attacking existing educational institutions they insisted upon a most generous public provision for the welfare of the democracy. They defined democratic public policy in terms of anarchy with a schoolmaster. *

Thus far, our evidence for the tendency of the workingmen's political devices to reduce to education has come from the writings and addresses of bona fide members of the early workingmen's movement. But the same tendency may also be illustrated by the writings of more radical exponents of working-class needs who were on the fringes of the workingmen's movement proper. To the extent that committed radicals turned to education, in fact, their thought constitutes even more compelling evidence that the idea of public education gained an extraordinary hold upon early social agitation in the United States.

One of the clearest examples of this development is the thought of Seth Luther, perhaps the leading "labor" agitator in New England during the early 1830s, and later a prominent figure in the Dorr Rebellion in Rhode Island. In 1832, for example, his "Address to the Working Men" foretold the inexorable degradation of the American producing classes through monopoly and avarice unrestrained by legislation, and predicted that the factories of New England would soon duplicate the gross inhumanities that mine and mill inspectors' reports already revealed in old England. Given these views, Luther might pardonably have appealed to the right of

---

* This summary of the workingmen's attitudes toward government does not take into account their tendency to support the National Republican party and Henry Clay's "American System" of internal improvements and protective tariffs. The significance of their commitment to an active national government will be dealt with as part of an analysis of democratic doctrine generally in Chapter VII.

revolution (as he was to do during Rhode Island's constitutional controversy) or at least have insisted upon giving priority to sweeping social reforms over all other innovations. Yet apart from an incidental reference to the limitation of hours of work by law he did not invoke social legislation. Instead his address held forth (in the words of its title) "On the State of Education, and on the Condition of the Producing Classes in Europe and America"—and it made the neglect of education its major reproach to the "aristocracy"! [8]

Similarly, the radicals of New York City, who derived many of their political conceptions from British rather than American sources, concurred none the less in Luther's optimistic belief in democratic education. The dogmatic Scotswoman Frances Wright, one of their chief spokesmen, told her audiences that existing evils might be done away with only through "radical" and "universal" reform; but in announcing the necessity that the people unite in a single compelling reform she explained in 1829 that "this measure will be found in a plan of equal, universal, and republican education . . . alone commensurate with the two great objects we have in view— the relief of the present generation, and the improvement of the next." [9] The chief advocate of a plan of equal, universal, and republican education, however, was Robert Dale Owen, son of the English philanthropist and social reformer. His devotion to public education is the more striking in view of the fact that he had come to the United States in 1825 as a member of his father's abortive communitarian experiment at New Harmony. The elder Owen had been interested in educational innovations (his Indiana colony attracted both Joseph Neef and William Maclure) but only as a supplement to complete and utopian social reorganization. The son adjusted to the American scene, and put education first. He was willing, he said in the New York *Daily Sentinel* in 1830, "that the subject of General Education should become—as it appears it will —the Shibboleth of our cause. We cannot have a better Shibboleth. It is the chief—We had almost said the *only*—essential of our political creed." [10]

The educational plan these two leaders sponsored called for state guardianship over children during their formative years, lest parental wealth or poverty or the children's out-of-school haunts miseducate them for a democracy. Clearly, Owen's scheme was drastic to the point of being utopian, and it promptly alienated a large number of New York workingmen, who read Owen and his faction out of their party. But what is significant for our purposes is that the Owenite scheme called for reform through education. Even more than the workingmen proper, Owen and his followers deprecated merely political approaches to social reform and reduced self-government to schooling.[11]

Hence the only significant opposition that radical agitators offered to the workingmen's belief in education came from still another leader of the New York workingmen, Thomas Skidmore. An agrarian leveler whose social theory derived largely from Thomas Paine, Skidmore agreed that general education is indispensable but insisted that the first requisite of reform is economic leveling through the confiscation of inheritances. "Political dreamers! Reformers, if ye prefer that I should call you so!" he charged his contemporaries. "Feed first the hungry; clothe first the naked, or ill-clad; provide comfortable homes for all; by hewing down colossal estates among us, and equalizing all property; take care that the animal wants be supplied first; that even the *apprehension* of want be banished; and then will you have a good field and good subjects for education. Then will instruction be conveyed without obstacle; for the wants, the unsatisfied wants of the body will not interfere with it." But Skidmore's faction was ousted from the Working Men's party even before Owen's, and—lest there be any mistake—Frances Wright herself denounced his "crude schemes and ill digested arguments" in 1830. Skidmore's thought marked an exception to democratic values, not a challenge to democratic belief.[12]

It followed that Paul Brown, another New York agrarian, should adopt education as a major element of social reform. In *The Radical: And Advocate of Equality*, which he published in 1834, Brown treated agrarianism as a utopian ideal and concentrated instead on typical democratic reforms: improvement of the judicial system, further broadening of the suffrage, destruction of artificial privileges, and above all "assurance of the same access to all useful knowledge that others have; that no set of men may in future have the advantage of superior knowledge to cheat us out of any of our rights."

This meant, he said gloomily, that "a rational system for educating the rising and future generations of the common people, is confessedly necessary to ensure the perpetuity of that reform for which we ought to contend. To establish this in full operation, may be the work of half a century. Alas! our oppressors will prevent it being commenced." [13] But his despair was faintly ludicrous. Like most agitators of the period, what he wanted was not radicalism but education, which the very classes whom he accused of oppression would soon adopt as their own vehicle of politics.*

SECOND THOUGHTS ON EDUCATION: THE 1830s

In their first enthusiasm for democratic reform, workingmen and radicals alike believed that universal public schooling would solve contemporary problems and secure universal justice. Under the best of circumstances their proposals would have been vulnerable to failure, but even before they had measured the practical value of education many workingmen adopted other kinds of reform. One main difficulty with education was that it must wait a generation to take effect; the worsening plight of the workingmen suggested that more immediate measures were necessary if republican institutions were to be preserved. During the 1830s, therefore, a number of craftsmen and mechanics turned to trade-union activities to secure urgent economic ends, while others intensified the crusade against chartered monopolies and banks and other forms of special privilege by supporting Andrew Jackson in his war with the "monster bank" or by lending their strength to the radical antimonopoly movement that flourished briefly during the mid-1830s.[14]

Yet the belief that public education is an indispensable ingredient of democracy survived virtually unchallenged in their thought. During the 1830s workingmen's conventions and "unions" and newspapers, although they now clearly subordinated educational reform to the attack on legal privilege, also continued to sponsor familiar proposals for public schools. The main difference between the origi-

* Chapters IV and V discuss the extent to which spokesmen of the major political parties adopted the workingmen's identification of democracy with education. Chapters VI and VII discuss the educational reforms that ensued.

nal and the newer view of education lay in the fact that workingmen who still hoped for political reform treated education as an object rather than a vehicle of that reform. George Henry Evans summed up the transition in their thought when he wrote in *Man* in 1834 that "we have made up our minds to believe that Universal Education is not to be obtained till another great reform is accomplished. . . . We must . . . elect men to office who will abolish monopolies, and by thus getting rid of the aristocracy they engender, remove the only obstacle to Universal Education." [15]

Meanwhile, even trade-union activists divorced from the political reform movement often voiced a commitment to education. One of the chief purposes of union organization was a shorter workday, which gained widespread support because it promised working people leisure time for education. At the same time, the ten-hour day attracted the support of political agitators. In 1835, for example, the Trades' Union Convention of the District of Columbia proclaimed that "the ten-hour system, is one of vital importance to workingmen, so long as they are free and wish to continue so." In Massachusetts, meanwhile, both the Boston Trades' Union and the New England Association of Farmers, Mechanics, and other Working Men pressed for the ten-hour day, and during the early 1840s a "Ten Hour Republican Association" formed in the mill towns to petition the state legislature for a statutory reduction of hours on the grounds that it would ensure "free, intelligent, well-educated, contented and thriving workmen." [16]

As these instances suggest, not only was education still valued by reformers and working-class spokesmen alike, but it was valued in substantially the same terms that had been employed by the workingmen a decade earlier. The hope of achieving political ends directly through universal education had indeed diminished, but the sense that education is an invaluable political asset had not. At the same time, the hope of achieving the social and economic ends of democracy through education remained as powerful as ever: in 1842 Lowell petitioners asked for a reduction of hours for reasons of health and personal affairs, and because *"they would have more time for mental and moral cultivation,* which no one can deny is necessary for them in future life—(it ought not to be supposed that those who work in the mills will do so as long as life lasts)." [17] The most significant innovation in the petitioners' argument was their belief that shorter hours would benefit adults as well as children. Having begun by demanding formal schooling, working-class spokesmen now proposed that opportunity for informal education also be extended, to the end that the present as well as the rising generation might be protected in their rights and privileges.

In dealing with republican advocates of popular education we recognized that informal means of education were never adequate to serve democratic purposes, and we know that the early working-men's movement repudiated existing formal institutions because they could not provide equally for the whole population. Nevertheless, the demand workingmen made for shorter hours during the 1830s in order to facilitate self-culture did not mean that they now accepted inequalities they had formerly charged against republican provisions for schools. Rather, they continued to press for universal public education at the common school level, believing that it would provide a necessary minimum of training beyond which every individual might be expected to acquire knowledge according to his needs and his capabilities. Together, public schools and the ten-hour day would make possible a general diffusion of knowledge that had been impossible under republican auspices.

In some respects, therefore, while the workingmen's faith in education had weakened, it had by no means disappeared. The thought of even the most insistent political reformers implied that if existing evils could be overcome, democratic education would suffice to prevent other evils from arising. The thought of trade-union advocates of a ten-hour day and of political reformers alike suggested that education was an indispensable instrument of social and economic equality, one that must be maintained and extended even if other approaches to reform were uniformly successful. Although the workingmen's original hope for spontaneous political reform through the democratization of education had virtually disappeared by about 1835, that is, their solutions to contemporary social problems continued to depend heavily upon liberty and education.

The extent of this dependence is most strikingly illustrated by the platform and history of the Equal Rights or Locofoco faction within the Democratic party of New York City. This left-wing anti-monopoly movement, which attracted the support of a number of former adherents of the Working Men's party, insisted that the Democratic party actively oppose all forms of legal privilege, paper money, and chartered banks. But it also insisted upon a radical improvement of the common schools, and whereas its extreme anti-monopoly position gradually alienated many of its own followers, its demands for better education proved attractive to all.[18] We may well conclude that neither the tendency of some workingmen to enter politics, nor of others to turn to trade-union activities, altered the fundamental belief of their class in public education. In the long run, elementary schools together with opportunity for further education would remain a characteristic objective of democratic reform when the particular issues the workingmen raised had been either settled or forgotten.

THE SOCIAL FUNCTIONS OF DEMOCRATIC EDUCATION

Like the workingmen's agitation of the 1820s, the agitation of the 1830s ultimately focused in education. Moreover, it embraced democratic rather than republican concepts of the diffusion of knowledge: education must be formal, public, and equal—not an uncertain mixture of formal and informal institutions, public and private responsibilities, "aristocratic" and pauper training. The nature of the educational commitment workingmen and reformers expressed during both the 1820s and the 1830s takes on added significance if we apply to it the same analytical scheme that we employed in evaluating colonial and republican commitments to popular education. Those commitments, we remember, were instrumental, hierarchical, authority-oriented, and limited in scope. By contrast, although the workingmen advocated public schools for clearly instrumental reasons, in other respects their educational doctrine constituted a stunning departure from republican precedent.

In the first place, the workingmen obviously repudiated a hierarchically oriented education. Not only did they denounce private schools and colleges for their "aristocratic" pretensions, but they also focused their constructive efforts on building up a genuinely democratic educational system. It is true that they made relatively little effort to extend this democracy to higher levels of education, but only because they were sure that elementary schooling would serve their political and social ends.

By the same token, their definition of the relationship between authority and education drastically modified the traditional sense of that relationship. On the one hand, their theory called for a popular education that would abridge—not enhance—the authority of established leaders of the society. They proposed both to eliminate encroachments on popular liberty and to protect the electorate against new political impositions. On the other hand, in educating that electorate against contemporary evils, they also proposed to make schools serve a new authority, that of the people. Whereas republican educational institutions had been intended to serve the *needs* of the people, democratic institutions were much more likely to respond to their *wants*. Common schools were only the first of many educational innovations that democratic authority would produce.

Still, it was schools rather than other kinds of innovation that the workingmen sought to impose on their country. Far from enlarging the scope and authority of government, they intended to reduce it, save only for committing it to vastly increased expenditures on public education. Here too they tended to reverse republican precedents, until in the final analysis their social theory assigned to education and to education alone almost all of the responsibilities for social welfare that state governments had previously exercised. In the long run, whereas colonial and republican education had been limited in scope, education was the one function of democratic government that might continue to expand even when political evils had been dealt with by limiting the scope of government. A good many republicans had hoped to diminish the activity of government, but none had really contemplated substituting education for it.

Abandoning republican precedents, the workingmen also modified the social and political perspectives of the British liberals from whom many of their doctrines were derived. For example, the workingmen's attack on chartered institutions closely followed

Adam Smith's analysis of monopolies in *The Wealth of Nations,*
while their thought also echoed most of his other economic principles. Yet in two major respects they transformed his thought. In the
first place, they advocated democracy, whereas Smith and the English liberals who succeeded him were slow to adopt it. Secondly,
while Smith proposed that the modern state educate the "laboring
poor" in order to protect mankind against degradation and the
state against disorder, he also criticized all forms of education that
depended for their support upon either private or public charity.[19]
In other words, he advocated laissez faire in education as well as in
other realms, although he would modify it out of necessity, whereas
in America the workingmen who adopted his liberal economics also
demanded public schooling as the very source and definition of
free government.

Hence the American workingmen may remind us instead of the
English Chartists, who began during the 1830s to form workingmen's political associations and to press for universal education as
a way of securing democratic privileges. Nevertheless, transatlantic
differences in the agitation of workingmen were almost as striking
as transatlantic differences in Liberalism. Chartist spokesmen increasingly repudiated mechanics' institutes and lyceums as a vehicle of reform because they were sponsored by middle-class reformers who wished to discourage aggressive political action by the
working classes. By contrast, American workingmen enthusiastically
imitated these English devices; they were insensitive to the political
implications of self-help as a vehicle of social reform, and complained only that such institutes could not be effective unless they
were grounded upon universal public schooling. In the long run,
moreover, Chartist extremists grew skeptical of schools themselves,
and even a moderate Chartist like William Lovett was apprehensive
of state control over public education. In America, extremists and
moderates alike insisted upon public schools under state control.[20]

We can understand why the American workingmen's movement
was so much less radical, so much more confident of the power of
education, than its British counterpart. Most American workingmen already exercised the suffrage; American society was neither
so stratified nor so impoverished as Great Britain's; American work-

ingmen had not yet despaired of achieving middle-class status. But the reasons are less important than the fact: American workingmen pressed for public education while British workingmen came increasingly to distrust it as an agency of the status quo. When monopoly had been eradicated, the Americans' thought suggested, they would be content with liberty and schools—with what I have called "anarchy with a schoolmaster" in extension of Thomas Carlyle's gibe at British liberals for believing only in "anarchy plus a constable."

It followed that the American workingmen would speak to a wider public than their British counterparts. The political history of the 1830s and 1840s, to which we now turn, is in large part a history of the impact of their liberal principles upon other areas of American social thought.

iv. The Broadening of Democratic Doctrine: The Democratic Party of the 1830s and 1840s

THE Democratic party was our first major party to commit itself to liberal economic doctrine and hence our first major party to equate democracy with public education.

Chance played a large part in this development. The miscellaneous coalition of political factions which put first Andrew Jackson and then Martin Van Buren into the White House was by no means a monolithic body devoted to a single cause. Indeed, many of its beliefs were simply rationalizations for the economic interests of its partisans, yet because of their practical interests it generally advocated a minimal role for government in the American economy. Its liberal economic sentiments appealed to southern and western farmers, and to small-town merchants and bankers and entrepreneurs who sought nothing so much as a free field for their economic endeavors, and who expected little of government save economy and liberty. As a result, the exaggerated liberalism of the Locofocos found a ready hearing in the party during the 1830s and gradually converted what had been a general orientation into a settled doctrine. By the middle of the 1840s the Democratic party was adamantly liberal in its economic theory.[1]

Yet the party was equally committed to the doctrine of popular sovereignty, and while it demanded retrenchment in government it also sponsored the extension and especially the democratization of popular education. At the level of national politics, of course, Democratic spokesmen focused their attention on eradicating the agencies of economic privilege; nevertheless, the party's leaders in the state governments developed in unmistakable terms the theory that popular rule is identical with public education no less than with economic liberty. They were more prudent in their hopes than the early workingmen, for no group in American society save the professional educational reformers was likely to advocate public education with the extraordinary enthusiasm the workingmen's parties originally displayed. But the dogma of popular education was a more plausible belief for middle-class entrepreneurs than for the uneasy victims of industrial progress, and in the long run Democratic philosophy and Democratic policy conspired to establish public schools as one of the few lasting responsibilities of government. In their way, Democrats as well as workingmen subscribed to anarchy with a schoolmaster.

THE IDEAS OF PARTY PROFESSIONALS

The consolidation of Democratic party commitments is apparent in the public statements of its leading figures during the 1830s and 1840s. Voicing the demands of an outspokenly "Democratic" party that had outgrown the assumptions of its "Democratic-Republican" predecessor, party professionals gradually adopted an unambiguously democratic perspective on economic policy and popular education in place of the more complicated republican perspective that had prevailed since the turn of the century. We may trace this development most conveniently in the two key states of New York and Massachusetts, postponing any consideration of events in the West or the South to other chapters of this analysis of democratic thought.

Governor William Marcy was the transitional figure in New York State. When he took office in 1833 he proposed to the state legislature that public expenditures on canals cease until revenues from canals already in operation had replaced public funds spent in their building. In subsequent years his messages to the legislature were more equivocal in dealing with internal improvements, for although the state was already in debt additional canals seemed necessary to complete its transportation system, but in other respects he advocated characteristic liberal reforms. In particular, he urged stringent limitations on banks and the incorporation of banks, a ban on small bills, and a reform of the state's judiciary, and throughout his governorship he insisted that state interference in the natural workings of the economy threatened society with worse evils than government inactivity. In none of his messages was Marcy truly adamant, and he never ceased to recognize practical objections to strict laissez faire, but even during the course of his five years in office (1833–38) he became more doctrinaire and more insistently liberal in his economic thinking. By the time of the Panic of 1837, in fact, he had become something very close to a Locofoco.[2]

While Marcy gradually diminished the role he assigned government in the conduct of the economy, however, he also rapidly enlarged its responsibility for popular education. In 1833, echoing Jefferson, he commended agriculture as the primary safeguard of free institutions, but in 1834 and again in 1835 he pressed the legislature to appropriate funds for public education, not only to supplement the income from the Common School Fund but also to facilitate the training and supervision of common-school teachers. In 1836 he went so far as to criticize men who worked with their hands and lacked education themselves but failed to support it as vigorously as they should. Even in 1837, when the state was beginning to feel the effects of the panic, he continued to champion the same measures, on the grounds that "education in all its branches, but particularly in that which includes the common schools, is the highest object of public concern."[3]

It is clear that in many respects Marcy urged public support for elementary education for reasons that we have identified as republican rather than democratic. His message of 1834 favored it explicitly as a "republican" necessity, while his message of 1837 voiced an old-fashioned perspective in proposing to a business-oriented people that "public virtue and intelligence" are more important than the acquisition of wealth. Similarly, in urging normal training Marcy implied that ordinary common schooling would not be adequate to support all the demands of government. But he held popular education to the highest possible standards because it was the one truly significant duty of government. "The mere imposition of tasks, which are usually performed as an enforced duty," he said in 1834 in pointing to the need for better teaching, falls far short of the ends that should be aimed at. Emulation should be awakened in the minds of the pupils, and the acquisition of knowledge made a desirable object. When they once become sensible of the great advantages of education in the ordinary pursuits of life, and of the numerous enjoyments springing from the cultivation of their mental faculties, the difficulties of the work are nearly overcome, and the duties of the government are in a great measure performed. They then become their own teachers, and will seek opportunities, and furnish themselves with the means, of instruction.[4]

In other words, the measures Marcy proposed were intended to support democratic purposes as well as diffuse available knowledge, and in conjunction with his increasingly liberal economic attitudes they were clear evidence of a tendency to define Democracy in terms of liberty and common schools. If education was not the only positive function Marcy's thought assigned government, it was undoubtedly the most basic.

In practice, converting New York's established school system from an inadequately organized and inadequately supported instrument of republican policy to a full-fledged public network had to wait at least a decade, until the rural population of the state abandoned its opposition to the high cost of educational innovations. But though Marcy met with indifferent success in his campaign for better schools, he was only one of several prominent Democrats who sponsored educational reform. Samuel Young, a vigorous advocate of extreme Democratic principles during the 1830s, was very largely responsible for securing the passage of a bill to establish district libraries in 1835. John A. Dix, secretary of state under Marcy and ex officio superintendent of schools, and Young, who held the post during the 1840s, showed great zeal in promoting public education. Calvin Hulburd, also a radical Democrat, was mainly responsible for establishing a state normal school. His work in turn made it relatively easy for Governor Silas Wright to rebuke rural voters in his message of 1846 because they objected to the "undemocratic" tendency of this state institution to centralize public authority over education. The leaders of the Democratic party in New York obviously favored expanding and improving public education at a time when they were withdrawing the state government from other areas of activity.[5]

In New York the Democratic party was the dominant force in state politics. In Massachusetts, on the other hand, it was slow to reach power, and as a predominantly rural party it was also slow to sponsor improved public education as one of its main goals. Furthermore, the system of schools the state had inherited from the eighteenth century was already more effective than comparable systems in other states, and in addition educational reform was vigorously pressed by adherents of the ruling National Republican (later Whig) party; there was every reason for the Democratic party not to insist upon public education. Yet by 1839, when it first won the governorship, the party was well on the way to adopting liberty and education as its program for reform.

As in New York, the Democrats in Massachusetts were influenced by radical political sentiments such as had originated with the workingmen. During its unsuccessful campaigns of 1840 and 1841, the party endorsed the ten-hour day, proposed unlimited personal liability for stockholders in banking corporations, and urged abolition of all imprisonment for debt together with an elective judiciary. In 1842, moreover, it was to sanction the democratic revolution in Rhode Island, and to demand "free suffrage" and equal education in Massachusetts. Meanwhile, in his first message to the state legislature, Governor Marcus Morton had recommended a general banking law instead of special incorporations, the suppression of small bills, stringent limitations on other forms of incorporation, retrenchment in state expenditures (particularly in expenditures for internal improvements), and the democratization of education. There are very few objectives of common as distinguished from partial interest, he explained, hence few objectives that warrant the activity of government. These are justice, police, free schools, and good education.[6]

Insofar as it dealt with education, the main burden of Morton's message was the need to apply public funds to common schooling rather than higher education, and the need to reestablish local control over the schools in place of the centralized authority established by the state board of education the Whigs had recently created. The committee on education of the House of Representatives responded with a partisan attack on the board for its "Prussianizing" influence, and proposed incidentally that teacher training be left to competitive private enterprise among the state's academies in place of the normal schools the board of education had established. Nevertheless, although such reactions to contemporary educational reform indicated that the Democrats of Massachusetts would oppose innovations their party had supported in New York, they also reflected an acute sense of what a popular education should be in order to serve democratic ends. Significantly, Morton's message pictured the common school as an epitome of American society. As he saw it, the district school fostered natural equality, taught that virtue brings rewards, and inculcated the great principles of freedom in such a fashion that they could not be obliterated.[7]

Elected again in 1842, Morton reiterated most of his proposals in his message to the legislature. Again he championed a liberal economic system in which everyone would be protected in the pursuit of his own prosperity and in which government would attempt to secure no more than justice and police. In particular he proposed tax reforms that would reach the rentier class rather than their tenants, a general incorporation law providing for unlimited stockholder liability, retrenchment rather than expansion of public expenditures, and a constitutional limitation on the borrowing power of the state. Apart from these reforms, he thought that contemporary problems could be met through a fuller democratization of politics and education. He expressed sympathy with the political aspirations of the unfranchised people of Rhode Island, insisted upon the "universal diffusion of mental and moral light" in Massachusetts, and renewed his plea for additional state aid to common schools under local control. Although he pressed for local control of schools because it accorded best with grass-roots democracy, like his antagonists he sanctioned a considerable improvement of common schooling. Because he believed that it is impossible to legislate religion or morality he thought that "the universal diffusion of knowledge" was essential to secure "the prevalence of virtue."[8]

This was what Robert Rantoul Jr., the first Democratic member of the Board of Education, also felt. "The leading idea of the American policy is freedom," he said at Scituate in 1836. "The sole purpose of government is to prevent the rights of the citizen from being infringed or encroached upon. Every man should be left in the full enjoyment of his natural liberty, so long as he does not thereby interfere with any of the natural rights of his neighbor. . . . Within these limits . . . the whole object of government is negative. It is to remove, and keep out of his way all obstacles to his natural freedom of action." Given this assumption, education was the one indispensable instrument of democracy. Rantoul pointed out to the American Institute of Instruction in 1839 that the United States was the scene of the world's great experiment in the peaceful democratization of social institutions. "Upon our capacity for the improvement of advantages never before vouchsafed to any portion of the children of men," he declared, "depends the issue of man's history. Universal education will determine this capacity." [9]

In two key states, that is, the leaders of the Democratic party lent its growing strength to the belief that democratic government is very nearly reducible to education. They aligned themselves more or less with the workingmen in their criticisms of educational systems dating from the previous generation, and they also held out hope that an effective system of popular education would deal with most contemporary problems. But New York and Massachusetts had led the nation in providing for the education of their people even during the republican era. We may well ask, therefore, what was the policy of the Democratic party in eastern states that had neglected public education during the preceding generation.

Pennsylvania offers us an instructive answer. The first eastern state to adopt Jacksonian democracy, it also confronted entrenched hostility to public education on the part of its German-speaking population and many of its pietistic sects. In addition, the Democratic party was slow to draw supporters from the workingmen and from the Scotch-Irish inhabitants of the western counties, who most strenuously advocated public schools. In this context, the fact that Governor George Wolf eloquently supported common schools against the wishes of many of his constituents is significant evidence of the party's growing commitment to democratic education, while his personal leadership in obtaining Pennsylvania's first important school law in 1834 and in protecting it thereafter is even more significant. In 1837, moreover, when the governorship and the house of representatives had fallen to the Whigs as a result of divisions within the Democratic party, a committee of the Democratic senate reported out a bill establishing compulsory education of factory children that compared favorably with those being debated at the same time in other states. The committee's action suggests that education had become a particularly attractive version of Democratic reform.[10]

Recognizing this possibility, we must not ignore the fact that Pennsylvania Democrats lagged behind their counterparts in other states in their enthusiasm for public schools. But it is also important to recognize that they lagged in other respects as well. Although Pennsylvania was a stronghold of the Democratic party, the party was slow to adopt the Locofoco attitudes that characterized it in New York and Massachusetts. For the time being, that is, the Democrats of Pennsylvania approached both economic liberalism and public education tentatively and cautiously; but in the long run they too would adopt both as their definition of democracy.

Within these limits, the attitudes of political leaders in three major states, heirs to different political and educational histories, suggest strongly that at least in the Northeast the Democratic party sponsored public education in much the same terms the workingmen had used. In practice, of course, the party was no better able than any amalgam of political forces and economic interests to carry out a single-minded reform of its society, and Democratic legislatures often fell far short of, or went far beyond, the recommendations even of Democratic governors. But while most Democrats sought economic and political reforms before they demanded education, and while their willingness to adopt reforms that strict economic liberals demanded was uneven and irregular, in the final analysis their policies resolved themselves into free enterprise and public schooling. In the states, Democracy usually meant less government and more education.

DEMOCRATIC PARTY IDEOLOGY

Besides its professional leaders, who helped to convert the Democratic party of the 1830s and 1840s into an agency of democratic liberalism, the party also claimed a number of essentially literary figures among its most prominent members. Because they bespoke democratic reform in language untrammeled by compromise, they helped to impose a radical orientation on the party even as a political organization. We cannot understand the impact the party made on American thought without also examining the doctrines put forward by these ideologues, who constantly pressed their party to assume extreme positions on contemporary public issues.

Perhaps the most striking element in their political thought was the conviction that the people must rule but that in order to rule properly they must be educated. One of the most dogmatic Democratic spokesmen suggested, indeed, that the people are invariably competent to rule irrespective of their education. "Democracy is the child of light; and adopts every enfranchising truth, that time and genius and the public mind may develope," George Bancroft told the Democrats of Springfield, Massachusetts, at their Fourth of July celebration in 1836. In an oration before the Adelphi Society of Williams College in 1835, in fact, he had ventured to suggest that the accumulated wisdom of the race is irrelevant to truth. Hence it was easy for him to suggest in 1836 that the most important safeguard of popular wisdom might be the inaccessibility of mind to the organs of government, inasmuch as in a democracy "tyranny cannot reach the public mind; and tyranny in a democracy is therefore an impossibility." [11]

Yet in both orations Bancroft also insisted on the importance of public education to the progress of truth. In the first, he explained that "the world can advance only through the culture of the moral and intellectual powers of the people. To accomplish this end by means of the people themselves, is the highest purpose of government." Hence he "deduced" a "universal right to leisure; that is, to time not appropriated to material purposes, but reserved for the culture of the moral affections and the mind." This was, perhaps, a superfluous deduction, but it culminated in a specific assertion of the "right to universal education," and in his oration of the following year Bancroft pointedly if mistakenly identified the early New England colonists as convinced democrats who had established popular education because of their political convictions. Outside of Massachusetts, he added, it is the areas boasting common schools that have joined with the Democracy, above all the state of New York, which is "pledged to internal improvements, to free labor and to free schools." [12]

This was as close as Bancroft came in either exhortation to a political program, although the oration at Springfield was decidedly partisan. (Two years later he was to become Collector of the Port of Boston, and thus prominent in the state's Democratic party.) But in an address at Hartford in 1840 he elaborated the principles of his party more specifically. After bombastic declamations against "aristocracy" and a pointed attack on the Whig principles of balanced constitutional government, he explained that Democracy chooses the policies that leave government nearest to the people. They include, he said, universal suffrage, honest elections, popular instruction of legislators, rotation in office, direct election of the executive, an elective judiciary, jury trial as to law as well as facts, and equal and simple laws that do not (like the protective tariff and the national bank) convert government into an auxiliary of the money power. He went on to rail at the social theory he imputed to the Whigs, that "artificial" legislation filters prosperity down to the laboring class—"So indifferent are the whigs to popular freedom and popular education." Clearly, Bancroft's program reduced to the democratization of existing political institutions, elimination of all special privilege, and popular education.[13]

In New York, William Cullen Bryant and William Leggett, the editors of the New York *Evening Post,* acted as theorists for the radical wing of the Democratic party. Whereas Bancroft owed much of his democratic doctrine to German transcendentalism, the New Yorkers identified democracy with a doctrinaire economic liberalism that derived almost unchanged from Adam Smith. "Liberty," Leggett wrote in the *Post* in 1834, "is . . . nothing more than the total absence of all MONOPOLIES of all kinds, whether of rank, wealth, or privilege," and he urged laissez faire as a universal reform for contemporary evils. Leggett's theory was so doctrinaire, in fact, that he even opposed public services like the post office and the public weighmaster, and he attacked incorporated schools and colleges, not to mention state subsidies to private academies that acted as normal schools, because their privileged status prejudiced free competition in education. Yet despite the extraordinary lengths to which both Bryant and Leggett were willing to carry their economic liberalism, neither repudiated public schools. Apparently each believed that education was a proper function of the state.[14]

Furthermore, during the 1840s Walt Whitman, another Democratic advocate of extreme economic liberalism, spoke up enthusiastically for public schools. Whitman's main interest lay in contemporary pedagogical innovations because they encouraged the individuality of each child, but he also recognized the social implications of American educational institutions. The difference between the United States and Europe, he wrote in the Brooklyn *Daily Eagle* in 1846, is the difference between aristocratic waste and democratic public works. "American liberality," he said, "is shown not in matters of vain and childish display—not on baubles and gew-gaws, and robes of state, and gilding and satin-cushioned carriages for officers of state—but in munificent grants for the support of Free Schools, in huge outlays for internal improvements, in the construction of mighty and useful works, such as the Croton aqueduct—a performance which all Europe cannot parallel!" As this passage suggests, Whitman's laissez faire was less consistent than Leggett's. Yet Whitman usually insisted upon minimal government, and what is most significant about his social theory is not that it was inconsistent but that one of the few public enterprises for which it made provision was elementary education.[15] Whitman by his explicit statement, and Bryant and Leggett by their tacit acceptance, treated common schools as a necessary service of government to the people.

Meanwhile, spokesmen for the national Democratic party also treated education as one of the few necessary and proper functions of government. Although few national controversies involved public education, and although all thought of a national scheme of education had disappeared with the republican generation of 1800–1828, during the late 1840s the *United States Magazine and Democratic Review* served as a vehicle for both laissez-faire economic dogma and current educational thought.

The magazine's explicit statements of the political and social purposes of education were less frequent than other kinds of social analysis, but they were significant. For example, in a classic statement of Democratic liberalism written for the first issue of the *Review*, John L. O'Sullivan upheld the right of the people to rule on the grounds that the "general diffusion of education" in the United States nullifies the aristocratic pretensions of the better classes "to the sole possession of the requisite intelligence for the management of public affairs." But O'Sullivan also denied the right of any people to regulate economic and social affairs, which should in all cases be left to the operation of the "voluntary principle." Obviously, he took public education for granted in spite of the doctrinaire quality of his economic liberalism.[16]

Other statements in the magazine reinforced O'Sullivan's doctrine. In April of 1840, for example, the editor appended to an article describing contemporary French politics a footnote in which he attributed both the poverty and the radical "fanaticism" of the French laboring classes to their inferior education, intelligence, and enterprise, together with the "clogs" upon their industry and their lack of arable land. In July a contributor criticized William Ellery Channing's "On the Elevation of the Laboring Portion of the Community" because it put provision for the mind before provision for the body. Yet he also identified provision for the body with removal of unnessary "clogs" upon business, and left the elevation of the laboring classes to the same self-culture that Channing preached as an accessory to common schooling. In October, it is true, another contributor denied that popular intelligence depends upon education, in that the divine will may work uncorrupted through ignorant men yet be corrupted by the sophistries of learning. But like George Bancroft, who might indeed have written the article, the author concluded by recommending to the people "the simple elements of learning, *with the means of educating themselves*," in place of the "hot-house system" sponsored by the aristocracy, which creates idle men and aristocrats. In one way and another the *Democratic Review* strengthened Democratic belief in the power and the necessity of common schools.[17]

Clearly, Democratic theorists as well as Democratic politicians supported public elementary education in spite of their devotion to laissez-faire economics. Indeed, they took public schools so much for granted that they were not even aware that public education created a logical inconsistency in their thinking, which in all other respects tended to be uncompromisingly opposed to active government. Equally clearly, they conceived of education as a powerful social engine which would facilitate individual competition and encourage individual enterprise. Although strict liberalism might have dictated leaving practical education to individual initiative, Democratic theory embraced it for the advantages it could bestow. In these terms, Democracy consisted of liberal institutions plus a liberal education.

Only one prominent Democratic theorist repudiated public education, and his reasons discredited him rather than challenged established Democratic belief. That dissident spokesman was Orestes A. Brownson, who devoted several essays in the *Boston Quarterly Review* to the proposition that social reform must precede education in order to make it effective. "We have little faith in the power of education," he wrote in his famous essay on the laboring classes, "to elevate a people compelled to labor from twelve to sixteen hours a day, and to experience for no mean portion of the time a paucity of even the necessaries of life, let alone its comforts. Give your starving boy a breakfast before you send him to school, and your tattered beggar a cloak before you attempt his moral and intellectual elevation." True reform, he argued, requires at the very least the abolition of all special privileges—including the inheritance of property itself.[18] In other words, Brownson was close to being an agrarian leveler, and as such he was an embarrassment to the Democrats. Although he intended his essay as propaganda in behalf of the reelection of Martin Van Buren, it was promptly repudiated by no less an authority than George Bancroft. Like Thomas Skidmore among the workingmen, Brownson had become a leveler first and an advocate of education second, and like Skidmore he was read out of his party. He deviated, that is to say, in both political and educational theory at the same time, and his deviation serves as one measure of accepted Democratic ideas.

Not every Democratic voter supported public education as a cure for contemporary evils or treated it as an irreducible function of free government. By the same token, neither Democratic leaders nor Democratic theorists devoted themselves to educational reform with the same energy that they devoted to their crusade against "aristocracy" and "monopoly." Yet the tendency of both Democratic policy and Democratic sentiment was to visualize public education in substantially the same terms that the workingmen had adopted once their first great enthusiasm for educational reform had passed. While some Democrats obviously reached this position only because of insistent Locofoco pressures, in fact, the similarity of views went deeper than mere political convenience. Whether they were middle-class liberals or spokesmen for the workingmen, Democrats advocated economic liberty and public schools.

It is almost redundant to point out that in doing so they also conceived of education as a major instrument of democratic rather than republican values. Obviously they repudiated any thought of an hierarchical education such as had seemed appropriate to republican sponsors of the diffusion of knowledge; they interested themselves in the common schools and left higher education to its own devices. Furthermore, they asserted the authority of the people in place of the authority of the few, not only in government but also in education itself. The district school and the local school committee were intended to maintain popular authority in the one area of community life that was important to every democrat. Finally, they sponsored many of the same political and economic reforms as the workingmen, almost all of which tended to limit the scope of government and thereby to extend the responsibilities of education. If in their eyes education was sometimes a residual rather than a primary function of government, it was also the one function that gained importance during their onslaughts on privilege. In all significant respects, Democratic attitudes toward education answered to democratic tests originally propounded by the workingmen.

v. The Conservative Response to Democratic Thought: National Republicans and Liberal Whigs

WHILE popular agitation for social and economic reform encouraged leaders of the Democratic party to adopt many of the doctrines that workingmen had originally championed, it also caused apprehension in the minds of prominent Americans who shared the traditional republican belief that government should oversee the economic activity of its citizens. They reacted by joining in first a National Republican and then a Whig opposition to Jacksonian Democracy, which responded to novel democratic dogmas by pressing for a more effective educational system than the founding fathers had established. Nevertheless, these conservatives found themselves unable to sustain their political and economic policies in the face of determined popular antagonism. Hence the long-range effect of their activity was to strengthen American educational theory and practice, not to preserve the traditional attitudes on which their resistance to the Democrats was often based. In the end, they had no alternative but to accept the two democratic commitments, popular liberty and public education—whereupon they succeeded in making their own educational imperatives a major element of American social theory.[1]

CONSERVATIVE ATTITUDES IN NEW ENGLAND

The changing nature of conservative social theory during the 1820s and 1830s is most strikingly demonstrated in the shifting attitudes of leading New Englanders. On the one hand, many of the area's intellectual elite fought bitterly against contemporary political innovations, and consequently they attempted to employ popular education restrictively, in behalf of traditional ways of thinking. On the other hand, on both political and philosophical grounds other conservative spokesmen abandoned the intellectual assumptions that required them to belabor democracy, and turned instead to considering how education might elevate democratic standards of intelligence and morality.

The typical vehicle of the traditionalists was the Phi Beta Kappa oration, and its most characteristic answer to contemporary problems was an appeal for the extension of New England's established educational institutions. In 1826, for example, in addressing the Phi Beta Kappa chapter of Harvard College, Joseph Story took as his text the unusual intellectual accomplishments of the age in which he lived. The Massachusetts Republican challenged Americans to produce higher achievements in the arts; but he also pointed out that "the unavoidable tendency of free speculation is to lead to occasional extravagances" and that, in Edmund Burke's words, "to innovate is not to reform" in either philosophy or law. Therefore he hoped that the same general diffusion of knowledge which seemingly provoked modern aberrations would also rectify them, by "working its way to universality, and interposing checks upon government and people, by means gentle and decisive, which have never before been fully felt." [2]

In 1826 Story was moderately optimistic; by 1834, however, he insisted that public education must be made over in order to diminish contemporary hazards to persons and property and to the Constitution. Addressing the American Institute of Instruction, he appealed to its members to encourage the teaching of political science, which would serve in the absence of ancient institutional bulwarks against radicalism to control the impact of public opinion upon the government. The next year, Theophilus Parsons Jr. appealed not to politicial science but to the influence of educated men to achieve the same purpose. "The demon brood of sin and self-ishness are awake and at work," he told the Phi Beta Kappa chapter of Harvard College; "shall there be none who will labor against them? Shall the whole direction of public opinion, be left to the demagogue who pays for the votes which give him place and pelf, . . . the expected price of flattering falsehood; to the raving infidel . . . ; to the wild and dangerous fanatic . . . ?" Parsons's address culminated in the suggestion that educated men might take the place of the "chivalry" of old who had maintained law and order and had put down Wat Tyler and the rising in the Netherlands. His point was that "the sword has lost its power" and that to "conquer in this warfare" it was necessary to use education as a weapon of truth.[3]

Perhaps the most striking advocate of this sort of conservative education, however, was the Reverend Horace Bushnell, the outstanding exponent of liberal Congregational theology. In 1837 Bushnell delivered a jeremiad against contemporary political economy before the Yale Phi Beta Kappa. "Under the supposed auspices of the new science," he complained, "a new era of misgovernment is . . . inaugurated," which deifies trade and degrades patriotism while it creates class distinctions and encourages class hostilities. But he refused to despair at the interregnum of "mischief and misrule." Instead he appealed to young people to take up careers in education, the noblest office they could aspire to, which (together with a national literature) might yet teach that "LIBERTY IS JUSTICE SECURED." Obviously his liberalism in theological matters did not extend to public affairs, and he proposed to restore the political and social virtues of the founding fathers by spreading truth among the people.[4]

The belief Phi Beta Kappa speakers expressed, that the "scholars" whom they addressed must save the republic through campaigns of popular education, echoed in their orations until 1861 and even afterward. Nevertheless, it was also possible for an impeccable spokesman of New England conservatism like Edward Everett to urge popular education on much more democratic grounds. In 1833, for example, in addressing the Yale Phi Beta Kappa, Everett acknowledged that education had always been mildly republican, in that it provided for an aristocracy of intellect rather than one of force or heredity. But he insisted that it had also been the engine of the few, whereas "it is the great glory of the age in which we live, that learning, once the instrument of this bondage, has become the instrument of reform." [5]

Still, Everett thought of popular education in 1833 in terms that might be described as generously republican rather than unreservedly democratic. It was not until he became governor of Massachusetts in 1836 on the basis of Whig and Antimasonic support against Marcus Morton that he openly recognized education as a democratic instrumentality. Then, in his first annual message, he told the state legislature that "free governments entirely reverse the theory, on which arbitrary governments rest, that there is a necessary war between Institutions and Public Opinion, requiring that the former should be upheld by force, and the latter contemned or defied. On the contrary, no free government can long exist, but in the cordial alliance between its Institutions and the Public opinion; an alliance which tends to render the institutions popular and opinion steady." And by "free government" he meant substantially what democratic theory held it to be. His opening remarks, congratulating the people of the state on their happy liberty and democracy, pointed out that "our system looks to the People not merely as a whole, but as a society composed of individual men, whose happiness is the great design of the association." To this credo he added one major qualification: "Almost the only compulsion exercised toward the citizen, in his private affairs, by the State, is that which compels him to provide the means of educating his children." [6]

The rest of Everett's message vaguely deprecated monopoly, recommended the abolition of imprisonment for debts contracted before the law against it had gone into effect, suggested that taxes be levied on the income of banks rather than their capital, criticized usury laws, and opposed the banning of small bills because it would contract the currency; Everett was sensitive to contemporary agitation but hardly a radical innovator. Yet he was an energetic advocate of educational reform. In 1837, in his second annual message, he urged that the state's share of the federal surplus be applied to "rendering education better, cheaper, and consequently more accessible to the mass of the community." Speaking at the Williams College commencement, moreover, he depicted education as the basis of civilization and the assurance of individual well-being, and insisted that common schools and higher institutions alike must achieve both "discipline and training of mind to the highest point of intellectual excellence" and "diffusion of useful knowledge among the community at large." Hence he was prepared to ask, "May not a great increase be made in the number of those who receive a good education, and may not the education of all be made much better?" [7]

The difference between Everett and contemporaries like Parsons and Bushnell lay in the fact that the latter, die-hard conservatives, demanded so much of public opinion that they could not reasonably expect any ordinary means of public instruction to serve their purposes. Accommodating himself to some democratic demands, on the other hand, Everett also hoped to elevate public opinion by improving formal education. It was not that he held no conservative opinions, but that he depended upon a more plausible guarantee of popular wisdom than the upper-class crusades the die-hards proposed. Although his hopes for an extension of higher education at state expense were reminiscent of republican schemes for an hierarchical system of popular education, in urging the improvement of elementary education he held it to a test that was compatible with democratic sentiment. In large measure, his conservative program consisted of better education for all the people.*

We may suspect that Everett sponsored limited economic reforms and extensive educational innovations chiefly because he was eager for public office in an age in which liberal democratic dogmas were growing increasingly powerful. Nevertheless, his attitudes toward popular education were faithful to the ideas of other leading New Englanders who held no political office. The extent to which conservative opinion paralleled democratic educational sentiment may be measured in the pages of the *North American Review* as well as in Everett's orations.

During the 1820s and 1830s this house organ of New England Unitarianism increasingly lent its columns to the new social outlook. In 1817 Edward T. Channing and in 1821 Jared Sparks each con-

---

* Significantly, the chief accomplishments of Everett's four terms as governor were the state board of education, provision for state normal schools, and state aid to the Western Railroad. Everett was hardly responsible for the board of education, which followed many years of agitation in the legislature by James G. Carter, but his general political orientation and the pressure of popular agitation for reform made it a most logical conservative innovation.

tributed an essay expressing traditional republican reasons for popular education, while in 1824 George Ticknor contrasted colonial provision for education with contemporary measures and criticized the poor for resisting tax support of *grammar* schools. By 1830, however, Samuel Sewall had tentatively committed the magazine to a version of the reform hypothesis. "Much of the existing evil in the world may be removed or lessened by human agency," he wrote in April of that year. "What now is, and always has been, regarded as the most powerful means for improving the condition of our race, is education." [8]

The magazine's chief exponent of liberal conservatism, however, was the Reverend Orville Dewey, a Unitarian clergyman and humanitarian reformer. After some preliminary explorations, he developed a comprehensive theory of democratic schooling in a remarkable discussion of "Popular Education" that appeared in the issue of January, 1833. The occasion made the discussion even more striking, for the ostensible subject of Dewey's article was the political and moral *Class Books* of William Sullivan, which were extremely conservative and old-fashioned in their approach to contemporary problems. Dewey praised each of the class books, and he made clear that he did not propose any incomplete or superficial education as a preventive or cure for social and political evils, but the main body of his essay was a passionate avowal of his belief in education as a vehicle of democratic progress, where previously he had only tentatively accepted "improvements." [9]

Dewey opened his essay with an apostrophe to the great new age that approached, an age in which individual men but not kings nor noblemen nor any products of a "feudal and artificial society" would achieve distinction or special privilege. The reason, he said, is the dissemination of knowledge among the people. For knowledge is power: "The relation of knowledge to freedom . . . is . . . immediate, strong, and indissoluble. It is the relation of cause to effect. Knowledge will invariably and inevitably produce freedom. The question, whether a people shall be educated, amounts to the whole question, whether they shall be free." Hence he attributed the American Revolution to the triumph of intelligence and principle, and he did not draw back from the contemporary social implications of his reference to the revolutionary past. For the Revolution had merely illustrated a principle. "We say again," he wrote, "that the question about free institutions is brought within a small compass. A man has only to decide, whether or not the human mind was made to be educated, made to be intelligent." [10]

As a conservative faced with contemporary radicalisms, Dewey was also apprehensive about the political effects of the revolutionary experiment. The diffusion of intelligence, he pointed out, has everywhere brought men to demand freedom and toleration and personal dignity; they are not satisfied with an inferior status. In Europe, therefore, the people are demanding social democracy, "and . . . there are, in our own country, combinations of the employed to procure higher wages, political working-men's parties, and fearful signs of resistance to the highest authority in the Federal Union." The same developments appear in domestic life, he added, where the aristocratic influence is declining: "There are abolitions of peerages in our towns; there are reform bills in our families; and our children are educated so freely, as to threaten rebellions, if not combinations for securing their rights." Yet his jocular tone belied his anxieties, and in the middle of his lament he drew attention to the "paradoxical" power of education to cure the evils it created. There are, he said, "tendencies to a radical reform, so radical, indeed, that if not restrained it will tear up every social institution by the roots, and leave nothing behind but disorder, waste, and ruin. But we confess, without intending to say anything paradoxical, that we look to the very power which has given the impulse to control it. That power, undoubtedly, is education, the diffusion of knowledge, the spread, among nations, of juster information concerning the nature of human rights and the action of governments." [11]

Here was something more than the opinion to which even the most ardent old-republican advocates of universal education adhered; it was a declaration not of national independence but of social freedom and equality to be created and nurtured by education. In this context Dewey added that "education, at present, is imperfect, and its result crude," and the remainder of his essay dealt with the necessity of a complete and effective schooling. Hence he wanted to challenge his countrymen: "The idea too much prevails among us, that schools have a kind of talismanic virtue to promote and preserve free institutions." But it was a friendly challenge, and even in the midst of his pedagogical discussion Dewey reverted to his progressive theme, criticizing the knowledge "which has not sought freedom" and with it the feudal age in which he said it had flourished. He also emphasized the fact that education destroys artificial social distinctions, and condemned the "poetic argument" in favor of an established aristocracy by saying that while aristocratic estates are beautiful we also have recollections of "the game laws and of the corn laws, and of all the oppression connected with them." Even in the writings of a professed conservative, the dogmas of liberal politics and democratic education could become a striking manifesto and a rebuke to traditional fears.[12]

Of course Dewey was unusual among his class, and being neither politician nor legislator he could perhaps afford to exaggerate strenuously. But after such an essay had appeared in the pages of the *North American Review* anything might happen. In 1838 it did: Robert Rantoul Jr. preached a lead article in behalf of democratic education.[13] Even more symptomatic of the spread of the new idea, however, was the argument an obviously extreme conservative developed in 1839 in favor of democratic education properly understood:

Let any man, dwelling in the United States, consider this fact; that he is living in the midst of some millions of human beings, having strong bodies, strong wills, clear heads, and mighty passions; let him consider, further, that these millions suffer him to pursue his business, and sleep quietly at night, because they see it to be their interest, or feel it to be their duty, to do so, but that, as soon as they cease to see their interest, or feel their duty, they may pull his house about his ears and hang him upon the nearest tree;—and he will feel, to his heart's core, the necessity of wide-spread moral and religious education *to his own safety.*[14]

From one point of view the writer's opinion revived that of Daniel Webster, who had described popular education in the Massachusetts constitutional convention of 1820 as a "wise and liberal system of police" that inhibits crime and serves as a political safeguard "as well against open violence and overthrow, as against the slow but sure undermining of licentiousness." From another point of view, however, this was a remarkable testimonial, for Webster had not implied that his salutary system of police was the *only* form of social organization and control.[15] In these terms it began to look as if a conservative might accept popular anarchy in spite of himself, provided that it included public education.

CONSERVATIVE DOCTRINE IN NEW YORK AND PENNSYLVANIA

Because of the survival of established educational institutions, and because of the influence that conservative spokesmen maintained against the onslaught of Jacksonian Democracy, the political transition of New England was in many respects unusually placid. Nevertheless, a similar reorientation of conservative attitudes also took place in other areas which lacked New England's special social and political characteristics. In New York and Pennsylvania as well as in Massachusetts the attitudes of leading conservatives very nearly duplicated those of liberal Democrats.

William H. Seward bore the main burden of elaborating a modern social theory for the opposition party in New York. His proposals as opposition leader and his program as governor (1839–43) consisted of an extraordinary mixture of traditional republican hopes with novel democratic demands, which came to a focus in the extension and improvement of public education. Beginning with a social perspective that was manifestly opposed to Democratic attitudes, in fact, Seward arrived at a synthesis of democracy and education that no thoughtful democrat could turn aside.

During the 1830s Seward repeatedly criticized Democratic doctrines that seemed to him to be out of keeping with the achievements and the perspectives of the founding fathers. He was especially scornful of the Democrats' limited views of public policy, and he reminded them frequently that the early leaders of the republic had not hesitated to serve the general welfare. "No such absurdity was then conceived," he told the state legislature in 1840, "as the proposition that while a nation may employ its revenues and credit in carrying on war, in suppressing sedition, and in punishing crime, it cannot employ the same means to avert the calamities of war, provide for the public security, prevent sedition, improve the public morals, and increase the general happiness." [16] Hence, although Seward thought that the federal government could do little to promote the public welfare, he urged a wide variety of innovations on the state government. In his annual messages to the legislature, he proposed that the state adopt an enlightened penal system, reform its judicial and administrative organization, devise electoral safeguards, bar state banks from circulating out-of-state banknotes, and put an end to feudal tenures even where they had been entered into voluntarily.[17]

The core of Seward's program for New York, however, was internal improvements and education, which he linked repeatedly in his public statements. In 1835, speaking at a celebration of the Owasco River works, he was anxious that "improvements of the minds of the people keep progress with those of our territory, if we would preserve [our] institutions." In his first message to the state legislature he proposed enlargement and extension of the Erie Canal and state support for railroads together with state supervision of common schools and academies, normal training, and district libraries. He was confident, he said, that government had power to enlarge the national prosperity, "equalize its enjoyments and direct it to the universal diffusion of knowledge." Even in rebuking Martin Van Buren in 1840 for his veto of the Whigs' Distribution Bill he invoked the same twin principles. The federal government does not build canals and the federal government does not educate, he argued, and therefore the states should be permitted to spend its surplus revenue on both.[18]

Moreover, criticizing the defects of contemporary education, Seward challenged the American people to make their educational system match their democratic hopes. In a discourse on education he delivered at Westfield Academy in 1837, for example, he stressed the "fearful truth, that we are rapidly approximating towards the maximum of population and maturity of national character, wealth and power, and yet have made no corresponding advance in moral and intellectual cultivation." Yet though he portrayed the history of the preceding fifty years as one of "deterioration" in virtue and intelligence, he urged his audience not to recover the standards of 1787 but to exceed them. The question, he said, is not what we have already accomplished, but "are the people of this country as highly educated as they might and ought to be, in order to maintain and perpetuate the peculiar government committed to their care?" "Just so far and so fast as education is extended," he told a Sunday-school celebration in 1839, "democracy is ascendant." [19]

Although Seward continued to press for public aid to canals and railroads, that is, in other respects his plan for an active government incorporated the liberal and egalitarian hopes voiced by the Democratic party in New York. "The highest attainable equality," he announced in an address he delivered in 1839, "is to be accomplished by education and internal improvement, as they distribute among the whole community the advantages of knowledge and wealth." Even more significantly, at Westfield Academy he argued that statesmen like those of the early republic could not solve modern problems because the proper means of public improvement is not beneficent control, exercised from above, but self-control and self-government, which can be achieved only through popular education. In other words, Seward proposed so far as possible to educate the whole people to the responsibilities of statesmanship, and in the Westfield address he described as his ultimate goal a society in which neither vice nor crime existed and in which "mutual truth, justice, and forbearance . . . would, more than human laws can do, protect us all in our personal rights; enlarged views of public policy and disinterested patriotism would engage us all in continued national improvement, and faction would be banished from all our borders." He was a republican who would make every man free and equal.[20]

The test and the symbol of Seward's determination to educate a whole people to liberty and democracy was his attempt to secure public funds for the schooling of New York City's growing immigrant population. Alienated by the nondenominational Protestantism that the Public School Society fostered, Catholic parents frequently chose not to send their children to school at all. Their only alternative was to send them to parochial schools, but during the 1830s the Catholic Church had not established an adequate school system of its own, and in any event most immigrants could not afford to support the education of their children under Catholic auspices any more than they could afford to educate their children by other private means. Hence Seward pressed the state legislature to support elementary schools under Catholic control as generously as it already supported Protestant education.[21]

The ground of his proposal was twofold. On the one hand, Seward was forced by the opposition his plan created to adopt an increasingly illiberal form of argument. Whereas he proposed the education of immigrant children as an inevitable consequence of free institutions and untrammeled immigration in his first message to the legislature, in his third message he told the same body that "I solicit their education, less from sympathy, than because the welfare of the State demands it, and cannot dispense with it. As native citizens, they are born to the right of suffrage." Yet even in 1841 he did not stop with an appeal to the security of the republic. Citing Thomas Jefferson's dictum that error may be tolerated where reason is left free to combat it, he sanctioned aid to Catholic education as part of "the education of the entire rising generation in all the elements of knowledge we possess, and in that tongue which is the universal language of our countrymen. To me the most interesting of all our republican institutions is the Common School." In a letter to Benjamin Birdsall he expressed an even more visionary hope for a nation in which classes formed along lines of birth, language, and religion should disappear, and a "homogeneous people, universally educated and imbued with the principles of morality and virtue" should take their place.[22] If Seward's proposal failed, it was not because he had not gone far enough in meeting democratic needs but because he had gone too far.*

In Pennsylvania as well as New York the outstanding leader of the opposition party contributed both sanction and definition to the democratic principle of education. When rural voters and religious zealots attempted in 1835 to repeal that state's permissive

* The controversy Seward's messages started eventuated in the complete divorce of the city's schools from sectarian administration, as an alternative to aid to different religious groups including the Catholics. This outcome defeated Seward's original purpose, inasmuch as the Catholic Church set its face against nonreligious public schooling, but at least it led to absorption of the Public School Society's functions by public authority, and so marked a major step toward democratization of education in the state.

school law of 1834, Thaddeus Stevens delivered before the lower house of the legislature a speech that echoed through the country. It reads badly today, and even for 1835 it was rather old-fashioned in most of its arguments, but in its setting it was a bombshell, the equivalent politically of Seward's plan for Catholic education, a call to educate in spite of religious differences and in the name of humanitarian and democratic sentiments. According to Charles Sumner's eulogy of Stevens in 1868, "Not a child in Pennsylvania, conning his spelling book beneath the humble rafters of a village school, who does not owe him gratitude; not a citizen rejoicing in that security which is found only in liberal institutions, founded on the equal rights of all, who is not his debtor." Stevens's famous speech was in fact a rather pale reflection of the attitudes of the Vermont of his birth, where the monotonously successful Whigs adopted both the egalitarian principles and the egalitarian education that had been proposed by the earliest sponsors of democratic social reform.[23]

Not every Whig capitulated to democracy by 1840, and not every such democrat adopted popular education with the enthusiasm these leaders voiced. But men like Everett and Seward and Stevens anticipated the direction that all American political thinking, Whig as well as Democratic, would take during the 1840s. They were friendly to democracy; they identified it with the furthest possible extension of liberty; they supported an education for all that would be truly accessible to all; and they suggested in criticism that the only trouble with democratic education was that there was not enough of it and that it was not yet good enough for a free people.

In most respects, therefore, they outdistanced their most optimistic republican predecessors. While Everett and Seward continued to urge public support for academies and colleges, for example, they obviously made effective elementary schooling their primary educational goal. If they also sponsored a hierarchy of educational institutions above the common school, it was because they valued the services of that hierarchy to the democracy at large. Again, in pressing for extension and reform of contemporary education, men like Everett and Seward hoped to elevate public opinion; but they were less concerned to shape opinion according to an authoritative definition of public policy than to make sure it was well informed and deliberate. Their educational innovations were authority-oriented only in the sense that they were intended to impose the highest possible standards of political virtue and intelligence on the exercise of democratic authority. (By contrast, as we shall discover, those who found it difficult to accept democratic authority and democratic policy also tended to deprecate the possibility of educating the democracy through the schools.) Finally, leading Whigs virtually conceded by 1840 that government should be limited in scope and that its traditional positive functions should be assigned so far as possible to organized education. If enough of the people were well enough educated, their theory implied, the responsibilities of government would be very nearly fulfilled.

What most clearly differentiated the Whigs' perspective on education from the Democrats', therefore, was not its traditionalism but its progressive orientation. Because they were conservatives, Whigs insisted upon the fullest possible provision for public education. Yet because they saw education in a democratic social context, they proposed to make it serve the widest possible range of public purposes. Education was not the only function of Whig government, as it sometimes was of Democratic, but it was none the less a popular agency of almost unlimited scope and promise.

v i. Educational Reform and
Democratic Liberalism

ALTHOUGH conservative political thinkers typically urged elaborate provisions for public education because they believed in positive government, some of them viewed educational reform instead as a necessary concomitant of laissez-faire social theory. We have already confronted one instance of this development in the writings of Orville Dewey, whose Unitarian theology helped him to accept economic liberty and popular education as the twin principles underlying modern progress. But it is a development that requires some consideration in its own right because of its profound influence on American democratic thought. On the one hand, a small body of essentially religious commentators whose first impulse in any political or social crisis was unmistakably conservative none the less advocated a drastic limitation on the authority of government. On the other hand, having denied the authority of government, these same conservatives urged pedagogical innovations in American schools well beyond anything that Democrats or Whigs ordinarily proposed. Their two commitments worked together to contribute a powerful liberal orientation to the educational system of the United States. Nor was their influence important only in the realm of educational practice, for in their role as educational theorists for the democracy these conservative reformers could not help but make a major contribution to American social theory.

EARLY APPROACHES TO EDUCATIONAL REFORM

Pedagogical innovations hardly originated during the Jacksonian era. Not only was there a long-standing tradition of educational experimentation in Quaker Pennsylvania, and not only had visionary writers proposed pedagogical reforms in their national plans of education at the turn of the century, but also such distinguished republican leaders as De Witt Clinton in New York and Levi Lincoln in Massachusetts had interested themselves almost as much in the improvement of teaching methods as in the extension of public schools. Moreover, republican leaders often pressed vigorously for the reorganization of existing school systems because they recognized that unless education were made universally effective it could not serve the political and social purposes they assigned to it. Pedagogical innovation was entirely compatible with a traditional republican attitude toward public schooling.[1]

When such latter-day republicans as William H. Seward and Edward Everett interested themselves in the improvement of public education, therefore, they drew heavily on the precedents early leaders had set. For example, because Seward envisaged educating the whole people so far as possible according to standards that had once obtained only for the elite, he proposed extraordinary additions to the curriculum even of the common school. He also urged that the people abandon their prejudice against aristocracy to the extent of holding schools of every kind to the highest possible standards. Yet he took relatively little interest in conditions that affected learning, and he seems not to have thought of education as a process to be developed but as a service to be performed. By the same token, although Everett had been a professor of Greek at Harvard College, and although he had also studied in Germany where pedagogical reform was in the air, his writings give little evidence that he was interested in teaching and learning so much as in the standards of achievement that were to be applied to them.[2]

Hence the public figures who were most likely to approach popular education from a pedagogical point of view were not political leaders who wished to encourage the diffusion of knowledge among the people but more philosophical commentators who were concerned with the nature of man. Among the writers we have already considered, the two leading innovators were staunch Democrats. One was George Bancroft, who followed Everett to Germany and who established an American version of the German Gymnasium

At the same time, Wayland was also an educational reformer and an advocate of popular education. In *The Elements of Political Economy* he viewed the widest possible diffusion of useful information through the common schools as a proper function of government, and in *Thoughts on the Present Collegiate System in the United States* (1842) he insisted that colleges must revolutionize their organization and curriculum in order to serve the needs of the whole public and not simply those of prospective members of the learned professions. Like Adam Smith, Wayland believed that one of the main reasons colleges failed to serve contemporary needs, and individual faculty members failed to be effective scholars and teachers, was that they were protected by public and private charity against the economic consequences of their inadequacies. Hence he proposed to college trustees that they introduce a merit system into the allocation of faculty salaries, and he suggested that they raise academic standards rather than lower fees in order to attract customers. Similarly, he advocated competitive examinations and public awards as means of stimulating intellectual achievement among college students. So strong was his belief in the natural laws of economic liberty, in short, that he would remake contemporary education in their image. He was a radical educational innovator because he was a liberal economist.[7]

In imposing the tenets of economic liberalism on the college curriculum and organization, Wayland adopted a line of thinking that was so narrowly utilitarian that it precluded any truly thoughtful consideration of the teaching process. Yet these practical shortcomings of his educational scheme obviously reflected defects in his imagination, not his purposes, for Wayland made clear in *The Elements of Political Economy* and *Thoughts on the Present Collegiate System* that he believed an improved education was necessary to secure public morality as well as to encourage material progress. As he explained in a letter to his son during the 1860s, "Democracy must prevail, but can be a blessing only by the intellectual and moral education of the people. This education must be a reality, and must not consist in spending years in hammering on Horace and Virgil, and Graeca Majora."[8] In other words, he recognized the need to make educational techniques responsive to the real needs of democracy, but his doctrinaire economics (and very probably his Calvinist training) hindered him from adopting a truly liberal attitude toward the educational process.

Consequently it was left to other religious commentators to explore the full range of possibilities that educational reform offered for cultivating democratic individualism. Most important among these commentators was William Ellery Channing, the Unitarian elder statesman whose influence extended far beyond the confines of Boston. Once a Federalist, more recently a Republican, more recently still disengaged from politics, Channing proposed to his countrymen that they deal with social problems by active reference to liberal religious principles. A humanitarian reformer who considered Americans' headlong pursuit of wealth degrading, and who was active in promoting pacifism, temperance, antislavery, improvement of the conditions of labor, and public education, he was afraid more than anything else of the degradation that stems from the lack of individual self-reliance, the lack of what he called "manliness." The highest interest of individuals and communities alike, he explained in an election sermon in 1830, is a nonmaterial one, the primacy of "spiritual freedom." Indeed, civil or political liberty is valuable only as it "invigorates" spiritual liberty, not through legislation but by removing the restraints on freedom. Those laws are best that represent not the authority of some men over other men but an acceptance of the human obligation to self-government.[9]

As a result, Channing frequently warned the laboring classes against their tendency to band together in associations intended to rectify contemporary social problems. On the one hand, he argued in "Remarks on the Associations Formed by the Working Classes of America" (1832) that there were no classes in the United States, only the rich and the poor, and that social stratification and distinctions based on wealth could not be severe where there was neither royalty nor nobility to burden the poor. On the other hand, he warned that distinctions of wealth are inevitable in any society, and while he approved of such reforms as abolition of debtor imprisonment, streamlining of the legal system, and militia reform, he insisted that many of the workingmen's difficulties arose from their own mistaken craving for wealth. Indeed, in his famous "Lec-

tures on the Elevation of the Laboring Portion of the Community"
(1840) he expressed the fear that "it is possible, that the laboring
classes, by their recklessness, their passionateness, their jealousies
of the more prosperous, and their subserviency to parties and political leaders, may turn all their bright prospects into darkness, may
blight the hopes which philanthropy now cherishes of a happier
and holier social state." [10]

Clearly, Channing was a conservative social philosopher, rebuking contemporary unrest in much the same terms that any apologist
for the status quo might have used. But his insistent demand for
spiritual freedom also led him to attack philanthropic associations
formed by impeccably orthodox defenders of public morality.
Whereas spiritual leaders like Lyman Beecher were prominent in
the movement to organize temperance societies and sabbatarian
societies and other voluntary associations intended to fill the vacuum left by disestablishment of the Congregational Church, Channing repudiated their collective efforts as well as those of the workingmen. He was in this sense an extreme liberal and a consistent
advocate of individual self-government and self-reliance.[11]

But he was still an advocate of spiritual values. Hence he took an
active interest in public education and in all the opportunities that
education offered, both formally and informally, for encouraging
spiritual development. This meant that in his remarks on workingmen's associations he condemned those who would tear down
higher schools and colleges, which opened educational careers to
talented students irrespective of their parents' wealth or birth. It
also meant, in his "Remarks on Education" (1833), that he placed
teachers in the front rank of society, before parents and clergymen
and statesmen, because "intellectual and moral culture" were the
foundation and the source of the "particular reformations" that were
in turn the basis of all human progress. Above all it meant that he
urged teachers and friends of education to sponsor educational
methods that were in keeping with the spiritual promise of mankind. In "Remarks on Education" he praised teachers who were able
to deal sympathetically with children in terms of their own needs
and criticized those who sought to crowd children's minds with
factual information and mechanical skills. And he concluded the

first of his two "Lectures on the Elevation of the Laboring Portion of the Community" with an exhortation to education to liberate the human spirit:

Great ideas are mightier than the passions. To awaken them is the highest office of education. As yet it has been little thought of. The education of the mass of people has consisted in giving them mechanical habits, in breaking them to current usages and modes of thinking, in teaching religion and morality as traditions. It is time that a rational culture should take place of the mechanical; that men should learn to act more from ideas and principles, and less from blind impulse and undiscerning imitation.[12]

As Orestes Brownson pointed out, Channing prescribed education for men who might better have demanded radical social reform. But what is important here is that in urging the widest possible encouragement of education on grounds that can only be considered socially conservative Channing also insisted that the educational process itself be revolutionized. Far from restricting his hopes to an expansion and improvement of the common schools, moreover, Channing proposed that men of every age and condition engage resolutely in self-culture, employing their daily tasks, contemporary political discussions, and free institutions themselves as means of further education. He thought that all life would become a source of spiritual strength when improved teaching in the common schools had opened the way to the exercise of spiritual freedom.

Channing died in 1842 before the New England reformers hit full stride. His successors tried out variations of his basic theme before going on, most of them, into the great crusade against slavery. A number evinced interest in cooperative or associative reform, but the more characteristic bearers of the New England conscience maintained and extended Channing's belief in the development of the individual. To do a great and unique man the injustice of brevity, this was Emerson's role, and we have no more pertinent critique of the organized do-gooders of his day than his "New England Reformers." More nearly like Channing, and more typical, was Theodore Parker, who helped to spread the gospel of Transcendentalism throughout the country.[13]

Parker often spoke like a radical social reformer, and it is not possible to ignore his conviction that there is sin in a society that permits some men to work sixteen hours a day in order that others may live in idle luxury, nor to deny his belief that "there is no nation in Europe, except Russia and Turkey, which cares so little for the class which reaps down its harvests and does the hard work." Yet the recommendations he made for social improvement were monotonously like Channing's. Hard work is not incompatible with self-culture, and it will bring extra rewards to the farmer or craftsman who approaches it with a small reserve of "mental capital"; many workingmen are themselves responsible for not leaving time in their pursuit of wealth for leisure thought and meditation; wealthy men ought out of Christianity, reason, and conscience to pay adequate wages, but "no law can regulate this matter." The passion that the sight of social evils engendered did not lead him to deny the primacy of spiritual freedom.[14]

At that, Parker was more willing than Channing to sanction moral reform through legislation. His great sermon to "The Mercantile Classes" drew their attention in 1846 to the good they could do through their customary control of the legislature. They should take it upon themselves to promote freedom, to forward public education, to "frame particular statutes" that would encourage the weak, the poor, convicts, and drunkards; they should cooperate with the clergy in weeding out "licentiousness, intemperance, want, and ignorance and sin" so as to "turn all the nation's creative energies to production—their legitimate work." Yet there was a decidedly individualistic character to most of these humanitarian suggestions, and in addressing the American Institute of Instruction in 1841—with no merchants to harangue—Parker had already described the ultimate measure as one of education.[15]

Like Channing, he also made reform of education itself the most important step of all. "We all know," he said, "there are certain things which society owes to each man in it. Among them are a defense from violence; justice in matters between man and man; a supply of comforts for the body, when the man is unable to acquire them for himself; remuneration for what society takes away. . . . But there is one more excellent gift which society owes to each; that is, a chance to obtain the best education the man's nature will allow and the community afford." In Massachusetts, he continued, we have only begun. We have schools for all, but "our system of popular education, even where it is most perfect, is not yet in harmony with the great American idea. . . . It is an old transatlantic system of education which is too often followed, not congenial with our soil, our atmosphere, our people." [16]

In such terms, and for reasons that included a traditional belief in the moral authority of the ministry as well as a novel religious orientation, Channing and Parker extended the theory of educated liberty American democrats had proposed as their definition of free institutions. They added one critically important injunction: educate with a scrupulous regard for the individual, and all life will then be educational. There was no other attitude consistent with their theology. Granting the transcendent importance of the individual, even schools geared to republican necessities were false institutions; only by restoring education to its root meaning could it be made to serve the human soul. But their theological commitment to pedagogical reform was also consistent with democratic attitudes. A reformed popular education offered a way in which progress and morality might be served without force or coercion or political machinations; it promised to support liberty with liberty. At their best, religious reformers challenged American education to live up to the theory of educated anarchy.

THE PROFESSIONAL EDUCATIONAL REFORMER: HORACE MANN

Clearly, religious agitation during the 1830s and 1840s helped to produce a theory of education that lent support to, even if it did not stem from, the democratic commitment to limiting the scope of government. One outgrowth of this agitation was Emerson's Transcendentalism, which broke completely with orthodox traditions in social theory and repudiated every influence that one man might attempt to exercise over another. Another outgrowth, however, was Horace Mann's work as an educational reformer. According to Emerson, writing in his journal in 1839, Mann was "full of the modern gloomy view of our democratical institutions, and hence the inference to the importance of schools." [17] But Emerson's criticism really missed the point: Mann was also the country's leading pedagogical reformer, and he became one of the country's leading social theorists. If his philosophy fell far short of Emerson's Transcendentalism, it nevertheless did much to make American education an agency of liberal democracy.

As a Unitarian, Mann was predisposed to visualize the education of children more hopefully than many of his contemporaries. Most of his *Ninth Report* (1845) as secretary of the Board of Education of Massachusetts was devoted to explaining methods of classroom instruction that would cultivate the native abilities and natural goodness of common school pupils, and his other writings consistently urged teachers and school committees to adopt liberal pedagogical methods in place of the tyrannical methods employed in the past. Although Mann demanded over and over again that the common schools inculcate morality, he treated moral education as a consequence of good teaching, and he blamed bad teaching for contemporary threats to the moral order of society. Furthermore, stressing the proposition that knowledge is power for good or evil according to the moral framework in which it is presented, Mann also insisted that the common schools practice self-government. "He who has been a serf until the day before he is twenty-one years of age," he wrote in 1845, "cannot be an independent citizen the day after; and it makes no difference whether he has been a serf in Austria or in America. As the fitting apprenticeship for despotism consists in being trained to despotism, so the fitting apprenticeship for self-government consists in being trained to self-government." In every way Mann represented educational reform as a pressing necessity of democratic government.[18]

Yet despite his theological and pedagogical liberalism Mann was far from being an uncritical advocate of democracy. It is clear in his writings that he regretted the materialism and the craving for personal success that marked the age, and equally clear that he conceived of popular education as a vehicle carrying not only morality but truth itself to those who might otherwise neglect them. Thus, he complained in his valedictory *Twelfth Report* (1848) that "education has never yet been brought to bear with one-hundredth part of its potential force upon the natures of children, and, through them, upon the character of men and of the race," and he insisted that a nondenominational Christianity must be inculcated in order to overcome the "moral oscillation" to which all human beings are susceptible. In most important respects he accepted the conservative fears and the conservative injunctions that spokesmen for orthodox Calvinism subscribed to.[19]

Like many other advocates of educational reform, that is, Mann thought in terms that were socially conservative yet pedagogically liberal. When he examined the Prussian educational system in his *Seventh Report*, for example, he praised its efficiency in instructing the whole population, but he was also sensitive to its pedagogical innovations because they stimulated intelligence and the ability to think. Conservative though he was in discussing American institutions, moreover, Mann criticized the Prussian monarchy for depriving its subjects of an opportunity to exercise their intellectual and moral faculties in elections, legislation, the conduct of public affairs, or the practice of religious freedom. He also predicted that a well-educated people would ultimately demand the right of self-government, and he pleaded with the king to liberalize his government rather than precipitate a revolution.[20]

Mann's plea may well have been disingenuous, intended to confirm American institutions rather than to challenge Prussian practices. But it lent support to a striking statement of his educational theory. Mann went on to argue that the lower classes throughout the rest of Europe were poverty-ridden, burdened with militarism, deprived of genuine religious freedom, and brutalized and ignorant because "vested interests" prevented their education. By contrast, the United States was exempt from most European evils; but in its indifference to education and to educational reform it had failed to eliminate vice and pauperism and ignorance and the political evils that threatened American liberty. By this means Mann identified hostility to educational reform in America with hostility to education in Europe. More than this, he offered American conservatives the strongest possible reason for adopting liberal principles in education. He believed that all men have a natural right to education, which European nations ignored; but quite apart from natural rights

ent in the *Seventh Report* also suggested that when popu-
on has been initiated it cannot be stifled and must there-
ried to its logical extreme. In Mann's analysis, democratic education demanded educational reform.[21]

Although Mann was wont to emphasize the conservative and
preservative character of public schooling, moreover, in his final
report he spelled out a theory of progress grounded upon the widest
possible diffusion of education and popular liberty. Now he emphasized not the hazards to which even the United States might be
subject but the opportunities "intellectual education" offered for
encouraging universal prosperity and removing class distinctions.
On the one hand, he differentiated American social theory from
European doctrine: "According to the European theory, men are
divided into classes,—some to toil and earn, others to seize and enjoy. According to the Massachusetts theory, all are to have an
equal chance for earning, and equal security in the enjoyment of
what they earn." On the other hand, he insisted that Massachusetts
as well as Europe was threatened by industrial feudalism, and he
urged that

Now, surely nothing but universal education can counterwork this tendency to the domination of capital and the servility of labor. If one class
possesses all the wealth and the education, while the residue of society
is ignorant and poor, it matters not by what name the relation between
them may be called: the latter, in fact and in truth, will be the servile
dependants and subjects of the former. But, if education be equably diffused, it will draw property after it by the strongest of all attractions;
for such a thing never did happen, and never can happen as that an
intelligent and practical body of men should be permanently poor.[22]

In 1848, that is, he accepted virtually the same diagnosis of contemporary social evils that workingmen had first voiced, and he
proposed virtually the same cure.

The one major point in democratic criticism of the existing social
order that Mann refused to accept was the charge that some men
are poor because other men are rich. Rather than seek to divide
established wealth, he argued, men should recognize the extraordinary resources education offers for creating new wealth.[23] Here
was a conservative argument that might justify maintaining every

other detail of the status quo on the grounds of what education would bring in the future. But it was a conservative doctrine that reflected contemporary radical sentiments. Like most Democratic liberals, Mann anticipated an almost infinite human progress, guaranteed by free institutions and supported by public schools. If he was a conservative social theorist he was also an extreme advocate of liberty and education.

Mann was unusual among professional educational reformers in that his interest in the extension and improvement of public education led him increasingly to adopt liberal democratic sentiments where other reformers often remained explicitly and exclusively conservative in their social thought. Nevertheless, his career as an educational reformer, which converted him from an advocate of improved standards of instruction and school facilities to an avowed proponent of democracy, foreshadowed a development that affected educational reform throughout the country. Once the possibilities of educational reform had been recognized, in a society which prided itself on its free institutions, it could not help but serve democratic rather than conservative purposes.

This development was apparent even in the fate of the Western Literary Institute. Conceived as a vehicle of religious and political orthodoxy during the 1830s, the Institute disappeared during the 1840s as professional educators turned to the practical tasks of raising Ohio's educational standards. In the long run, Calvin Stowe's report on the Prussian schools led not to orthodoxy but to improved democratic education. Similarly, the work Henry Barnard accomplished in Connecticut and Rhode Island, and the writings of other sponsors of pedagogical reform, all contributed to the development of a nation-wide system of public schools organized and administered in the interests of a liberal democracy. True, even during the 1850s it was necessary for Barnard to defend pedagogical innovations against the charge they were an illiberal Prussian invention; practical achievements did not come easily.[24] But the long-range tendencies of American education had been accurately if unsympathetically delineated as early as 1840 by Andrew Peabody in the *North American Review*. Examining contemporary schoolbooks and pedagogy, Peabody wrote sarcastically:

Mathematics are taught by toys; geography and history must be mixed with equal portions of Peter Parley's mythology; the mysterious differences between active, passive, and neuter verbs, instead of being beaten into children's brains, as of old, by hard blows, are more kindly, yet not more wisely, illustrated by the picture of a whipping; while all the mooted points in moral philosophy, which have baffled the wisdom of ages, are despatched in a thin 18mo, which treats but of tops and whistles, broken glass, and stolen sweetmeats.[25]

Yet Peabody was notoriously conservative even in his own day; his lament testified to changes in educational doctrine that he could not share.

What had happened in American thought, in short, was that educational reformers converted the limited enthusiasm with which men of conservative temperament witnessed the rise of democracy in the United States into a generous enthusiasm for democratic education. Their motives were obviously conservative in that the reforms they introduced were intended to protect the republic against the consequences of an excess of democracy. But the tendency of their thought was unmistakably liberal. Advocates of educational reform like Wayland and Channing insisted that education must observe the laws of human liberty, and professional innovators like Mann and Barnard sponsored pedagogical reforms because they would enhance political and moral freedom. When their work had been completed, the public schools would be a vehicle of demo·cratic liberalism on the Jacksonian model.

VII. Recognition of the Common Principle

IN spite of obvious disagreements, workingmen and Democrats, Whigs and educational reformers established universal public education as the indispensable institution of the American democracy. Nevertheless, even their powerful educational commitment might have been ineffective had contemporary circumstances not made it virtually impossible for die-hard conservatives to maintain their deep-seated prejudices against public schooling. We shall find that only critics of American society who repudiated democracy itself could consistently repudiate the education of the people at public expense. Others, whose attitudes we shall examine here, found that history had converted them to democracy and public schools.

Their willingness to adopt both democracy and public schools, reluctant as it may sometimes have been, helped in turn to make possible constitutional enactment of the liberal principles that Jacksonian Democrats had originally imposed on American political life during the 1830s. During the 1840s and 1850s, when virtually every state in the Union revised its instrument of government to accord with democratic doctrine, the American people defined their political consensus in terms of popular liberty and public education. Their quest for self-government ended in virtue and intelligence.

CONSERVATIVE OBSTACLES TO PUBLIC EDUCATION

The obstacles and objections to systematic instruction at public expense have traditionally attracted the attention of historians of education. Their bias is understandable: educational reformers and political leaders who interested themselves in public education during the 1830s and 1840s confronted resolute opposition from well-to-do taxpayers whose children attended private schools and academies, from farmers and rural democrats who saw no great need for educational institutions more elaborate or more expensive to maintain than those their fathers had attended, and from orthodox religious leaders who refused to surrender moral and intellectual education to schoolteachers whose religious beliefs might be unorthodox or noncommittal. Furthermore, to the extent that the educational awakening called for state-wide supervision of elementary schooling, or threatened in other ways the autonomy of the district school and the local school board, educational reform was bound to create opposition even where public education was an accepted fact. The obstacles were severe, and the struggle to overcome them took the better part of at least three decades.[1]

Still, the struggle was successful, and for reasons that were implicit in the opposition. Taxpayers who worried about paying for two educations for every child—one private and one public—also worried about the thrust of democracy into American life. On the one hand, they hoped that good public education might stabilize contemporary social attitudes, and they feared that poor public education might very well unsettle them. (Horace Mann's reports as secretary of the Massachusetts Board of Education were often addressed to these hopes and fears.) On the other hand, they also recognized that the development of a factory system of production in the northern mill towns threatened to create an industrial proletariat inaccessible to the moral and intellectual influences common to small-town life. Even though millowners often balked at it, one of the first steps the movement for educational reform took was legislation requiring the education of child laborers. Typically, these early measures enjoined education without providing schools, but though in this respect they followed colonial precedent they also anticipated the day in which prosperous citizens would demand universal elementary instruction at public expense.[2]

Rural taxpayers were less likely than city dwellers to urge significant educational reforms. Isolated from most of the intellectual currents that influenced even the workingmen, and devoted more often than not to orthodox Calvinism, which tended to be intolerant of liberal pedagogical practice, they also confronted much more difficult problems of school organization and tax support. Even in eighteenth-century New England the moving school and the district school had been the only plausible way to make education accessible to a widely scattered population, and during the nineteenth century the spread of population westward in hit-or-miss fashion fixed the district school almost irrevocably on the country as a whole. Although the proliferation of district schools lowered academic standards and inhibited adequate school taxation, however, the farmers' resistance to educational reform did not preclude a devotion to education itself. Controversy arose because educational reformers sought to develop rural educational institutions more rapidly than most farmers intended to, but not because there was any lasting issue between them over the importance of public schools.[3]

The gravest obstacle to the development of an effective common school system throughout the United States, therefore, was neither urban taxpayers' parsimony nor rural complacency but religious intransigence. During the 1830s and 1840s prominent spokesmen for most of the Protestant sects, and for the Catholic Church as well, insisted that sectarian religious training was indispensable to the maintenance of public morality. In 1845, for example, a committee of the Presbyterian Synod of New Jersey attacked public schooling on the grounds that "the race of irreligious and infidel youth, such as may be expected to issue from public schools, *deteriorating more and more,* with the revolving years will not be fit to sustain our free institutions." In their place it proposed to establish Presbyterian parochial schools, which the General Assembly of the church initiated in 1847. By the same token, during the late 1830s a group of religious conservatives led by Frederick Packard, secretary to the American Sunday School Union, accused Horace Mann and the Massachusetts Board of Education of conspiring to drive the Bible and religion itself out of the public schools. The fact that Mann and most of the board were Unitarians added zeal to the attack, but fundamentally the controversy arose because Mann wished to restore moral instruction to the schools without imposing the kind of teaching that would offend against individual conscience. He proposed to teach a nonsectarian Protestantism, which his opponents condemned both because it resembled Unitarianism and because it abandoned sectarian principles.[4]

Yet the most significant fact about the controversy in Massachusetts was the way in which it was resolved in favor of Mann. So long as devout men of various sects identified Mann's nondenominational morality with his Unitarianism, they could ally themselves against him despite their own religious differences. But as soon as spokesmen for religious training in the schools revealed themselves as in effect advocates of established religion the alliance was doomed. Thus the Universalist journal that had pressed the attack against Mann in 1838 for proposing to teach religion in the schools lined up behind him in 1839 and denounced Packard on the same grounds. After two attempts to destroy the Board of Education had failed in the legislature, it was out of danger. What happened was dramatized in the shifting opinion of the Universalists. Men who had every reason to disagree bitterly in religion agreed to disagree in such a fashion as to preserve the common schools which sustained their common social order.[5]

Nevertheless, although Mann and the Board of Education survived the attack on their principles, and although what happened in Massachusetts was duplicated elsewhere in less dramatic form, the politics of religious dissidence were hardly sufficient to convert die-hard advocates of sectarian instruction into enthusiastic supporters of nondenominational public education. The chief vehicle of this conversion was probably the nativist crusade of 1830–60, which attracted support from both political and religious conservatives.[6]

Two phenomena made Protestant bigotry especially significant in our educational history. One was the fact that when orthodox Protestants were confronted with a demand for public aid to Catholic schools, even the most dedicated sponsors of religious training usually opted for nondenominational common schools as a lesser evil. Significantly, when Governor Seward proposed to subsidize the Catholic schools of New York City, the state legislature responded by depriving the Protestant Public School Society of its subsidy and by barring state aid to religious education. Between 1844 and 1860, moreover, nine northern and midwestern states prohibited state aid by constitutional enactment: New Jersey, Wisconsin, Michigan, Ohio, Indiana, Massachusetts, Iowa, Minnesota, and Kansas. Protestants were obviously more eager to bar aid to Catholic schools than to make sure that public education was inoffensive to Catholics (during the 1850s the Maine supreme court and the Massachusetts legislature required reading of the King James Bible as a part of school exercises), but their very zeal to limit Catholicism taught them the virtues of undifferentiated Protestantism.[7]

Furthermore, the terms in which some of the most vigorous Protestant bigots mounted their attack on the Catholic Church also served to reinforce the prevailing American commitment to nonsectarian moral and intellectual instruction. In his famous *Plea for the West* (1835), for example, the Reverend Lyman Beecher urged New England Protestants to interest themselves in western education on the ground that "the great experiment is now making, and from its extent and rapid filling up is making in the West, whether the perpetuity of our republican institutions can be reconciled with universal suffrage. Without the education of the head and heart of the nation, they cannot be; and the question to be decided is, can the nation, or the vast balance power of it be so imbued with intelligence and virtue, as to bring out, in laws and their administration, a perpetual self-preserving energy?" While this phase of his argument reflected little more than a traditional eastern exhortation to educate the West, the book as a whole described "the conflict which is to decide the destiny of the West" in terms of "a conflict of institutions for the education of her sons, for purposes of superstition, or evangelical light; of despotism, or liberty." Although Beecher was soliciting aid for Lane Seminary and other sectarian academies, in its broader reaches his argument had the effect of placing common schools in the balance against Catholic parochial schools.[8]

Indeed, the only significant point of educational controversy between nativist agitators and the sponsors of nonsectarian instruction in the public schools was the extent to which the latter were willing to go in removing the King James Bible from the schools in order to make them acceptable to Roman Catholic pupils and their parents. In 1844 a convention of Ohio Presbyterians and Congregationalists declared bluntly that "the liberty to *worship* God accord-ing to the dictates of conscience, conceded to our citizens by the Constitution, cannot, by any principle of legitimate interpretation, be construed into a right to embarrass the municipal authorities of this Christian and Protestant nation in the ordering of their district schools." *The Sons of the Sires,* an anonymous prospectus of the nativist American party, adopted the same attitude in 1855: "Our revolutionary sires held that the Bible, the sabbath, and the com-mon schools, were the strong bulwarks of our national freedom and prosperity. Whatever denominational distinction may exist, the nation cannot live and prosper without the Bible and the sabbath." Anti-Catholic sentiment remained powerful until the Civil War, and it helped to prevent the development of a common school sys-tem that Catholics as well as Protestants might attend, but in other respects it lent strength to the movement for universal popular edu-cation in nondenominational public schools.[9]

Conservative Protestants themselves recognized the change that had taken place in their thinking. Horace Bushnell expressed it in classic terms in 1853: "We can not have Puritan common schools—these are gone already—we can not have Protestant common schools, or those which are distinctly so; but we can have common schools, and these we must agree to have and maintain, till the last or latest day of our liberties. These are American, as our liberties themselves are American, and whoever requires of us, whether directly or by implication, to give them up, requires what is more than our bond promises, and what is, in fact, a real affront to our name and birthright as a people." [10] For reasons that must always be an embarrassment to Americans who truly respect religious idio-syncrasy, orthodox Protestants ultimately adopted the nonsectarian public school as the fundamental guarantee of democratic liberties.

It is important in the history of American thought, moreover, that writers like Beecher and Bushnell, who were conservative in their social philosophy and who regretted the passing of the religious establishment of their youth, should have been led by religious bias to sanction nondenominational instruction at public expense. They were not like Channing, whose religious liberalism forced him to share contemporary democratic principles, nor even like Wayland, whose economic dogmas had much the same effect, but unmistakable conservatives who turned voluntarily to the same educational institutions that contemporary democrats and educational innovators had originally sponsored. The educational awakening in the United States was never a device conservative die-hards invented so much as a liberal development they acquiesced in on substantially the terms in which it had been proposed.

THE LIBERAL CONSENSUS

During the period between 1840 and 1860, even conservative leaders like Beecher and Bushnell became reconciled to most of the democratic innovations that had seemed so threatening during the 1830s. Meanwhile the American people turned with extraordinary unanimity to consolidating and perpetuating the liberal achievements of the Jacksonian revolution. From the early 1840s through the early 1850s constitutional conventions in one state after another wrote into the fundamental laws of the land the principles of popular rule, limited government, and public education that had caused such a stir during the 1830s. In doing so they fixed the doctrines of educated anarchy irrevocably on American political thought.[11]

Democratization of politics came easily. The conventions generally abolished restrictions on the suffrage, removed qualifications for office-holding, and eliminated the property basis of representation in both houses of the legislature. Responding to the use Andrew Jackson had made of the presidency, and reacting against the incompetence and the corruptibility of state legislatures, they also extended the power of the executive and restricted the power and even the duration of the legislature. By 1860 white manhood suffrage and popular authority were commonplaces of American government.[12]

By contrast, the consensus Americans reached on limiting the scope of their state governments was arrived at only through struggle. In general there were partisans of three distinct points of view at work in each convention: dedicated Locofocos who wished to abolish incorporated banks and other corporate enterprises and to eliminate internal improvements at public expense; die-hard Whigs who believed that the state legislature should continue to shape economic life through selective incorporations and appropriations and other special uses of political authority; and a large middle group—comprising both Whigs and Democrats—who wanted the benefits of banks and incorporations and internal improvements but not the special privileges nor the extraordinary public expenditures that had accompanied them in the past. Nevertheless, the existence of the middle group made compromise possible. It usually took the form of authorizing general banking and incorporation laws within stipulated limits both on the process of incorporation and on the operations of the companies after they had been chartered, while simultaneously limiting the authority of the state to go into debt, to undertake internal improvements, or to appropriate its funds or lend its credit even to enterprises affected with a public interest. The laissez-faire liberalism of William Leggett and William Cullen Bryant during the 1830s came close to being the settled policy of the states during the 1840s and 1850s. Not governments but individual human beings freed from government, under "free government," were to secure national prosperity.*

* American historians may object that laissez faire was not adopted either in theory or in practice before the Civil War, and within the last fifteen years we have had a number of close analyses of American thought and legislation to prove their point. Yet it seems that in employing an absolute distinction between government and the economy to define laissez-faire practice such studies have often exaggerated the American commitment to an active government before the Civil War. Complete laissez faire has never been practiced anywhere under any government, but some governments have obviously adopted it as a general principle; in this sense the abstract theory is not an adequate criterion of what constituted liberal economic practice. Furthermore, it is not necessary to adopt the theory formally in order to hold to its most important tenets. Indeed, some of the arguments that have shown liberal economic doctrine was foreign to the United States have succeeded mainly because they relied upon a clearly academic definition to prove the point.

Behind the issues of definition lie two overwhelmingly important facts. First, the path American politics took in the decades before the Civil War lay in the direction of an extreme economic individualism that severely limited the authority of government. Over the years, and in spite of notable exceptions, American state governments abandoned most of the social and economic responsibilities they had once exercised as a matter of course. Second, the major exception to laissez-faire practice consisted of government aids to internal improvements. By the 1850s, indeed, even internal improvements had come under the interdict of democratic theory, but it was only after most of the canals had been built and means had been found to finance railroads without the use of government funds that objections to them could safely arise. The

Extending popular participation in government while limiting the scope of legislation, the conventions of the 1840s and 1850s also adopted constitutional provisions strengthening common schools. The burgeoning liberal consensus is apparent in the different ways in which the Pennsylvania convention of 1837–38 and representative state conventions a decade or more later dealt with the problem of popular education. In these conventions, indeed, men who differed radically on other issues of public policy agreed in supporting constitutional provisions for education, while others who for various reasons opposed burdening the constitutions themselves with such matters represented every shade of opinion with respect to political and economic issues. In this sense public education was a commonly held principle even before the states had fully adopted economic voluntarism.*

---

reason was that all internal improvements—turnpikes, bridges, canals, railroads—were the necessary preconditions of economic individualism. If they had to be built under government auspices to be built at all, they were none the less compatible with less government in every other realm of society.

So far as domestic economic policies are concerned, that is, the states and by the same token the nation adopted something tantamount to laissez faire during the 1840s and 1850s. Moreover, even the advocates of a protective tariff, who quarreled bitterly with the Democratic party's free-trade policies, increasingly visualized an almost completely unregulated economy behind the tariff barriers they proposed. The tariff issue divided Whigs from Democrats, northern industrialists from southern planters, producers from consumers, but it did not threaten the widespread American belief that economic individualism is the surest guarantee of material and moral progress.

Further elaboration of this point is impossible within the confines of this study. Most of the relevant literature was thoughtfully reviewed by Robert A. Lively in "The American System: A Review Article," *Business History Review,* XXIX, No. 1 (March, 1955), 81–96, which will serve any interested reader as a guide to the problems of definition and research. He should also consult Joseph Spengler, "Laissez Faire and Intervention: A Potential Source of Historical Error," *Journal of Political Economy,* LVII, No. 5 (October, 1949), 438–41, and James W. Hurst, *Law and the Conditions of Freedom in the Nineteenth-Century United States,* chs. 1–2. Spengler suggests that legislators may have passed regulatory acts out of deference to traditional sentiments but knowing that they would not be effective; hence even statute law may not be evidence of a genuine commitment to active government. Examining legal as well as legislative practice, Hurst holds that government activity intended to protect and enhance individual economic opportunity denied laissez faire. Strictly speaking, of course, he is correct; but in this case as in others I think that logic may obscure history.

* Educational attitudes and achievements in the South were influenced by conditions peculiar to that region, which are discussed in Chapter VIII. Therefore the discussion here ignores the achievements of the southern state conventions.

Because the Pennsylvania convention met while the struggle between Jacksonian Democrats and the Whig and Antimasonic opposition was at its height, the delegates accomplished relatively few changes in the political structure of the state and imposed relatively slight limits on the power of the legislature. Moreover, they finally refused to alter the constitutional provision of 1790 which provided only for free education of acknowledged paupers. In every respect the results of the convention provided but inconclusive evidence of the triumph of democratic principles in either politics or education.[13]

Nevertheless, the debates the delegates engaged in show us better than the amendments they finally proposed the light in which both reformers and conservatives already visualized public education. There was every possible reason why the convention should have left the subject of education alone. It was an especially delicate issue in Pennsylvania; the legislators who had enacted the school law of 1834 had been made to suffer at the polls; the political issues between Locofocos and conservatives seemed irreconcilable; and the two parties were evenly balanced in the convention. In this complicated situation a number of delegates urged their colleagues not to endanger revision of the constitution by introducing so controversial an issue among the amendments to be submitted to the people. Among the advocates of such prudent silence, Walter Forward and Thomas Earle conceded (in Forward's words) that education was probably the most important topic "that has been, or can be, brought before the convention." Earle was a radical on the question of banks and a firm democrat who would in 1840 become a vice-presidential candidate of the Liberty party, Forward a staunch conservative who was to become President Harrison's comptroller of the currency and President Tyler's secretary of the treasury. Other men who supported them in the convention were well distributed among its different political factions.[14]

On the other hand, the three most vigorous proponents of a constitutional establishment of state-wide education, including a superintendency or other central control, were Charles Jared Ingersoll, Joseph R. Chandler, and James M. Porter. Ingersoll had been prominent as a Jeffersonian Republican and was now a Democrat who spoke for a specie currency. Chandler had once been a candidate of the Philadelphia Working Men's party, edited the National-Republican *Gazette of the United States,* and was an advocate of banks, while Porter was a college professor and the candidate of the Democratic party for president of the convention. The next most vociferous trio of educational reformers was Thaddeus Stevens and Thomas Sill, conservative on banks and suffrage, and John McCahen, appointed postmaster by President Van Buren, sent to the convention by Philadelphia workingmen, and allied with the radical critics of banks.[15]

The delegates who feared that educational reform might cause a rejection of the amended constitution were very probably correct, for it was ultimately adopted by a popular majority of only 1,212 votes in a total of nearly 227,000. For our purposes it is more important, however, that the reasons given in the convention in support of public education were generally the same throughout and certainly followed no party division. McCahen, Porter, Stevens, and Sill argued that education would protect the people against demagogues, preserve their liberties, and maintain constitutional and republican government. As might be expected, conservatives (Chandler, Sill, Stevens) emphasized its role in encouraging constructive and informed self-government, but the nearest thing to a truly conservative sponsorship came from McCahen, who although uneducated himself argued that "an educated and well instructed people [are] the best stay of a republic"—and quoted Daniel Webster to prove his point. (He also criticized free education past the age of sixteen and opposed state grants to colleges.) Conservatives pointed to the social and economic benefits a diffusion of knowledge would bring—prosperity for all, and the encouragement of practical genius—but Thomas Earle was equally concerned to achieve these same advantages. And John Cummin, an insistent Democrat and radical opponent of banks who objected to introducing the educational question when there were more critical reforms at stake, none the less told the conservative Stevens that an extension of education automatically justified an extension of the suffrage, provided (he added provocatively) it was an education in benevolence, virtue, and honor. The failure of the Pennsylvania convention to act on education reflected special circumstances and obstacles that another decade would remove.[16]

New York's convention nine years later also debated common schools. Not surprisingly the issues it faced were mainly administrative: should the constitution abolish educational rate-bills; precisely how should the Common School Fund and the United States Deposit Fund be applied; should the state or the school district bear the cost of schools? For fear of rural taxpayers' resistance the convention finally abandoned its plan to require completely free schooling for all children between the ages of four and sixteen, even though the amendment providing for it was to be submitted to a separate popular referendum. But it felt no need to debate the underlying logic of education at any length, and its action in dropping compulsory tax support was in point of fact the product of deference to a powerfully situated minority of the electorate. After two referenda held on its own initiative the state legislature accomplished nearly everything the convention had originally set out to do.[17]

In Illinois in 1847 there was less readiness than on the eastern seaboard to require free common schools, at least in part because the state was bankrupt. Therefore, although the convention's committee on education proposed an elaborate constitutional injunction, the delegates evinced greatest interest in measures intended to protect the common school fund against misappropriation. Significantly, however, the majority responded favorably to the committee's recommendation that a state superintendent of schools be appointed by the governor. It provoked some criticism from Thompson Campbell, a Democrat born in Pennsylvania, but only because he wished to make the superintendency elective, while the leading advocate of an appointive superintendency was William Bosbyshell, also a Democrat born in Pennsylvania, who made obeisance to universal public education as if to articulate what was already common doctrine.[18]

In the Ohio convention of 1851 there was considerably more controversy about education, in part because of the influence of a New England population with set ideas on the subject, but also because of the issues that educational proposals raised between town and country, native-born citizens and immigrants, northern and southern delegates. Yet the most striking fact is that the alignments were usually alignments over details rather than over essential principles, and that there was no identifiable party line either favoring or opposing fundamental provision for education. A clause requiring its "encouragement" was sustained over the token objections of Charles Reemelin, a German immigrant and Locofoco Democrat, and the more determined negations of William Sawyer, Virginian by birth and representing a district inhabited by former southerners. Reemelin objected mainly to the stirring up of unnecessary trouble, in which he was joined by opponents of his Locofoco extremism, while Sawyer's opinions reflected nothing so much as the self-conscious reactionary provincialism that had begun to infect southern political and social thought, which was fighting a losing battle in the old Northwest Territory. On the other hand the leading advocate of a general system of education was Joseph McCormick, who wanted a minimum annual expenditure, an elective superintendent, and normal schooling provided for in the constitution, and who was a Locofoco believer in unlimited liability although not a friend to a specie currency. His sturdiest ally was Samuel Quigley, a Locofoco with respect both to banks and banknotes, and a member of the committee on education. Meanwhile the immigrant Democrat Reemelin pressed most vigorously for a complete ban on state aid to sectarian schools, with mixed support from Democrats and Whigs and equally mixed but actually quite perfunctory opposition.[19]

Ultimately the provisions for a superintendent of schools and normal schooling were dropped, while a general provision for the encouragement of education and the safeguarding of school funds, together with a prohibition on sectarian aid, was sustained. McCormick had lost his fight for a constitutional appropriation in support of schools and their improvement, but no one had thought in the course of haggling over details to gainsay his basic political premise: "We may construct the laws of the State as we please; unless the minds of the people are educated, the legislation is in vain. As we improve in general intelligence we shall approximate to that point where legislation may be dispensed with. Educate the mind of man, and the heart, and little legal restraint upon his conduct will be required." [20] He spoke for a state, and more generally for a nation, that had adopted popular freedom and popular education as the basis of its politics.

VIRTUE AND INTELLIGENCE

As the constitutional achievements of the states indicate, by mid-century the great body of Americans agreed in almost every respect upon the political order under which they lived—the Constitution of the United States, the state constitutions, extra-constitutional arrangements like political parties, separation of church and state—and they knew from experience that the social controversies of the 1830s had been successfully resolved. Writing in the *Atlantic Monthly* in 1859, in fact, a shrewd journalist looked back comfortably on the lessons the Democratic thirties had taught. On the one hand, C. C. Hazewell felt that at that time American politics had received a "large infusion of Socialism" because of the workingmen's influence in the Democratic party. On the other hand, he also pointed out that the workingmen had not really been agrarian levelers or revolutionaries (they had had no intention of surrendering their own right to property, he said) and that in any event they had not dominated the party. "For five years after the veto of the Bank Bill, in 1832," he wrote, "the Democratic party was essentially radical in its tone, without doing much of a radical character. In 1837, the monetary troubles came to a head, and then it was seen how little reliance could be placed on men who were supposed to be attached to extreme popular opinions. . . . From radical practices we have always been free, and it is improbable that our country will know them for generations." [21]

Because the Americans believed in their political and social institutions they also established a democratic educational system. Their object was to perpetuate the social order all of them knew so that all of their children might benefit from it, and education was instrumental to what all of them wanted. The aphorism that "knowledge is power" runs through the literature of the era. In the context of the American Revolution it meant that knowledge is an intellectual resource against arbitrary and unrighteous force. In the context of the concrete achievements of the age—roads and turnpikes, power machinery, canals, steamboats, railroads—it meant that knowledge enables men as individuals and as a nation to share in the mastery of a continent. In the context of the Protestant Reformation, on the other hand, it meant that care must be taken as to what kind of knowledge men have and how they use it; they must be made proof against the temptations of poverty or wealth, the leadership of demagogue or atheist. Knowledge was power to be like every other American—free, republican, prosperous, active, moral—and education offered every man the opportunity to know his duty and to profit from it.

Commonplace psychological assumptions reinforced the tendency to invoke education as the bulwark of a democratic society. They owed something to John Locke's optimistic *tabula rasa* psychology, but by 1850 most Americans, following the Scottish philosophers, had repudiated the more obviously mechanistic and materialistic corollaries of Lockean sensationalism in order to dwell on the spiritual aspect of mankind and the role of the three faculties (reason, affections, will) in determining action. It followed that a proper exercise for the three faculties, and more loosely for the human faculties generally, would produce virtuous individuals capable both of self-government in the personal sense and of democratic self-government. As a result, formal religious training seemed less and less necessary to ensure public morality, which could be secured instead through nonsectarian moral instruction. Indeed, this was what made liberty work. Virtue produced a diffused cultural control over intelligence, which might otherwise (in the absence of complicated legislation) get out of hand.[22]

But intelligence was necessary too; the Americans simply converted intellection to "intelligence" as they changed sectarian belief to "virtue." Nevertheless, we must remember that they had relatively little suspicion that what they called intelligence differed fundamentally among individuals. "Intelligence" tended instead to connote a combination of specific quantitative knowledge with a universal common sense, and thus to imply equal access to at least the essential truths of politics and mechanics and morals. Not that there were no differences in talents and capacities conceived of; everyone could not be equally wise in all matters even with equal education. But as Irvin Wyllie has shown in his study of *The Self-made Man in America,* "genius" was suspect, and the whole burden of the social thought of the period pointed toward a genuine possibility of effective universal diffusion of knowledge through preliminary public schooling and the habitual practice of lifelong self-improvement. A favorite illustration of the proponents of such diffusion was Benjamin Franklin, who rambled through their exhortations not as a brilliant scientist but as the methodical apostle of all the middle-class virtues. His flirtation with deism forgotten or passed over in silence, Franklin was a much more suitable example to democrats than the august Washington or the philosophically inclined Jefferson.[23]

"Virtue and intelligence" were thus the great desiderata that education could communicate, and men could do the rest. We find the phrase occasionally in the writings and speeches of republican friends to education, where however the emphasis is on a dispensation of what learned men have acquired. We find it or its equivalent on the other hand flooding the expression of democratic advocates of education, orthodox and liberal in theology, Democratic and Whig in politics. The doctrine is so universal as to seem meaningless, except that it is in reality a precise definition of what American education was intended to achieve for American democrats. In broad terms they proposed to substitute their virtue and intelligence for political leadership and religious authority, to substitute educated anarchy for government. "Here is an equalizing power—a leveling engine, which we may rightfully and lawfully employ," wrote Horace Eaton in his first report as Vermont state superintendent of schools. "Its operation will not undermine, but consolidate and strengthen society. Let every child in the land enjoy the advantages of a competent education at his outset in life—and it will do more to secure a general equality of condition, than any guarantee of 'equal rights and privileges' which constitution or laws can give. And if we would preserve this life giving spirit, as well as the form, of our republican institutions, we must rely mainly upon popular education to accomplish our purpose."[24]

The practical consequences of the common faith are well known. No one phenomenon defines the public-school idea, but Massachusetts, which established a Board of Education in 1837, and Ohio, which adopted an effective school law in 1838, took unmistakable first steps in the establishment of truly common schools. Massachusetts promptly surpassed all other states including New York, where the elaborate machinery of supervision initiated during the 1800s had deteriorated for lack of public support. Within little more than a decade the practice of democratic public education was irrevocably fixed in American life. By 1850 almost every northern state was well on the way to a permanent and systematic provision for common schools controlled by state officials and supported largely if not exclusively by public monies, and there was no turning back.[25] In the following decade a number of the states of the South, where there were inbred resistances to free schooling, also moved in the same direction.*

Among those men who subscribed without reservation to the country's liberal institutions, moreover, only the very wise or the exceedingly doctrinaire were likely to recognize any limitations on the effectiveness of its educational experiment. Although few writers expressed misgivings as to the utility of public common school education in guaranteeing popular liberty, an examination of their views will help to place the more commonplace democratic attitude in secure perspective.

The prominent American writers who were skeptical of the power of public education included the economist Henry Carey and the political philosopher Francis Lieber, the jurist Frederick Grimké and the publicist George Sidney Camp. In systematic analysis of American institutions each described a society that depended not on formal education but on other advantages to perpetuate its freedoms. Carey's position was essentially that of a doctrinaire advocate of laissez faire in domestic policy, Lieber's the consciousness of a refugee from Prussia that education "is not liberty itself, nor does it necessarily lead to it."[26] Camp's little treatise on *Democ-*

---

* Peculiarly southern attitudes toward education, and the institutional peculiarities that accompanied them, are discussed in Chapter VIII. The table on page 120 illustrates the success of the common school awakening and indicates the extent to which education depended upon public funds.

racy for Harper's Family Library almost wholly ignored education in its discussion of the basic institutions (chiefly constitutional republicanism and laissez faire) that characterized American self-government, while Grimké's *Considerations upon the Nature and Tendency of Free Institutions* argued that the most effective safe-

ATTENDANCE OF STATE POPULATIONS (WHITE) AT EDUCATIONAL
INSTITUTIONS, 1850

State	Attendance at all educational institutions (in percent)	Proportion at publicly aided institutions (in percent)	State	Attendance at all educational institutions (in percent)	Proportion at publicly aided institutions (in percent)
Maine	34	97	Michigan	28	98
New Hampshire	26	93	Wisconsin	20	95
Vermont	32	93	Ohio	25	96
Massachusetts	19	92	Indiana	17	96
Connecticut	21	90	Illinois	15	96
Rhode Island	17	92	Iowa	16	96
New York	24	93	Kentucky	9	83
New Jersey	18	88	Tennessee	12	90
Pennsylvania	19	94	Missouri	9	84
Maryland	25	74	Alabama	5	79
Delaware	12	81	Mississippi	4	70
Virginia	18	87	Arkansas	5	77
North Carolina	13	91	Louisiana	6	81
South Carolina	4	69	Texas	5	69
Georgia	5	76	California	0.2	22
Florida	4	60			

Explanation: Attendance is average attendance as reported by institutions at every scholastic level. The percentage of "public" attendance includes all institutions supported even in part by public funds, and thus exaggerates the percentage of what we would today consider public education, particularly for the southern states. Moreover, for some of the southern states the large proportion of youth attending academies and even colleges supported in part by public funds probably exaggerates the apparent diffusion of education.

Total school attendance, as reported by families, was 112 percent of the total attendance reported by the institutions polled, and may indicate that all percentages for public education should be reduced, on the assumption that private institutions would be less likely than public ones to be surveyed. Alternatively, it may suggest that many heads of households claimed schooling for their children because a social stigma attached to absence from school.

The figures on which these percentages are based are those of the Census of 1850 as tabulated in J. D. B. De Bow, ed., *Statistical View of the United States . . . Being a Compendium of the Seventh Census* (Washington, 1854) and correlated in Lawrence A. Cremin, *The American Common School: An Historic Conception*, p. 180.

guard of liberty is not education but the habits of republican freedom. "The diffusion of property and education," he wrote, "are not
sufficient to produce the degree of reflection which is requisite to
maintain free institutions. The acquisition of property, notwithstanding its manifold benefits, has a tendency to undo all that education has done. The affluent become too contented, too self-
complacent, to be either virtuous or wise. The ever enduring
struggle for equality is the only agent which, united with property
and education, will conduce to the right ordering of society." [27]

Although these commentators obviously dissented from the vulgar
faith in free schools, they help by their very uniqueness to define
that faith. In the first place, all of them were struggling to articulate
principles of political theory that were practiced without thinking
by most Americans. In this sense they were talking about something foreign. Lieber was in fact an immigrant political scientist
and arch-conservative who sought to lecture the Americans on
their ways, while Camp wished to find coherent principles behind
contemporary American practice. For his part, Grimké apparently
hoped to refute Tocqueville's criticisms of democracy in America
by turning him on his head and demonstrating how his systematic
analysis missed the whole point of American liberalism, while Carey
moved from economic theory to sociology in his attempt to com-
prehend American institutions. Yet most Americans were interested
not in analyzing the nature and tendencies of their institutions but
in reinforcing habitual institutional behavior through proper training in the schools. That is, they assumed the advantages the theorists
set out to demonstrate, and attempted only to cultivate the practices
they assumed.

Secondly, it is of some significance that although these writers
interested themselves in more fundamental social characteristics
than any that could be created by the common schools, they did
not entirely renounce education as a bulwark of American liberty.
In *Civil Liberty*, for example, Lieber wrote that education alone
could not create freedom, but he also declared that it was "indispensable to liberty." By the same token, his *Manual of Political
Ethics* explained that education perpetuates the social order and
helps to inculcate desirable traits in individuals. For his part, Camp

virtually ignored contemporary educational developments, but he argued that together American schools and the institution of private property would protect the country against any dangers to be expected from the vast flow of immigrants. And despite his skepticism, Grimké observed that popular education was at least highly desirable, inasmuch as it could train the people for free institutions by incapacitating them for any other, and that by equipping them to do things for themselves it would reduce the scope of government.[28]

It was in the context of his discussion of public schooling, moreover, that Grimké entered his demurrer to doctrinaire laissez faire, arguing that it is not an absolute principle separating "private" from "public" affairs but that "it depends upon who can most effectually and most advantageously, for both government and people, preside over the one and the other." Similarly, in his *Principles of Political Economy*, Henry Carey criticized Britain and France for inhibiting voluntary education through burdensome taxation and centralized authority, yet he praised Massachusetts and the Northeast generally for establishing schools at public expense: "Here we see the people providing for themselves the means of education, and placing those means within reach of all who require instruction. In Europe, we find a general system of centralization, whereas in the United States a tendency to diffusion is every where to be remarked." This was an important point at which to extend the scope of government. It implied that the extremest liberalism of American practice—what I have called "anarchy"—would be interrupted first and foremost by public provision for common schooling.[29]

Lastly, what this handful of writers suggested was that education is not all-powerful, that its success as a social institution depends in the first instance upon the prior existence of a functioning liberal society. But of course this is precisely what virtually all Americans believed, after their first enthusiasm for education as a reforming agency had passed. By 1850 American writers representing every shade of political opinion recognized that education was a powerful instrument of popular authority, best employed to safeguard equal rights and encourage individual prosperity. Schools were intended not to discover and achieve liberty but to sustain it.

This was an attitude to which Ralph Waldo Emerson raised

powerful philosophical objections. "Our culture has truckled to the times,—to the senses. It is not manworthy," he said in one of his essays. "If the vast and the spiritual are omitted, so are the practical and the moral. It does not make us brave or free. We teach boys to be such men as we are." [30] But only a thinker as radical as Emerson in his devotion to human freedom could challenge contemporary institutions so fundamentally and so irrevocably. Even philosophical advocates of liberty like Carey and Lieber, not to mention Camp and Grimké, believed that Americans must teach boys to be exactly such men as they were. The difference between these philosophical writers and the American public lay not in any hope for political innovation but only in their sense that even at its best common school education was limited in scope and inadequate to preserve liberty and democracy singlehanded. At worst they were friendly critics of a naive faith.

VIII. Irreconcilable Dissent from Anarchy

BY 1860, the bulk of the evidence suggests, radical reformers and die-hard conservatives had found common ground in a devotion to public education. There were of course exceptions to consensus: religious leaders still resisted the introduction of secular and nondenominational common schools; statesmen still conceived of government as an active agency of the public good; political agitators favored radical social measures and frowned on education as a useless panacea; and many voters remained skeptical of pedagogical reform and of the reorganization of their school systems. Meanwhile the state legislatures continued to use their power in ways that were not compatible with strict liberalism, while they often left to its own devices the educational reform they had initiated because American liberty depended upon it; the grounds and the rhetoric of the faith in education were sometimes clearer than the individual commitment and the practical example. But in spite of these exceptions the only significant and lasting dissents from the commonplace theory of liberty and education were those entered by thinkers who began by denying the very premises of American liberalism. Like the exceptions to any rule, however, disagreements as fundamental as these tended rather to reinforce the common principle than to undermine it.

IRRECONCILABLES, NORTH AND SOUTH

Among the thinkers who all but repudiated public education because they could not accept democracy were conservative irreconcilables who spent their declining years lamenting the nature and tendencies of American political institutions. They form a distinctive opposition, united not so much in their specific social and political attitudes as in their characteristic rejection of both democracy and democratic education.

One of them was John Randolph of Roanoke, the intransigent Virginia Republican who found the public policies of even the presidents from Virginia tainted by political expediency. Characteristically, in the Virginia constitutional convention of 1829–30 Randolph delivered a long harangue against "King Numbers" and all modern political innovations, in the course of which he turned vehemently on the idea of public education:

Among the strange notions which have been broached since I have been on the political theatre, there is one which has lately seized the minds of men, that all things must be done for them by the Government, and that they are to do nothing for themselves: The Government is not only to attend to the great concerns which are its province, but it must step in and ease individuals of their natural and moral obligations. A more pernicious notion cannot prevail. Look at that ragged fellow staggering from the whiskey shop, and see that slattern who has gone there to reclaim him; where are their children? Running about, ragged, idle, ignorant, fit candidates for the penitentiary. Why is all this so? Ask the man and he will tell you, "Oh, the Government has undertaken to educate our children for us. It has given us a premium for idleness, and I now spend in liquor, what I should otherwise be obliged to save to pay for their schooling." [1]

The vehemence of Randolph's remarks makes it clear that despite his laissez-faire prejudices he could not easily be reconciled to democratic principles.

Another irreconcilable conservative was Chancellor James Kent of New York, who distinguished himself in the New York constitutional convention of 1821 by fighting with rhetoric and vituperation against the slightest extension of the suffrage. In 1831, addressing the Yale Phi Beta Kappa, he praised the colonial fathers for founding a system of free schools that had "communicated to the people of this state, and to every other part of New England in which the system has prevailed, the blessings of order and security, to an extent never before surpassed in the annals of mankind." But this public statement was misleading. In 1830 Kent wrote privately to Daniel Webster that the mass of the people *cannot* be virtuous and able, and in 1847 to Townsend Harris that free public education for the masses can "only enlarge their capacity for mischief and add a fresh stimulus to delinquencies and to novelties, to change and revolution and contempt for the ordinary restraints of law, morality and religion." No more than John Randolph was Kent willing to accept either democracy or democratic education.[2]

Both Randolph and Kent had come of age during the eighteenth century, and their intransigence in the face of democratic innovations was as much a product of an earlier generation as an instance of latter-day conservatism. What is most significant about their attitudes, therefore, is not the fact they were carried forward into the Jacksonian era but the form they took: they expressed simultaneously a radical dissent from democracy and a radical dissent from popular education at public expense. Yet even while they lived, Randolph and Kent spoke for a lost cause. In dissent they identified but could hardly threaten the common American faith.

Speaking from an entirely different point of view, Roman Catholic spokesmen experienced much the same inability to make themselves heard in the United States. There were good as well as bad reasons for their failure. We have already taken note of the fact that legitimate Catholic demands for public school funds and legitimate Catholic attacks on the reading of the King James Bible in the schools helped to reconcile many conservative Protestants to common schooling. Here we may consider instead how far and in what ways Catholic doctrine when systematically pursued proved incompatible with the common faith in democracy and education even when it was purged of a Protestant bias. The writings of Orestes A. Brownson, after 1844 a doctrinaire convert to Catholicism, reveal Catholic opposition at its most irreconcilable.

In 1845 Brownson wrote two essays for his *Quarterly Review* that amounted to a declaration of war upon American democratic education. He agreed with Protestant reactionaries in arguing that "there is no foundation for virtue but in religion, and it is only religion that can command the degree of popular virtue and intelligence requisite to insure to popular government the right direction and a wise and just administration." But he condemned even Protestant sectarianism because it prevented a "common moral culture" and he insisted that "Protestantism is not and cannot be the

religion to sustain democracy; because, take it in which stage you
will, it, like democracy itself, is subject to the control of the people,
and must command and teach what they say, and of course must
follow, instead of controlling, their passions, interests, and caprices."
He concluded that "the Roman Catholic religion, then, is necessary
to sustain popular liberty, because popular liberty can be sustained
only by a religion free from popular control, above the people,
speaking from above and able to command them,—and such a religion is the Roman Catholic." [3]

In other words, having repudiated nondenominational moral instruction on the same grounds as Protestant conservatives, Brownson also repudiated denominational moral instruction outside the
Catholic Church. Furthermore, he insisted that the Church was the
only agency that could preserve the American republic from the
twin evils of anarchy and despotism. Religion, he said in 1854, "if it
is to serve our purpose, and save our republic from degenerating,
on the one hand, into social despotism, and on the other, into individualism and anarchy, must be a constituent element of society,
and stand on a basis of its own, independent both of the individual
and the state." His doctrine was consonant with his premises, but it
was also in direct and explicit conflict with the common ideal of
educated democratic freedom.[4]

At that, by 1854 Brownson was almost ready to quarrel with his
adopted church over the merits of common school education. He
urged Catholic parents to send their children to public school, provided only that it did not offend against conscience, and five years
later he openly criticized parochial schools as "a system of schools
which will train up our children to be foreigners in the land of their
birth." Yet it was significant that he put forward these propositions
on an entirely practical basis. "Our children," he wrote in 1854,
"have got to take their stand in American society with others, and it
is our duty to do all in our power to enable them to do so with as
little disadvantage as is possible with fidelity to our holy religion.
When all others are educated, it will not do for us to suffer our children to grow up in ignorance." More significantly still, he wrote in
conscious defiance of prevailing Catholic opinion, asserting the right
of private judgment in matters not dogma; to this extent he leaned

toward the very autonomy he had condemned in Protestant individualism during the 1840s. But his defiance was ineffective and
short-lived. In the long run he and his Catholic critics alike challenged the working agreement that had been reached by different
Protestant sects to keep religion out of the schools entirely in order
to make them work for common ends. Failing to accept those ends,
he could hardly do otherwise.[5]

Nevertheless, although Brownson's thought clearly took issue
with prevalent American beliefs, his position as spokesman for a
minority religion isolated him from the main stream of American
thought even more completely than the doctrines Kent and Randolph had voiced isolated them. At best, he would be ignored; at
worst, he would convert his Protestant antagonists to the very doctrines he repudiated.

THE SOUTHERN PROSLAVERY ARGUMENT

Arch-conservative and Roman Catholic opponents of democratic
educational innovations were politically too weak to impose their
principles on the United States. By contrast, when southern proslavery thinkers opened their attack on northern liberal institutions
they spoke for a region and a generation that wielded great power
in American politics. As a result, they helped both to inhibit common schooling in the South and to foster an ideological cleavage
between the North and the South that culminated in civil war. In
the long run, however, southern opposition to northern institutions
served like conservative and Catholic dissent to reinforce northern
dogmas about democracy and education.

Even had slavery not become an issue between North and
South, educational reform would have labored under significant
handicaps in the South. For one thing, the income from many of
the school funds the southern states had established, and on
which as agricultural communities they depended more heavily
than did the partly urbanized northern states, was appropriated
wholly or chiefly to pauper education, and seemed to meet current
needs. Any surplus usually went toward the support of private

academies, and sometimes paupers were sent to fill out the ranks of private schools on a tuition basis, a practice that made an additional reason why it would be difficult to break away from tradition. Still further, the arrangement of local government in the South gave county courts rather than townships or school districts control of the schools. Not only were these county courts relics of prerevolutionary social organization, obsolete vehicles of charity, but also in the upper South (the area of greatest educational achievement) they long remained nonelective bodies playing a role mixedly juridical and benevolent. In the North the school district was the bane of existence for educational reformers, but at least it displayed an intense if often bigoted interest in education for its own children. In the South the school district was an appendage of the county court that only slowly acquired self-government.[6]

In addition to regional custom there were also positive obstacles to public provision for education in the area that were more serious than the obstacles in most northern states. The most important was the perpetual conflict between lowlands and uplands, plantation country and farm country, slave economy and mixed or free-labor economy. "In a country like ours, the component parts of which are so essentially different from each other," wrote one of Virginia's educational reformers, ". . . no uniform plan of education can easily be devised to provide for the real wants or is likely to accord with the opinions and wishes of all." Particularly in the upper South the plantation oligarchy fought a long delaying action against the triumph of the upcountry. One of their most energetic efforts was to prevent reapportionment of the legislatures, lest loss of their power there result in discriminatory taxation of their estates and slaves for the benefit of internal improvements and public education, in which they had slight interest on their own account. The planters were willing to provide education but it would be at their own option and in their own way, and it would not readily approach a truly democratic system.[7]

Again, the sparseness of population characteristic of some northern states was characteristic of almost the whole South, and there was hardly any artisan class to counterbalance the reluctance, not to say the inability, of a predominantly rural population to pay for adequate education. Moreover, the back-country population—influenced by its isolation and by its long-standing antagonism toward the more cosmopolitan lowland—was also prone to an exaggerated religious fundamentalism which promoted conflicting orthodoxies and helped both by orthodoxy and by conflict to inhibit systematic schooling. Where intrastate political conflict was minimal, as in the lower South generally, frontier isolation and orthodoxy were more common. Given the lack of a tradition of vigorous public support for education there was little reason to expect such areas to overcome difficulties easily and promptly, or to establish an expensive educational system even when consensus was possible.

Beyond all this there was the fact that to many southerners democracy was more nearly political than social. In the upper South, upcountry spokesmen usually favored public education as an adjunct to the democratization of politics, and much of the pressure they put upon the lowland aristocracy resulted from the latter's failure to provide schools. Yet the demands these spokesmen made were by no means as insistent as those made in most northern states. At the Virginia constitutional convention of 1829–30, for example, western delegates who pressed for a broader suffrage were relatively uninterested in education either as justifying or as sustaining democracy. Two men expressed a hope that the legislature would provide public education once general suffrage had been established, but five argued that Virginia might safely broaden the suffrage simply because her citizens (being farmers) were already intelligent, virtuous, and patriotic. Meanwhile democracy in the sense of white manhood suffrage triumphed so abruptly in the lower South as to precede by many years the more gradual achievements of the northern states, but it did not connote all that it finally meant in the North. Presumably the presence of a slave caste made the pressure for social democracy less urgent; presumably also the absence of either the difficulties or the opportunities of an industrial society minimized social sensibilities once purely political aims had been satisfied. To southern political agitators, at any rate, education seldom held the political or the social importance that it had in the North. If sometimes they were democratically unwilling to accept a pauper education, they were often quite willing to go without.[8]

All told, therefore, the South did not offer fruitful conditions for educational growth. Although republican roots continued to bear, there was relatively infrequent legislation apart from public grants to academies and universities. Most laws that were passed authorizing district or county taxation were not acted upon by the districts even in upland counties whose leaders had spoken in behalf of universal public education. During the 1850s, it is true, several states took the first effective steps toward publicly supported and publicly controlled education. The Virginia constitutional convention of 1851 and the Tennessee legislature of 1854 levied capitation taxes, and North Carolina in 1853 and Alabama (a leader among the states of the lower South) in 1854 created effective state superintendencies. Kentucky had made a somewhat earlier beginning, but it was not until 1848 and 1849 that its school fund was amply protected against misapplication and a state-wide property tax levied. Of all the southern states, however, Maryland and Virginia had the most widely diffused education when the Civil War broke out, and in both it still rested upon a strong private tradition paralleling the public contribution. In other states progress toward a universal public system, essential though it might be to the democratization of education, was only beginning.[9]

But slavery and the sectional controversy that grew up around it created a much more fundamental distinction between northern and southern attitudes toward democracy and education than this comparative institutional approach reveals. As the sectional crisis developed, southern political thought moved toward deliberate secession from northern principles. Other differences might have been resolved, but differences over slavery gradually converted many southerners into irreconcilable opponents of liberal democratic institutions.[10]

Their doctrine took shape in an explicit defense of slavery as a mode of social and political organization. It involved both an affirmation of the worth of southern institutions and a pointed criticism of northern freedom, such as reached its climax in James H. Hammond's famous mudsill speech before the United States Senate in

1858. "In all social systems," Hammond declared during debate over admitting Kansas into the Union under the proslavery Lecompton Constitution,

there must be a class to do the menial duties, to perform the drudgery of life. That is, a class requiring but a low order of intellect and but little skill. Its requisites are vigor, docility, fidelity. Such a class you must have, or you would not have that other class which leads progress, civilization, and refinement. It constitutes the very mud-sill of society and of political government; and you might as well attempt to build a house in the air, as to build either the one or the other, except on this mud-sill. Fortunately for the South, she found a race adapted to that purpose to her hand—a race inferior to her own, but eminently qualified in temper, in vigor, in docility, in capacity to stand the climate, to answer all her purposes. We use them for our purpose, and call them slaves.

The North, the South Carolina senator went on, has abolished slavery in name only. Those who are in fact its slaves "are your equals in natural endowment of intellect, and they feel galled by their degradation." [11]

Thus far Hammond's argument was wholly racial, like the argument of others who shared his views, and as such it supported an aggressively democratic theory of both politics and education. In 1842, for example, Henry A. Wise of Virginia announced to the House of Representatives that "the principle of slavery was a levelling principle; it was friendly to equality. Break down slavery, and you would with the same blow destroy the great Democratic principle of equality among men." Applying the same principle to educational reform, Governor Joseph E. Brown of Georgia insisted to the state legislature in 1858: "Let [there] be a Common School, not a Poor School System. Let the children of the richest and poorest parents in the State, meet in the schoolroom on the terms of perfect equality of right. Let there be no aristocracy there but an aristocracy of color and conduct." [12]

Yet even Governor Brown bespoke aristocracy of a sort, and the idea of an aristocratic South runs through proslavery thought. "I accept the term," Hammond told the House of Representatives in 1836. "It is a government of the best. Combining all the advantages, and possessing but few of the disadvantages, of the aristocracy of the old world . . . it gives us their education, their polish, their munificence, their high honor, their undaunted spirit. Slavery does indeed create an aristocracy—an aristocracy of talents, of virtue, of generosity and courage. In a slave country every freeman is an aristocrat." However rhetorical in spirit, such a statement stood as a direct rebuke to contemporary democratic sentiment in the North, which had resolved to eradicate not only aristocratic privileges but also aristocratic influences both foreign and domestic.[13]

Moreover, dedicated proslavery theorists tended to argue that even in a society in which common laborers are set apart racially the remainder of the population must also be organized in hierarchical rather than egalitarian fashion. Chancellor William Harper of South Carolina spoke for these extremists when he addressed the South Carolina Society for the Advancement of Learning in 1835. Urging southern planters to cultivate knowledge, he observed: "Whatever may have been said in the fervor of their zeal by those who were in pursuit of the greatest practicable liberty . . . natural equality and universal freedom never did and never can exist. We are lovers of liberty, and republicans." Harper toyed with the idea that southern republican liberty might be understood in purely racial terms, but he ended by appealing to the white elite to recognize and act on their special responsibilities. His appeal was irrelevant to race, negated white equality. The essential proposition of the extreme proslavery thinkers was not that the existence of two races creates slavery but that their coexistence in the same geographical area makes easier for all an aristocratic social system that is already both inevitable and desirable.[14]

It followed that public education of the whole people is both impossible and dangerous. In a free society all men must labor, and, laboring, they cannot be well educated. According to Matthew Estes's *Defence of Negro Slavery* (1846), "The superior Common School System of the New-England States, enables the larger portion of the population to acquire the first rudiments of education; but when they reach mature years, they are necessarily so much engaged in bodily toil that they have no leisure for mental culture." More than this, they threaten society itself. As Chancellor Harper expressed the idea in his essay on "Slavery in the Light of Social Ethics" (1837), "Men of no great native power of intellect, and of

imperfect and superficial knowledge, are the most mischievous of all
—none are so busy, meddling, confident, presumptuous, and intolerant. . . . Of all communities, one of the least desirable, would
be that in which imperfect, superficial half-education should be universal." [15]

As Harper's words suggest, extreme proslavery thinkers finally
made northern educational institutions a basis for repudiating northern liberal principles. The *Southern Quarterly Review* summed up
the southern argument in 1852 in an article devoted to "Instruction
in Schools and Colleges." Rebuking contemporary "cant" on the
subject of popular education, and observing that "in spite of the
falsehoods which constitutions proclaim to the contrary, the privileged few must govern," it went on to argue that

Men whose lives are spent in humble toil, have little time for reflection.
They are as susceptible to evil impressions as to good. Education exposes
them to the danger of attacks from the demagogue, as well as to the
wholesome admonitions of the patriotic. As we go northward in our
country, we find every phase of political doctrine. The spirit of agrarianism is rife. In New-York the landlord has had to resort to military force
to collect his rents. Throughout the whole country, from the Hudson to
the Bay of Fundy, a settled determination exists to abolish slavery at
the South. . . . The diffusion of education in New-England is likely to
effect a dissolution of the Union.[16]

By the same token, in his "Anniversary Oration" Chancellor Harper
complained in 1835 that "already among our confederate States, in
which universal suffrage exists, and domestic slavery is excluded, we
hear of schemes of universal education at the public expense, and
of agrarianism." [17] In the final analysis the proslavery argument
treated public education as a positive evil in American society.*

Of course, few southerners adopted the proslavery argument in
its entirety. Even the *Southern Quarterly Review* sometimes published favorable accounts of contemporary educational innovations,

---

* Significantly, although proslavery theorists denied that mudsills could be
educated, they also shared a common southern fear that slaves might in fact
acquire some education and become restive because of it. In conceding that the
education of Negroes was dangerous, southern writers and southern legislators
alike paid unexpected tribute to liberal democratic belief; in effect, they accepted the northern commonplace that the spread of universal education would
destroy tyranny everywhere.

and for that matter some of the South's principal apologists for slavery were among its leading educational reformers.[18] Nevertheless, the defense of slavery as a social rather than a merely racial institution obviously weakened the South's commitment to universal public education. At its best, it helped to perpetuate the aristocratic traditions of republican education into a democratic era. At its worst, it denied democracy everywhere in the United States.

THE NATURE OF ILLIBERAL DISSENT

What the extreme proslavery theorists finally said nay to was liberty for anyone. This was the burden of George Fitzhugh's books, not only *Sociology for the South* but also his mordant commentary on northern life entitled *Cannibals All! or, Slaves without Masters.* Proving that free society had failed, he proposed a normative alternative: "Liberty is an evil which government is intended to correct." [19] Other writers would not go so far as to elevate government, and preferred instead to speak of "society" or "civilization" as the mode of human organization that would cure liberty. But underneath it was all one. Because they began by denying liberty to Negro slaves they ended by denouncing freedom in all of its customary manifestations.

Moreover, these southerners were critical of northern liberty *as anarchy.* They pointed to precisely the institutional arrangements in which northerners took greatest pride—the very anarchy with a schoolmaster they had adopted—as an example of what the South could not accept for itself. Much has been written about the Jeffersonian democracy of the soil that proslavery theorists repudiated. Yet they renounced not simply the agrarian republic of the past but also the educated democracy of the present. Northern democrats had substituted education for social organization; southern proslavery sociologists substituted social organization far beyond anything republicans had visualized for both liberty and schools.

Here was the common principle that linked truly irreconcilable dissenters from northern democratic practice, not only in the South but also in the North. What ultimately characterized genuine anti-

liberals was not a belief in specific public policies that were threatened by contemporary innovations, nor a predilection for slavery as
such, but a conviction that unorganized freedom, freedom without
severe limitations, is impossible. To their way of thinking order took
precedence over liberty because liberty without order was incredi-
ble. Neither Protestant reactionaries nor doctrinaire Catholics nor
proslavery southerners were willing to entrust the national destiny to
public education together with the practical social conditions—
liberal democracy, geographical dispersion, material wealth—which
most Americans believed would preserve and enhance freedom.
Idiosyncratic as their thought may have been at times, dedicated
reactionaries commonly assumed that a far more compelling structure was necessary in human affairs than the self-regulating arrangements of popular liberty and public education.

Under some circumstances, indeed, they actually articulated
their common assumptions. In spite of his religious convictions, for
example, Orestes Brownson wrote like a Protestant nativist in
praising the sectarian schooling of the Puritan fathers in preference
to contemporary liberal practice. During the 1850s, moreover, he
became an outspoken defender of slavery.[20] Again, during the last
desperate struggle of the slave states, George Fitzhugh wrote in the
Southern Literary Messenger that "we begin a great conservative
reaction. We attempt to roll back the Reformation in its political
phases."[21] Finally, in 1835 Samuel Finley Breese Morse, one of
the earliest and most vitriolic of nativists, developed an argument
against the naturalization of immigrants that proved equally serviceable in the defense of slavery. In Imminent Dangers to the Free
Institutions of the United States through Foreign Immigration he
denied that immigrants have a right to political privileges in America on the grounds that the social state introduces limitations and
duties that abrogate natural rights. Twenty-eight years later, in
1863, he published an "Argument on the Ethical Position of Slavery
in the Social System, and Its Relation to the Politics of the Day"
in which he held that human freedom is disobedience to God, who
has ordained a fourfold "system of restraints" upon it: civil government, the matrimonial relationship, parental authority, and servile
status. But, he complained, "Great is the Goddess of Freedom!"

Not slavery but antislavery impiety has brought civil war in its train, "the legitimate fruit of humanitarian doctrines." [22]

The fact that both a Brownson and a Morse adopted a proslavery stand during the sectional crisis should not blind us to differences among the positions of Catholics, nativists, and southerners respectively. It was necessary to fight a civil war to put an end to proslavery attacks on northern liberalism, whereas the passage of time and the pressure of circumstances gradually outmaneuvered both reactionary Protestants and doctrinaire Catholics who challenged the political assumptions northern democrats shared. But all had in common that they were repudiated by American history, and that they had no opportunity to persuade American democrats that there were shortcomings in both social leveling and common schools. Contrary to Tocqueville's famous dictum, it was not true that Americans would tolerate neither diversity nor distinction; their enthusiastic reception of immigrants indicated otherwise. But it was true that, consciously and unconsciously, they perceived the terms on which their democratic experiment must be made to operate, and they paid no attention to dissidents who began by saying that it would not or it should not. They repudiated hierarchy; they repudiated superior authority; they repudiated all criticisms leveled against the common school as the palladium of American liberties; they made public education the instrument of their freedom. The outcome of the Civil War would only confirm their common faith.

Part Three

CONFLICT AND CONSENSUS AFTER

THE CIVIL WAR

IN church it occurred to me that it is time for the public to hear that the giant evil and danger in this country—the danger which transcends all others—is the vast wealth owned or controlled by a few persons. Money is power. In Congress, in State Legislatures, in City Councils, in the courts, in the political conventions, in the press, in the pulpit, in the circles of the educated and the talented, its influence is growing greater and greater. Excessive wealth in the hands of the few means extreme poverty, ignorance, vice, and wretchedness as the lot of the many. It is not yet time to debate about the remedy. The previous question is as to the danger—the evil. Let the people be fully informed and convinced as to the evil. Let them earnestly seek the remedy and it will be found. Fully to know the evil is the first step toward reaching its eradication.

Rutherford B. Hayes, 1887

IF I had not read two books, Henry George, in the early eighties, and later Bellamy, I should have grubbed along and never thought anything was wrong. Those books set me thinking how the things we grow and make are divided up.

Anonymous farmer, 1903,
quoted by John Graham Brooks

IX. National Reconstruction

through Formal Education

NORTHERN victory in the Civil War had lasting significance for the American people's commitment to liberal democracy and popular education. It automatically confirmed the social and political principles that proslavery arguments had repudiated, and by the same token it encouraged northern leaders to attempt the education of the defeated Confederacy. Completing the emancipation of the slaves, it also invited northern advocates of Negro rights to see to the education as well as the liberation of the freedmen. For a decade after Appomattox, northern philanthropists vied with northern politicians in training the southern population to be democrats, and after Congressional Reconstruction had been abandoned both philanthropists and legislators continued to press for universal education in the South.

The vindication of northern principles in the war also encouraged national leaders to apply popular education to the solution of problems that were only remotely connected with the war. During the 1880s and 1890s, statesmen and professional educators alike looked to an expansion of the country's school systems to ensure national progress and safeguard republican institutions despite recurrent agrarian unrest, violent labor strife, the rise of the city and the political machine, an unprecedented influx of immigrants. Even had no war taken place, Americans would undoubtedly have turned to education to fulfill their national promise, but the way in which northern opinion after the war linked southern secession and southern backwardness to southern ignorance lent added force to the idea that education could be a national panacea.

Nevertheless, the attempt that national leaders made to overcome contemporary evils in both the South and the North by means of education was doomed to failure. Conditions in the South were not immediately amenable to the diffusion of knowledge, and national problems accumulated much more rapidly than educational innovations could hope to deal with them. Furthermore, many of the prominent advocates of a national educational awakening were conservatives, spokesmen for a traditional social and political order that was increasingly incapable of promoting either individual prosperity or the general welfare. Hence while the clamor for extending formal education drew on an established popular belief in the efficacy of public education it also threatened in the long run to disabuse the people of that belief. The attempt to reconstruct the nation through an expansion of formal education challenged as well as extended American democratic commitments.

REDEEMING THE SOUTH

In the first flush of victory, northern spokesmen treated the education of the South as one of the prerogatives of a conqueror. As uncharitable toward southern civilization as they had been toward southern slavery, public figures like James Russell Lowell insisted that the antebellum South had produced neither education nor art nor literature nor science worthy of the name, and they proposed to make up these deficiencies by "Americanizing" the defeated region. The North, a missionary spokesman wrote in the Atlanta *Christian Index* in 1866, "should teach the South line upon line, precept upon precept, by military garrisons, by Bureau courts, by Congregational churches, by Northern settlers, by constitutional amendments, by christian missionaries, by free schools, lectures, newspapers and reading rooms, what be the first principles of social order, political eminence, moral worth and industrial success." [1]

Nevertheless, the punitive impulse to educate the South was less important than the intellectual assumptions that suggested using education as a tool of reconstruction. Francis Wayland expressed a fundamental northern conviction when he told the National Teachers' Association in 1865 that "it has been a war of education and patriotism against ignorance and barbarism." Long after the antagonisms engendered by the war had begun to disappear, northern spokesmen assumed as a matter of course that secession had been the fault of popular illiteracy. In 1882, for example, Representative Horatio Bisbee of Florida, a transplanted Republican from Maine, told the House of Representatives that if the white masses of the South had been educated they would have been too wise to go to war in a losing cause. Two years later Senator Henry W. Blair of New Hampshire reduced the issues of the war to those of ignorance. "Had common schools been universal throughout the country there would have been no civil war," he told the Senate in 1884; "for intelligence among the masses of the people would have abolished the causes which led to it, and the chains of the bondmen would have dissolved like the mists of the morning in their warmth and light, instead of awaiting to be broken by the terrible hammer of Thor." [2]

Even if we discount Blair's argument on the grounds that he was an indefatigable champion of federal aid to education, we cannot ignore its significance. Early and late, northern spokesmen visualized the coming of the war as well as the redemption of the South in educational terms. Ignorance explained both the tragedy of war and the difficulties of reconstruction; education would solve the problems each had left in its wake. Even during the heyday of Congressional Reconstruction Senator Henry Wilson of Massachusetts, who had led the antislavery forces in that state, urged compassionately that half of the proceeds from the sale of public lands should be devoted to common school education in the "slave-cursed and war-smitten South." In 1880 President Rutherford B. Hayes proposed an even more generous appropriation to the Congress. "Whatever Government can fairly do to promote free popular education ought to be done," the apostle of reconciliation between North and South said in his fourth annual message. "Wherever general education is found, peace, virtue, and social order prevail and civil and religious liberty are secure." Four years later Senator Blair described federal aid to education as "the logical consequence and true conclusion of the war." "This work belongs to the nation," he told the Senate in 1882. "It is a part of the war." [3]

Both the punitive and the redemptive impulses to educate the South naturally came to a focus in attempts to educate the freedmen.

In 1866, for example, the *Freedman's Record* urged northern whites to recognize that "in the coming struggle with the spirit of rebellion and slavery . . . we must have the freedman on our side. As we stand by him, so may we expect him to stand by us. Every teacher you send to the field is a pledge to the freedman of your determination to see justice done him; it is a pledge to the disloyal rebel that you will not yield to him in the future." In 1871, on the other hand, Representative William Clark, a Republican from Texas, urged the education of both white and black races in order to improve the relationships between them. Similarly, in 1872 Representative George F. Hoar of Massachusetts advocated devoting the proceeds of land sales to common school education in both the South and the North. He argued that only popular instruction would counteract encroachments on constitutional rights and privileges, stimulate prosperity, and encourage the distribution of wealth. Eleven years later, moreover, Representative John Sherwin of Illinois pressed for federal aid to education in the South on the grounds that whereas that region had once been victimized by the illiteracy of its whites it was now victimized by the illiteracy of its Negroes. The impulse to educate was more basic in American thought than the wish to penalize former rebels.[4]

Meanwhile, Negroes themselves had enthusiastically sought education as soon as they were freed. "Some of the most pathetic sights I have ever witnessed in my life," Senator Benjamin Harrison of Indiana told his colleagues in 1884, "I saw when the advancing armies of the Union were brought in contact with the slave population of the South. Aged colored men, slaves from their mother's womb, came into our camps as into cities of refuge. I have seen old men past the meridian of life, yes, well on toward its end, after a hard day's work in the company's kitchen, lying prone upon the ground before the camp fire with spelling-books in their hands painfully trying to fasten in their memories the names and outlines of the letters of the alphabet." Negroes as well as whites testified to the fact: Booker T. Washington remembered in 1900 "a whole race trying to go to school."[5]

Furthermore, the freedmen originally embraced education in the same social and political terms that had influenced northern democrats just before the war. Especially in their first enthusiasm, they hoped to acquire literary and sometimes even classical training, while they ignored or even scorned practical instruction because it reminded them of their bondage. Southern historians are wont to identify southern Negroes' quest for a bookish education with the invasion of New England schoolteachers and missionaries who followed upon the heels of the northern armies, and there was of course a connection between them. But it is a mistake to overlook the fact that the freedmen themselves thought like the New Englanders. For many Negroes, to be educated and to be free were literally inseparable, and they demanded the same schooling that white southerners had received before the war as both a badge and a guarantee of their freedom.[6]

Following unconsciously in the footsteps of early advocates of classless education, in fact, some Negro spokesmen hoped that racial prejudices might be overcome by integrated common schools. But these were probably in the minority. The latest beneficiaries of Jacksonian liberalism, most freedmen wanted not assimilation between the two races but schools and the vote. Together these institutions promised to deliver to the Negroes the power they had never wielded before, to make them equals of the whites in the only sense that mattered. They saw in universal suffrage their weapon against oppression, in formal schooling the primary instrument of their independence and prosperity. Senator Blair described this early faith acutely when in 1886 he recalled to the minds of his colleagues the Negroes' first enthusiasm for literacy. "We all remember," he said, "the condition of things at the close of the war. We know how the colored population had an idea that education was their real liberty, their real enfranchisement, their real political salvation; and they poured into the schools, established in whatever way they might be; they sought the opportunity to be educated, to learn to read and to write." According to the platform of the National Colored Labor Union, adopted in 1869, education was "one of the strongest safeguards of the Republican Party, the bulwark of American citizens, and a defense against the invasion of the rights of man." [7]

On the other hand, most Negroes had reason to grow skeptical of education as a vehicle of their liberty and equality; Senator Blair's recollections were in large part a lament for a golden age. Many freedmen discovered to their surprise that learning was hard work and abandoned it for themselves even if they sought it for their children, while others soon realized that literacy alone could not solve the pressing problems of making a living and raising a family. More important, even before Congressional Reconstruction ended Negroes began to discover that education could not protect their suffrage or secure their other civil rights against the determined opposition of southern whites, and the end of Reconstruction left them with no other means but education to confront the terrifying consequences of their forcible liberation.[8]

This is not the place to detail the events nor to assign the blame for the ugly path that the reassertion of white supremacy took in the South. So far as Negroes were concerned, there was often little to choose between southern conservatives and the radicals who succeeded them; the period after 1876 was marked by an unrelenting white effort to fix the Negroes in their place at the bottom of society, which reached its climax in the virtual disfranchisement of the race between 1895 and 1909.[9] What is important here is not the reasons for their plight but its consequences in American thought. Given the frauds and the deprivations practiced on the Negroes once northern troops had been withdrawn from the South, how did both white and Negro advocates of Negro rights react? In particular, to what extent and on what terms did the American faith in education survive the Negroes' experience?

White advocates of Negro rights relied almost exclusively on public education of both whites and blacks to rectify pressing evils. In 1890 some Republicans toyed with the idea of establishing federal protection of the national suffrage, but apart from this stillborn measure they put their faith in federal aid to common schools and in philanthropic endeavors to encourage public education in the South. On the eve of withdrawing the last troops from the South, for example, President Hayes looked to universal education to safeguard Negro rights, and even in 1880, after he had repeatedly complained of infringements against them, he held that "the best and surest guaranty of the primary rights of citizenship is to be found in that capacity for self-protection which can belong only to a people whose right to universal suffrage is supported by universal education." In subsequent years other Republican presidents recommended that Congress appropriate funds in aid of common school education everywhere in the United States. Their messages urged a liberal construction of the Constitution to sanction such unprecedented appropriations, but made clear in the same instant that the national government would adopt no means other than education for the protection of human rights.[10]

Although Congress debated a number of educational measures during the 1870s and 1880s, it never actually appropriated federal funds to aid common schools. In the absence of federal appropriations, northern philanthropists and missionaries continued to do what they could after 1876 to encourage education in the South. The most effective work in behalf of Negro education was probably that undertaken by the Peabody Fund, which was administered by northerners and southerners together in aid of public but not integrated schools. The Fund's grants helped to overcome both the traditional southern resistance to free education and the post-bellum reactions against it, and they encouraged the white population of the southern states to expand and improve their incipient public school systems. These were important gains. Yet it was of great significance that such advocates of universal education dwelt on the promise education held out to the South quite apart from the original aims of Reconstruction, and indeed with a due regard for the peculiar sensitivities of southern whites. They fought for Negro education, it is true, but they fought for it precisely in the terms of the existing social structure.[11]

Of course there were no practical alternatives to acquiescence once the federal government had withdrawn its military forces from the South, yet under the circumstances education could hardly be counted upon to solve contemporary problems. More than this, in the hands of its disciples the faith in education threatened to degenerate into a platitude—as the words of the Reverend A. D. Mayo, a trustee of the Peabody Fund, may serve to indicate. Speaking of the need to develop a new social order in the South to replace antebellum institutions, he told the American Social Science

Association in 1882: "Only the American school, in all its beautiful variety of operation, is adequate to this great work. The South needs the people's common school for discipline of character, mental training, instruction in manners and morals and in the habit of living and working together for the common good." [12] Despite its heartfelt enthusiasm for education, his statement obviously ignored the fact that the common good was likely to be defined in oddly one-sided ways in the postbellum South. How education might rectify this difficulty neither Mayo's words nor the experience of the Negroes revealed.

Nevertheless, the greatest Negro spokesman of the post-Reconstruction era also viewed education in much the same terms as philanthropic whites. Assuming from the first that a radical reconstruction of southern institutions was impossible, Booker T. Washington spent a lifetime teaching his people to make a better living on southern terms. In his famous address before the Atlanta Exposition in 1895, for example, he expressed a tentative hope for eventual racial equality, but he also postponed its realization indefinitely. "The wisest among my race," he told an audience composed of both whites and blacks, "understands that the agitation of questions of social equality is the extremest folly, and that progress in the enjoyment of all the privileges that will come to us must be the result of severe and constant struggle rather than of artificial forcing." In time, he thought, Negroes' efficiency as farmers and mechanics would diminish southern race prejudice, but for the foreseeable future he did not intend to work against inequality so much as to increase Negroes' economic opportunities within a two-caste society in which one caste kept political power. [13]

As a result, he urged practical rather than literary education on his race. One who is white cannot condemn his choice with impunity, but it seems legitimate to suggest that Washington conceded a great deal, and that the practical training he advocated was an inadequate economic substitute for the large-scale political reforms universal literary education had once been intended to safeguard. Whatever Washington's hopes for the long run, there was scant reason to think his approach would serve them well during the lifetime of those who heard him speak. Not only did he acquiesce in the Negroes' disadvantaged position—in their political inferiority, their social inferiority, their educational inferiority; he also acquiesced in it on the supposition that the education southern whites permitted the Negro would ultimately redeem his race from its second bondage. The Atlanta compromise, as Washington's theory was later derisively labeled, surrendered rights for education.[14]

In recent years Negro leaders who are more determined than Washington have renounced his acquiescent stance, and they have also tended to read back into the 1880s and 1890s a decided cleavage between him and more radical Negro contemporaries. Their retrospect is misleading, however. Not until 1903 did William E. B. Du Bois break with Washington over vocational training, and during the 1880s even so radical an advocate of equal rights as T. Thomas Fortune both urged industrial training and deprecated higher education—and Fortune lived in the North. More important still, although the radicals condemned white infringements on Negro rights, they also invoked popular political education to complete the work that Reconstruction had left undone. In 1885, for example, Fortune advocated national aid to education on the grounds that the whole nation had been implicated in slavery, and he demanded universal literacy "that the people may more clearly know their rights and how best to preserve them and reap their fullest benefits." So far as Negro leaders were concerned, that is, education continued to seem a powerful instrument of both liberty and progress. The differences between Washington and his opponents were differences over tactics, not strategy, and both conservatives and radicals still relied upon forms of education to achieve the ends of Reconstruction after more than a generation of frustrations and disappointments.[15]

Because of their experience, Negroes might pardonably have decided that education was a useless nostrum. Similarly, the Negroes' helplessness in the face of a hostile and unreconstructed southern white population might also have taught northern whites to be skeptical of the supposed power of education to serve democratic ends. But Negroes had an extraordinarily difficult role to play in American society, one which made education the only plausible vehicle of their hopes, and their white sympathizers were content

to encourage their education while discouraging more radical assertions of their rights.[16] Meanwhile most whites ignored their
plight entirely. Ignoring the Negroes' fate, the whites had little occasion to perceive the ways in which popular education might also fail
to serve all white interests equally. White democrats continued to
believe in liberty and schools even when conservative advocates of
national aid to education mounted a crusade to redeem the North as
well as the South from its political errors.

REDEEMING THE NATION

Not all conservatives supported national aid to education, and
not everyone who supported it was conservative; the postbellum
era gave rise to a wide variety of political valuations of formal
schooling, which it is one purpose of this volume to explore. Nevertheless, the interest northern spokesmen took in redeeming the
South and elevating the freedmen through public education led
directly to a conservative effort to uplift and protect the whole nation by means of federal aid to common schools and colleges. As
early as 1872 congressional sponsors of federal aid urged illiteracy
rather than race or section or population as the criterion by which
federal funds were to be awarded to the states, and by the 1880s
(when Senator Blair's bills were debated) illiteracy everywhere in
the United States was commonly advanced as the major reason
for aiding common schools.[17] Nor were congressional spokesmen
alone in their attitude. In 1882, for example, the American Social
Science Association submitted a memorial to Congress urging it
to take "prompt and efficient measures" to support common school
education throughout the United States on the grounds that "a
Government resting on the suffrage of the majority of the people
cannot preserve itself from corrupt influence nor secure a high
degree of civil freedom unless education is generally diffused
among all classes of voters." [18]

Inevitably, the advocates of federal aid to education employed
the enthusiastic terminology that had characterized the educational
awakening before the war. In 1876, for example, Representative
Gilbert Walker, a Conservative Democrat from Virginia who in-

troduced a bill to devote the proceeds from the sale of public lands to common school education, urged the House of Representatives to "educate the present generation, and those which succeed it will take care of themselves. Once lift the dark pall of ignorance which overshadows the land and the light of universal intelligence will never again be obscured." In 1882 Representative Bisbee of Florida urged the House to adopt a slightly modified version of the Blair Bill, then pending in the Senate, on the grounds that education is indispensable to a government founded on liberty, popular law-making, and the absence of a standing army. Meanwhile Senator Blair himself had exhorted his colleagues: "We have gained all that we possess by reason of the education of the individual, and we hold it upon the same tenure. What we hold for ourselves we hold for mankind, and we hold it for both upon the same condition by which it was gained." "Educate the rising generation mentally, morally, physically, just as it should be done," he challenged them, "and this nation and this world would reach the millennium within one hundred years." [19]

Nevertheless, in attacking illiteracy throughout the United States, the sponsors of federal aid to common schools clearly sought to up-lift public deliberations at least as much as they wished to strengthen popular liberties. In 1881, for example, former Senator James W. Patterson of New Hampshire, who was now that state's Superintendent of Public Instruction, praised popular education extravagantly only to advocate national aid on much restricted grounds. "The Republic carries with it, written or implied, the right to perpetuate itself," he told the National Educational Association at its annual meeting; "and national education being essential to that end, its maintenance will be found necessary to transmute the blind, brutal instincts of ignorant masses into intelligent forces of strength and prosperity. We have not yet realized the full measure of dis-aster possible to a free state based upon popular ignorance." [20]

Patterson was a New Englander and a professional educator be-sides; hence his anxiety may seem unrepresentative. But other pub-lic figures were equally insistent that national survival depended upon education. In his inaugural message, President James A. Gar-field urged that the danger from an ignorant suffrage "covers a field far wider than that of negro suffrage," and echoed Patterson in asserting that "we have no standard by which to measure the disaster that may be brought upon us by ignorance and vice in the citizens when joined to corruption and fraud in the suffrage." By the same token, in supporting the Blair Bill in 1886, Senator Howell Jackson of Tennessee invoked two powerful arguments against those who had constitutional objections to federal aid. Like Patterson he stressed the democratic virtues of universal education at public expense, but like Patterson he also insisted that if the republic were to be preserved "we must take wiser precautions than any have ever yet taken, by diffusing far and wide among our people that intelligence which will alone constitute the safeguard and protection of our political institutions." Two years later Senator William Stewart of Nevada told the Senate: "If this Government perishes, it will not fall before a foreign foe; it will go down because the people are incompetent to understand the wants and the complicated machinery of this great Government. My position is that notwithstanding this bill may not be in the best possible form, I ought not vote against a proposition to extend aid for the education of the people. I regard money expended for such a purpose as a contribution for the preservation of our free institutions." [21]

Moreover, the argument advanced by advocates of nationwide aid to education was often conservative in a narrowly specific sense, focused on northern cities. Introducing his first bill to aid common school education into the Senate in 1882, Senator Blair himself urged that the whole nation must act to overcome the weaknesses appearing in its politics: evil threatened as much from northern cities as from illiterate Negroes. Senator Thomas Bowen of Colorado insisted in 1888: "We are confronted to-day with the fact that not only in some of the Southern States, but in dense populations in the North as well, fair and free elections have become a mere travesty. A government professedly based upon universal suffrage becomes under such circumstances a national lie; and what are we going to do about it? . . . There is no peaceful solution of this problem save that which is afforded by a more general education of the people and the higher state of civilization which will follow." "This illiteracy is not confined to the Southern States," Blair told the same session of the Senate, explaining that

I am not one of those Northern men or American citizens who are at all inclined to hold up their hands in holy horror and say, "These poor outcast States of the South! See how ignorant they are!" I admit that there is as much danger to-day to the institutions of this counry from the illiteracy of the North as there is from the illiteracy of the South. The great cities of the North to-day are, in my belief, increasing in the dangers that grow out of ignorance and worse-resulting vice, misrule, and tendencies to anarchy, and there is as great danger in the large cities of the North to-day to the good of the whole country as results from the condition of the South.

Indeed, he added, "There is one peculiarity in regard to the situation of States in the North which does not exist at the South. There is no great Northern State that is not practically under the control of some great city, or it may be more than one great city within its limits." [22]

The debates also made clear that the core of the problem the city posed was its immigrant population. In each of his major speeches Senator Blair referred to the illiterate "balance of power" that prevailed in every northern state, and other speakers repeatedly employed the same formula. It was significant, indeed, in that grave public questions might be decided by the changing opinions of a body of illiterate voters, but Blair's arithmetic implied that such voters would inevitably vote the wrong way, and as a monolithic body, if they remained untaught. Hence there was no mistaking the restrictive intent that lay behind seeking to educate them. In sponsoring a bill to divide income from land sales and patent-office receipts among the states on the basis of their school-age populations, Senator Justin Morrill expressed alarm at the influx of uneducated immigrants into the country and urged support for common school education to overcome the alien traditions they brought with them. Presumably a senator from Vermont had no reason to fear repercussions from his words at home; other congressional advocates of national aid to education were more guarded in their language but not in their meaning.[23]

Voicing an unusually outspoken antagonism toward immigrants, moreover, Senator Morrill also exemplified the point of view expressed by congressmen who urged federal aid to higher education during the postbellum era. Most of the debate over federal grants revolved around aid to common schools, but the Vermont senator

any kind often expressed similar ideas, and hardly anyone denied either the general political utility of education or the national emergency in which it had been invoked. (Significantly, there was hardly any difference in perspective between southern spokesmen for the conservative Redeemer governments and northern spokesmen for the Republican party.) The Senate and the House of Representatives, and public figures who followed their deliberations, agreed that popular education must elevate and improve and purify American life by teaching freedmen and white illiterates and immigrants their duties and responsibilities as citizens. Advocates of federal aid continued to speak from time to time in the accents of the common school awakening, with its emphasis on the protection of individual liberty and the encouragement of individual prosperity, but even the most generous spokesmen among them portrayed an education that would limit rather than multiply the paths that the democracy might take. In every sense the first national attempt to stimulate public education since the days of the founding fathers was both conservative and republican.

THE USES OF FORMAL EDUCATION

The Blair bills failed to reach the floor of the House of Representatives, and (with the exception of the second Morrill Act) every other proposal for national aid to education was unsuccessful.* Nevertheless, the failure of national aid indicated only that the constitutional and political objections to federal intervention were compelling, not that the American people were unwilling to support common schools. During the period between 1865 and 1900 both northern and southern states engaged in a slow but steady expansion and improvement of their public educational facilities.

Because of their backwardness before the war, because of the war itself, and because of Reconstruction, most southern states had all they could do to establish universal elementary schooling. Slowly

* Successive bills passed the Senate by comfortable majorities in 1884, 1886, and 1888, with support from each of the major regions of the nation. They never came to a vote in the House because they were sidetracked by Speaker John Carlisle of Kentucky, an inveterate opponent of every measure that might justify increasing the tariff.

at first, but with growing effectiveness, they provided (at least for their white populations) an educational system that was probably the equivalent by 1900 of the best that northern states had created before the Civil War. Meanwhile northern states built on their earlier beginnings. Western states and rural regions of the East, which had often been slow to adopt the educational innovations sponsored by reformers like Horace Mann, soon matched and sometimes exceeded the accomplishments of their urban neighbors. Already committed to improving public education, moreover, and alert to the influx of illiterate immigrants, the crowding of their cities, and the perseverance of child labor in their factories, the heavily populated states of the Northeast and Middle West pioneered in establishing compulsory education for the school-age population, in consolidating district school systems and bringing schools and schoolteachers under more effective supervision, in increasing their expenditures per pupil and the days of schooling each pupil received, and in opening public high schools to serve those who required more advanced training than the best common schools could give. Hardly 8 percent of the eligible population attended public high school as late as 1900, and much remained to be accomplished in improving teacher training and modernizing both curriculum and pedagogy in both common schools and high schools, but there was no mistaking the American commitment to public education.[28]

Insofar as the nation's expanding educational system embodied a political philosophy, however, it was distinctly conservative. With few exceptions the prominent sponsors of educational expansion in the states shared most of the attitudes expressed by the sponsors of national aid to common schools and colleges. (Often, of course, they were the same persons.) Merle Curti has analyzed their political and social orientation extraordinarily well in *The Social Ideas of American Educators;* suffice it to say here that while professional educators before the war had often been apprehensive over popular illiteracy and concerned to prevent ignorance and vice from undermining the republic, they had seldom expressed themselves so narrowly as the professionals—college presidents, superintendents of schools, school board members—who gathered at the annual meetings of the National Educational Association after 1870. Horace Mann and his contemporaries had pressed for educational reform because it promised to open so many opportunities for individual prosperity and national progress. Their successors continued to believe that education would serve both individualism and progress, but they stressed its political uses. As early as 1874, in a "Statement of the Theory of Education in the United States of America" which was circulated by the federal Bureau of Education, leading educators distinguished between the urgent political necessity of universal education, irrespective of sex, social rank, wealth, or ability, and the less critical need for diffusing intelligence in order to support the nation's productive industry.[29]

Hence even pedagogical reform was often geared explicitly to conservative purposes. One of the leading topics for discussion in the NEA during the 1880s and 1890s was the question of what forms of instruction would be most conducive to desirable social ends. "We take the position, here and now," George H. Atkinson of Portland, Oregon, said in 1888, "that the true aim of the public school must be to teach and guide, and if need be compel, its youth to be law-respecting and law-abiding citizens. If, in time past, mere school-learning and discipline have been or have seemed to be the main objects in view, while the dignity and responsibility of good citizenship have been only incidental, the time has come to reverse the process." Speaking to the same point, B. F. Tweed of Cambridge, Massachusetts, observed that it was necessary to use the liberal atmosphere of the classroom to inculcate the "habits of obedience" that make up good citizenship. In 1892, moreover, the resolutions committee of the association pointed out that the American school was a unique influence for "patriotism and good citizenship," while in 1895 the full convention voted to recommend flag ceremonies and national patriotic holidays to inculcate patriotism, respect for law and order, and respect for the rights of society and property. Indeed, even the industrial education movement that flourished during the final decade of the century was commonly defended for its putative effects in creating a disciplined and cooperative labor force as well as its enrichment of purely literary training.[30]

Furthermore, professional educators now treated the extension

and improvement of formal education as almost the whole definition of their educational responsibilities, while they tended to ignore or even to deprecate the informal educational influences that
their predecessors had counted upon before the war. The great
task in 1840 had been to provide everyone with a necessary start,
which he might improve for himself by means of lectures or lyceums
or libraries, not to mention newspapers and sermons. Fifty years
later the professional educators threatened to assume almost all of
the responsibility for democratic education. Their motives included
professional zeal, the growing complexity of the society and the
economy, and the errors perpetrated in American political life by
uninformed voters. "If our republican institutions are to stand,"
President James B. Angell of the University of Michigan explained
in 1891, "it will be because there are found in every part of the
land, in the smallest village and on the farms as well as in the great
centers of population, men and women of sufficient intelligence and
education to make the triumph of charlatans in medicine and in
theology and of demagogues in politics impossible." [31]

While the belief in education was far from moribund as an
American political commitment, therefore, the restricted and often
restrictive purposes shared by the advocates of improving American schools presented contemporary democrats with a difficult problem. Historically, the American people had visualized education
as the instrument of their liberties, the agency of their authority;
now both the design and the purposes of formal schooling were
slipping out of their hands. We have seen that the Negroes' political
fate, and the fate of Negro education in the South, might have suggested the futility of popular education as a tool of democratic
policy. Even without glancing at the Negroes' problems, white
democrats confronted in the activities and opinions of professional
educators another significant challenge to their educational faith.
We must turn to the movements of popular protest that flourished
after the war to discover how and on what terms American democrats preserved their belief that popular education would guarantee
both democracy and liberty.

x. The Farmers: "Organization and Education"

NEXT after the Negroes, the farmers of the United States were the most nearly ingenuous heirs of the Jacksonian era. Their rural virtues identified them as democrats who deserved to be free, and their self-reliant labor marked them as the ideal productive entrepreneurs of the antebellum image. Therefore no obstacle should have stood in the way of their prospering, once they had embodied democracy in their state constitutions and nurtured it in their schools. After the successful conclusion of the war to end aristocracy everywhere in the United States they set out confidently to live the part democratic theory had assigned them.

Many of them soon confronted difficulties they had not foreseen. Commercial farmers, they discovered after the war that they were being cheated out of their prosperity by the mechanisms of modern capitalism: by railroad and grain-elevator combinations, by inadequate banking facilities and high interest rates, by a national debt made doubly burdensome by provision for its redemption in gold rather than wartime greenbacks, by high prices for tools and supplies and low prices for agricultural commodities. Although many of these handicaps to their well-being were an inevitable outgrowth of the triumph of liberated democratic capitalism, farmers were slow to recognize the fact. Instead they turned to classic Jacksonian techniques for dealing with pressing social problems. They proposed to restore democracy through popular education and occasional corrective legislation.[1]

THE EXPANSION OF FORMAL EDUCATION: THE GRANGE

One of the measures farmers proposed to employ in their behalf was formal schooling. Whereas rural spokesmen had tended to discount public schools before the war, farm spokesmen and farm organizations took an active interest in them after it was over. Well before the end of the century the National Grange of the Patrons of Husbandry had constituted itself both a sponsor and a watchdog for American education, while even the more radical farm organizations that flourished momentarily during these troubled years also sought to make the schools more effective for the farmers' ends.

The Grange's interest in public education operated at several different levels. In the first place, its leaders consistently rallied to the support of ordinary common schools against supposed threats to their integrity or effectiveness. In this sense they literally carried forward the doctrines of the common school awakening. In 1879, for example, the Worthy Master of the order invoked its aid in protecting the common school system against unnamed evils. "Let us watch with sleepless eyes, this glorious palladium, the common school," J. J. Woodman urged. "Let no profane hands be laid upon it. Let none seek to destroy, or pervert it from its legitimate end, the free and untrammeled diffusion of knowledge throughout our land." Woodman's exhortation was undoubtedly aimed at the Catholic Church, which had renewed its efforts to share public school funds, but like the anti-Catholicism of the nativists his prejudice committed the Grange to serving a wide range of democratic values through the public schools. They "are specially designed to aid us in the education of our children," he explained, "and not only ours, but the sons and daughters of the rich and the poor, native and foreign-born, who may meet alike together, and receive the materials of a good and respectable education; an education far superior to that enjoyed in the old world by king, prince, or emperor three centuries ago." [2]

Responsive to rural Protestant prejudice, the Grange also lent its support during the 1880s to both compulsory school laws and national aid to education, measures aimed primarily at an urban and immigrant population. But it also developed an abiding interest in the nature and quality of schooling available to its own kind. State granges in particular sought to influence school boards in their choice of textbooks, which were often inadequate and which sometimes bore the additional taint of "monopoly" origins. Even

more significantly, state granges also interested themselves in raising the standards and improving the teaching in the public schools.
Although their interest was unprofessional, and although the rank
and file of the order undoubtedly lagged behind its leaders in their
enthusiasm for educational innovations, any expression of interest
was striking among a group that had been critical of professional
educators before the war. Clearly the common schools were not
simply an established popular institution, to be defended at all
hazards against alien encroachments, but a promising vehicle for
deliberate social progress.[3]

In particular, Grange spokesmen sought two kinds of improvement in the schools. On the one hand, they insisted again and again
that three fourths of the farm population would receive no schooling beyond the primary grades; hence the order must see to it that
primary schools provided all the elements of knowledge that were
necessary to citizens and democrats. On the other hand, they were
equally insistent that common schooling embrace practical subjects
as well as the traditional academic disciplines. One of the ends
grangers had in view in urging practical training in the schools was
the dignity of labor. Like the Jacksonian democrats they believed
that common schooling in the manual arts could and should be
used to combat contemporary tendencies to look down upon productive labor. But they also had great hopes for practical education
as an economic asset in every farmer's career. In 1883, for example,
the national convention's Committee on Education urged that the
work of the Grange would be incomplete unless it encouraged "a
system for the schools by which the minds of the young may be
more effectually developed and disciplined for the self-education by
which the farmer may gather for himself the practical knowledge
he needs, from the various sources that are open to him in his daily
life. In an enlightened public sentiment it seeks the instrumentality
with which to effect this end." [4]

At the same time, the Grange renounced the farmers' traditional
hostility to higher education, insisting instead that colleges must
meet the vocational needs of farmers as effectively as they already
met the needs of other classes. As early as 1874 the Committee on
Resolutions devised a "Declaration of Purposes" in which the

Grange committed itself to "advance the cause of education among ourselves and for our children, by all just means within our power. We especially advocate for our agricultural and industrial colleges that practical agriculture, domestic science, and all the arts which adorn the home, be taught in their courses of study." In subsequent years other spokesmen for the order reiterated the idea, applying it to high schools as well as colleges, on the premise the Worthy Master expressed in 1885. "We want," he said, "a class of schools and system of instruction, which shall bring the means of a practical education suited to the wants of every condition of life, within the reach of every child in the community." Not only had the farmers adopted the common school; they had also begun to think of high schools and colleges as necessary instruments of their social and economic values.[5]

But the grangers also conceived of their order as an educational institution in its own right, which they could employ to overcome the shortcomings inherent in formal schooling. From the beginning the Grange organization attempted to teach farmers to be more efficient producers and more effective businessmen, while simultaneously showing farm wives how to help their husbands prosper. In the early years it also sought to instruct men and women alike in the mysteries of producers' and consumers' cooperation, and generally it worked to bolster the farm family's position in the modern world by spreading technical and practical information through the subordinate granges. As the Worthy Lecturer of the order explained in 1888, "In as few words as possible, the Grange is teaching the farmer to 'mind his own business,' as a *producer*, as a *man* and as a *citizen*. In a single sentence the Grange means EDUCATION. It teaches the farmer that he has mind as well as muscle, brains as well as land, and that it pays him to cultivate the one as well as the other, for 'knowledge is power.' "[6]

Significantly, Grange spokesmen frequently referred to their order as a "school." Obviously the term was a useful rhetorical device, as is apparent in a statement the Worthy Master of the order made to its annual convention in 1875: he anticipated the day "when our Order is crystallized and embalmed in the hearts of all its members, when the Grange in every agricultural neighborhood becomes as much a matter of course as the school-house." Yet the image appears too often in Grange literature to be thought of as merely rhetorical. In 1878, for example, the Committee on Education of the national body described the order as "a public educator" and "a superior finishing school." During the 1880s two regional spokesmen described it expressly as the farmer's school, and in 1893 the Worthy Master summed up more than two decades of activity by saying that "education is the chief end and purpose of our Order, and the good work goes steadily on. About twenty seven thousand Subordinate Granges have been already organized, every one of which has been, and is a school for the farmer and his family." So prevalent was the imagery of formal education in explaining the voluntary activities of the Grange, indeed, that in 1894 a sympathetic commentator writing in the *Annals* of the American Academy referred to it enthusiastically as a "national university." [7]

The regularity with which Grange spokesmen referred to their order as a school suggests even more strongly than its practical educational activities the extent to which farmers built upon the traditional techniques of Jacksonian liberalism in order to deal with unfamiliar problems. Confronted with increased productivity, falling commodity prices, discriminatory railroad rates, and other deepseated economic evils, they might have invoked strenuous measures of social reform, or at least have grown skeptical of the power of education to ameliorate human affairs. Yet the Grange entered politics only briefly, during the 1870s, and although the antimonopoly measures it sponsored during these years fell far short of restoring farm prosperity, the order soon repudiated political partisanship and turned instead to education to serve the ends politics had failed to reach.[8] Far from abandoning education in the light of experience, grangers extended the idea of schooling both vertically and horizontally: vertically, to include high schools and colleges; horizontally, to include the informal influences of the Grange itself.

Even during the course of their political agitation, moreover, Grange leaders remained surprisingly faithful to liberal democratic precedent. The measures they sponsored during the 1870s, regulating railroads and grain elevators, were intended not to destroy but to restore free competition in agriculture. They recognized that some new measures of social control were necessary to protect economic individualism, but they believed that if the channels of trade were free the individual entrepreneur would prosper. Hence in the very act of calling upon farmers to band together in order to protect their interests, Grange spokesmen appealed not to personal and group advantage but to justice and equal rights, which they proposed to achieve through education. In 1875, for example, the master of the Kentucky State Grange welcomed the delegates to the national convention as a body of conservative, prudent, liberal, wise, and hard-working men whose actions were awaited by millions. "They hope and believe," he said, "that you will establish a system of education, so much needed by the agriculturists of our land, and will fix plans by which equal justice can be given to all industries, and which will cause moneyed monopolists hereafter to cease oppressing the laboring classes among us." Like the Jacksonian democrats, the grangers trusted to liberty and education to serve democratic social ends.[9]

The form their political agitation consistently took, therefore, was an appeal to "organization and education"—organization for the sake of education, education in order to disseminate just principles. The founder of the order, Oliver H. Kelley, told its national convention in 1877: "Let the education of the masses be the great object. . . . Our membership generally is composed of a class who never have been organized before; it is rough material to work with, and it will require time before they learn the necessity and advantage of being prompt. Such a body has to be educated for years before it will be ready to embark in any great enterprise." Three years later the Worthy Master of the order blamed discriminatory legislation in Congress and the states on public indifference, and urged that "such a condition of affairs can only be averted in this country by educating the wealth producing classes to understand their privileges, and in the full exercise of their political rights, demand a fairer representation in the legislative departments of the government, and equal protection to their interests." From this point forward, nonpartisan organization and education epitomized the political activities of the Grange.[10]

Even during the 1870s, that is, and increasingly during the 1880s

and 1890s, Grange spokesmen *substituted* organization and education for politics. Moreover, their annual proceedings and other
vehicles of opinon make clear that the substitution was conscious
and deliberate. In 1890, for example, at a time when other farm
groups were turning to politics, the Executive Committee of the
Minnesota State Grange counseled the state convention that "everything comes to those who wait. And in the meantime we must continue to prosecute our purpose of educating the toiling farming
class. The work is slow, but it will be successful if we simply persevere with rational means." Four years later the Worthy Master
of the national order exhorted its annual convention: "The party
worker wishes to win the battle, whether right or wrong. The farmer
wants the Right to triumph in any case. The Grange will teach him
how to know the right." Praise for education obviously deprecated
politics.[11]

Under the circumstances, the belief in education could only be
conservative: in the long run both schools and the granges were
more likely to serve private economic ends than to achieve democratic social purposes. Significantly, in 1893 the Committee on Education of the National Grange pointed out that the true purpose of
agricultural education was not to make better farm laborers but to
make better farmer-leaders. Labor can be bought, they argued, but
informed leadership comes hard. Again, in 1895 the same body
praised the work of the Grange in improving agricultural methods
and in strengthening public education, but it also urged farmers
not to care so "sentimentally" for other classes.[12] Such statements
implied that grangers had decided to make their own way in a
hostile world, using education not to dissolve social evils but to
benefit individuals who chose to be educated. This view not only
sanctioned a passive role in politics; it also involved overtones of
political and social exclusiveness, of willingness to accept an hierarchical social order and to abandon the quest for universal justice.
By the end of the century the Grange and its education had become
little more than a way of profiting from the existing social and
economic system, an auxiliary to what the Worthy Master had described in 1885 as "condition of life."

Yet it was still possible for the Committee on Education to say in 1894, "The subject of Education underlies all other subjects, and not only is the fundamental principle of our Order, but is the fundamental principle of progress and advancement in all classes of society, and all industries relating to human welfare." [13] The committee's declaration suggests that it was easy for grangers to adopt a conservative political outlook partly because education held broader connotations than the limited uses to which they now put it. On the one hand, it promised to bridge the gap between the interests of the farmers and the interests of the rest of mankind. On the other hand, it promised to solve problems of social organization and social justice through nonpolitical means. Here was the other side of the grangers' reliance on education as a social panacea. Not only did their traditional laissez-faire orientation tend to make education the only solution they could conceive of for contemporary evils, but their belief in education helped to justify their conservatism in the face of pressing social problems.

Nevertheless, Grange leaders had visibly limited the purposes and functions that farmers might attribute to education at any level or in any form. Most of the farmers who joined the Grange were in all probability content with its conservative stance, but not all farmers joined the Grange. Above all it could not speak for the angry men who found their way into the People's party during the 1890s. Far more significantly than the Grange, the Populist movement tested Americans' traditional commitment to liberal democracy and popular education.

THE EXPANSION OF INFORMAL EDUCATION: THE POPULISTS

The People's party drew its main strength from the northwestern and the southern Farmers' Alliances of the 1880s, agricultural organizations patterned after the Grange but committed almost from the start to some form of political activism. Recognizing that contemporary social and economic evils could not be dealt with effectively by the traditional measures of liberalism, the Alliances sponsored a variety of legislative innovations which the People's party incorporated into its platforms during the 1890s: banking and currency reform, public warehousing for farm products, government ownership or operation of the railroads and the telegraph. At the same time, the party adopted major electoral reforms (the Australian ballot, direct popular election of senators, direct primaries, the initiative and referendum), not to mention the eight-hour day and other measures intended primarily to attract support from the labor movement. In many important respects, that is, the aggressive farmers' movement that reached its climax in the congressional elections of 1894 either repudiated or transcended the laissez-faire principles and the antiquated political machinery that the Jacksonian revolution had fixed on the United States.[14]

In spite of its radicalism, however, the political movement the Alliances sponsored ultimately degenerated into William Jennings Bryan's empty free-silver crusade of 1896, which treated the unlimited coinage of silver at 16 to 1 as a vehicle of comprehensive social reform. Admittedly, important practical considerations helped lead the Populists in Bryan's direction: the inflationary effects of free silver would have helped the farm economy temporarily, while fusion with the Democrats offered an opportunity to acquire power immediately rather than in the distant future. But it was not practical considerations alone or even predominantly that brought the Populists to adopt free silver. Instead, their writings inescapably suggest, they were influenced by an exaggerated version of the democratic educational hopes that had persuaded the Grange to enter politics momentarily during the 1870s. They defined their political opportunities in terms not of exercising power but of furthering popular education, and they enlisted in Bryan's crusade because they believed that a decade of organization and education had come to fruition in it.[15]

Like the Grange, the Alliances took an active interest in formal education. Often they simply followed Grange precedent in demanding technical education in elementary schools and high schools and a better agricultural education in the land-grant colleges, but sometimes they invested even formal schooling with major social responsibilities. At their joint convention in Shreveport in 1887, for example, the Agricultural Wheel and the southern Farmers' Alliance adopted a Declaration of Purposes in which they demanded a comprehensive system of public education for the producing classes. Intellectual, moral, physical, and industrial training, they held, "will strengthen the attachment of these classes to their profession . . . ; will better qualify them for success and happiness in life; will render the farm more attractive and remunerative; give the means and time for more general thought and useful study; increase the opportunity and inclination to adorn the home and practice the social virtues; broaden the spheres of their knowledge and usefulness, and give character and influence to husbandry and labor." Such a declaration was the more striking in that it reflected the opinions of southern farmers, who had been even less eager historically than their northern counterparts to establish a full-fledged educational system.[16]

Nevertheless, the main focus of Alliance efforts lay in informal political education. On the practical level, Alliance lecturers sought to make the farmers thoughtful and articulate about a wide range of social problems, introducing them to works like those of Henry George and Edward Bellamy as well as to books by farm spokesmen like W. Scott Morgan and James B. Weaver, and encouraging them to read and circulate reform magazines like the *Arena*. Similarly, local alliances sponsored or encouraged countless popular newspapers, while for a time the *National Economist*—the official organ of the southern Farmers' Alliance—ran weekly essays in history, economics, and political science, and weekly "educational exercises" for the use of sub-alliances. Hardly an opportunity for informal dissemination of knowledge and propaganda went untested by Alliance leaders.[17]

On the theoretical level, Alliance spokesmen invested their informal educational activity with extraordinary significance. Anticipating the St. Louis meeting of the northwestern and southern Alliances in 1889, for example, C. W. Macune wrote: "The delegates who meet at St. Louis in December should be prepared to devise or adopt some practical plan for the systematic education of the producers and workers there represented upon the economic, industrial and political questions in which they are so vitally interested. This special work has not hitherto received the attention which its importance deserves." By the same token, *The Riddle of*

the Sphinx and *The Farmer's Side,* two of the most famous Alliance
tracts published during the 1890s, mingled radical criticism of the
country's economic system with a considered evaluation of farm
organizations as educational institutions. The Alliances' belief in
political education was unmistakable.[18]

They held much the same belief, in fact, that Grange spokesmen
had expressed during the 1870s: organization will ensure the education of the producing classes, while education will guide and also
elevate that organization. Typically, the preamble to the constitu-
tution of the Iowa State Alliance declared that it was that body's
first purpose "to labor for the education of the agricultural classes
in the science of economical government in a strict non-partisan
spirit, and to bring about a more perfect union of said classes for
the promotion of their interests socially, politically and financially."
Urging fiscal reform and railroad regulation, a committee of the
Agricultural Wheel of Arkansas reported in 1887: "It is the belief
of your committee that if we ever succeed in raising and placing
the agricultural and toiling masses upon the broad plane of equality
it must be through organization and education of the masses." Indeed, from time to time Alliance spokesmen invoked the image of
the common school to explain their movement, much as Grange
spokesmen had been wont to do. "Our organization means education, and every sub-Alliance is a school-room," the president of the
Texas State Alliance declared in 1891. "We teach our members political economy and the science of pure democracy from a non-
partisan standpoint." [19]

When the nonpartisan Alliances gravitated into the organized
Populist movement, therefore, their spokesmen inevitably viewed
that partisan activity in educational terms. Urging a third party in
the columns of the *National Economist,* for example, Thomas J.
Davis observed in 1891: "The first purpose, principles and aims of
the Alliance and all other industrial organizations are education.
The second purpose is the action, the good, the benefit we may obtain as a result of such education." From these premises the Indiana
Populist inferred that "the Alliance is purely educational, but is
surely political. It brings the laborers and wealth producers together
and encourages them to study, to think; to investigate the gigantic

evils which surround mankind, and impresses upon our mind, the duty, the responsibility that rests upon us as American citizens." Similarly, in 1891 the Vincent brothers compiled a *Populist Hand-Book for Kansas* as an educational contribution to the farmers' movement. The volume as a whole detailed Populist successes and Populist trials in Kansas; the preface observed that "a *thoroughly-informed* people cannot be enslaved, nor kept in slavery long after they become educated concerning the means used to bind them." [20]

As the Alliances adopted an increasingly partisan stance, it is true, disgruntled leaders who were reluctant to enter politics often invoked informal education as an alternative to organized political activity. Even in September, 1891, for example, the *National Economist* insisted in a lead article that the primary purpose of the Alliance was education rather than politics. "Educate, educate thoroughly, and trust to that education for results," it urged.[21] To this extent the farmers' belief in education worked against rather than supported political activism, as the doctrines of the Grange also indicate. But even the most dedicated Populist activists continued to believe that their role could be fundamentally educational. As Populist agitators contemplated the crisis of the early 1890s they portrayed a radical social upheaval that was destined to succeed, not because the Alliances had organized a class-conscious political movement to secure the farmers' ends, but because they had achieved the universal diffusion of true democratic principles.

There was no mistaking the Populists' belief that they had set in motion a radical transformation of American society. In July of 1892 the *National Economist*, hitherto reluctant to commit itself to overt political agitation, hailed "THE REVOLT" of that month— the decision of the farming classes to abandon the major parties and to unite behind their own presidential candidate—and in subsequent numbers it regularly printed the modernized version of the Declaration of Independence drafted by the People's party convention justifying agrarian "revolution." [22] Meanwhile other farm spokesmen had enthusiastically identified their movement with a "revolution" or an "uprising," as even the titles they gave their political tracts make clear. Among them were W. Scott Morgan's *History of the Wheel and Alliance, and the Impending Revolution*

(1889), James B. Weaver's *A Call to Action: An Interpretation of the Great Uprising, Its Source and Causes* (1892), and Tom Watson's *Not a Revolt; It Is a Revolution* (1892), all of which insisted that drastic social and economic changes were necessary to secure justice in place of special privilege.

Yet these same spokesmen also insisted that peaceful revolution was possible. Typically, Morgan argued that violent revolution impended only if the legitimate demands of the producing classes were not met, while Watson looked no further than legislative adoption of the People's party platform—especially the agricultural subtreasury plan and government ownership of the railroads—to restore liberty and equality. Similarly, in his intemperate and often vitriolic *The American Plutocracy* (1895), Representative M. W. Howard of Alabama exhorted farmers to achieve their ends by constitutional means. "Now it need be only a battle of ballots," he said. "But if we prove recreant to our duty and betray the trust which our fathers have reposed in us, then constitutional methods will not avail, and this continent will be shaken by a mighty revolution." Revolution might indeed impend, but Populist spokesmen commonly hoped to achieve its ends without bloodshed.[23]

The element in the Populists' thought that reconciled and made plausible their contradictory hopes for drastic social change by peaceful legislative means was their belief in the power and authority of education. Obviously, even the most militant Populist advocates of education assumed that informal measures of persuasion would convert farmers themselves to Populism. At the same time, they also assumed that informal education would persuade right-thinking men and women everywhere—not simply farm families—to adopt the farmers' cause. Indeed, the idea that informal education would influence all of the people had accompanied the first gestures the Alliances made toward popular instruction. "We must teach our principles," the chief lecturer for the southern Alliance wrote in 1889. "We must create public opinion; it controls the world—*vox populi, vox Dei,* the voice of the people is the voice of God—and we must make that voice." Two years later the Vincent brothers reported that in Kansas "the education furnished in Alliance halls stimulated the latent energies of the rural classes, gen-

eral reading became more universal, all available sources of information were utilized, and gradually the masses realized that cun-
ning greed had kept country and city arrayed against each other,
though many of their interests are common." [24]

Consequently there was no limit to what the farmers might accomplish. A radical Kansas writer promised in 1895 that the farmers'
movement

will not stop at the remonetization of silver, nor at the system of bond-
ing the nation and the nation's children to the millionaires. It will demand the restitution of Nature's gifts—the land and all which the term
implies—to the equal use of all. It will take from private corporations all
public utilities and operate them for the benefit of all. It will emancipate
woman from economic dependence and political nonenity. It will make it
possible for men who are willing to work to live, accumulate wealth, and
become prosperous. All this it will accomplish by the irresistible force of
education, agitation, and peaceable revolution.[25]

Alliance leaders and Populist spokesmen alike assumed that education was an effective tool of politics and that it would suffice to
achieve "revolutionary" ends.

By visualizing a campaign of universal popular education as the
vehicle and in some senses the definition of their political activity,
however, the Populists also placed themselves in a position in which
any evidence of public sympathy with their demands would appear
to them to be a constructive answer to the farmers' needs. Mindful of Populist victories in the election of 1894, for example, Con-
gressman Howard wrote in 1895 that "a great tidal wave of reform
is sweeping over the land, and the people are not quite such blind
followers as they have been. They are beginning to think for themselves, and understand that the great beating of drums, sounding of
tom-toms, blast of trumpets and blazing of torches are a ruse to lead
them away from the real issue and make them become the cele-
brants of plutocracy's triumph over labor's downfall." Hence they
gravitated naturally and almost automatically into Bryan's free-
silver campaign of 1896, abandoning or at least putting aside other
more comprehensive measures of economic and social reform in the
belief that Bryan's candidacy opened the way to all they had striven
for. Die-hard Populist leaders protested against accepting Bryan

as their party's candidate, but at the party's national convention its first leader, James B. Weaver, nominated him, seconded by a galaxy of farmer-agitators including "Sockless" Jerry Simpson, Ignatius Donnelly, and Mary Ellen Lease. "To your devoted efforts," Weaver told the assembled delegates, "is largely due the revival of economic learning in this country, which has enabled the Democratic party to assume its present admirable attitude. Your work now promises much to mankind, and is about to break forth in complete victory for the industrial masses." [26]

Events were to prove that Weaver was mistaken. Not only was Bryan unable to win the urban East, but soon after his defeat the People's party disappeared as an effective political force; Henry Demarest Lloyd, who had quarreled with the decision of the delegates to the 1896 convention, had plausible reasons for thinking of free silver as "the cow-bird of the Reform movement." [27] Yet Lloyd underestimated the extent to which the Populists' enthusiasm for informal popular education had encouraged farmers to respond to Bryan's appeals, the extent to which the events of 1896 were implicit in the movement from the beginning. In spite of the educational work the Alliances had accomplished, but also because of it, Bryan succeeded in diverting almost all of the farmers' indignation to his cause.

THE USES OF EDUCATION: THE FARMERS

The Farmers' Alliances and the Populist movement challenged the belief American farmers had inherited from Jacksonian democracy, that minimal government will secure the general welfare if the people are adequately educated. To an extent Jacksonian social theorists surely would have repudiated, they proposed that government act to safeguard the farmers' prosperity, not only by protecting them against monopolies but also by providing them with credit and by rearranging the financial system for their benefit. Had the People's party continued to be effective, therefore, it would have marked a major shift in American democratic opinion, and education would have borne an unfamiliar responsibility for reconstructing American society according to a novel economic plan.

On the other hand, the fact that the People's party soon disappeared suggests that the agitation of the 1890s was far less radical than its spokesmen supposed. Its conservatism is also apparent in the later history of the attitudes the Populists adopted toward formal education. Significantly, the belief in formal vocational training survived the farmers' most visionary schemes for social reconstruction. Even when the Alliances turned to politics to achieve agrarian ends, they never repudiated the same kinds of practical training in schools and colleges that the Grange had sponsored, and after the campaign of 1896 the farmers generally repudiated politics and turned instead to technical training to improve their lot. One of the main achievements of the Populist administration in Kansas, indeed, was a reform of the state agricultural college that committed it firmly to practical agricultural training, and Populists in other states were in the forefront of the campaign to hold the land-grant colleges to their original purposes. More generally, the failure of the farmers' political movement coincided with the beginning of a truly effective program of agricultural education conducted by the land-grant colleges, agricultural experiment stations, and the Department of Agriculture. Almost the only practical outcome of nearly a decade of "revolutionary" agitation was better technical training and a greater interest among farmers in learning about technical advances in agriculture.[28]

But the farmers' renewed devotion to practical education was more than a mere reflection of their fundamental political conservatism; as the attitudes of the Grange suggest, the belief in education probably facilitated as well as reflected that conservatism. Logically, members of the Farmers' Alliances should have been dismayed by the collapse of their political agitation, and they might well have turned against all forms of education as an inadequate tool of farm prosperity. In practice, however, they accepted their political failure peacefully, and they turned instead to practical education to achieve their ends. Obviously, they expected to profit from practical training; the significant fact is that they expected to profit from it in spite of their earlier belief that prosperity is impossible without revolution.

This is not to deny that the farmers were influenced by other circumstances besides the belief in education, nor to overlook the fact that the gradual return of agricultural prosperity even before the election of 1896 removed many of the pressures for radical social reform. But the way in which radical political doctrine all but disappeared while the farmers' interest in various forms of practical education flourished suggests that the belief in education helped to renew the farmers' conservative political orientation by providing them with a developed theory of social organization and social progress to replace the aggressive radicalism of the Populists. Almost from the beginning, grangers had been willing to substitute education for politics; after 1896, it seems, so were most Populists.

In this sense, the Grange spoke for the farmers after all. But it was more than the granger philosophy that survived the crisis of the 1880s and the agitation of the 1890s. Far from challenging the farmers' belief in education, the closing years of the nineteenth century witnessed a revival of Jacksonian doctrine in very nearly classic terms. In 1900 even more than in 1875 or 1890 the farmers were advocates of liberty and schools.

x i. The Labor Movement: Accommodation

and Education

IN spite of their difficulties, American farmers could maintain
the stance and identity of Jacksonian democrats after the Civil
War. Therefore the fact that they continued to think of education
as a major instrument of social policy is hardly surprising. By contrast, industrial workers increasingly found that any hopes they may
once have had for restoring social and economic equality through
measures of liberal reform were illusory. Hence the attitudes spokesmen for the labor movement adopted toward forms of education
after 1865 were even more significant than the farmers' attitudes in
defining the uses the American people would make of their traditional liberal panacea. The farmers belonged to the past, whereas
organized labor spoke for the future.

In broad terms, the history of the labor movement between 1865
and 1900 is one of accommodation: accommodation to the proliferation of corporate enterprise, to the development of an unmistakable
class structure, to the disappearance of traditional democratic hopes
for a society of independent small craftsmen and entrepreneurs.
Although the outcome of industrial agitation was far from settled
by 1900, it is accurate to say that the labor movement survived the
century mainly by accepting for its members the very working-
class status it had been the first purpose of earlier reformers to
abolish.

The uses successive spokesmen for organized labor proposed for
education corresponded to the shifting perspectives in which they
saw American society. In the eyes of the dedicated Labor Reformers
who appeared during the 1860s and 1870s, for example, education
seemed to be a promising vehicle for drastic social reform, comparable in both form and function to the education the Farmers'

Alliances were to urge as a corollary of farm organization. In the eyes of the Knights of Labor, who succeeded the Labor Reformers and who attempted to employ massive organization and producers' cooperation to put an end to the wage system, it appeared to be a necessary first step toward working-class solidarity. In the eyes of the American Federation of Labor after it had come to dominate the American labor movement during the 1890s, on the other hand, education seemed to be little more than a serviceable vocational asset, defined for the most part in terms of what training was available through the schools. Far more than the Grange, the AFL accommodated its educational hopes to those of the established social order.

While the labor movement gradually narrowed the scope and limited the functions it assigned education, however, it never wholly abandoned the original democratic belief that an informed people is the best safeguard against political evils and a universal diffusion of knowledge the most effective guarantee of social progress. Indeed, the extent to which and the ways in which the traditional belief in education survived the experience of American labor make a significant chapter in the history of American thought. The doctrines of the AFL as well as the doctrines of the Labor Reformers suggest that even in the postbellum world the idea of education was not simply the by-product of a group's perspective on society but also an influence in shaping that perspective.[1]

LABOR REFORM THROUGH EDUCATION

Strictly speaking, the labor movement that originated during the 1860s could not speak for labor and was in no real sense an organized movement. Instead, it was a state of mind shared by humanitarian reformers like Wendell Phillips, advocates of social and economic panaceas like Ira Steward, and organizers of idealistic labor "congresses" and "brotherhoods" like Charles Litchman. Still, occupational and class lines were not yet so severely drawn that they could not be crossed, and the social agitators who flourished during the 1860s and early 1870s spoke to and for a large number of bona fide workingmen who had not yet reconciled themselves to industrial capitalism. Hence the ideas these reformers expressed were probably as representative of contemporary labor opinion as was the hostility to political agitation expressed by those few trade unions which survived the end of the war.[2]

The career of William H. Sylvis illustrates the political orientation that even a man who worked with his hands might adopt during the 1860s. President of the Moulders' International Union from 1863 to his death in 1869, Sylvis was also a leading figure in the National Labor Union, which upheld eight-hour legislation in its 1866 congress, producers' cooperation in 1867, and currency reform in 1868, all in an attack on wage slavery. Impatient with reformers who spoke of a harmony between capital and labor, Sylvis pressed vigorously for producers' cooperation because it would ultimately reduce capitalists and laborers to a single producing class. Characteristically, however, he also held that the evils American society experienced could be attributed to maladministration of its institutions rather than a settled policy of despotism, and he believed that the diffusion of knowledge would elevate the working class.[3]

While he stressed the need for a fundamental reorganization of the economy, therefore, Sylvis also supported the movement for shorter hours as a means of political education. "It is true," he explained at a Moulders' convention in 1864, "that churches are erected, schoolhouses are built, mechanics' institutions are founded, and libraries, free and otherwise, are ready to receive us, to instruct our understanding and shape our judgment; but alas! we lack *the time to use them.*" Although his lament may remind us of Thomas Skidmore's scathing indictment of common schools, it eventuated in no more than a plea for practical opportunity to secure informal education. Moreover, Sylvis reiterated the classic Jacksonian doctrine, which Orestes Brownson had been quick to challenge, that education will put an end even to European despotism; the liberation of the European masses, he argued, requires only that they have leisure. "Give them but *time* and *opportunity* to think," he wrote in the *Workingmen's Advocate,* "with even limited education, and neither the heat of furnaces, the clang of machinery, the stifled air of manufactories, nor the heat of midsummer's sun, would be sufficient to chain them to the contracted sphere assigned them by the aristocracy of intellect." In America, he added, "the elements of self-elevation are more accessible to the masses; and, if properly applied, neither mind nor body need be fettered." Clearly, Sylvis drew on political categories that had originated in the workingmen's movement of the 1830s, which he maintained by extending the scope and vehicles of education to meet new social needs. He substituted informal means of education for formal schooling, but left politics to education still.[4]

Sylvis was not alone in portraying the eight-hour movement in substantially Jacksonian terms. Ira Steward, the chief theoretical exponent of shorter hours, who looked to the eight-hour day much as Sylvis looked to producers' cooperation to revolutionize the American economy, also based his hopes on informal political education. A prominent member of the International Union of Machinists and Blacksmiths, which was traditionally more reformist than the Moulders, Steward championed shorter hours because leisure would educate the working classes up to the point at which they would be capable of political and social reform. In the United States, he explained in 1868, we have a free press, educated mothers, and common schools; further reform depends upon giving the working classes leisure. In these terms he assigned to informal vehicles of education the political responsibilities that Jacksonian labor agitators had assigned primarily to the schools.[5]

At the same time, Steward was sure that "we shall accomplish our purpose so gradually and acceptably that men will wonder why they ever opposed us. We do not mean Agrarianism! We mean the progress of Social Science, as slow and as natural as the growth of the oak." Not only did he anticipate the education of the working classes; he also expected informal means of persuasion to convert even the possessing classes to his scheme. Significantly, the eight-hour plan he drafted for the Boston Trades' Assembly in 1863 held: "Since this cannot be accomplished until a public sentiment has been educated, both among the employers and the employés, we will use the machinery of agitation, whether it be among those of the religious, political, reformatory or moneyed enterprises of the day." In Steward's eyes, that is, effective popular education was both the first objective and the fundamental method of labor reform; he substituted the progress of social science through popular discussion for more drastic measures of working-class organization.[6]

When the National Labor Union adopted the eight-hour day as its own main project of social reform, it too assumed that the processes of agitation and popular education would achieve its social ends. More generally, labor reformers who refused to limit themselves to the pragmatic techniques of trade unionism commonly relied upon the same educational processes to shape American social policy. Their commitment was most clearly expressed by Wendell Phillips, who ran for the governorship of Massachusetts on a Labor Reform ticket in 1870 with the active support of the National Labor Union.[7]

A vigorous democrat and a tireless agitator of public questions both before and after the Civil War, Phillips believed that rational deliberation was the indispensable basis of free government, and he visualized the American democracy as a vehicle of popular education. On the one hand, inverting the usual assumption that education is intended to guide the people, he held that democratic politics educate statesmen and public figures to deal with social problems they might otherwise be tempted to ignore. "Therefore, on every great question I turn instantly to politics. It is the people's normal school," he told the International Grand Lodge of the Knights of Saint Crispin (alias the shoemakers' union) in 1872. On the other hand, he also praised democracy because it guaranteed that public figures would educate the people. The grant of universal manhood suffrage, Phillips remarked to a workingmen's meeting in Faneuil Hall in 1865, "means taking a bond from the wealthy and learned to educate the poor—the machinery of God's College to ensure the education of the masses." Hence he was an enthusiastic and even undiscriminating advocate of labor organization. Rally for what you will, he told the Knights of Saint Crispin—eight hours, division of profits, cooperation, monetary reforms—"Only organize, and stand together." In his eyes organization promised to solve contemporary problems, not by enabling the working classes to exercise power themselves, but by persuading the political leaders of the commonwealth to exercise it wisely in the light of popular aims. Labor organization terminated as well as originated in education.[8]

Obviously Phillips was far from being a representative figure in the labor movement, yet equally obviously a sizable element of that movement identified itself with him. Furthermore, Phillips had in common with other advocates of labor reform the belief that informal processes of popular education were sure to redeem contemporary society from pressing evils without necessitating class-conscious organization or divisive political activity on the part of the labor movement. (Even the Labor Reform party was intended to compel the major parties to honor workingmen's demands, not to countenance a separate political interest.) To this extent his thought testified to the continued influence of Jacksonian belief in popular liberty and public education in the postbellum world. Not only did labor reformers invoke informal popular education to solve problems they would have assigned to formal education in an earlier generation; they also trusted to that education to solve them in spite of the fact that the schools had failed to prevent them from arising.

ORGANIZATION AND EDUCATION: THE KNIGHTS OF LABOR

The Labor Reformers were often visionary and always theoretical, qualities which suggested that spokesmen for the working classes would not long subscribe to informal political education as a primary vehicle of social reform. Nevertheless, during the 1880s the Knights of Labor continued to identify the labor movement with nonpolitical organization and education of the working classes. Attempting to organize a single comprehensive union incorporating semiskilled and even unskilled workers as well as skilled craftsmen, the leaders of the Knights addressed themselves to a critically important problem, the increasing anonymity and replaceability of individual workers under modern industrial conditions. While they recognized that workingmen had become little more than interchangeable cogs in the industrial machinery, however, the Knights' leaders proposed to deal with the fact by substituting a utopian economic system for the degrading wage system. In the long run they looked chiefly to producers' cooperation to achieve their goal; for the immediate future they sought to diminish the strife between labor and capital and to convert the whole of society to their panacea.[9]

The testimony spokesmen for the Knights presented before the Senate Committee on Education and Labor in 1883 indicates the extent to which they conceived of education as their principal means for protecting and elevating the working classes. "How do you propose to pass from the condition of the wage-worker across the chasm to the condition of the capitalist?" Senator Blair asked Robert Layton, Grand Secretary of the order, when he appeared as the committee's first witness. Layton replied that the Knights relied upon producers' cooperation to achieve their ends, but explained that it depended in turn upon "a process of education in which no legislative means can be adopted." He also told the committee that short of remaking the wage system the first aim of the order was arbitration (i.e., negotiation) of industrial disputes, and he volunteered the belief that "arbitration is a matter up to which the people have to be educated, and we hope to educate not only the wage-worker but the employer, so that they will both understand arbitration and its advantages better than they do now." [10]

As Layton's testimony indicates, leaders of the Knights thought that informal popular education would simply dissolve all of the obstacles to equal rights; if education were successful, his words suggested, social reform would follow as a matter of course. To this extent at least the Knights shared with the Labor Reformers an optimistic belief in the power of knowledge to sway all social classes, including both those which protested and those which benefited from social injustice. (Significantly, the order denied membership only to bankers, lawyers, and saloonkeepers.) More than this, the testimony suggests that because they believed democracy depends upon popular education they were also led to believe that an industrial labor movement might be effective if it devoted itself solely to informal agitation and classless organization. Certainly the ideal of "organization and education," which appealed both to the early Grange and to the Farmers' Alliances, also entered very largely into the thought of leading figures in the order.

It appeared, for example, to be a plausible alternative to strikes. Albert A. Carlton, a spokesman for the order in Massachusetts, told the committee: "We do not desire to indulge in strikes, although, apparently, to the first men who band themselves together a strike appears to be the only effective weapon that we have at hand; but by means of these organizations they are educated to something higher; they are educated to a realization of their position and condition, and are also expected to conduct themselves as men and as citizens who take pride in their country." By the same token, Terence Powderly, the Grand Master Workman of the order, customarily repudiated even strikes intended to secure recognition of a union local as bargaining agent, and at one point in his career he argued that essay-contests would be preferable to an eight-hour struggle. Similarly, both Powderly and Charles Litchman (Grand Secretary of the order, and formerly Grand Scribe of the Knights of Saint Crispin) hoped that if education could not prevent all strikes it would at least be effective in discouraging strikes for excessive wages. Education was tantamount to organization.[11]

As Albert Carlton's testimony suggests, moreover, leaders of the order generally conceived of organization and education as an alternative to politics. Asked whether the Knights supported James G. Blaine for president in 1884, Powderly replied in the *Journal of United Labor* that the order was an educational and not a political body. "There are men who join our Order only to vote," he wrote; "they have no intention of teaching men *how* to vote; they wish to rush things, they think that now is a good time to rush." Two years later Benjamin W. Goodhue, lecturing for the Knights in Illinois, insisted that those who expected the order to be a political agency were mistaken. "Our order was founded for one great and grand purpose," he said, "the unification of labor and the education of the masses." He added that both depended on organization. For that matter, Robert Layton urged Congress not to legislate an eight-hour day but simply to enforce it in federal employment, whence it would spread automatically to other employers, while Powderly devoted part of his annual address to the Knights' General Assembly in 1883 to reading a letter from Judge Jeremiah Black of Pennsylvania praising the order as a nonpartisan educational agency. The idea that

education would achieve all the legitimate purposes of labor organization was extraordinarily powerful.[12]

The techniques of education the Knights sponsored corresponded
to their definition of its responsibilities. In general, they paid little
attention to formal schooling, which was not likely to serve their
political ends nor to help semiskilled workers economically. The
order condemned child labor and approved of legislation compelling school attendance, but it urged no more than narrowly
utilitarian extensions of the common school curriculum and it opposed public high schools because its members thought that high-
school education was class education for which its beneficiaries
should pay. On the other hand, the order supported the *Journal of
United Labor* and sponsored other newspapers; it championed
statistical investigations of the conditions of labor; it pressed for the
eight-hour day "so that the laborers may have more time for social
enjoyment and intellectual improvement"; and it sought means to
convert American labor and the American people to producers' cooperation. Because formal education was relatively useless for the
Knights' purposes, in short, they explored the avenues of informal
education.[13]

Yet their basic commitment was to education as a vehicle of
social amelioration—not to formal education as such nor to informal
education as such, but to whatever educational devices might
promise to achieve their ends. Significantly, Terence Powderly employed the rhetoric of organization and education in urging the
Knights' General Assembly to make sure that all children went to
school. "The sword may strike the shackles from the limbs of the
slave," he told them in 1886, in words that later became the motto
of his *Thirty Years of Labor* (1890), "but it is education and organization that make of him a free man. He is still a slave whose
limbs alone have been freed."[14] Operating on this premise, the
Knights broadened their definition of education to solve new problems, where other men might have inferred from experience of the
same problems that education of any sort was a hopeless instrument
of social reform. We must conclude that education was not only
a convenient technique but also a fundamental assumption in their
thought.

EDUCATION AS A BUSINESS ASSET: THE AFL

During the early 1880s the Knights of Labor seemed to carry all opposition before them. Their apparent successes forced even the national trade unions, organized along craft lines and devoted to gradual improvements of working conditions, to waver in their devotion to business unionism. When a wave of strikes and boycotts initiated by the rank and file of the Knights culminated quite coincidentally and illogically in the Haymarket bombing of 1886, however, both the order and its policies rapidly lost popular support. Within a few years the American Federation of Labor had achieved a dominant position in the American labor movement. With it triumphed a much more restricted view of the role of labor organization and a correspondingly limited view of the uses and authority of popular education.[15]

Adolph Strasser identified the social and economic orientation of the trade unions when he testified in behalf of the International Cigar Makers' Union before the Senate Committee on Education and Labor. "We have no ultimate ends," he announced. "We are going on from day to day. We are fighting only for immediate objects—objects that can be realized in a few years." Neither Strasser nor Samuel Gompers, who succeeded him as spokesman of the new unionism, wholly abandoned the idea that a slow accretion of minor changes might ultimately revolutionize the wage system, but the focus of trade-union efforts was the antithesis of that of the Knights. The leaders of the Knights dwelt in the future and compromised with the present only for the sake of the future; the leaders of the Federation dwelt in the present and were willing to let the future take care of itself.[16]

As a result, they also visualized popular education in narrowly pragmatic terms. Between 1886 and 1914 the American Federation of Labor formally supported compulsory school laws and the prohibition of child labor, free textbooks for school children and reading rooms for their parents, public high schools and industrial or vocational training in the public schools, not to mention shorter hours and improved working conditions. Although many of these measures had attracted the support of labor reformers as well as trade unionists, it was clear that most of them appealed to the AFL primarily because of the economic advantages they might bring. The benefit to be derived from free textbooks is obvious. Compulsory school attendance, the prohibition of child labor, and shorter hours were intended to help make work and to protect adults against low wages. Moreover, only when the trade unions recognized that public secondary education and common school industrial training were not likely to threaten craft monopolies did they urge either. Such facts can hardly detract from the intrinsic merits of the Federation's demands, but what is significant here is that spokesmen for the unions commonly treated education as no more in theory than what it might be in fact, a useful assistance to men and women who wished to improve their economic status within the social order in which they found themselves.[17]

Among the educational reforms the AFL advocated, indeed, only the adult reading rooms carried forward the labor reformers' belief in informal vehicles of education, and in the eyes of the AFL even these enterprises were intended primarily as a means of self-improvement for the individual rather than as a way of altering the social order. Typically, the official pronouncements of the order emphasized its devotion to formal schooling and made relatively little mention of the promise or the possibilities of public discussion or other devices of informal education either within or without the labor movement. Oriented to immediate gains and eschewing ultimate ends, the AFL had little or no use for the kinds of organization and education that appealed to the Farmers' Alliances and the Knights of Labor.

Whenever trade-union spokesmen invoked informal education as one of the functions of the labor movement, therefore, they were more likely than not to speak of it in an unconvincing or perfunctory manner. Testifying before the Senate committee, for example, Adolph Strasser prefaced his pragmatic description of the labor movement with a series of references to its educational activities, but in the telling these reduced to ways of aiding the trade unions in their daily struggle for better working conditions. To the extent that it had any place at all in Strasser's thought, informal education was clearly subordinate to union organization.[18]

Not only was the idea of educating the masses obviously subordinate to organization; it was sometimes employed to discredit the very kinds of social and political agitation Labor Reformers and the Knights of Labor had sponsored. In 1894, under pressure from advocates of political action, a committee of the AFL reported to its annual convention: "We heartily concur in the sentiment . . . that education shall be the watchword of the labor movement, in order that the masses may fully realize the importance of unity of action, regardless of creed, color or country." The language was reminiscent of the Labor Reformers, but the circumstances suggest that deference to education was no more than a way of avoiding politics and political agitation. Samuel Gompers turned informal education into a conservative platitude when he addressed the convention of 1898. Repudiating utopian social theory, he insisted:

Much of our misery as enforced wage-workers springs, not so much from any power exerted by the "upper" or ruling class, as it is the result of the ignorance of so many in our own class who accept conditions by their own volition. The more intelligent, realizing their inability to *create* a millennium, will not descend to trickery or juggling with terms. They seek to benefit themselves and their fellow men through trade unions and trade union action, and, by bearing the brunt, be in the vanguard in the cause, and hasten on the process of education that will fit humanity even to recognize the millennium when it arrives.[19]

Nevertheless, in spite of their pragmatic attitude toward formal schooling, and in spite of the limited purposes to which they put informal education, leaders of the AFL invested both with some of the same hopes that earlier reformers had attached to them. In particular, they assigned formal education an important role in safeguarding democracy and in overcoming social and economic evils. Testifying before the United States Industrial Commission in 1899, for example, Gompers represented the prohibition of child labor as a make-work device but described compulsory universal education as a moral benefit to children, an economic asset to all, and a means of making Americans "great defenders of liberty and of right in the ever-present contest for the establishment of humane conditions and fair dealing between man and man." Similarly, in a statement presented to the same body, a spokesman for the Cigar Makers' Union of Chicago described schools and trade unions as complementary agencies of general social improvement. "Encourage the unions, encourage good wages," George J. Thompson said, "and you assist in creating a consuming population, a population that will ultimately make better men and women, for it is through our trade unions that we are enabled to earn sufficient wages to keep the children—who are now forced into the factory at miserable wages to compete with the bread-winning head of the family—in schools. More schooling and less factory life makes better and more desirable citizens, and, finally, a higher and more ideal social and economic state." [20]

In other words, while statements invoking popular education were often mainly rhetorical, echoes of earlier labor doctrine rather than expressions of a full-fledged trade-union commitment, they apparently also expressed beliefs genuinely held by the leaders or by the rank and file of the trade-union movement. Two circumstances helped to make this belief possible. In the first place, although it was obvious by 1900 that education could not remake American society, schooling clearly offered one way in which individuals might rise within it. Indeed, formal training offered greater opportunities for self-advancement than informal education; if schools were a poor substitute for "organization and education," they also promised to compensate for some of the deficiencies of the existing social order. The idea of education remained powerful in the thought of the American labor movement partly because it had retained some of its original practical significance.

Secondly, the fact that the labor force was increasingly made up of immigrants or children of immigrants may have lent added strength to the idea that formal schooling would compensate for serious social and economic problems. The influence this alien population exercised after the Civil War should not be overemphasized; the American labor movement drew heavily upon European attitudes and immigrant leadership throughout the nineteenth century, and (for that matter) the AFL adopted restrictive nativist policies after it had supplanted the Knights of Labor. But the mid-century labor movement had derived in large part from English or at least English-speaking sources, whereas the new unionism also attracted immigrants from the Continent to whom opportunity for formal education at public expense would appear an immense blessing. As a result it was entirely plausible even in 1900 that spokesmen for organized labor should place great faith in schools as an agency of social progress, a faith comparable in some respects to the faith Negroes had expressed after their emancipation.

In any event, the circumstances can only make more plausible what was apparent in the statements of spokesmen for the AFL: shorn as it was of many of its radical meanings, formal education appealed to labor leaders and labor agitators who had grown skeptical of the power of informal education to achieve their social ends. Schools were by no means the only agency the trade-union movement invoked, nor were they its main focus of interest, but they were unmistakably important to it. In the long run, the experience and origins of the new working class served to preserve rather than to challenge the American belief in education.

THE USES OF EDUCATION: THE LABOR MOVEMENT

Clearly, it took little more than three decades for the American labor movement to come to terms with industrial capitalism. In accommodating itself to modern economic conditions, organized labor also redefined the uses to which it would put popular education, and the very techniques of popular education it would employ. By the end of the century, labor leaders who had witnessed the failure of radical exhortation, and who had discovered the power of close-knit organization to extract benefits piecemeal from employers, visualized education as an incidental device of social amelioration. Whereas the early labor agitators had appealed to an education that was political, radical, and ineffectual, pragmatic unionists turned to forms of education that were economic, conservative—and effective within their limits.

In many respects, therefore, the experience of industrial wage-earners threatened to diminish the value that the American people had traditionally put upon education, and suggested that they might value it even less in years to come. Yet a belief in education continued to affect the thinking even of tough-minded advocates of business unionism. When men like Gompers spoke of popular education as a promising vehicle of social change, it is true, they were often pious and sometimes disingenuous, for they clearly repudiated the whole intellectual apparatus of "organization and education" that old-line labor reformers brought to the consideration of social problems. But when they spoke of schools and formal training they were obviously serious. Although they could not believe that schooling would solve every industrial problem, they expected to make use of it wherever it promised to increase prosperity or to facilitate upward mobility. In the long run, in fact, their devotion to better schools became in their eyes a claim upon the loyalty of the whole labor movement.[21]

By returning education to the schools, indeed, trade-union spokesmen helped to revive Jacksonian liberalism in very nearly classic terms. Whether or not the influx of an immigrant population into the American labor force helped to protect the popular faith in education during a time of drastic social change, immigrants can have provided only an additional motive and not a fundamental definition for American belief, as a comparison between the educational ideas of the AFL and those of the Grange suggests. Putting aside politics, eschewing social reform, the Grange and the AFL concentrated on improving the economic welfare of their members. The AFL employed collective bargaining whereas the farmers remained individual entrepreneurs; to this extent the two groups could hardly have been more unlike.[22] But both groups treated formal education as a vehicle for individual prosperity, and both also advocated extending formal training to meet new economic needs, whereas the Farmers' Alliances and the Knights of Labor concentrated on extending the scope of informal education in order to achieve extensive social reforms, and the Knights even opposed public aid to higher education. In these terms the two producing-class organizations that survived the turn of the century—the Grange and the AFL—carried forward the original Jacksonian commitment. By comparison at least with other spokesmen for the producing classes they advocated minimizing government and maximizing schooling.

Hence it is legitimate to suggest that they employed popular education for impeccably conservative purposes. It is even more important, however, to recognize that their belief in education justified and probably even facilitated their conservatism; that they accepted the established social and economic system at least in part because improvements in public schooling promised to achieve so much within the confines of that system. In this sense the idea of popular education remained an obstacle to the radical rethinking of American social theory even when utopian hopes for a restoration of economic equality had been frustrated by experience.

XII. Middle-Class Liberalism after the Civil War: Popular Education and Civil Service Reform

CONSERVATIVE though American farmers and trade unionists may have become by the close of the nineteenth century, during the intervening years their agitation of social and economic questions frequently struck terror into the hearts of spokesmen for the professional and business classes. At the same time, many middle-class spokesmen were equally repelled by the excesses of monopoly capitalism and by the influence corporate interests had achieved in American politics. Many of them were outspoken advocates of laissez faire who attributed contemporary evils to the unwarranted activities of government, while even those who repudiated strict laissez faire were reluctant to employ the powers of government constructively to solve pressing social and economic problems. Characteristically, they sought to overcome every kind of evil by reasserting the classic definition of liberty that Locofoco Democrats and liberal Whigs had established before the Civil War.

Therefore they had every reason to turn to popular education to eliminate unnecessary social inequalities, restore an open society, and redeem traditional political values. To some extent they did; but their commitment to education was fundamentally conservative if not actually reactionary. While they rebuked the excesses of capitalism they were unwilling to reshape the capitalist system, and in the long run they employed antebellum liberalism as a counterweight to postbellum social agitation. Hence they seldom put their faith in formal education save as a vehicle of their own authority, and as that authority dwindled they called even informal popular education into question. In their search for a vehicle for their conservatism, indeed, middle-class spokesmen finally abandoned most of the generous hopes that antebellum democrats had attached to the education of the people. Some virtually abandoned democracy itself when they decided that popular education would not support their definition of liberty.[1]

COLLEGE EDUCATION AS AN INSTRUMENT
OF LIBERTY

After the Civil War, the forum for upper-middle-class liberalism shifted gradually from the lecture platform to the new weekly and monthly magazines, especially the *Nation,* the *Century,* the *Forum,* and *Scribner's.* Nevertheless, the Phi Beta Kappa oration and the college commencement address continued for many years to serve as a model for scholarly liberals. Almost until the end of the century they believed that if they spoke out on public questions they might exercise an informal educational influence in American politics out of all proportion to their numbers.

The main ground of their belief was the victory of northern principles in the Civil War, which seemed to represent a triumph of liberty made possible by scholarly leadership. George William Curtis, an antislavery spokesman before the war and a prominent advocate of middle-class reform after it, gave voice to this belief in a lecture he delivered repeatedly during 1865. "Human history," he said, "is the history of [the] Good Fight, of the effort of man to attain that universal liberty to which he feels himself born." The war had demonstrated, he continued, "that a popular government, under which the poorest and most ignorant of every race but one are equal voters with the richest and most intelligent, is the most powerful and flexible in history." But more than this he felt that "the national mind has gained a clear perception of the relation of morals and politics—the strict dependence of civil order and national prosperity upon morality." This was the great achievement of the American people, who had firmly decided to make liberty universal, and it augured well for the future destiny of the republic.[2]

Hence scholarly spokesmen for the middle class were much more fully committed to democracy than their antebellum predecessors.

In 1865, for example, E. L. Godkin of the *Nation* took European commentators to task, in an essay on "Aristocratic Opinions of Democracy," for ignoring the actual workings of American institutions in their haste to condemn them. Similarly, in describing the American democracy to an English audience in 1884, James Russell Lowell praised it for its idealism, its conservatism, and its ability to recognize and to follow great men like Lincoln and Emerson. When Charles W. Eliot addressed the Harvard Phi Beta Kappa Society four years later, moreover, he insisted that Alexis de Tocqueville had been mistaken in his criticisms of American political mediocrity, for the American people had decided the great issues of the Revolution, the Constitution, and the Civil War wisely and deliberately. Throughout the postwar decades, the great events and the great men of the crisis years seemed to vindicate democracy.[3]

Some middle-class spokesmen even expressed the belief that the very processes of democratic deliberation would educate public opinion. Again and again in his public addresses President Eliot urged that democracy educates. "The ballot is not the only political institution which has educated the American democracy," he told the Harvard Phi Beta Kappa. "Democracy is a training-school in which multitudes learn in many ways to take thought for others, to exercise public functions, and to bear public responsibilities." Reviewing current proposals for economic and social reform in the *Forum* in 1889, moreover, Edward Atkinson criticized each of them sharply but held that "in the end, the common sense of the people will seize upon and hold fast every element of truth that is to be found in each and all of these proposed reforms, and will reject all that is shallow, fallacious, or purely selfish. In that way society grows and reforms itself." [4]

Nevertheless, these middle-class advocates of democracy also qualified their democratic faith. Significantly, Godkin wrote a companion piece to "Aristocratic Opinions of Democracy" in which he castigated democratic errors and suggested limiting the suffrage to those who could read and genuinely understand a newspaper, while Lowell differentiated in 1888 between the defense he had made of democracy before an English audience and the attitudes American college men must adopt. At Birmingham, he said, he had dwelt upon the good points of democracy; "but here among ourselves it is clearly the duty of whoever loves his country to be watchful of whatever weaknesses and perils there may be to the practical working of a system never before set in motion under such favorable auspices, or on so large a scale." Similarly, Atkinson urged that public deliberation on economic matters must be better informed if it were not to be disastrous in its effects, while Eliot argued: "Experience has shown that democracy must not be expected to decide wisely about things in which it feels no immediate concern. . . . Questions of war, peace, or human rights, and questions which concern the national unity, dignity, or honor, win the attention of the many. . . . But it is curiously difficult to secure from multitudes of voters effective dealing with questions which relate merely to taxation, expenditure, administration, trade, or manufactures. On these lesser matters the multitude will not declare itself until evils multiply intolerably." [5]

To solve the problems democracy created, Eliot proposed that the people be taught to recognize the wisdom and authority of experts in the conduct of public affairs. "Democracies will not be safe," he wrote in the *Outlook* in 1897, "until the population has learned that governmental affairs must be conducted on the same principles on which successful private and corporate business is conducted." In invoking the expert, however, Eliot was atypical of middle-class spokesmen, who tended instead to call on the leadership and influence of "scholars in politics" to achieve similar ends. The scholar in politics was not an expert but a college graduate whose claim to authority lay in his moral stature as an educated man rather than in his special technical competence; the mere fact of his possessing a liberal education qualified him to help guide public opinion. In addressing a commencement gathering at Union College in 1877, for example, George William Curtis remarked: "In this annual celebration of faith in the power and the responsibility of educated men, all the colleges in the country . . . form but one great Union University." What was important, he added, was not formal scholarship but "education as a power in human affairs, . . . educated men as an influence in the commonwealth." [6]

In other words, while they continued to praise democracy, spokesmen for the professional and business classes also urged college men to take up the task of shaping public deliberations. Sometimes they had in view no more than a benevolent intellectual influence on public opinion. After reviewing the educational influence that leading men had exercised in all the great crises of American history, Alexander H. Bullock told the Phi Beta Kappa Society of Brown University in 1875 that "a duty remains for each generation of intelligent, educated citizens. The day of intellectual guidance never goes by." But more characteristically they treated their own scholarly influence as an indispensable part of the democratic process, necessary to raise popular deliberation above popular standards. "This, then, is the great office of education in the Republic," Carl Schurz explained in concluding a Phi Beta Kappa oration at Harvard College in 1882: "it is to insure the durability and success of democratic government by guiding and moderating with knowledge and high sentiment that discussion which has to grapple with the great problem of the present and the future; which has to reform and to preserve, and which alone can lead the people through all the clash of opinions and interests, to a peaceable understanding and harmonious action." [7]

So eager were the scholars in politics to establish their own ethical and political attitudes as the criteria of popular deliberation, in fact, that they frequently held up colonial precedents of educated leadership as a model for contemporary college men. Schurz began his Harvard Phi Beta Kappa address by recalling the precedent of the Puritans, who had founded a college because, he said, they anticipated that public opinion was to govern and realized that "to be safe under all circumstances" such a government "must be one of instructed public opinion." Addressing an anniversary gathering at Cambridge four years later, James Russell Lowell pointed out that colonial society had followed "certain recognized, authoritative guides, and the College trained them as the fashion of the day required." We no longer exercise a monopoly over these guides, he went on, but "the office of the higher instruction, nevertheless, continues to be as it always was, the training of such guides; only it must now try to fit them out with as much more personal accomplishment and authority as may compensate the loss of hierarchical prestige." Clearly, the advocates of college training sought to employ education conservatively, as a vehicle of superior leadership.[8]

In the long run, indeed, they proposed not only to guide public deliberation but to control it and even to reverse its operation. Both George William Curtis and E. L. Godkin exemplified this ultimate tendency of their thought, Curtis in praising popular government and Godkin in reacting against its evils. Writing in the *Nation* in 1876, Godkin deplored the impact of egalitarian ideas and institutions on American public life. "We have for forty years been trying to govern without education," he wrote, "and the experiment is now, we hope, in its last stage." Invoking American history to support him, Curtis told an alumni gathering at Brown University in 1882 that the educated American "has faith enough in the people to appeal to them against themselves, for he knows that the cardinal condition of popular government is the ability of the people to see and correct their own errors." Twelve years later, responding to the political agitation of the 1890s, Godkin informed educated men that their highest duty was to prick the false speculations of the lower classes. Nor were these isolated instances of scholarly conservatism. However much they rebuked the social and economic evils of their era, middle-class spokesmen commonly conceived of higher education as a way of limiting the exercise of popular power.[9]

It followed that the scholars in politics advocated the formal education of the people primarily because it would open the public mind to the influence of scholarly authority. Significantly, Carl Schurz told the Harvard Phi Beta Kappa Society that two levels of formal education were necessary in the United States: "the elementary popular education which does not impart a high degree of knowledge and culture, itself, but makes . . . men open, accessible, susceptible to the influence of superior knowledge and culture when they come in contact with it; and that higher education which enables and incites . . . those to whom it imparts superior knowledge and culture, to make their influence felt." By the same token, in his address at Brown University Alexander Bullock suggested that the increasing diffusion of knowledge necessitated even more strenuous efforts to overcome its hazards. "All these agencies and methods of a more diffused intellectual life," he said, "all these potent influences of a more distributed education over more numerous gradations of intelligence only render essential a higher standard for the higher masters." Clearly, the first purpose of education was to maintain scholarly standards in politics.[10]

In these terms, middle-class spokesmen both carried forward and severely modified traditional democratic doctrines of politics and education. On the one hand, they visualized democratic politics as a great exercise in scholarly persuasion, which they originally undertook hopefully because the experience of the war had taught them that truth and liberty would prevail. Many years after the event one of their number recalled visiting Godkin in his office at the *Nation* on Election Day in 1884 and expressing surprise at finding him serene and hopeful, only to be rebuked with the comment that "I have been sitting here for twenty years and more, placing faith in the American people, and they have never gone back on me yet, and I do not believe they will now." [11]

On the other hand, in relying upon education to maintain liberty they converted schooling itself into an agency of their political conservatism. For the most part, indeed, the scholars in politics ignored primary and secondary education save as vehicles for shaping public opinion; the object of popular education was not individual prosperity but the success of scholarly principle. "The public end of education," George William Curtis said at Kingston Academy in 1891, echoing John Stuart Mill, ". . . is not to make accountants or engineers, or specialists of any kind, but enlightened, patriotic, upright, public-spirited citizens." [12] In the eyes of these middle-class liberals, democracy was a vehicle for popular self-denial enforced by educational institutions geared to support the political influence of gentlemanly scholars.

SCHOLARLY INDEPENDENCE AND CIVIL SERVICE REFORM

Thus far we have concerned ourselves with the abstract theory of scholarly leadership spokesmen for the professional and business classes voiced before college audiences. So far as we have examined their thought, these middle-class liberals believed that disembodied scholarship—the expression of right opinion in a government conducted by discussion—would serve their high purposes. Hence the only organized institutions they appealed to in order to enforce their standards were educational rather than political. In a strict sense, although they had assigned the schools new tasks and extended the educational apparatus of democracy to include the colleges, they continued to put their faith in anarchy with a schoolmaster.

At the same time, many advocates of a scholarly politics also recognized that mere statements of principle would not protect democracy against all its faults; Godkin among others was quick to point out that educated men could hardly expect to exercise a decisive influence in American politics simply by exhorting the voters. Consequently middle-class liberals tended more and more to suggest institutional devices that would strengthen the influence of scholarship and restrict the evils of democracy. Typically, they turned to political independence and civil service reform to achieve their ends. Two characteristics of these reforms are particularly relevant here. In the first place, both were educational, in the sense that they adapted forms of education to middle-class purposes. In the second place, both were conservative to the point of being hostile to democracy. Almost without sensing the fact, middle-class reformers supported independence and the merit system as alternatives to democratic processes of public deliberation and popular education.[13]

One of the motives that led spokesmen for the professional and business classes to consider limiting the processes of democratic politics was sheer ethical revulsion at the spoils system. More characteristically, however, the reformers deplored contemporary politics because it corrupted discussion of public issues. According to their scholarly diagnosis, which George William Curtis articulated in 1886, "The legitimate and healthy contest of parties in a republic is not to be deprecated. It is the controversy of principles, the argument of policies, the great contention to which the political genius of the English-speaking race especially inclines. But patronage destroys legitimate party action, and the reckless party spirit, against which Washington bequeathed us his last and most solemn warning, constantly strives to substitute personal and private ends for public purposes, and to make party contest a struggle for the public money in the emoluments of petty place instead of a great appeal to the country for a public policy." [14]

On this view, both patronage and the party system were evil influences in American politics. Most scholarly reformers agreed in principle with Curtis that "the legitimate and healthy contest of parties in a republic is not to be deprecated," but they also indicted most of the activities in which parties necessarily engaged. "Under every form of representative government," James Russell Lowell explained in 1888, "parties become necessary for the marshalling and expression of opinion, and, when parties are once formed, those questions the discussion of which would discipline and fortify men's minds tend more and more to pass out of sight, and the topics that interest their prejudices and passions to become more absorbing. What will be of immediate advantage to the party is the first thing considered, what of permanent advantage to their country the last." Hence it was easy for them to denounce out of hand the whole apparatus of patronage that helped to keep parties alive. In 1893, indeed, Carl Schurz, who succeeded Curtis as president of the National Civil-Service Reform League, ridiculed the "curious conceit that the spoils of office are necessary to hold political parties together, to create an interest in public affairs among the people, and to give life and spirit to our political contests." Like many reformers, he supported his argument by appealing to the experience of England, which had until now been rebuked by most American liberals for its monarchical and aristocratic government.[15]

Denouncing party politics, the reformers sought to cure their consequences through political independence, the exercise of discriminating judgment between the major parties in order to punish each by refusing to support it when it failed to heed principle. Because the close numerical balance between the two major parties made every vote count, the Independents believed that they guided democratic politics, forcing the upright Hayes on the Republicans in 1876, defeating James G. Blaine's nomination in 1880 and his election in 1884, letting a disappointing Cleveland go down to defeat in 1888, vindicating him against a worse Harrison in 1892.[16] Their practical achievements are less important here, however, than the political theory that supported them. Whereas the theory of scholarly leadership assumed only that college men might exercise an educational influence in their society, the theory of independence inevitably suggested that they should control the exercise of political power.

The evidence is unmistakable. Although George William Curtis customarily appealed to no more than "the courageous independence of the individual citizen," James Russell Lowell clearly held in "The Place of the Independent in Politics" that "it is for the interest of the best men in both parties that there should be a neutral body, not large enough to form a party by itself, nay, which would lose its power for good if it attempted to form such a party, and yet large enough to moderate between both, and to make both more cautious in their choice of candidates and in their connivance with evil practices. If the politicians must look after the parties, there should be somebody to look after the politicians." Even more strikingly, addressing himself to political parties and party leaders in a speech he delivered before the Independent Republican Association of New York City in 1880, Charles Francis Adams Jr. took the view that "we do not care which [party] is in office and which in opposition; we only ask that one shall be in office and one in opposition; we who manage the schools, the press, the shops, the railroads, and the exchanges will take care of the rest. We, not you, are moving this country; you run the political machine." Other reformers, less disdainful of politics than Adams, spoke frequently of returning educated men to authority in the republic.[17]

The theory of independence shaped the use its advocates made of education. If the people were to have the final voice in electing candidates for office, the Independents proposed nevertheless to educate only a limited segment of the population; they intended to carry the day for virtue by tipping the electoral balance in its favor. In this sense, and although they were slow to acknowledge the fact, Independents expected educated leaders to function in isolation from the people. Charles Francis Adams Jr. pointed up the limited scope of their appeal to education when he told the Independent Republican Association that

the New York *Nation* is to-day more generally read and has a wider, deeper influence upon the rising generation of college graduates of this country than any, or probably than all other newspapers combined. And I think we can be pretty sure that in our own country's future the youth nurtured on the *Nation* as his college pabulum is likely to be something of an independent in politics.

Now this I hold to be what we want; it is what I am here to try to elaborate. We do not want more organization—more discipline—more "machine." . . . We want more men of thought and character who are able to stand up before us in the full dignity of their personality; and we don't want so many organs.[18]

There was a notable discrepancy between this vision of politics and the traditional image of the democratic process as universal popular deliberation.

Middle-class liberals also championed civil service reform in the hope that it would deprive political parties of their ability to win political campaigns by corrupt means. According to its advocates, appointment to office by merit established by competitive examinations was an egalitarian as well as a purifying innovation in American politics. In his pioneering *Civil Service in Great Britain: A History of Abuses and Reforms and Their Bearing upon American Politics* (1880), Dorman B. Eaton emphasized the fact that examinations offered equal opportunity to all, and he contrasted the merit system with the patronage system that was characteristic of monarchical and aristocratic governments. Introducing Eaton's book to the American people, moreover, George William Curtis argued that the unreformed civil service in both Great Britain and the United States was "founded upon the theory of feudal times, that public offices are the property of the ruler." By contrast, Curtis explained to the National Civil-Service Reform League in 1883, "in a republican government it is desirable constantly to bring the fresh intelligence and ability of the people into the direction of public affairs. This is undeniable. And it is because the spoils system arbitrarily excludes this intelligence and ability from every branch of the public service that it is dangerous to republican government." [19]

In the eyes of its advocates civil service reform also extended the traditional American commitment to popular education. Because Americans so clearly believe in education, Eaton argued, they should see to it that the "ratio of well-educated persons in official life" increases rather than decreases. His book also stressed the stimulating effects civil service reform in Great Britain had already exercised on popular education there. In 1890, moreover, Curtis invoked the educational ideals of the United States against the opponents of reform. "To win a cheap cheer," he told the League at its annual meeting, "I have known even intelligent men to sneer at the scholar in politics. But in a republic founded upon the common school such a sneer seems to me to show a momentary loss of common sense. It implies that the political opinions of educated men are unimportant and that ignorance is a safer counsellor of the republic." [20]

Nevertheless, the idea of purifying the civil service also presupposed that a renovated public administration would serve to control democratic politics as well as elevate public discussion. Even in arguing that the ratio of well-educated persons in public office should be increased, Eaton implied that educated officeholders would limit the effects of popular ignorance; other advocates of reform made clear that they intended to forestall unwarranted influences on the legislative process, not to increase popular political power. Significantly, Charles J. Bonaparte told the League in 1890 that

a politician may as well, so far as his self-respect or his public utility is affected, be owned by a rich man or a rich corporation as by the Farmers' Alliance or the Knights of Labor or the Grand Army of the Republic: he is a bale of the same goods, whatever may be his trade-mark.

To rid our country thoroughly and once for all of these dangerous and noxious counterfeits of statesmen, and to thus make room for the genuine article, which we produced in good measure a hundred years ago, we have only to do away with the incidents of public life which have arisen within those hundred years and made it no fit career for honorable men.

Curtis went even further when, in addressing the same group in 1888, he equated reform of the civil service with restraints on party spirit. "In a Democratic Republic, where the majority of voters is sovereign," he said, "the vital question for liberty is that of the ability of the voters to restrain themselves." [21]

Under the circumstances, it is not too much to suggest that having found informal political education inadequate to their purposes, middle-class liberals made formal education a criterion for appointive office in order to check contemporary democracy. Two characteristics of their thought lend weight to this proposition. One is the fact that they fought for the merit system, not in order to introduce expert knowledge into the management of public affairs, but only to restrain political abuses. In 1882, for example, Dorman B. Eaton criticized the spoils system because it rewarded partisanship instead of industry and sobriety. Obviously this was a moral rather than a technical defect. In 1889, moreover, Charles J. Bonaparte stated explicitly at the annual meeting of the League that civil service reform was a moral and not an administrative question, while in the following year he argued that contemporary legislators would be competent to solve public problems if they could be guided by scholarly influences. "When there is neither 'money' nor 'politics' in a proposed measure," he said, "the average American politician is a very fair legislator, provided that reputable citizens will take the trouble to tell him just what he should do." After Charles W. Eliot became president of the League in 1909, it is true, he helped to convert it to efficiency rather than purity as its standard of politics, but during the nineteenth century its members spent their energies on preventing democratic mistakes rather than strengthening public administration.[22]

Secondly, some of the most vigorous advocates of civil service reform also considered other devices, nominally grounded in education, to limit popular political authority. One of the most illustrious of these men was E. L. Godkin, editor of the *Nation* and for thirty years the most consistent advocate of laissez-faire liberalism in the United States. During the 1860s Godkin suggested that illiterate Negroes and other uneducated voters should be deprived of the suffrage by a rigorous literacy test. What made his suggestion especially significant was not the idea of a literacy test, which the nativist legislature of Massachusetts had enacted in 1857, but the fact that an advocate of civil rights for the freedmen none the less thought it was more important to limit Negro suffrage through a formal educational test than to ensure universal education. Typically, Godkin also opposed national aid to education, even to education in the South.[23]

Toward the end of the century, moreover, Godkin virtually despaired of democracy, and his despair led him to propose two anomalous political innovations. In the emergency of 1892 he was willing to invoke the influence of the wealthy classes whom he had once vigorously criticized. He thought they might be reliable at least on the basic questions, and he urged on them "the work of persuasion through voice and pen. . . . There is no nobler nor more fascinating game than the work of changing the opinions of great bodies of men, by inducing them to discard old beliefs and take on new ones, or arresting their rush after strange gods." And this was but a harmless tutelary pastime compared with what he finally recommended to them, indifferent to the traditional criteria for scholarship in politics. "Public functionaries are becoming more and more the puppets of the managers outside," he observed, "and the managers are whatever public opinion lets them be or insists on their being. The coming rulers of men are those who mould the thoughts or sway the passions of the multitude." [24]

Six years later, in *Unforeseen Tendencies of Democracy*, Godkin virtually closed his public career with a dismaying catalogue of the ways in which democratic government had failed to attract the wisest men to public office or to stimulate the necessary techniques of public discussion outside of it. The saving grace of democracy, he decided, had been not the wisdom of the democrats but the salutary effect of common and fundamental law, but there had been no equivalent protection against the democratic tendency to use public offices as mere agencies of the popular will. Yet he wished to preserve what was good in democracy. He concluded that only if the scope of legislation were reduced by referring details of policy to trained administrators, and major political issues to infrequent constitutional conventions, could it be restored.[25]

Godkin was not alone; the turn of the century saw a number of treatises like his, proposing the strengthening of constitutional obstacles to popular rule. In its ultimate reaches, middle-class liberalism threatened education itself as a vehicle of democratic politics.

THE LIBERAL USES OF EDUCATION

Because few middle-class reformers attacked democratic errors so vigorously as Godkin, it may seem that the political theory underlying their reforms was more democratic than this analysis suggests. Yet it is significant that the measures spokesmen for the professional and business classes proposed in order to redeem the faults of democracy all substituted the authority of small groups of educated citizens for the authority of the people as a whole. Phi Beta Kappa speakers commonly proposed that college graduates attempt to control public opinion on contemporary questions. Advocates of political independence praised a small body of educated men, acting to govern the consequences of political deliberations rather than shape the deliberations themselves, by maintaining a balance of power between the two major parties. For their part, and although they invoked both democracy and democratic education, civil service reformers sought primarily to take politics away from contemporary political parties, secondarily to limit the scope of politics itself. Even the idea of expert management of public affairs connoted deliberate limitations on popular rule. To the extent that it was common for one man to sympathize with all these measures, indeed, it is difficult to escape the conclusion that middle-class reformers worked consistently to curtail democracy.

This conclusion is reinforced by the fact that they typically honored only the forms of popular education and missed its ultimate political significance. Wendell Phillips pointed out the shortcomings of their appeals to education in addressing the Harvard Phi Beta Kappa Society in 1881. "A chronic distrust of the people pervades the book-educated class of the North," he charged; "they shrink from that free speech which is God's normal school for educating men, throwing upon them the grave responsibility of deciding great questions, and so lifting them to a higher level of intellectual and moral life." A moralist as well as a democrat, Phillips made no attempt to conceal his own dismay at the politics of corruption and the power of political bosses, but he demanded that educated men remain faithful to the democratic experiment even so. "Trust the people," he continued, "—the wise and the ignorant, the good and the bad—

with the gravest questions, and in the end you educate the race."
This was the one kind of education the scholars in politics were
unwilling to tolerate, albeit the one also closest to Jacksonian
ideals.[26]

Middle-class reformers commonly restricted the definition of popular political education; at the same time they all but forgot the
practical vocational advantages antebellum democrats had hoped
to secure through universal schooling. Here too the scholars' prejudice challenged popular belief, and had they stood alone among the
professional classes they might have precipitated a vigorous popular reaction against their narrow educational doctrines. (As it was,
the Knights of Labor—but not the American Federation of Labor
—publicly opposed civil service reform.) [27] But professional advocates of education also spoke for the American middle class. Their
espousal of extensive educational reform, it seems plausible to
suggest, helped to protect middle-class opinion against popular
retribution.

The suggestion is plausible only because professional educators
and their allies clearly shared the political attitudes of the middle-
class reformers. We have already taken note of the conservative
social values that the professional advocates of educational reform
typically voiced before the National Educational Association; here
it need only be said that they also repeatedly echoed the warnings
of scholarly reformers like Curtis, Godkin, and Schurz.[28] But the
educators also concerned themselves with improving and extending
formal education: with industrial and technical training, with the
development of secondary education, with reform and elaboration
of the college curriculum, all for vocational as well as political ends.
Hence their actions identified them in spite of their political prejudices as true servants of democracy.

Rhetoric as well as practice committed them to democratic
values: they referred to both high schools and state universities
as "democracy's colleges." It will not do to charge them with deliberately manipulating public opinion, however; their very profession
caused them to share a basic commitment of the American democracy, the belief that public education should be a vehicle of personal success as well as of political rectitude. In 1881, for example,

when the newly elected president of the NEA suggested to its annual convention that the public school would eliminate the threat of communism, the reasons he offered were appealing in spite of his conservatism.

> The greatest preserving power in the world [he said] is hope. Take hope from a man and you do what you can to make a bad father, a bad neighbor, and a bad citizen of him. But has he no hope, has he no ambition? He sees that it is not wealth that rules, but that it is intelligence that rules. He sees the children of the poor entering the door of the public school, and that there they have equal advantages with the proudest and the best. He sees that by reason of the public school, which he could not maintain himself, the humblest have a chance to climb up. He looks around him and sees that they are climbing up, climbing up in every direction of life. It is a matter of common observation. It is borne in upon him that his children may have a chance, and that he may secure a precious legacy for them. Hope and ambition are revived. The grass looks greener, and the skies are bluer; and he looks up and thanks God and toils on a cheerful man and a good citizen.[29]

This was 1881, but even during the crisis of the 1890s public education appeared in the hands of its professional advocates to be a personal asset as well as a device to limit popular agitation. "When the farmers demand special legislation in their behalf," Henry Raab declared in a classic statement before the NEA in 1892; "when they propose to form into a political party by virtue of their occupation; when they expect the government to purchase their surplus produce and store it; when they demand the unlimited issuing of paper money without any funds to redeem it; then citizens, and especially teachers, will respectfully differ with them; but when they strive to improve their social, intellectual, and financial condition, every one may well contribute his share towards the consummation." [30] Unlike the scholars in politics, who progressively narrowed their definition of education to fit their narrowing political purposes, the educators expanded theirs to meet every modern evil.

Obviously, the professional educators were not the only middle-class advocates of extending the education of the people. Testifying before the Senate Committee on Education and Labor, for example, Edward Atkinson rebuked contemporary agitators for demanding social reform through legislation and invoked popular education in its stead. "The destruction of the poor is their poverty," he said. "But what is that poverty? It is not want of money so much as want of intelligence—want of knowledge; how to earn, how to save, and how to spend. You can in some degree promote education throughout this land, and thus you may remedy this wrong. In that way, and in that way only, can you relieve us from the evils which press upon us, for neither you nor I nor any man can help those who cannot help themselves." By the same token, witnesses as different as Jay Gould and Francis A. Walker urged further aid to public education as a vehicle of social amelioration compatible with economic liberty.[31]

But the social doctrine of the educators illustrates most dramatically how the idea of extending popular education must have reconciled American democrats to middle-class conservatism. Sharing the political prejudices of the professional and business classes, the educators also proposed to educate everyone for prosperity as well as citizenship. Hence it is logical to suppose that the idea of popular education, fostered primarily by its professional spokesmen, helped to create a mood of popular acquiescence in the contemporary social order. By 1900, at least, farmers and industrial workers were pragmatically ready to accept education if its promise seemed real, and the educators worked to make it as real as possible. Not only did they offer to serve the whole public in all its different interests; it was in the nature of their enterprise that they would constantly discover new services. Education was by no means a necessary element in personal success before 1900, but the educators had already begun to do everything within their power to convert it to that purpose, and with the sanction of an amenable people.

Because of the inadequacy of even the best kinds of schooling to overcome mounting social problems, it is possible to argue that the idea of popular education the educators appealed to amounted to a colossal fraud on the Americans' social consciousness. If it was, however, it was a fraud in which nearly the whole people was implicated. The professional educators' profession, not their Machiavellian intelligence, enabled them to speak for so much of American social thought. Like most Americans, they carried forward into the postbellum era the naive Jacksonian faith in liberty and schools.

XIII. Keepers of the Middle-Class Conscience

CHARACTERISTICALLY, spokesmen for the professional and business classes reacted to mounting social problems after the Civil War by denying their significance for democratic government. During these same years, however, a handful of middle-class commentators attempted to convert American opinion to a new vision of social justice. Although they supported reform measures as diverse as the social gospel, the single tax, and Christian socialism, they had in common a powerful ethical commitment to the amelioration of contemporary social problems, which they proposed to overcome by extending their own ethical outlook to other members of society.

In their basic political strategy, however, they remained adamantly liberal: they wished to convert other individuals, not organize collective political action. Keepers of the middle-class conscience rather than working-class radicals, they relied upon ethical agitation and popular education to achieve their social ends. In various ways advocates of the social gospel like Washington Gladden and Lyman Abbott, utopian agitators like Henry George and Edward Bellamy, and Christian economists like Richard T. Ely and John R. Commons all trusted to forms of education to solve the problems of industrial capitalism without jeopardizing middle-class values.

THE SOCIAL GOSPEL: "CHRISTIAN SOCIOLOGY"

By contrast with middle-class liberals like E. L. Godkin, the clergymen who developed the social gospel considered contemporary agitation of social and economic issues as evidence of serious social problems. Washington Gladden insisted that there was a labor question at a time when Godkin insisted there was not, while John Bascom, Gladden's erstwhile teacher at Williams College, observed pointedly in his *Sociology* (1887) that "it is surprising how sharp is the criticism on the mistakes of the poor, as if the rich had not been making their mistakes since the dawn of the industrial era." Although they often criticized the excesses of labor organization, therefore, socially conscious clergymen undertook to solve contemporary industrial problems as the only way to bring industrial peace.[1]

In their eyes, the solution for these problems was justice, which they defined in terms of the impact of industrial organization on human character. "As the church, the state, and the school are to be measured by the character which they produce," Lyman Abbott wrote in *Christianity and Social Problems* (1896), "so is the industrial system. One standard of value cannot be applied in one case and another standard of value in another. The social and industrial system is to be measured, not by the wealth it produces, but by the men it produces; not by the abundance of material things, but by the kind of men developed in the process." Hence they were tolerant of contemporary socialism, which recognized the necessity of remaking social institutions in order to secure humane ends. According to Abbott, who was a relatively conservative advocate of the social gospel, "Socialism and Christianity . . . agree in two fundamental respects. They both aim to secure the reorganization of society, and such a reorganization of society as shall give a greater diffusion of virtue, intelligence, and power." [2]

Nevertheless, the reorganization such clergymen proposed was not socialist but Christian in its orientation, as befitted ministers of the gospel. "The principal remedy for the evils of which socialists complain," Washington Gladden wrote in *Applied Christianity* (1886), "is to be found . . . in the application by individuals of Christian principles and methods to the solution of the social problem." Similarly, Abbott devoted a large part of *Christianity and Social Problems* to explaining the difference between socialism and Christianity. "Broadly speaking," he said, "Socialism puts environment first and character second; Christianity puts character first and environment second. It is not true . . . that intelligent Christianity—the Christianity which follows the teaching of the Master—disregards social conditions. But it is true that the social reformer puts the emphasis on the condition; the Christian disciple puts the emphasis on the individual character." [3]

Therefore clerical reformers were reluctant to appeal to legislation to achieve justice. At various times both Abbott and Gladden proposed government regulation or ownership of railroads and public utilities, federal regulation of corporations, government restrictions on the use of land and other natural resources, and legislation establishing shorter hours and minimal conditions of labor, not to mention municipal building codes and sanitary legislation. Meanwhile other clergymen, less progressive than they, none the less supported a number of legislative infringements on the rights of property. Yet their radicalism was often tendentious, a prediction that drastic reforms might become necessary rather than a full-fledged commitment to them. Significantly, the only legislative measures that Gladden approved unequivocally in *Applied Christianity* were those that clearly reflected an individualistic rather than a collective moral standard. The Christian will insist upon two reforms, he wrote: "Certain outrageous monopolies exist that the state is bound to crush," and "Another gigantic public evil that the state must exterminate is that of gambling in stocks and produce." Otherwise, he observed only that "the time may come when the nation will be compelled to take under its control, if not into its ownership, the railroads and the telegraphs, and administer them for the common good. They are falling, in far too large a degree, into the hands of men who use them for the spoiling of our commerce and the corruption of our politics. But the wisdom or the equity of this measure is not yet so clear that it can be demanded as an act of public justice, and therefore the Christian moralist will not yet venture to pronounce upon it." [4]

Instead, the advocates of the social gospel turned to informal education to achieve their social ends without socialism and so far as possible without legislative action. Tentatively during the 1870s, and with increasing conviction during the 1880s and 1890s, socially conscious ministers undertook to teach their congregations and all others whom they could reach that the prosperous classes bore a special responsibility for the welfare of the less prosperous classes. The reforms they proposed varied somewhat but the underlying principle held constant: Christian charity in modern times requires that entrepreneurs infuse the economic system with human values. Employers should share their surplus profits with their wage workers, either in the form of special bonuses or in superior working and living conditions. Landlords and other members of the possessing classes should take into account the lives and interests of their tenants and dependents as well as their own need to achieve a reasonable return on their investments. Everyone engaged in economic activity should accept a larger personal responsibility for the welfare of society.[5]

The ministers were well aware that ethical instruction of this sort required more than informal pastoral injunctions to charity, however. Hence they spent a major part of their reform effort in developing what they thought of as "Christian sociology." Christian sociology was the marshaling of empirical data that illustrated the failure of the contemporary social order to serve ethical purposes. It sometimes connoted a knowledge of techniques of social reform, but more generally it consisted of collecting and disseminating vivid examples of the social effects of an industrial age in the hope they might stimulate a prudent charity. Acting out their sense of social responsibility, clergymen made their pulpits a source for miscellaneous sociological information, and beyond that encouraged their congregations to interest themselves in the actual conditions of the poorer classes of the community.[6]

Preaching voluntary social reform through Christian sociology, moreover, writers like Abbott and Gladden made clear that clergymen must address themselves to the intelligence as well as the sympathy of the prosperous classes. "There are plenty of people in our churches to-day," Gladden wrote in 1886, "who give every evidence of having been soundly converted, but who are conducting themselves continually in such a manner as to cause this [industrial] trouble, instead of curing it. . . . If a man . . . has got into his head the idea that *laissez faire* is the chief duty of man, the gospel, in the ordinary acceptation of that term, will not correct the defects in his conduct towards his work people." By the same token, Henry

C. Potter, Episcopal Bishop of New York, told the United States Industrial Commission in 1900 that "the problem in modern life in any organized society is to prevent alienation and . . . misapprehension of classes; that, from the growth of wealth in a republic is just as great as in an empire. . . . So, when issues between labor and capital come about, the element that is discreditable in it is the profound ignorance of intelligent people as to what brought them about." The reform principle involved adding informal social and economic education to the abstract preaching of the Gospel.[7]

In this fashion the social gospel both built upon and reshaped the established American belief that popular education rightly employed would solve problems of social organization and social progress that had baffled other societies. True, the original impulse to educate probably stemmed from pastoral tradition rather than educational precedent. Moreover, much of what the proponents of the social gospel wrote—their vocabulary as well as their social theology—derived from English clerical agitation, and it would be a mistake to attribute Christian sociology to American invention. But neither the pastoral roots nor the British origins of the social gospel were so important as the fact that the developed doctrine sanctioned liberty and education as the chief vehicles of Christian social responsibility. Significantly, while Bishop Potter opposed most forms of social legislation he specifically excepted "all law which involves the turning on of the light. That is another question." Similarly, R. Heber Newton told the Senate Committee on Education and Labor in 1883 that "I believe the solution of the labor problem is to be chiefly found in education; education of both factors in the problem—capital and labor—though I should not count the education of one less important than that of the other." In common with other members of the American middle class, socially conscious clergymen visualized education as the necessary basis and instrument of urgent social reform.[8]

In preaching the exercise of ethical responsibility by employers and landlords, however, these clergymen adopted a thoroughly elitist definition of reform. Despite the deference they paid to utopian ideals like industrial democracy, industrial partnership, and the end of the wage system, the whole burden of their teachings

was that if the wealthy behaved righteously there would be no reason for social unrest and, at least by implication, no need for a
greater popular participation in the direction of the economy. In
1884, for instance, Newton pointed out to the New York Chamber
of Commerce that contemporary commercial and industrial associations had already begun to establish a corporate society on the
model of the medieval guilds, and he enthusiastically suggested
that to solve the industrial problem they needed only to build on
these natural tendencies. In 1893 Nicholas P. Gilman, a prominent
clerical spokesman for profit sharing in industry, observed in his
Socialism and the American Spirit that "we rightly condemn the
obvious excesses of the Knights of Labor; but even-handed justice
will inquire what the aristocracy of the industrial world are doing
to make the Knights of Labor superfluous." "Every approximation
toward a community of goods," said Washington Gladden, quoting
the German economist Wilhelm Roscher, "should be effected by the
love of the rich for the poor, not by the hatred of the poor for the
rich." [9]

Hence the education the clergymen proposed was extraordinarily
limited in its scope and significance. On the one hand, they conceived of Christian sociology almost exclusively as a middle-class
vehicle for converting the prosperous classes to social reform. Significantly, Gladden is unclear in *Social Salvation* as to whether the
evils that popular agitation has condemned, or the issues that Christian conscience has discovered, constitute the social problems of
the day, while in *Social Facts and Forces* he appeals to an undefined
and unstructured "public opinion" to remedy contemporary evils.
Employers are partly responsible for social problems, he says, and
employees have many faults that they may correct, "But there are
some things that you and I, who are neither workingmen nor employers, can do, and must not fail to do. We can study this whole
problem, and thus be able to help in forming an intelligent and
humane public opinion concerning it; and it is public opinion, after
all, that must be depended on to settle most of these questions." [10]

On the other hand, advocates of the social gospel also interested
themselves in reforming the established school system. But their
primary interest lay in innovations that could be expected to foster

social discipline or encourage a new social orientation among the working classes. Typically, R. Heber Newton urged that the schools adopt industrial education, yet his writings stressed the ethical purposes rather than the vocational advantages of educational reform. Criticizing the contemporary educational system for its narrowness and its utilitarian outlook, moreover, Washington Gladden wrote in 1902 that "somehow the school must find a way to cultivate the social temper, the habit of coöperation, the spirit of service, the consciousness of fraternity," and he called upon Christian ministers to act as "guardians" over this enterprise. He also advocated manual training, not to teach a trade but to cultivate character, which he defined as self-discipline, dignity, and self-reliance. Even more than Newton, Gladden made popular education a vehicle of working-class discipline to complement the ethical teachings he hoped to impress upon the entrepreneurial class.[11]

Perhaps the elitism of the social gospel was attributable in part to its British origins; perhaps it also owed something to native traditions of humanitarian reform. But it was also traceable to postbellum middle-class liberalism. Politically speaking, the social gospel tended to be a gospel of the professional classes, a gospel of scholarship modified by greater humanity and flexibility than dogmatic scholars in politics displayed, but none the less a gospel of guardianship by a special group of educated men. Certainly the clergymen's sense of the role, the strategy, the very techniques of education was very much like that of the doctrinaire liberals. They hoped to achieve leadership or at least influence in their society; they contemplated using that influence to discourage if not to suppress social unrest; and they preached a superiority to material values that worked more effectively to disarm the poor than to inhibit the rich. So far as advocates of the social gospel were influential in American social thought, they employed education in ways that challenged most of the political values that had originally given it its authority.

UTOPIAN RADICALISM: HENRY GEORGE AND EDWARD BELLAMY

The clerical advocates of social Christianity were not the only spokesmen for ethical social theory, however. During the postbellum era other middle-class agitators, clearly religious in spirit if not in their formal commitments, pressed criticism of the contemporary social order to the point of demanding a radical revision of its liberal economic institutions. More insistent than advocates of the social gospel that social inequalities must be totally destroyed, Henry George and Edward Bellamy were also more willing to invoke popular political opinion to support their comprehensive economic measures. They turned to untrammeled popular education to achieve their social ends. But their very belief that the people as a whole might be educated to sponsor extensive social reforms served paradoxically to limit the specific reforms they demanded. Had either George or Bellamy fully sensed the difficulties of popular education, it seems plausible to say, neither would have been satisfied with the panacea he urged. Relying upon the informal education of the people to secure justice, however, both George and Bellamy failed to grapple decisively with the social problems they described.[12]

Henry George's reliance upon popular education is especially striking in view of his declared skepticism, many times reiterated, of the power of schooling to solve contemporary problems. He pointed out in *Social Problems* (1883), which was his most pragmatic discussion of contemporary reforms, that the consolidation of wealth and power enslaves not only the bodies but also the minds of the people, and he recognized that traditional devices of education could hardly liberate a people so oppressed, inasmuch as they would inevitably be victimized by received attitudes and knowledge. In *Progress and Poverty* (1879), moreover, he argued that universal education could not elevate the "mud-sills" of society so long as an artificial economic system siphoned off all they earned except for what was necessary for minimum subsistence. He also insisted that the educated worker is the end product and not the cause of a high standard of living; only a high standard of living will permit him to indulge in the relative luxury of education. "Deny him leisure," he wrote in unconscious imitation of Thomas Skidmore, ". . . and you cannot, even by running the child through a common school and supplying the man with a newspaper, make him intelligent. . . . Poverty is the Slough of Despond which Bunyan saw in his dream, and into which good books may be tossed forever without result." [13]

George concluded that only confiscatory taxation of the unearned income from land would destroy economic inequalities and create an ethical social order, one in which universal education as well as other middle-class institutions would be feasible. Urging the single tax, he also subscribed from time to time to other legislative reforms; but almost invariably these reduced to innovations that would simplify government and liberate the economy. Asked by the Senate Committee on Education and Labor to describe the measures he would take if he were given dictatorial power, George repudiated dictatorship but answered: "I would abolish all forms of taxation save taxation upon land values, and raise the public revenue in that way. If it was necessary to go further to raise more revenue I would raise whatever more was needed by a tax on legacies, or something of that sort. Then I would add to the functions of the Government as soon as possible telegraphing and railroading; I would abolish the Navy and Annapolis and West Point; I would abolish the collection of debts by legal process, and simplify as much as possible our whole legal system." He thought, in short, in terms of liberal panaceas at a time when traditional liberal institutions had worked against humane values.[14]

In the same instant, George also turned to informal education as his primary political technique. Not only did he repudiate the idea that he might act the part of a dictator; he also declared that a dictator could not achieve social reform. "You cannot go much ahead of the general intelligence of the people," he told the Senate Committee. "If you do you are building upon sand." The belief in education runs through his writings. Even *Progress and Poverty* suggests that demagogues and radicals will pervert the reform movement if the public is not educated, and *Social Problems* explains that "the progress of civilization requires that more and more intelligence be devoted to social affairs, and this not the intelligence of the few, but that of the many. We cannot safely leave politics to politicians, or political economy to college professors. The people themselves must think, because the people alone can act." Hence it argues that "the great work of the present for every man, and every organization of men, who would improve social conditions, is the work of education—the propagation of ideas. It is only as it aids this that anything else can prevail." [15]

In other words, while George believed that formal schooling would not solve contemporary economic problems, he was also convinced that informal education must precede and support his economic panacea. There were two major elements in his belief. On the one hand, he thought that education was necessary to overcome the political obstacles that the contemporary social system put in the way of reform. Formal education could not overcome poverty or secure social justice, but informal education must overcome popular apathy and popular ignorance so that the voters would adopt proper measures of reform. This was the basis on which George justified discussing the single tax before the Senate Committee in spite of the fact that the federal Constitution forbade (or was thought to forbid) confiscatory taxation. "All our Government," he explained, "depends ultimately upon the thought of the people, and therefore the investigation of these subjects by either branch of Congress is good, in the way of stimulating thought and getting information circulated among the people." [16]

On the other hand, George's panacea also depended upon popular education in the quite different sense that unless the public shared his ethical values the restoration of a competitive economy would not serve his larger social purposes. The only basis on which he could hope to achieve his ultimate ends was to assume that somehow a higher spirit would spread among mankind, a spirit that would hold up the standard of duty in place of self-interest. "In that spirit, and in no other," he wrote in concluding *Social Problems*, "is the power to solve social problems and carry civilization onward." Here a faith in religious conversion as well as a faith in secular education was necessary to support his social theory;

George took it for granted. Given land reform, he wrote rhapsodi-
cally in *Progress and Poverty,* government would be transformed
into the agency of a great cooperative society, greed and corruption
would be eliminated from public and private life, and "the sterile
waste would clothe itself with verdure, and the barren places . . .
would ere long be dappled with the shade of trees and musical
with the song of birds." [17]

Yet his language was not exclusively religious: insofar as George
offered his contemporaries more than a visionary hope for social
reform, it rested upon informal popular education. If the ethical
reorientation of society demanded an ethical reorientation of the
whole population, the reorientation of society seemed possible because of George's belief in informal persuasion. His criticisms of
formal schooling were the criticisms of a man who expected to
make informal education effective for ethical social ends. [18]

George's social theory eventuated in laissez-faire liberalism, albeit a liberalism modified by a handful of legislative reforms and
infused with unfamiliar ethical perspectives. By contrast, Edward
Bellamy advocated a collectivist economy democratically regi-
mented to produce material equality as a condition for individual
self-development. Abandoning middle-class liberalism, Bellamy
might therefore have abandoned education as a tool of social
change. In the event, however, he turned to informal processes of
education much like George's to achieve his drastic social ends.

Bellamy devoted most of his exposition in both *Looking Backward* (1888) and its sequel, *Equality* (1897), to portraying the
perfections of the American economic system in the year 2000. Especially in *Equality,* however, he also accepted the responsibility
for explaining how such radical innovations had come about, whereupon he described a great peaceful revolution that had reached and
destroyed the economic sources of tyranny, which the political revolution of 1776 had left untouched. Like George, he would not be
content with charity but demanded the establishment of a just
social order.

The revolution his novels prescribed was peaceful because it
was grounded on universal conviction. Even more than Henry
George, Bellamy looked to a species of religious conversion to ac-

complish radical social change. Mr. Barton explains to Julian West in *Equality* that "the great enthusiasm of humanity which over-threw the old order and brought in the fraternal society was not primarily or consciously a godward aspiration at all. It was essentially a humane movement. It was a melting and flowing forth of men's hearts toward one another, a rush of contrite, repentant tenderness, an impassioned impulse of mutual love and self-devotion to the common weal. But 'if we love one another God dwelleth in us,' and so men found it." Indeed, Bellamy could not avoid the very terminology of conversion. "The Great Revival," Dr. Leete says to Julian, "was a tide of enthusiasm for the social, not the personal salvation, and for the establishment in brotherly love of the kingdom of God on earth which Christ bade men hope and work for." [19]

Nevertheless, while Bellamy obviously counted upon some sort of ethical revival to reconstruct the social order by peaceful means, he also argued that secular popular education would produce that revival. On the one hand, borrowing something from Karl Marx, he described an inevitable process of social and economic development which would culminate in a revolutionary reorganization of society. On the other hand, he described this developmental process in terms not of institutional changes but of educational influences. Thus, *Equality* represents the labor leaders who precipitated the great wave of strikes in 1887 as unconscious pioneers of revolution. They were unaware of the need to destroy the established economic system, Dr. Leete explains, but they were none the less significant in that they rebelled and in that their rebellion taught the well-to-do classes that something was wrong. Again, in a chapter devoted explicitly to causes of the revolution, Leete attributes it to the general diffusion of intelligence during the nineteenth century, coupled with worsening economic conditions. Economic distress, he says, "awoke Americans from their self-complacent dream that the social problem had been solved or could be solved by a system of democracy limited to merely political forms, and set them to seeking the true solution." Indeed, the novel explains at one point that the critical stage of the revolution depended not upon a change of human character but upon a "new spirit and intelligence"; Leete elaborates by saying that popular intelligence was required to put into effect a social system that writers like Plato had been able only to wish for.[20]

Clearly, Bellamy relied upon informal vehicles of education to achieve his utopia. Dr. Leete says in passing that if the reformers had controlled the public press "they would have converted and carried the country in a month." The statement acknowledged the apparent failure of informal means of education at the time Bellamy wrote, but it also justified failure and implied that a more protracted education would be successful. Significantly, Bellamy has Dr. Leete describe early working-class agitation, with all its short-comings and inevitable failures, as an educational process affecting the whole people. "Nothing but just this discipline of failure, disappointment, and defeat on the part of the earlier reformers," Leete tells Julian, "could have educated the people to the necessity of attacking the system of private capitalism in its existence instead of merely in its particular manifestations." Bellamy solved the problem of social reorganization by equating inevitable institutional developments with popular education. Because he believed in education he could hope to achieve radical ends by peaceful means.[21]

Advocating informal popular education, Bellamy also took an interest in the problems of formal education and recognized that pedagogical reforms were indispensable in the schools if they were to serve ethical purposes; *Looking Backward* prescribed educational reforms as well as other innovations in contemporary social institutions. In Bellamy's eyes as in Henry George's, however, reform of the educational system depended upon reform of the social order. Thus Bellamy shared with George and with advocates of the social gospel alike a sense that the problems of an industrial social order negate pure individualism and require more than public schools to safeguard humane values. But Bellamy and George also differed from advocates of the social gospel in that they demanded on the grounds of justice what the clergymen urged finally on the grounds of charity. Hence they turned to the informal education of the whole people to ensure universal respect for justice, and they postponed reform itself to the day on which their elaborate economic tracts had converted the American public. Recognizing why the schools had failed, in short, they turned to informal education to achieve the ends the schools had failed to reach.

THE LABOR MOVEMENT AS A VEHICLE OF MIDDLE-CLASS REFORM

The defect of the social gospel was its elitism, which left social reform primarily to the charitable impulses of the wealthy classes. The defect of the single tax and Bellamy nationalism was their utopianism—not simply the economic panaceas George and Bellamy urged but also the educational influence they counted upon to revolutionize American social thought. Together these defects suggested that significant social reform might be either incompatible with democracy or unattainable through education. During the 1880s and 1890s, however, a handful of social theorists began to explore the possibility that the gap between working-class protest and middle-class idealism might be overcome by special vehicles of informal popular education. In particular, they looked to sympathetic middle-class collaboration with the labor movement to guide popular discontent into constructive channels. Instead of thinking of popular education as a way of controlling social unrest or as a way of transcending disparate class interests, they began to visualize it as a process of interaction between middle-class scholars and working-class agitators, a process of adjustment from which successive social reforms would emerge piecemeal as their necessity became evident.

Two of these theorists were Richard T. Ely and his student John R. Commons, professional economists who hoped to make their discipline a tool of ethical social change rather than a bulwark of the status quo. In *The Labor Movement in America* (1886), which was the first sympathetic study of the subject by a scholarly writer, Ely suggested that the labor movement would make significant contributions to contemporary social reform, and he intimated that it would respond most constructively to men who sought to help industrial workers in overcoming their difficulties, not to limit their action nor to define their problems away. Moreover, in *Social Aspects of Christianity* (1889) Ely suggested that modern scholarship must illuminate as well as identify social problems. "The ethical school of economists," he explained, "aims . . . to direct in a certain definite manner, so far as may be, this economic, social growth of mankind. Economists who adhere to this school wish to ascertain the laws of progress, and to show men how to make use of them." In other words, Ely vaguely sensed that democratic social reform must be guided equally by working-class voters who have directly experienced modern problems and by scholars who have been trained to understand them theoretically, on a reciprocal educational basis.[22]

Commons was even more hopeful of achieving democratic social reform through a harmony of efforts between scholars and voters. The educated man who stubbornly obeys the exhortations of the scholars in politics to act independently, he wrote in *Social Reform and the Church* (1894), is likely to become "a self-righteous and negative scold." Instead, he urged the well-to-do classes to enter into practical politics in sympathy with the working classes in order to counterbalance the power that wealth already wielded in American society. But he would not leave contemporary problems to be solved only by educated men. The electorate must study social questions, he said,

And having found what is wanted, the next thing is to find how to get it. Legislative reform in the shape of proportional representation and direct legislation is indispensable to facilitate both. These reforms would educate the people as no other institution could do, and would furnish the unfailing machinery for enforcing the plans which education has led the people to adopt. So important are these as a key to all social reforms, that with their adoption we might expect greater social progress in five years than the present bungling methods permit in twenty-five years.[23]

Like Ely, Commons looked to the discipline of experience, aided by the disciplines of scientific scholarship and new techniques of popular education, to achieve an ethical social order.

Other writers of the late nineteenth century also looked to a process of education grounded in contemporary organizations and illuminated by sympathetic scholarship to bring about necessary social reforms. Among them was Henry Demarest Lloyd, who first achieved prominence as a leader of the Liberal Republican movement during the 1870s, but who became a vigorous advocate of social and economic reforms during the 1880s and 1890s. *Wealth against Commonwealth* (1894), Lloyd's best-known work, shows that he used empirical research mainly as the vehicle of a universal moral revival; to this extent he was an agitator like Edward Bellamy even though he could not accept Bellamy's utopian scheme. But his other writings suggest that he recognized discrete interest groups within the social order as an important vehicle of democratic reform. Part of the time, that is, Lloyd realized that men must see the world from a point of view governed by their interests and their experience, and he recognized that they cannot be expected to adopt overnight a disembodied universal morality as their standard of social values.[24]

Lloyd developed the educational implications of his position in some detail. On one level, he was sensitive to contemporary developments in formal education that were bringing schools into ever closer contact with daily life. On another level, he was eager to see the labor movement and other social groups grow in strength and authority, believing that they would acquire both responsibility and wisdom in the process. On still another level, Lloyd visualized a fruitful interchange between experience and formal learning in which both scholars and the people would participate. Although there was a distinctly elitist undercurrent in his thought, which led him to suggest in 1896 that only an academy of experts might be trusted with social legislation, Lloyd nevertheless believed that scholarship would answer to popular needs and that the people would respond to scholarly explorations of contemporary problems. For all his moral preconceptions he saw no easy way out, foresaw no act of conversion that would transcend daily existence and obviate social controversy. Only the long hard discipline of experience, illuminated but not prejudged by scholarly investigations in sociology and economics, would bring social democracy to fruition.[25]

Other social commentators adopted the labor movement even more enthusiastically than Lloyd or Ely and Commons. In *The Social Unrest* (1903), for example, John Graham Brooks argued on the basis of twenty years' familiarity with labor agitation that workingmen's views of contemporary economic and social institutions were far more accurate than any a priori liberal theories. But he refused to concede that labor's ways of getting what it wanted were always just; instead, he advocated joint management of corporations by unions and employers as a cure for social strife. Furthermore, he understood joint management primarily as a reciprocal educational relationship, not as a charitable concession on the part of employers nor as an absolute privilege of employees. In spite of his working-class sympathies, that is, Brooks valued the labor movement primarily as a vehicle of democratic education. Similarly, Walter Rauschenbusch, the radical Baptist clergyman who contemplated Christian communism with utopian longing and who urged his congregation to ally themselves with the labor movement in order to work toward ideal justice, also invoked education as the chief vehicle of social reform. Although Rauschenbusch wrote as if the evils of the day might be dissolved by a preaching of benevolence from the pulpit, he also urged ministers and other men of good will to join the labor movement in order to understand its resentments and to arm it with "scientific information and trained intelligence." Obviously, the idea of informal educational collaboration appealed to middle-class social reformers who sought more than Christian charity but less than universal conversion to solve contemporary social problems.[26]

While a number of writers explored the possibilities of collaboration between scholarly investigators and an anxious people, however, their devices of popular education were tentative and hortatory rather than developed and persuasive; their theory of democracy was more significant for the problems it raised than for the difficulties it solved. Still, it suggested that if sophisticated social reform were to be attempted within the framework of middle-class ideals and democratic politics it would depend upon new techniques of political education to inform public opinion and to raise the level of popular political deliberation. In proposing a constant process of educational interaction between middle-class scholars and working-class voters, in short, men like Ely and Commons and Brooks and Rauschenbusch both evinced a traditional democratic faith in popular education and anticipated the path that popular education must take if it were to remain effective for democratic social ends. Their ideas, much refined, would become the theoretical basis of the progressive movement.

XIV. Democratic Education in
an Evolutionary Society

UNLIKE most of the social theorists whose works we have discussed, leading spokesmen for ethical social reform participated actively in the progressive movement of the early twentieth century. Hence it is possible to treat progressive thought as no more than a direct outgrowth of their agitation. In order to understand the progressive synthesis of democracy and education, however, we must also recognize the influence that one other nineteenth-century phenomenon exercised on American social theory. This was the idea of social evolution, which appeared at the time of the Civil War, but which established itself in its full significance only by the close of the century.

Evolutionary social theory was not the property of a single group of American writers but a conviction that permeated the thinking of many writers representing many different points of view. For this reason it must be understood in abstract terms, as an idea that both confirmed and challenged the American commitment to popular education as the basis of democracy. On the one hand, it made little or no difference to the traditional American belief that universal instruction is an indispensable tool of liberty. On the other hand, it implied that effective government requires the application of comprehensive scientific knowledge to contemporary problems, and so raised the standard of political deliberation above the level of popular intelligence. Here was a challenge to democracy that it might not easily dismiss. The effect of both phenomena together was to force democratic theory toward a new calculus of politics and education.[1]

EVOLUTIONARY THEORIES OF DEMOCRATIC
EDUCATION

As it happened, two fundamentally opposed views of social evolution were broached during the postbellum era, one extremely pessimistic, the other correspondingly optimistic about the possibility of guiding social development. Each in turn made a peculiarly important demand upon education, the traditional core of American democratic theory.

William Graham Sumner, professor of political and social science at Yale University from 1872 to 1909, was the leading exponent of pessimistic evolutionary theory, which stressed the frightful hazards of meddling with the social structure. Indeed, Sumner refused to concede that evolution would automatically benefit men even if they permitted it to take place unimpeded. "Under our so-called progress," he wrote in "The Challenge of Facts," "evil only alters its forms, and we must esteem it a grand advance if we can believe that, on the whole, and over a wide view of human affairs, good has gained a hair's breadth over evil in a century." All that he could suggest was that by careful pruning men might eliminate some of the evils they had created.[2]

To be consistent with himself, Sumner should have left formal education to private initiative, as his English counterpart Herbert Spencer in fact did. Yet Sumner would not; his dogmatic lectures, his angry essays against social visionaries, were paralleled by long years of service on the Connecticut State Board of Education, which his social theory could hardly sanction. Some commentators have felt that Sumner's interest in modernizing American education, and his devoted public service to it in Connecticut, marked a "progressive" exception to his rigidly "conservative" ideas. It may be so. But universal public education was also an inescapable political corollary of his conservative social theory. Because he was an American conservative, it seems plausible to say, formal education held a place of extraordinary importance in his thought.[3]

Its importance lay in the fact that Sumner invoked public as well as private schooling to protect the evolutionary social process against "sentimental" meddling by democratic governments. The idea that an improved system of education will guard society against unwarranted political interference runs through his essays, interspersed with criticisms of the clamor for tax-supported innovations in the schools. Education, he explains in "Purposes and Consequences," is an instrument to train men and women to resist visionary impulses and to discipline crowd enthusiasms. In "Protectionism" he identifies schools and churches as a legitimate exception to strict laissez faire—not because of the good they will do individuals, but because "we know that society must pay for and keep up its own conservative institutions." Everywhere he treats effective education as an indispensable social asset, and limited public support for it as an unavoidable consequence of its importance.[4]

Hence it is legitimate to assert that although he ridiculed the attempt to impose human aspirations on the natural tendencies of social existence, Sumner clearly advocated it himself. Typically, he was critical of contemporary education because it would not enforce necessary principles. "In truth," he wrote plaintively during the 1890s, "half-culture is one of the great curses of our time. Half-culture makes men volatile and opinionated. It makes them the easy victims of fads and fallacies and makes them stubborn in adhering to whims which they have taken up. It makes them impervious to reason and argument because they hold to their pet ideas with a pertinacity which has a great deal of vanity in it." His doctrine was an anomaly, but an anomaly born of contemporary necessity and reflecting the American tradition. In spite of his skepticism regarding contemporary education, in spite even of his criticisms of those who demanded public education as a right, even a rigorous determinist like Sumner would hardly leave instruction in the political requirements of the cosmos to chance or to brute experience.[5]

At the other extreme from Sumner's adamant laissez-faire doctrine lay the social theory of Lester Frank Ward, who also insisted that governments must approach human experience empirically. Like Sumner, Ward felt that there is no such datum as inevitable progress. He also argued as stringently as Sumner that nature is amoral, and that there is no possibility of imposing a sentimental morality on its workings. Nevertheless he repudiated Sumner's conservative inferences. His answer to Sumnerian determinism lay in exploring the successive stages of life from amoeba to man—this is the subject of the first part of his *Dynamic Sociology* (1883)—and in demonstrating, on the strength of a genetic approach to social institutions, that there is a distinct opportunity for exercising deliberate control over social evolution. Mankind, he insisted, has made progress in the past by collectively subduing nature to its purpose, and there are no rightful boundaries to action: "In the control of nature as in its study, there are no arbitrary limitations. The right is always co-extensive with the power." [6]

For Ward, that power lay in man's unencumbered intellect. All social institutions, he argued, are the product of deliberate human action, but not often of self-conscious or effective choice among possible means. The problem of social techniques for the future, therefore, is one of "pure meliorism" that will go beyond the sentimental proceedings of contemporary humanitarians and achieve "the improvement of the social condition through cold calculation, through the adoption of indirect means. It is not content merely to alleviate present suffering, it aims to create conditions under which no suffering can exist." [7]

These were bold strokes in behalf of human self-determination, set within the very confines of natural forces that Sumner revered. Ward's social machinery was equally bold. He proposed to use universal scientific education to manipulate social development. "If society ever collectively realizes what the ultimate end of its being is, and comprehends the true relations of the hierarchy of means to that end," he wrote in *Dynamic Sociology*, "it will necessarily regard the distribution of knowledge as the one great function, outside of its regulative functions, which it is specially constituted to perform." Tracing his hierarchy of means back, Ward argued that the ultimate end of men is their happiness, the means to happiness progress, the means to progress "dynamic action," the condition of dynamic action "dynamic opinion," the condition of dynamic opinion accurate knowledge, the condition of accurate knowledge the dissemination of scientific truths. Education was no panacea, he insisted, but an essential first step before men could hope to manipulate their environment for their own purposes, and a step from which all else would follow.[8]

It was also a democratic principle. "The greatest of all desiderata in society," Ward explained in *The Psychic Factors of Civilization* (1892), "is a degree of uniformity of intelligence, or intellectual and moral homogeneity." Significantly, he spoke in *Dynamic Sociology* of the ultimate form of society as a "conscious anarchy of intelligence." In such phrases he both identified himself with the liberal democratic tradition and summed up the extraordinary responsibilities evolution might put upon education.[9]

Sumner and Ward were doctrinaire thinkers, however, and their social theories were probably too drastic to appeal to most of the American people. In any event, it was left to other writers, chief among them Andrew Carnegie, to define the more commonplace American response to the social teachings of evolutionary theory. Carnegie understood social evolution in terms that were compatible with Sumner's doctrines, but also far more hopeful. Far from accepting the painful struggle for existence as a universal human necessity, Carnegie visualized American society as one in which leading men engaged in that struggle in its most rigorous and most rewarding form, while other men willingly accepted and benefited from their economic achievements. In addition, he insisted that the wealthy had an ethical obligation to help the poor, not simply a political obligation to defend the conditions of material progress. Whereas Sumner was so insistent that the evolutionary process not be corrupted by ethical confusions that he all but forgot charity, Carnegie was so convinced that evolution is beneficial that charity gave him few theoretical difficulties, and he sanctioned a considerable extension of private and public benefactions beyond the limits that Sumner propounded.[10]

Carnegie's model charity was education, on both a public and a private basis. As a public institution it seemed, as he said in *Triumphant Democracy* (1886), a "true panacea for all the ills of the body politic." That volume gave it a predominantly political significance, but still not the narrowly conservative meaning lent it by Sumner, who urged public education only because he was so apprehensive of uncontrolled movements of social protest. "Educate man," Carnegie enthusiastically proclaimed, "and his shackles fall. Free education may be trusted to burst every obstruction which stands in the path of the democracy towards its goal, the equality of the citizen, and this it will reach quietly and without violence." At the same time, education made a most suitable model for private beneficence because it left so much to the initiative and diligence of the recipient. "There is really no true charity," Carnegie wrote in *Nineteenth Century*, "except that which will help others to help themselves, and place within the reach of the aspiring the means to climb." [11]

The principle lent special sanction to the famous gifts of public libraries. The public library, Carnegie said in his essay on wealth, is a useful extension of the public school and an inestimable contribution to the "genuine progress of the people." Hence "no millionaire will go far wrong in his search for one of the best forms for the use of his surplus who chooses to establish a free library in any community that is willing to maintain and develop it." Like formal education, indeed, the library would serve two distinct purposes equally well: it would aid the most deserving individuals to rise by their own efforts, and it would support the material progress of the country. But it was also an important exception to strict determinism, in the sense that Carnegie intended it to modify the rigorous effects of economic competition by sharing the advantages of the few with the many. Without recognizing the contradiction it created in his thought, Carnegie advocated generous provision for popular education in order to temper the effects of evolution. Unlike Sumner, who treated democratic education as a predominantly political phenomenon, Carnegie invoked it in behalf of both popular suffrage and popular welfare. [12]

Among the three evolutionary theorists we have discussed, therefore, Carnegie was closest in spirit to professional educators who put forward practical education in the schools as a preeminent device of deliberate social improvement. He was sufficiently optimistic about democracy to express none of their political fears, but in effect if not by intention he too substituted education for other kinds of social reform. For our purposes here it is not extreme to suggest that his belief in education amounted to a layman's interpretation of the professionals' idea, and that it drew on the same popular concepts.

Similarly, Sumner and Ward stood in sufficiently close relationship, respectively, to the scholars in politics and to the utopian Christian radicals to be identified with them here. The likeness between Sumner and Godkin is in fact extraordinary, if one disregards the evolutionary vocabulary. Not only was Godkin an adamant believer in laissez faire, but Sumner in his early career was an important political Independent and a strenuous advocate of civil service reform. He was also one of the first American writers to suggest that the difficulties of contemporary government stemmed from an unlimited application of democratic dogmas to American politics, which might be remedied only by restricting the participation of the people in the process.[13]

By the same token, although any parallel that is drawn between Ward on the one hand and George or Bellamy on the other is necessarily somewhat forced, it is a striking fact that both he and they should have turned to universal education to solve contemporary problems. Ward labored diligently to ground his system in evolutionary rather than ethical sociology, but his ideal of reform through scientific education was manifestly utopian: in its first draft, indeed, his book bore the title "The Great Panacea." Moreover, for all his materialism, Ward's vision of human progress was compatible with both George's enthusiastic hopes for, and Bellamy's matter-of-fact descriptions of, a perfected social order.

The precise degree of identity is not so important, however, as the general conclusion these parallels illustrate: evolutionary theory provided somewhat different language for familiar social doctrines. Examination of other social theorists influenced by evolutionary thinking would reveal the same phenomenon; indeed, many of the writers we have discussed incorporated echoes of Social Darwinism into their discussions without bringing their theories to fit its most basic tenets. Hence its revolutionary influence in both social and educational theory was to wait until the next century, when men would begin—however reluctantly—to contemplate themselves and their society in truly naturalistic terms. During the nineteenth century, far from being a decisive influence in American political theory, the idea of evolution sanctioned traditional techniques of politics and education.

THE EVOLUTIONARY CHALLENGE TO DEMOCRATIC THEORY

Although evolutionary theory served mainly to provide a new vocabulary for nineteenth-century political and social thought, in one respect it could not help but challenge traditional American views of society and education. Significantly, Sumner, Ward, and Carnegie all called for specialists to guide the social order. The specialist Carnegie respected was the successful businessman, while Sumner and Ward revered essentially academic heroes, but in important respects the basic principle was the same. Only the specialist could be trusted to govern social and economic development because only he would know enough.

This was an article of scientific faith for both Sumner and Ward. Although in many ways Sumner was simply conservative, he also advocated eliminating accumulated errors in social management like the protective tariff. Reform of this sort called for the most delicate scientific knowledge. If, as he wrote in "The Challenge of Facts," "It will take centuries of scientific study of the facts of nature to eliminate from human society the mischievous institutions and traditions which . . . statesmen, philosophers, and ecclesiastics have introduced into it," there was no room for amateur bungling. More than this, in at least one of his early essays Sumner insisted that laissez faire did not mean an absolute prohibition upon government intervention in the economy, but only that such intervention must be entirely scientific. "*Laissez-faire* is so far from meaning the unrestrained action of nature without any intelligent interference by man," he wrote during the 1880s, "that it really means the only rational application of human intelligence to the assistance of natural development." In these terms science was an instrument of statesmanship that justified exceptions to laissez faire. "Statecraft," Sumner concluded, "is to be guided all the time by the active reason and intelligent conscience. . . . If the statesman proposes to interfere with exchange, then *laissez-faire* comes in as a general warning, not as an absolute injunction: Let them manage for themselves. *Laissez-faire* is the only maxim which allows of the correct use of history and statistics to secure such knowledge as shall properly guide the statesman in his task." [14]

Statecraft was the real point. Sumner rebuked contemporary social theorists who confused ethics with science, but not the use of scientific inquiry to serve human ends. Hence his social thought bore finally on the question of who should guide reform rather than on whether reform might be attempted. During the 1870s he suggested in the *Journal of Social Science* that democracies must train voters to reach satisfactory technical judgments. "To educate millions of voters," he wrote, "to sufficient knowledge of a technical and scientific subject, involving self-denial, firmness, and persever-ance, in the presence of dull and passionless peace, and for a good which is not immediate, but remote, involves the severest test to which popular institutions have ever been put, one which hitherto they have never endured." [15] During the 1880s and afterward, how-ever, he suggested that it was wiser not to try. Nevertheless, this was more nearly a comment on democracy than on social science. The province of the social scientist was to guide popular govern-ment—if only he could find a way.

Ward described much the same problems as Sumner. Having accepted the legitimacy of human desires as a definition of society's goals, he none the less denied that they could be effectively served by anyone but trained social scientists, and he had slight patience with the ignorant democracy of his day. In *The Psychic Factors of Civilization* he blamed contemporary evils on institutionalized self-ishness, described the social will as a "mass of conflicting desires which largely neutralize one another and result in little advance movement in one settled direction," and ridiculed the idea of popular government. "The fundamental problem of social dy-namics," he pointed out in *Dynamic Sociology*, "is to show how legis-latures may be lifted up to the position from which they will of necessity, and as a matter of course, legislate according to the scien-tific method." Hence he projected a legislature that would be a "central academy of social science, which shall stand in the same relation to the control of men in which a polytechnic institute stands to the control of nature." [16]

Ward's outlook was conditioned by his fundamental evolutionary principle of achievement by indirection. According to this view, man does not wisely attempt to control natural forces directly, by means of brute strength: even if he can succeed in the attempt he will expend far too much energy in merely counteracting nature, and it is usually much simpler to trap natural forces into serving human ends. Arguing that the physical sciences develop ever more effective ways of dealing indirectly with natural forces, and that it is a mark of backwardness in the social sciences that they have not yet learned to use social forces in the same way, Ward proposed nothing less than the conscious manipulation, by his scientific academy, of the human environment. "It only requires a somewhat higher type of this same quality of mind," he said in *The Psychic Factors of Civilization*, "to tame the human animal and make him as harmless and as useful to society as domestic animals are to man." [17]

Although his objectives and his evolutionary techniques differed radically from Sumner's, therefore, Ward agreed with him in urging that only government by social scientists would avoid the terrible hazards of a meddling democracy. "Think," he said, "of trying to advance scientific discovery by a general convention!" [18] In the long run he anticipated that universal scientific education would make indirect manipulation of the people unnecessary. For the foreseeable future, however, his theory of government rested upon fears that Sumner might well have voiced, and eventuated in an elite academy of social scientists that Sumner might well have adopted. In this sense Ward's "conscious anarchy of intelligence" was every whit as utopian as universal conversion, a way of solving a problem of political democracy that did not deal with the problems of democratic politics.

Other writers who were less systematic social theorists than either Ward or Sumner also lent their support to a developing evolutionary elitism. For example, when David Starr Jordan explained in an address at Stanford University that " '*Laissez-faire*' is now a discredited principle," he also hastened to add that superior knowledge must be the guiding principle in any reforms that were undertaken. Moreover, he employed a metaphor that could have come from Ward. "All unscientific or sentimental tinkering with society, and law, and government," he said, "is still '*laissez-faire*.' The blind effort to do the impossible effects nothing. It is only the whirl of the water in the eddy of the stream, which in no way hastens or changes its flow. Man must first learn the direction of the currents. The efforts he puts forth must be in harmony with these currents, else his labors may hinder, and not help, real progress. The opposite of *laissez-faire* is not action simply, but action based on knowledge." [19]

Scholars in politics, E. L. Godkin for example during the 1870s, had sometimes voiced similar ideas, but in emphasizing the analogy with natural forces in a stream Jordan made scientific social engineering far more elitist and at the same time more indispensable than any traditional scholarship could be. So to some extent did men like Charles W. Eliot and Andrew D. White. It is not that there was no precedent for an appeal to scholarly science, but that under the influence of evolutionary thought reformers as well as conservatives would adopt specialized knowledge rather than the popular will as the necessary basis of modern government.

Some of the same currents of thought also affected the definition of the businessman's role in the contemporary social order. In developed evolutionary theory, the distinguishing mark of the business leader was not his charitable undertakings—these were only secondary distinctions—but his special organizational ability, and (in the circular logic of Social Darwinism) his superior organizational ability explained his personal success while his success in the competitive struggle testified to his superior fitness as a social leader. Carnegie exemplified this aspect of the theory when he hailed the millionaire as a benefactor, through his organizing genius, of the whole society; but Carnegie was by no means unique. Significantly, the Reverend Nicholas P. Gilman, one of the prominent advocates of the social gospel, observed in *Socialism and the American Spirit*: "Modern civilization is not due to mere distension of muscle; it is primarily the fruit of the intense action of the human brain, and the great mass of mankind can follow no surer path of welfare than that of high respect for the patient inventor, the busy manufacturer, and the master of commerce or finance, who may seem to be working purely for their own good, but whose efforts can never benefit themselves without producing an improvement in the lot of their fellow-men." [20]

Such beliefs had an important bearing on the theory that education is the basis of American politics. It was not an educated elite that Carnegie described and Gilman sanctioned; it was a business elite. But it was an elite based on superior fitness, and the fact forced democrats to seek new grounds for assertions of elementary democratic rights. Only if they could legitimately claim equal fitness to guide social and economic development could they justify their wish to regulate the economy. The basis of any such assertion of fitness lay perforce in superior knowledge. Thus the evolutionary theory of business leadership worked in a peculiar way to reinforce the elitist tendencies of the social scientists, and to make superior fitness based on knowledge rather than fundamentalist morality reflected in popular suffrage the necessary criterion of democratic social policy. From this point forward democrats would be compelled to take new steps to ensure the quality of popular deliberation if they were to protect the right of the people to rule.

THE AMERICAN BELIEF IN EDUCATION: RETROSPECT AND PROSPECT

By 1900, indeed, American democratic theory had reached a critical point in its history. Not simply evolutionary theory but experience itself threatened time-honored solutions to the problems of social and economic organization, and challenged the traditional belief in educated liberty. In the economy, the practice of freedom had engendered a fantastic growth of trusts and millionaires, until it was no longer possible to talk simply of destroying them and returning to the competitive model of the antebellum years. Democrats had to live with advancing economic organization and to learn how to manipulate it to serve their ends. Similarly, in politics Americans were now confronted with the permanence of political institutions like the boss and the machine, unanticipated in Jacksonian doctrine, and with growing difficulties in involving the whole people effectively in the process of public policy-making. Here too they had to learn to live with their political system, and to discover how to make use of it for democratic ends without seeking to destroy modern institutions wholesale. Above all, democrats had to find out how to harmonize the attitudes and judgments of ordinary men with the complex political necessities of modern life if they were to escape from the stultifying politics of the late nineteenth century, in which business interests conducted the affairs and swayed the politics of the country because the people had not learned how to reach the sources of their discontent and because the better-educated classes were fearful of popular ignorance.

Yet it was clear from the events of the postbellum era that even now Americans were likely to apply the education of the people, on a still more expanded basis, to the solution of their problems. Despite serious differences of opinion, each of the main groups of social reformers that appeared after the Civil War adopted a political strategy that depended to a notable degree upon some technique of education. Negroes and northern advocates of southern rights sought to achieve their ends by extending the common school awakening to the prostrate South. Restless farmers turned to informal political education to protect their entrepreneurial status, while they also explored the possiblity of improving formal schooling to benefit their own kind. Spokesmen for the labor movement also extended the definition of popular education; like the farmers, they appealed first to informal political education, then adopted formal schooling when the futility of political persuasion had become apparent. Yet their frustrations hardly undermined democratic belief that the political education of the people, if it were undertaken on a sufficiently broad scale, would redeem the United States from contemporary evils. Both Henry George and Edward Bellamy, and for that matter such writers as Richard T. Ely and Henry Demarest Lloyd, continued to treat the pressing problems of American society as amenable in the first instance to informal education.

Meanwhile conservative spokesmen had also redefined the education of the people to accord with their political and economic values. As the deliberations of Congress show, many men who were apprehensive over the radical tendencies of American society after the war believed that perfecting the country's school systems would itself safeguard American liberty. By contrast, the self-appointed scholars in politics came increasingly to believe that formal elementary education could not protect the republic; but though they very nearly abandoned the schools as agencies of their conservatism, they none the less turned to other political devices grounded in education to replace them. Furthermore, the advocates of the social gospel, whose political conservatism was tempered by a sense of ethical obligation to the working classes, coupled a narrow definition of formal education with a broadened definition of informal education as a vehicle of necessary reforms. Moreover, although conservative spokesmen generally were interested in formal education less as a source of popular advantage than as a vehicle of popular discipline, professional educators who were unmistakably conservative in politics pressed to extend public education on the most generous terms possible. Conservatives as well as radicals turned repeatedly to forms of education to solve national problems.

We must conclude that the idea of education remained a powerful commitment in American thought during the late nineteenth century. Spokesmen for different political interests might advocate technical schools, high schools, or colleges; granges, alliances, or labor unions; scholarship, sociology, or economics; but all these devices reflected the same fundamental strategy for controlling social events. Whatever the tactics different groups employed, they had in common that they substituted education for other techniques of social action. Most Americans continued to believe that liberty is the basis of social order and education the key to liberty.

Nevertheless, while the fundamental strategy of applying forms of education to the solution of contemporary problems was common to all branches of American social thought, its fragmentation into distinct and sometimes conflicting techniques argued that its influence was weakening and that it might abruptly disintegrate. Few Americans had recognized the inadequacy of education to meet contemporary needs, but if it proved too visibly a tool of contradictory social purposes it might yet lose its hold on their political imagination. This possibility defined the terms in which the idea must be restated if it were to retain its influence after 1900. It could not be merely conservative or merely utopian, nor could it be exclusively political or exclusively careerist, for it had to answer to a wide range of social pressures.

In the progressive movement the Americans would attempt once more to solve their social problems, to restore their liberal democratic utopia, by educational means. The task was in many ways impossible, but most of the currents of late nineteenth-century thought would funnel into the attempt: the movement of elementary democratic protest, the political anxieties of scholarly liberals, the social teachings of the Christian gospel, the complicating assumptions of evolutionary theory—both of society as a natural growth and of the necessity of skilled government. During the nineteenth century these currents of opinion had been in conflict at least as often as they had been in agreement; now, however, they must be joined if the quest were to be successful. As they joined, in turn, they would bring democratic education into a new relationship with democratic politics. During the nineteenth century the idea of education had been defined in different ways and oriented to different purposes. The progressive movement would seek to revitalize both democracy and education, would identify the one in the other, and so attempt to resolve the difficulties and divisions that threatened anarchy with a schoolmaster.

Part Four

TWENTIETH-CENTURY

INNOVATIONS

THE wisest of modern educators has declared that "the only way to prepare for social life is to engage in social life." The rule applies to society conceived as a school no less than to the school conceived as a society.

Herbert Croly, 1914

FAITH in the people must have as its corollaries faith in the facts, faith in the power of knowledge, faith in the free flow of ideas, and hence faith in education and the processes of education. These are the very pillars of our free society.

David Lilienthal, 1949

x v. The Progressive Synthesis

DESPITE its obvious debts to an earlier epoch, the progressive movement marked a turning point in American democratic thought. On the one hand, in their early enthusiasm the progressive generation attempted to solve all the economic and social and political problems that had accumulated since the Civil War by extending democracy and education to every phase of contemporary life. They reacted to pressing evils by treating them as instances of ineffective public opinion, which greater popular power and better popular education would be sure to remedy. On the other hand, in pressing both democratic politics and democratic education to their logical extreme as techniques of reform, the generation also opened democracy itself to charges of incompetence and irrelevance. Having institutionalized so many of the political ideas nineteenth-century democrats had cherished, indeed, progressives were ultimately led to doubt their own principles when their exaggerated hopes for reform failed to materialize. Hence the progressive definition of democracy stands as both the climax and the apex of liberal democratic theory in the United States.[1]

One of the phenomena that made progressivism so vulnerable to historic change was the unanimity with which different social groups representing different social interests adopted its basic political tenets. Much has been written in recent years of the differences between the progressive conservatism of Theodore Roosevelt and the obsolete liberalism of Woodrow Wilson. The distinction has some basis in fact: for various reasons (not all to his credit) Roosevelt sought to accommodate reform to the needs of modern corporations, while Wilson often spoke in the accents of nineteenth-century hostility to all concentration of power. Yet in most respects these champions of middle-class reform shared the same political beliefs even when they disagreed over the social and economic measures the government should adopt. Moreover, contemporaries who aligned themselves with one or the other of these two leaders generally subscribed to the same political doctrines. In its narrow meaning the progressive movement was simply a reform movement within the Republican party, but in its larger sense it was a common undertaking of organized labor and of business spokesmen, of farmer representatives and of professional men, in both major parties.

The common political principles of that larger progressive movement are the subject of this chapter. Responsive to the causes for popular protest, but mindful of its potential aberrations, progressive leaders sought to make reform effective by introducing drastic innovations into the democratic process: the direct election of senators, the direct primary, and the initiative, referendum, and recall; the recall of judges and of judicial decisions; presidential and party leadership; the systematic use of experts in the formulation of public policies; new forms of journalism. Each was in some measure conceived in educational terms, intended to develop the competence as well as to increase the political power of the people to deal with contemporary evils. Far more effectively than any of their predecessors, the progressive generation identified the expansion of democracy with the expansion of education, fused the two commitments in a comprehensive theory of politics.

THE THEORY OF DIRECT GOVERNMENT

In supporting direct popular participation in government, progressive spokesmen often urged no more sophisticated reasons than those axiomatic arguments in favor of democracy that had been a commonplace of American thought during the nineteenth century. "There can be no argument against the Initiative and Referendum," Professor Lewis Johnson of Harvard University wrote in 1912, "that is not an argument against popular sovereignty." Nevertheless, advocates of direct democracy also argued that direct participation in government would encourage intelligent popular deliberation, and they commonly assumed a distinction between the unthinking democracy of the past and the alert democracy of the future that contemporary political reforms would create. According to Delos

Wilcox in *Government by All the People* (1912), a handbook of the direct-legislation movement, "If the masses of the people are now qualified to select men to conduct the government, they certainly can become qualified by practice to participate in other ways in the service of the state. The country surely will suffer no harm from the increasing intelligence of its people." [2]

One of the reasons progressive spokesmen advocated direct democracy was that it was sure to confront the electorate with its fundamental political responsibility. In supporting the direct election of senators, for example, George Haynes wrote in 1912 that "under popular elections every candidate's record and qualifications would be under discussion for weeks before the election, and if the popular verdict proved to be not in accord with the evidence, the blame could be shifted by the voters upon no one else." Enumerating the advantages of the initiative and referendum, moreover, a committee of the National Economic League declared: "While enough power is thus left with the representatives, a salutary increase of responsibility is thrown upon the voter. It brings him, to some purpose, into closer touch with great affairs. It enables him to vote for measures apart from men, and for men apart from measures." Marshaling the rebuttals to critics of the initiative and referendum, indeed, a writer in the *Arena* acknowledged that the voters might not always be adequate to the complex task of evaluating legislation presented to them in a popular referendum. "But," Charles S. Lobingier wrote, "it may well be asked if this is not after all an indictment of popular government in general rather than merely of popular legislation, and whether as a matter of fact the people are not now, in the last analysis, required to determine these questions but to do so under a system which disguises and conceals the fact that they are involved?" [3]

But clarifying political responsibility also meant, in the eyes of the progressives, that the people would learn to confront events intelligently for themselves. "The world has enormously overestimated the educational value of that popular participation in political affairs which consists only in voting for candidates for office," the *Independent* pointed out in 1908. Voting "provides no incentive to study questions, to understand measures. All that is left to the legislator. Under the initiative and the referendum the voter turns his attention from men to measures and becomes an informed citizen. Altho years and generations may pass before more than a small minority of the people will thus become thoroly informed and interested, yet every year the number of such increases where direct participation in legislation is the rule, while under the merely representative system voters become more indifferent, more neglectful and more stupid." This was the basis on which Frederic Howe urged New York State to adopt the initiative and referendum in 1915. The experience of western states had already shown that the referendum was not likely to support radical purposes, he said. "But most important of all is the educative influence of referendum elections on measures initiated by the people themselves. They lead to constant discussion, to a deeper interest in government, and to a psychological conviction that a government is in effect the people themselves. And this is the greatest gain of all. It has been said that the jury is the training school of democracy. To an even greater extent is this true of the initiative and referendum." Not the will of the people, not even the present competence of public deliberations, but the possibility of educating the people to still greater political achievements was what both defined and validated democracy.[4]

On this view the prime enemy was obscurity—not only the "murky atmosphere" in which Haynes complained state legislatures often operated, nor yet the obstacles to individual perception of events, but all the institutional obstructions standing in the way of a clear direct perception of the consequences of popular choices and popular decisions. "These are the principles I would apply to government affairs," Howe told the New York Academy of Political Science. "Politics should be simple, rather than confused. Officials should be responsive, not irresponsible. There should be an end of checks and balances. There should be a direct vision between the citizen and his servant, and easy means for the community to achieve its will, and an equally easy means to change its decision when it finds itself in error." For the ultimate objective of politics was neither democracy as such nor the power of the people to secure the legislation they already knew they wanted; it was, as Howe also said, "fluidity, responsiveness, freedom; freedom of society, in its collective capacity, to develop its own political life; freedom to evolve, to grow by change, just as does the individual, just as does the whole animal and even the vegetable kingdom." To the typical progressive, democracy was a progressive institution, and progress depended upon an untrammeled popular education.[5]

Consequently, progressives argued that given a properly democratic politics even popular errors would educate public opinion. As William Mackenzie expressed the idea in the *Arena*, "The people may make some mistakes in voting directly on public measures, just as the average citizen may make mistakes in deciding upon the kind of house he wishes his architect to build for him, or in deciding to enter upon a legal suit; but in collective as well as in individual affairs, we learn wisdom through our mistakes. Better an occasional error of judgment with the chance to correct it, than blind submission to laws, however perfect, which are imposed from without." Growth was the end, the capacity for intelligent growth the condition, politics become truly educative the means of achieving bona fide democracy. "Civic education resulting from the adoption of Majority Rule is dynamic," Delos Wilcox explained in an apt summary of the progressive argument;

it is self-education, not the mere doing of tasks under direction. . . . After their long tutelage in public affairs by numerous well-recommended instructors, the people need, as the crowning feature of their education, the privilege of making independent use of the knowledge they have so acquired. The finishing touches can never be put upon knowledge except by the actual doing of things. Responsibility assumed as the result of free participation in the affairs of government, big and little, confers the degrees and issues the certificates of proficiency in civic affairs.[6]

All these attitudes came to a focus in the progressives' attack on the power of the courts to invalidate social legislation. Theodore Roosevelt articulated a common opinion when he advocated the recall of judicial decisions before the Ohio constitutional convention of 1912. "It is impossible," he said, "to invent constitutional devices which will prevent the popular will from being effective for wrong without also preventing it from being effective for right. The only safe course to follow in this great American democracy is to provide for making the popular judgment really effective. When this is done, then it is our duty to see that the people, having the full power, real-ize their heavy responsibility for exercising that power aright." Gilbert E. Roe, a prominent advocate of the recall of judges, was even more outspoken in the *Proceedings* of the Academy of Politi-cal Science. The recall, he said, "would be a good thing not only for the judge and his decisions, but for the people themselves, and after all that is the real reason why we want any of these demo-cratic measures. I am not at all sure that where there are direct primaries better candidates have been nominated than under the old system, but I do know this, that it has been a good thing for the people; the discussion, the agitation, the education, the interest ex-cited has laid broad and deep the principles of democracy in those communities, and that is why it has been good." [7]

Clearly, progressive advocates of direct democracy neither aban-doned nor wholly accepted the traditional political premises of the American democracy, but instead began to make them over on a new pedagogical model. The first tenet of progressivism was the right of the people to rule, but the devices of direct government were also intended to strengthen the educational force of political events in order to help the people to rule better. Progressive theory made their right to rule contingent upon the possibility of con-tinuing their political education by novel political devices.

LEADERSHIP, PARTISANSHIP, AND JOURNALISM

Adopting a contingent theory of democracy, the progressive generation was hardly prepared to stop with clearing the channels of democratic politics. The progressive movement also gave rise to an extraordinary attempt on the part of political leaders, scholars, and journalists to find ways of educating the self-governing public to a better understanding of contemporary problems. The most im-portant corollary of popular self-education through direct govern-ment was a whole cluster of techniques to further informal popular education and guarantee the success of the democratic enterprise.

The first of these techniques was self-conscious political leader-ship. Recognizing that the social and economic instruction of the people could not depend entirely upon their spontaneous acquisition of knowledge, the era's most prominent political figures deliberately sought to use public office as a vehicle of popular education. The first great progressive educator in this sense was Theodore Roosevelt, who worked tirelessly during and after his presidency to convince the American people that they must adopt new techniques of social engineering in place of both the empty laissez-faire practice and the equally empty antimonopoly dogmas of the past. Like other spokesmen of the period Roosevelt was first of all a moralist, often simply platitudinous, invoking the eternal verities to bear him witness, but he introduced a new force into American politics. In spite of their limitations his innumerable political sermons were attempts to shape public opinion on contemporary questions in such a fashion as to make it both relevant and constructive.

Moreover, Roosevelt was entirely conscious of his role; he conceived of his contributions to popular education not as dispassionate scrutiny of events but as personal leadership that focused and organized an unformed public opinion. Every act of his public career seems to have been calculated to achieve this effect. "People always used to say of me," he told one of his correspondents in 1916, "that I was an astonishingly good politician and divined what the people were going to think. This really was not an accurate way of stating the case. I did not 'divine' how the people were going to think; I simply made up my mind what they *ought* to think, and then did my best to get them to think it. Sometimes I failed and then my critics said that 'my ambition had overleaped itself.' Sometimes I succeeded; and then they said that I was an uncommonly astute creature to have detected what the people were going to think and to pose as their leader in thinking it." And, inclined to rodomontade as Roosevelt was, this was the light in which sympathetic contemporaries saw him. "Under his leadership," the sociologist Edward Alsworth Ross commented at the close of Roosevelt's presidency, "the people have become aroused as to the use of natural resources, the conditions of meat-packing, the purity of foods, the hygiene of industry, industrial accidents, child labor, the protection of the family." The central fact here was not that Roosevelt was wholly or even largely responsible for all of these developments, but that the President of the United States had used his office to educate the public to them.[8]

Other political figures also enthusiastically adopted the technique of educational leadership. While Roosevelt turned to it instinctively, Woodrow Wilson came to it as a result of his scholarly consideration of the workings of parliamentary government in Great Britain. In early studies of the political process, Wilson tended to idealize Parliament and to deprecate actual public opinion, but by the time he was a candidate for the presidency he found himself deferring to the wisdom of the people. Some of the time he seemed to say that the public needed only to be informed to put an end to contemporary evils. "Publicity," he argued in *The New Freedom* (1913), "is one of the purifying elements of politics. The best thing that you can do with anything that is crooked is to lift it up where people can see that it is crooked, and then it will either straighten itself out or disappear. Nothing checks all the bad practices of politics like public exposure." Yet he also believed that publicity depended for its effectiveness upon a leadership that would focus issues, organize the better judgment of the people, educate. In effect, he supplemented the devices of direct democracy (to which he gave only a grudging support) with the techniques of responsible leadership. "I think it will become more and more obvious," he explained in words that might have been written by Frederic Howe,

that the way to purify our politics is to simplify them, and that the way to simplify them is to establish responsible leadership. . . . The business of the country ought to be served by thoughtful and progressive legislation, but it ought to be served openly, candidly, advantageously, with a careful regard to letting everybody be heard and every interest be considered, . . . and this can be accomplished only by some simplification of our methods which will center the public trust in small groups of men who will lead, not by reason of legal authority, or the right to command, but by reason of their contact with and amenability to public opinion.[9]

At the same time, Wilson also championed the role of the political party in stimulating a public opinion that would otherwise be inarticulate. No less of a moralist than Roosevelt, Wilson put his theory in simplistic terms. What is important here, however, is the fact and not the form of what he proposed. "Organization is legitimate, is necessary, is even distinguished," he said, "when it lends itself to the carrying out of great causes. Only the man who uses organization to promote private purposes is a boss. . . . I honor the man who makes the organization of a great party strong and thorough, in order to use it for public service." However inadequate his distinction between good and bad organization, he made party and political leadership as important as publicity and the latent power of the people to the success of democracy; together he thought they might discipline popular government to achieve its legitimate ends. The secret of democracy in his eyes was not simply more democracy but a more realistic organization of the democratic process, which was at the same time the best possible guarantee of a better political education of the people.[10]

Furthermore, political leaders in the states also developed a theory of educative political leadership. Here the chief figure was Robert M. La Follette of Wisconsin, who in many ways spoke with the most authentic voice of the progressive movement. Typically, La Follette argued in his political *Autobiography* (1913) that pressing social and economic problems would be solved if only Americans sent honest and idealistic men to Washington; to this extent he made the processes of democratic politics seem simple and a matter largely of good will. But he also went beyond this simple doctrine into a functional analysis of contemporary political problems, and he intended the *Autobiography* as a whole as a kind of laboratory notebook recording his explorations of ways to overcome them.[11]

In particular, La Follette discussed the necessary role of political parties in the reform process. He thought of the party platform as a "covenant" with the voters binding the party to carry out specific policies and giving the voters a clear basis on which to make their choice of representatives, but he had no intention of letting the party's role be merely passive. He argued that party platforms should incorporate even nonpartisan planks so as to direct the voters' attention to matters of principle, and he pointed out that it is best to focus on only a handful of contemporary issues at one time in order to make their meaning unmistakably clear. The objective in either case was what La Follette himself referred to as "education," which he insisted must be a slow and deliberate process. "I have always felt," he wrote, "that the political reformer, like the engineer or the architect, must know that his foundations are right. To build the superstructure in advance of that is likely to be disastrous to the whole thing. He must not put the roof on before he gets the underpinning in. And the underpinning is education of the people." [12]

La Follette's words implied that party principles can achieve a valid educational significance for the people only when they are voiced by a forceful political leader, and this was a political conviction his career demonstrated over and over again. One of the recurring images in his narrative is his portrait of the responsible official using facts to educate. The same image justifies his disdain for patronage—patronage is not necessary to hold a party together, he argued, if its leaders constantly circularize the people—and it helps also to give point to his bitterness toward Theodore Roosevelt: "Roosevelt is the keenest and ablest living interpreter of what I would call the superficial public sentiment of a given time and he is spontaneous in his response to it; but he does not distinguish between that which is a mere surface indication of a sentiment and the building up by a long process of education of a public opinion which is as deep-rooted as life." No man who ran for public office could hope always to meet the standard La Follette proposed, but it was one of the political criteria of the age. An educative political leadership seemed to the progressive generation an indispensable device of popular self-government. [13]

Progressive spokesmen counted upon other educational resources than political leadership and partisan organization to make democracy work, however. One of the phenomena of the age, which lent additional force to the theory of popular reform, was a wide-ranging literature on public affairs that supported the leadership of extraordinary men by working to inform the political judgments of ordinary citizens. Significantly, there was no ironclad distinction in the progressive mind between scholarly investigations of contemporary problems and the literature of popular agitation. Many of the prominent advocates of political and social reform were serious students of contemporary institutions, among them such figures as Charles Beard, Frank Goodnow, Henry Jones Ford, and John R. Commons, while even Lincoln Steffens began his journalistic career in a scholarly search for a new science of ethics. In retrospect most of the works of progressive scholarship seem tendentious and unscholarly, handicapped by their insistent attempt to solve contemporary problems, but they were also a unique contribution of the progressive era to the machinery of democracy. In its behalf, scholars and publicists acted out a part assigned by democratic theory to all democrats, the acquisition of political intelligence, half aware that it was no longer logical to expect democratic self-education without having specialists to make it possible.[14]

The most characteristic literary expression of the age, it is true, was muckraking, which was first of all a vehicle of protest and indignation, and which saw in every contemporary evil a conspiracy by unrighteous men against the natural righteousness of the American democracy. Nevertheless, one of its essential characteristics was the extent to which some muckrakers converted the moral hypothesis underlying contemporary indignation into a sharper tool of political and social inquiry. Here Lincoln Steffens was a leader. If he charged the American people with "moral weakness," he also suggested that the moral scheme by which they were wont to judge politics was itself at fault. Somewhat ahead of most of his contemporaries he reached the conclusion that good government and democracy are not identical, and began to redefine corruption as failure to serve the people rather than as personal dishonesty. The words he used remained moralistic: the boss, he said, is "disloyal" to the people although sometimes "honest" in admitting it. But the lesson he taught was pragmatic: the true test of government is not the personal behavior of the people's agents but their effectiveness in gaining the people's ends. His criteria suggested that the people's traditional diagnosis of public affairs was at fault, represented their indiscriminate indignation as a form of political ignorance. Accepting fundamental democratic values, that is, Steffens sought to use his kind of scholarship to liberate the American political mentality.[15]

Other muckrakers were less sensitive than Steffens to the weaknesses of moral exhortation as a vehicle of political reform; they thought of themselves not as social scientists but as journalists, who would rouse the public to contemporary evils by overwhelming them with facts. "Facts, facts piled up to the point of dry certitude, was what the American people then needed and wanted," Ray Stannard Baker wrote in his autobiography many years later. Yet these journalists had in common with Steffens that they sought a functional as well as a formal understanding of contemporary institutions, and their investigations had an inescapable pragmatic significance. The veteran agitator B. O. Flower recalled in 1914 that the years from 1880 to 1900 had been filled with social visions, but that at the turn of the century practical books and magazines caught the public interest. His remark suggests that the difference between epochs was in large part the difference between Christian utopianism, which required only conversion, and deliberate social reform, which continued to depend upon conscience, but which also dealt in facts. A belief that only a knowledge of the facts could set men free was the common principle that underlay much of the journalistic enterprise of the period.[16]

While the muckrakers usually minimized interpretation of the data they collected, moreover, other popular writers sought to make up their oversight. One of the most prominent of these commentators, halfway between muckraking and scholarship, was E. A. Ross, whose *Sin and Society: An Analysis of Latter-Day Iniquity* (1907) blended moral indignation and social analysis into one of the most influential volumes of the period. Ross's essay was a tract in social ethics, and like many of its precursors it bespoke a regeneration of the public will. But the point of the book was that there were new sins abroad in contemporary society, made so not by the increase of individual vice but by the complexity and impersonal organization of the economy. Again and again Ross returned to the theme: men whose private lives are above reproach lend themselves, often unawares, to social evils. "Our social organization," he wrote, "has developed to a stage where the old righteousness is not enough. We need an annual supplement to the Decalogue. The growth of credit institutions, the spread of fiduciary relations, the enmeshing of industry in law, the interlacing of government and business, the multiplication of boards and inspectors,—beneficent as they all are, they invite to sin." He wished to substitute for the traditional ethical inquiry into the motives of personal behavior a pragmatic test of its social consequences. "This book deals with sin," his preface began, "but it does not entreat the sinner to mend his ways. It seeks to influence no one in his conduct. It does seek to influence men *in their attitude toward the conduct of others.* Its exhortation is not *Be good,* but *Be rational.*" [17]

Hence the main burden of the book was its attack on the people's ignorance, which Ross proposed to correct by teaching them to recognize the real nature of contemporary problems. This was also the purpose of his many magazine articles, some of which were gathered together in 1912 as *Changing America.* "The average man's mental picture of his society is at least two or three decades out of date," he wrote in the preface to that work, "so that half the time he is fighting windmills instead of grappling with the enemies that rise in his path. In this book I aim to bring the picture nearer to reality by describing certain contemporary social developments. . . . For it is only *living* tendencies that man can work with, curb, or guide." [18] In practice, it should be said, Ross's diagnosis of specific evils was ludicrously inadequate, and he must be charged with failure (typical among progressive social theorists) to understand the institutional developments he proposed to examine. His inadequacies as a social scientist are less important here, however, than the fact that he attempted as a matter of political principle to reconcile a scientific understanding of contemporary social problems with democratic politics. Like other progressives he sought to establish a viable technique of democratic reform; like them, too, he turned first to the education of the people.

THE PRACTICE OF FORMAL EDUCATION

Thus far we have understood progressivism as a development of informal devices of popular political education. Typically, progressive leaders and progressive spokesmen adapted and extended and improved upon informal political devices that had originated with nineteenth-century radicals and conservatives, reformers and standpatters. At the same time, however, the progressive era witnessed significant developments in formal education. Like the progressives' political achievements these educational innovations owed a good deal to nineteenth-century precedents; like them, too, they came to fruition only during the early years of the twentieth century. As educational historians have just begun to realize, the progressive movement in education and the progressive movement in politics were not simply parallel phenomena but variant forms of the same middle-class impulse.[19]

To some extent, indeed, progressives made direct political use of formal education. The focus of their interest was the university-trained expert. During the last decades of the nineteenth century major American universities had begun to reform their curriculums and to offer qualified students technical training in political science and economics in place of the traditional college courses grounded in moral philosophy. By the first decade of the twentieth century, therefore, there was a sufficient number of trained specialists available to warrant an attempt to employ scientific criteria in the formulation and administration of public policy. Drawing on the universities for expert advice, progressive leaders also charted a new political role for them. Far from imitating the conservative scholars of the postbellum epoch in wishing to subordinate democracy to trained intelligence, and (for that matter) far from imitating nineteenth-century democrats in being apprehensive of an educated elite, progressives saw in the higher learning a promising new apparatus of democratic social control.

The most striking statement of the progressive theory of the expert came from Wisconsin, where Governor La Follette's administration went far toward incorporating the state university into the governing process. Like Woodrow Wilson, La Follette distrusted legislative committees and special commissions because they too readily lent themselves to the stifling or distortion of reforms, but unlike him he saw in the university a way to secure the competent technical advice he needed without surrendering control of policy. He turned to the university's social scientists, who had demonstrated their sympathy with progressivism by supporting it politically, and who could provide detailed information that was indispensable for railroad rate regulation and other state activities in the public interest. We may suspect that their science lost some of its objectivity by being progressive, but from La Follette's point of view this was what made it a functioning political instrument. If scholars sacrificed some of their austerity, they also achieved a unique influence in democratic political deliberations.[20]

The chief proponent of the close collaboration between scholars and government in Wisconsin, however, was not La Follette but Charles McCarthy, head of the state's legislative reference bureau, itself one of Wisconsin's characteristic political innovations. McCarthy's *The Wisconsin Idea* (1912) is particularly significant because he was almost a conservative among reformers, a scholarly man who was sufficiently apprehensive of raw democracy to write at some points like a wholly unfriendly critic. Yet he was also confident that Wisconsin had found the way to reinforce democracy with intelligence in such a fashion as to make its expanding operations valid.

The secret, his book explained, was the right use of knowledge. McCarthy praised the state's policy of appointing administrative officials whose only purpose was to be expert agents of public ends, and he described the roles of the merit civil service, the legislative reference bureau, and above all of the university in the governing process. In his eyes the university's chief virtue was that it provided disinterested answers to questions before the legislature. If a legislative body cannot acquire expert advice except from private interests, he argued, "it will never reach the scientific basis of these great questions now before us which must be solved by the aid of the expert's technical knowledge." But he also believed that the university had achieved an important influence among the electorate, bringing factual information and the techniques of reform to their attention. Thanks largely to this fact, he saw in Wisconsin no serious difficulties to be apprehended from either legislative or popular ignorance. The goal and the practice were a democracy that was effective because it knew when and how to acquire knowledge.[21]

Nor was McCarthy's rather austere appraisal the only contemporary expression of a belief that Wisconsin had shown how superior knowledge might be incorporated into the democratic process without threatening at the same time to destroy it. In 1912, for example,

Frederic Howe indicated in his rhapsodic study of *Wisconsin: An Experiment in Democracy* that the state had achieved the dearest objectives of the direct-legislation movement. Howe reported enthusiastically that the university was truly "the fourth department of the state" and that the Wisconsin experiment was a success largely because the state had found ways to integrate scholarship into an active political life, to incorporate the higher learning as a functioning part of a functioning democracy. "Scientific efficiency is one of the university's contributions to the state," he wrote, "and efficiency is one of Wisconsin's contributions to democracy." Beyond lay the incalculable influence of the university in the whole life of the state:

Scientific thoroughness [he wrote in his preface] characterizes politics as in no other place in America. Legislation is preceded by exact knowledge of the abuses to be corrected and the ends to be achieved. Laws are made as simple and direct as possible. The politician has almost disappeared from the state-house. . . . There is an enthusiasm among officials that is a high tribute to the state. . . . Permanent party ties have been greatly weakened. Voters support men and measures, rather than empty emblems. The people themselves reflect the new motives in politics.

The essence of democratic reform was not simply the authority of the people but also the values they had come to respect and the standards they had learned to observe in their deliberations.[22]

Wisconsin was admittedly a special case, however, and in most states formal educational innovation meant extending and improving existing provisions for academic and practical training in the schools, high schools, and land-grant colleges. Even now, expansion of the established educational system took precedence over pedagogical reform; improvement was largely quantitative rather than qualitative. But quantitative improvement also acquired a qualitative importance for American education. During the late nineteenth century, educational reform had consisted primarily of organizing a truly common school system through consolidation of district schools, professional supervision of teachers, and the creation of minimum standards for school terms and school attendance. Hence it had also involved increasing public expenditures on education, which extended to public high schools in many urban areas, but it had not begun to approximate the achievements that were to come. During the first decades of the twentieth century, on the other hand, professional educators and taxpayers joined in extending modern educational standards to common schools throughout the nation, in providing improved professional training even for teachers in rural areas, and in increasing high-school enrollments and broadening the high-school curriculum. Meanwhile publicly supported universities began to serve the multitude of vocational purposes that the Grange and the Farmers' Alliance had originally stressed, while even private colleges took steps to modernize their curriculums. When the progressive era drew to a close the greatest achievements of the American educational system still lay in the future, but the accomplishments of the era pointed the way.[23]

Two progressive innovations were especially significant in preparing the way for later developments. One was the conversion of the public high school from a tax-supported equivalent of the nineteenth-century academy, which functioned primarily as a college preparatory school, to a public secondary school offering training in a wide variety of disciplines to all who wished to take advantage of them. During the first two decades of the twentieth century, high schools began to offer their students not only a widening range of academic subjects but also an increasing number of practical and vocational courses, all of which served to qualify students for a diploma. (Thanks to changes in curriculum design, the diploma came to stand for the completion of a given number of units of work rather than proficiency in a few traditional disciplines.) Partly because of the general prosperity of the era, but also because of these curricular changes, high-school attendance tripled between 1900 and 1920, while the proportion of male students and the proportion of students completing four years of work also increased, albeit less rapidly. Even in 1920 only one fourth of the eligible population was in secondary schools (over 90 percent of that fourth in public high schools), and not until the late 1930s was half of the eligible population enrolled, but in most respects the progressive generation designed the educational ladder that would ultimately serve the whole nation.[24]

The generation also made the first great strides since the common school awakening in reforming American pedagogical practice. The innovations sponsored by Horace Mann and other early reformers had been indispensable to a democratic educational system, but they had also been no more than beginnings, handicapped by an inadequate psychology and too easily converted by unimaginative teachers into routinized methods of instruction. During the postbellum era, pedagogical reform consisted largely of modifying but not of reforming the educational practices Mann and others had urged, and most of the discussion of educational methods revolved around the curriculum and not the child. During the first decades of the twentieth century, on the other hand, professional educators employed novel psychological perspectives to reshape American teaching. They repudiated factual information and "object" lessons in favor of intelligent understanding by the child; they attempted to take each child's personality and background into account in planning his education; they sought to encourage natural growth, geared to the child's experience and culminating in a fully developed individual. Some of their innovations—especially mental testing—were little more than mechancial fads, and none of them was wholly effective during the years before the First World War, but (like the expansion of high-school education) they initiated changes that a later generation would build upon.[25]

Obviously, these progressive innovations were political only in the sense that education has always been an indispensable tool of American political values. Like their predecessors, the professional educators of the progressive era sought to train citizens for the democracy. Unlike their predecessors, however, they viewed education itself in a new perspective. The earlier generation had worked within a restrictive political framework; acknowledging the economic and vocational needs of its pupils, it had thought primarily of safeguarding the republic against political aberrations. The progressive generation hoped as a matter of principle to serve the needs and interests of every child, and it was far less apprehensive over the dangers to be expected from contemporary political agitation. Because progressive political leaders had domesticated nineteenth-century democratic protest, progressive educational leaders were free to revolutionize American democratic education. They set to work with a will to supplement contemporary social and economic reform with a perfected educational system.

THE PROGRESSIVE IDEOLOGY

To its advocates, the progressive movement represented the long-delayed triumph of middle-class principles, and they moved forward confidently, expecting reason and justice and morality to overcome the accumulated evils of their time. "We turn our faces to the future with good hope in our hearts," Washington Gladden wrote in 1909 in concluding his autobiography. "There are great industrial problems before us, but we shall work them out; there are battles to fight, but we shall win them. With all those who believe in justice and the square deal, in kindness and good will, in a free field and a fair chance for every man, the stars in their courses are fighting, and their victory is sure." [26] Optimistic, expansive, reformist, they rested their hopes on the increasing intelligence of the people, which they proposed to support by every educational innovation they could devise.

As a result, the progressive ideology succeeded in fusing the contradictory political and educational doctrines that had flourished during the late nineteenth century into a single coherent belief. On the one hand, like the organized farmers and the labor movement of that earlier epoch, progressives commonly asserted the right of the people to rule. On the other hand, like the scholarly independents and professional educators, they also insisted that democrats live up to middle-class standards of public deliberation. Instead of employing informal popular education primarily as a vehicle of doctrinaire protest, or formal educational institutions as a vehicle of political conservatism, they sought to enhance the democratic process itself by making every part of it educational. They avoided conflicts between popular sovereignty and scholarly intelligence by insisting that American politics honor both.

By the same token, progressive spokesmen also overcame the conflicts of purpose and attitude that had separated advocates of ethical social reform during the postbellum decades. Although the progressives were generally middle-class, and therefore more likely to sympathize with the doctrines of the social gospel than with those of radical ethical protest, they purged that gospel of most of its paternalistic overtones, and they actively sponsored legislative reforms to secure many of the social goals the earlier generation of reformers had hesitated to entrust to government. Simultaneously, by opening the door to systematic social reform, progressive spokesmen also provided a practical outlet for the radical sentiment that Henry George and Edward Bellamy had helped to create. Significantly, a number of leading progressives owed their interest in social reform to George or the single-tax movement; even more significantly, however, they drew inspiration from the original movement but went beyond it in their willingness to attempt piecemeal practical reform. By establishing a middle ground between Christian utopianism and Christian paternalism, indeed, the progressive movement offered scope to such distinctive advocates of social reform as John R. Commons, who spent the early decades of the century at the University of Wisconsin developing an institutional economics that was Christian and pragmatic at the same time.

Under the circumstances it was hardly surprising that the progressive movement both stimulated and took the form of a comprehensive educational revival. But in the same instant it could not help but be vulnerable to the hazards that threaten any attempt to achieve lasting social reform by purely educational means. Certainly one of the difficulties that ultimately undermined progressivism was the progressives' economic theory, which also helped to make formal education one of their chief devices of social amelioration. Progressive political leaders were willing to legislate necessary social reforms when they could not achieve them by other means, but they also hoped wherever possible to restore the conditions of economic individualism, not change the structure of the economy. (This was as true of Theodore Roosevelt as of Woodrow Wilson; the difference between them was a dispute over what legislation could achieve, not whether individualism was desirable.) Given the necessary legal and educational conditions, they expected every individual to earn his own place in society. To this extent, although the progressives repudiated the grosser practices of late nineteenth-

century individualism, and although they were aware that positive
social legislation must be undertaken in behalf of permanently disadvantaged social groups, they were not far from the Jacksonian
democrats in their devotion to formal education to forestall social
evils and promote social progress. Formal education was at least
as important as social legislation in their definition of democracy,
and their political theory was not prepared to deal with any failure
of popular education and remedial legislation to secure their liberal
ends.[27]

Moreover, the economic assumptions that supported formal education also shaped the progressives' vision of the political process.
Progressives were willing to legislate for disadvantaged social
groups, and they were determined to make democracy work, but
they continued to think of politics itself as a form of ethical persuasion, and of the autonomous individual as its basis. E. A. Ross
was outspokenly critical of all manifestations of special interests
in politics, poor as well as wealthy; Theodore Roosevelt insisted
upon the right of workingmen to combine in asserting their own
special needs, but he also proclaimed the preeminence of righteousness over all partial truths; even Samuel Gompers, alert to the prevailing opinion of the age, wrote sometimes as if the reforms the
American Federation of Labor sponsored had a sure universal appli-
cability. In other words, the progressives' informal educational devices corresponded to progressive liberalism, which renounced the
economic policies of the Manchester school but was reluctant to
countenance a group-based struggle for economic advantage.[28]

This was the underlying weakness of the progressives' institutional innovations. On the one hand, the initiative, referendum, and
recall assumed that the responsible individual is the unit of politics, and progressives depicted him entering into rational discourse
with his neighbors, deliberating carefully upon the merits of different policies, making up his mind in the light of all the evidence,
and joining with others as a consequence of this elaborate practice
of judiciousness, independent of any interest or allegiance but truth
and like-mindedness. On the other hand, such devices as leadership
and scholarship and even muckraking meant that the progressives
were concerned to protect justice against all possible public vagaries,

not only popular ignorance and indifference but also faction and prejudice and selfishness. The idea of an educated and an educative politics rested upon ideally rationalistic assumptions, and although progressive theory embraced every conceivable device to make political education more effective it could not show why education should work. Rather, the progressives assumed that the criteria of politics are honesty, responsibility, and reason, and their faith in these qualities was such that (as Louis Filler has sadly observed) they thought every defeat was temporary, the result of insufficient education that more education would surely overcome.[29]

Hence progressive political theory was powerless to cope with the disappearance of popular support for progressive reform during Woodrow Wilson's presidency. Progressives at the time displayed some tendency to blame failing public interest on the international situation, and after the war many of them would blame the war itself for disrupting the reform movement. Whether or not their explanation was historically accurate, however, it did not explain how an educated generation could have become so indifferent to its own rightful purposes. Accordingly, it has become a commonplace of recent American historiography that the progressives sought only to institutionalize a mood. Yet the commonplace undervalues the most basic characteristic of the progressive impulse. If progressives virtually limited reform to education, and if they failed to anticipate the practical failure of their methods, they also undertook to structure the processes of popular education in functional terms. The tendency was evident in the deliberate practice of political leadership, in the attempt to fuse scholarship with democracy, in journalistic efforts to focus and inform public opinion, even in reforms of formal education. It is a mistake to complain that the progressives sought to institutionalize a mood without recognizing that this was also their most characteristic achievement.

x v i. The Progressive Philosophy

WHILE the progressive movement brought together in one comprehensive ideology most of the various strains of nineteenth-century American thought, it also gave rise to a novel philosophical inquiry into the nature and prospects of the American democracy. In different ways such thoughtful commentators as Herbert Croly, Walter Lippmann, and John Dewey reexamined democratic beliefs and sought to reshape the fundamentalist democratic faith of their countrymen. Critical and even skeptical of democratic dogmas though they may have been, they also testified in their own works to the political value Americans of their generation put upon democratic education. As philosophers they challenged but at the same time extended progressive belief.

HERBERT CROLY: IDEALIST

Aristocrat, idealist, and mystic, Herbert Croly was a powerful critic of the contemporary reform movement from both an historical and a philosophical point of view. He felt that for over one hundred years the promise of American life—the material and moral well-being of the people—had suffered from inadequate notions of democracy, and that in attempting to reinvigorate traditional democracy the progressives were no more likely than their predecessors to achieve desirable results. Democracy, he explained in *The Promise of American Life* (1909), has stood historically for jealousy of true distinction, distrust of government, and an absolute commitment to the rights of property and to the privileges of factional and regional interests. Now it must transcend these negative prescriptions and explore constructively the necessities of modern social organization. Above all it must recognize that the deliberate and artificial manipulation of social and individual interests by government is essential to the achievement of its long-standing purposes. Croly urged no monolithic state, but his sense of an inclusive national purpose held up an organic social test to which every institution and every privilege must be subjected. "All rights under the law," he said, "are functions in a democratic political organism and must be justified by their . . . functional adequacy." [1]

Croly defined his political reforms in the light of this functional principle. He was convinced that the central problem of democracy was one of prevailing upon democrats to accept qualified leadership instead of trying by all possible means to eliminate distinctions and hierarchy from politics. Hence he criticized direct-legislation reforms, because they undermined representative responsibility. He also hoped for a trained legislative council in place of the ordinary legislature, where current issues might be settled on their merits, or at least for an arrangement whereby the executive branch might initiate legislation. The method of valid democracy, he was certain, necessitated "expert, responsible, and authoritative leadership," and it demanded the grant of adequate power to government to act for the public good. [2]

But while Croly's reconstruction of American democratic institutions finally depended, as he also said, on "the ceaseless creation of a political, economic, and social aristocracy," in his view the only way to secure a trustworthy leadership—one that did not simply become a vested interest—was to find ways to involve the people themselves in the process of governing. One solution was the incessant recruitment of talented leaders from the ranks of the people by all of the time-honored devices of competitive selection. Yet the full participation of the people in politics also seemed important to him, and it involved an educational premise. "A democracy," he explained,

should encourage the political leadership of experienced, educated, and well-trained men, but only on the express condition that their power is delegated and is to be used, under severe penalties, for the benefit of the people as a whole. A limited suffrage secures governmental efficiency, if at all, at the expense of the political education and training of the disfranchised class, and at the expense, also, of a permanent and radical popular political grievance. A substantially universal suffrage merely places the ultimate political responsibility in the hands of those for whose benefit governments are created; and its denial can be justified only on the ground that the whole community is incapable of exercising the responsibility. Such cases unquestionably exist. . . . But wherever the whole people are capable of thinking, feeling, and acting as if they constituted a whole, universal suffrage, even if it costs something in temporary efficiency, has a tendency to be more salutary and more formative than a restricted suffrage.

Like other democratic doctrines, his rested upon the probability of an educative politics.[3]

The final chapter of *The Promise of American Life* elaborated still further on this fundamental educational concept. In it Croly criticized the American attempt to achieve social and political reform through educational uplift, but only because the effective use of education was undermined by a naive belief in the power of mere words. "The American faith in education," he wrote, "is by way of being credulous and superstitious, not because it seeks individual and social amelioration by what may be called an educational process, but because the proposed means of education are too conscious, too direct, and too superficial." True political education, he explained, must parallel the education of the adult individual: "His experience,—as a man of business, a husband, a father, a citizen, a friend,—has been made real to him, not merely by the zest with which he has sought it and the sincerity with which he has accepted it, but by the disinterested intelligence which he has brought to its understanding. An educational discipline which has contributed in that way to the reality of a man's experience has done as much for him as education can do; and an educational discipline which has failed to make any such contribution has failed of its essential purpose." Croly's idealistic and nationalistic mystique clothed all his words with ambiguities he never resolved, but his pedagogical principle was clear. Whatever the shortcomings of democratic politics were, they would be overcome only by a comprehensive process of education. Achieving the latent promise of American life depended in the last analysis upon popular self-education, self-education grounded in the wish and the capacity to continue learning from experience. Every truly democratic reform, Croly's book implied, must be based upon education.[4]

Progressive Democracy (1914) was a still more challenging statement of this fundamental principle. Encouraged by the already significant achievements of the progressive movement, Croly examined the political influences that continued to block the achievement of more thoroughgoing reforms. Although he felt that most of the democratic dogmas he had previously criticized continued to stand in the path of effective reform, he now thought that the major obstacle was not democratic liberalism but the constitutional organization of government. His criticism did not mean that he had simply joined with ordinary democrats in their attack on indirect government and the courts, for he pointed out that the people had originally sanctioned constitutional limitations on their power and that for decades they had voluntarily acquiesced in both the limitations and the decisions of the courts that enforced them. Rather, he felt that the role of "the Law" in the political process must now be modified to accord with democratic necessities.[5]

According to Croly, the defect of American constitutionalism lay in the fact that it was not educational. "The way to rationalize political power," he wrote, "is not to confine its exercise within limits defined by certain rules, but frankly to accept the danger of violence and reorganize the state so that popular reasonableness will be developed from within rather than imposed from without." Freeing the country from the stultifying rule of Law meant to Croly that neither the Law nor representative institutions should be permitted to interfere with popular political education, and he made clear that every political institution must ultimately satisfy his educational test. "The electorate," he said in commenting on different forms of government, "must be required as the result of its own actual experience and unavoidable responsibilities to develop those very qualities of intelligence, character, faith and sympathy which are necessary for the success of the democratic experiment." He was far from admitting the people's present political competence, but their shortcomings were a compelling reason for improving rather than stifling their opportunities for political education.[6]

This was the context in which Croly described the social and economic reforms he thought the country must undertake. He reiterated the necessity for an affirmative state and for regulation rather than destruction of modern industrial complexes, and he referred more than once to the proposition that a valid social order must respect both authority and liberty, both democracy and privilege. But significantly he spoke of the national life as a kind of collective pilgrimage toward an unmapped destination by an unknown route. His image indicated that there was no authority but their own to which the people might ultimately turn, and it implied that they must adopt an experimental approach to social problems, making not their will but their experience the criterion of reform.[7]

Here was the final meaning of Croly's strictures on the Law: the difficulty was not that the Law was intrinsically bad but that it limited democratic education in social necessities. Contrasting his vision of democracy with the traditional constitutional definition, Croly argued: "The alternative method is fundamentally educational instead of fundamentally pedagogic. The American nation is no longer to be instructed as to its duty by the Law and the lawyers. It is to receive its instruction as the result of a loyal attempt to realize in collective action and by virtue of the active exercise of popular political authority its ideal of social justice." Education was indeed the all-encompassing definition of Croly's democratic philosophy. "The attempt," he continued, "can be made more safely now than it could four generations ago, because the ideal of justice and the habit of orderly procedure have been wrought into the American national consciousness; but safety is not its peculiar virtue. It is the one method which may be able to call up moral and intellectual resources needed by a progressive democratic society." The progressive era had convinced Croly that American democrats were to be trusted with their freedom, but on the supposition still that freedom meant self-education. The value he put upon democracy not only depended upon that education but was identical in every way with democracy's meeting the highest educational standards.[8]

WALTER LIPPMANN: PRAGMATIST

Walter Lippmann approached the study of American politics with perspectives so different from Croly's that their joint editorship of the *New Republic,* which Croly founded in 1914, will always remain something of a mystery. A tough-minded pragmatist and an insistent critic of the rationalist and intellectualist fallacies of traditional democratic theory, Lippmann developed an elitist theory of democracy that revolved around political leaders' ability to recognize the nonrational sources of public opinion in order to manipulate them to serve rational public ends. The key terms in his political vocabulary were derived from such philosophers of irrationalism as Georges Sorel and Henri Bergson, and his political system as a whole stood in much the same relationship to Croly's as Sigmund Freud's new psychology to the best nineteenth-century mental philosophy. Like his first master Graham Wallas, however, Lippmann also valued modern democracy, and therefore he sought ways to make it work. As a result, during the progressive era he was converted like Croly to an educational diagnosis of American politics.[9]

Lippmann's first volume, *A Preface to Politics* (1913), was a handbook in statecraft comparable to Croly's first treatise, and in its own way it censured many of the same democratic errors. Especially, it criticized artificial constitutional contrivances for their destructive effect on the conduct of government, and rebuked democrats for systematically excluding all personality and hence all leadership from public office. But it also developed a highly idiosyncratic attack on the moralizing habits of democratic and reform thought, notably the habit of looking upon politics as an exercise in righteousness, and the comparable habit of judging all social problems in ethical terms that were both inapplicable and misleading as reform hypotheses.[10]

The cure Lippmann proposed was creative statesmanship, undertaken by leaders given their freedom to fit social and political arrangements to real needs instead of trying in vain to satisfy obsolete democratic dogmas. His picture of the political leader was as pragmatic as his description of the craft. Lippmann wanted above all to trust to men rather than institutions to achieve progress: he would install creative minds, give them real rather than merely nominal power, and limit them only by surrounding them with all the supports that scholarly criticism and scientific research could give, aware at the same instant that only experience could provide a conclusive evaluation of their policies. "We cannot wait in politics," he argued, "for any completed theoretical discussion of its method: it is a monstrous demand. There is no pausing until political psychology is more certain. We have to act on what we believe, on half-knowledge, illusion and error. Experience itself will reveal our mistakes; research and criticism may convert them into wisdom." For the core of his politics was not the belief in men but the belief in science: "If we are wise we shall become experimental towards life: then every mistake will contribute towards knowledge." [11]

Like Croly, therefore, Lippmann was only indirectly concerned with the political relationships that might exist between statesmen and their publics, and by the same token little interested in the possibilities of a popular political education. Nevertheless, in occasional remarks he indicated that he intended his proposals to revitalize democracy as well as remake statesmanship. "A large part of the unfaith in democracy," he observed at one point in his analysis, "of the desire to ignore 'the mob,' limit the franchise, and confine power to the few is the result of an unsuccessful attempt to make republics act like old-fashioned monarchies." Moreover, one chapter of his book explored in some detail the question of how the public might be brought to participate in the governing process. [12]

That chapter is concerned, significantly, with "the making of creeds"; it treats of the power of myths—imaginative constructs, whether valid or not—to motivate mankind. The lesson Lippmann wished to stress was that the true statesman must be willing to manipulate men for social purposes, either by appealing to their myths or by creating new myths that will enlist them in his cause. In spite of its antidemocratic implications, however, his doctrine suggested that the role of the statesman must finally be educational. "Looked at closely," he wrote, "the deliberate making of issues is very nearly the core of the statesman's task. His greatest wisdom is required to select a policy that will fertilize the public mind." The final chapter enlarged upon this fundamental idea. "The real preparation for a creative statesmanship," Lippmann wrote, "lies deeper than parties and legislatures. It is the work of publicists and educators, scientists, preachers and artists. Through all the agents that make and popularize thought must come a bent of mind interested in invention and freed from the authority of ideas. The democratic culture must, with critical persistence, make man the measure of all things." [13]

To this extent, at least, Lippmann invoked education to serve his purposes, and in the act he made clear that his purposes were democratic: "The democratic experiment," he went on, "is the only one that requires this wilful humanistic culture." Yet statesmanship required the subtlest kinds of social insight, which the people could only partly share, and therefore he distinguished between statecraft and contemporary democracy; from the point of view of democratic theory the lasting significance of his book was that while it stated what he thought were the necessary conditions of effective government it had only begun to explore the ways of relating statesmanship to democracy. In the end Lippmann suggested that leadership must be an integral rather than an isolated function in the democratic process, and that the commitment to new processes of statecraft must be a common rather than an unshared creed. Beyond this, he could say only that "the politics of reconstruction require a nation vastly better educated, a nation freed from its slovenly ways of thinking, stimulated by wider interests, and jacked up constantly by the sharpest kind of criticism." The problem, stated, was one of education, but the means were only dimly apparent.[14]

Lippmann's second book explored those means. *Drift and Mastery* (1914) was a challenging analysis of contemporary economic forces and tendencies, an essay in the kind of perspective the *Preface to Politics* had said the statesman must achieve. But, significantly, Lippmann no longer treated events chiefly as problems for statecraft and political manipulation. According to his new interpretation, each social group possessed its own political wisdom and also recognized the likeliest path of its own economic growth. One of his prime examples was the contemporary labor movement, which had demonstrated that it was learning from its practical experience how to accomplish socially desirable ends. Indeed, Lippmann took the labor movement as a kind of model to other social groups, which he thought must either learn from the actual exercise of power to be responsible and wise, or find themselves forced by external pressures to cooperate faithfully with social purposes. Lippmann's evaluation of these contemporary groups disclosed that he now thought the greatest promise of democracy lay within, and depended upon clearing the channels of self-education. "You cannot institute a better industrial order by decree," he said of the most pressing problem of the times.

It is of necessity an educational process, a work of invention, of coöperative training, of battles against vested rights not only in property but in acquired skill as well, a process that is sure to be intricate, and therefore confusing.

But that is the way democracies move: they have in literal truth to lift themselves by their own bootstraps. Those who have some simpler method than the one I have sketched are, it seems to me, either unaware of the nature of the problem, interested only in some one phase of it, or unconsciously impatient with the limitations of democracy.[15]

Lippmann followed his portrait of contemporary social forces with a discussion of the ideological obstacles to effective democracy. The core of his statement was his anxiety lest the electorate allow the undirected course of events—"drift"—to substitute for a conscious effort at "mastery," and he charged most of them with trusting to mysterious harmonies in nature or in history to rectify contemporary evils. Yet at the same time he reserved his sharpest criticism for radical social commentators, whose characteristic fault was not that they were radical but that they too relied upon drift. "At the only point where effort and intelligence are needed," he wrote, "that point where to-day is turning into to-morrow, there these people are not found. At the point where human direction counts most they do not direct." Here, indeed, was the universal shortcoming of the reform mentality: "Men will do almost anything but govern themselves. They don't want the responsibility. In the main, they are looking for some benevolent guardian, be it a 'good man in office' or a perfect constitution, or the evolution of nature. They want to be taken in charge. If they have to think for themselves they turn either to the past or to a distant future: but they manage to escape the real effort of the imagination which is to weave a dream into the turning present." [16]

This criticism of the widespread preference for drift over

mastery explained, as the *Preface to Politics* never had, how Lippmann proposed to use social myths for democratic ends. The myth
he championed was the ethic of scientific inquiry. On the one hand,
he believed that scientific methods alone promised to liberate men
from the errors of previous generations. "What we have learned,"
he wrote in contrasting modern man with the ancients, "is to
organize invention deliberately, to create a record for it and preserve its continuity, to subsidize it, and surround it with criticism.
We have not only scientific work, but a philosophy of science, and
that philosophy is the source of fruitful scientific work." On the
other hand, he hailed the scientific method less for its achievements
than for its potential influence on democratic deliberations. "The
scientific spirit," he wrote, "is the discipline of democracy, the escape from drift, the outlook of a free man. Its direction is to distinguish fact from fancy; its 'enthusiasm is for the possible'; its
promise is the shaping of fact to a chastened and honest dream."
And this, he thought, could become a creed for democrats, a "modern communion." He used the phrase fully conscious of its multi-
ple meanings. As a communion, science could be a shared outlook,
a common dedication of democrats to the true conditions of their
highest interest, a universal principle of social action and social
salvation.[17]

In his commitment to science and its open-ended attack on contemporary problems Lippman diverged to a notable degree from
Croly, who was always sure there was a unitary final goal even if it
did not reveal itself while he was writing. The extent of Lippmann's
divergence was measured in the final analysis by the greater degree
of responsibility he laid upon democracy. Croly urged it to be prin-
cipled and adult and true; Lippmann, to be constantly flexible, self-
critical, radical in thinking if conservative of values. Science and
democracy and education in politics were all the same, or should
be. In his eyes the promise of a scientific approach to contemporary
affairs was itself the promise of American life.

JOHN DEWEY: INSTRUMENTALIST

Confronted with popular political vagaries, both Croly and Lippmann turned to informal political education to redeem the democratic process. In the same instant, and despite their strictures on progressivism, they adopted its characteristic solution for the defects of democratic politics. Subscribing to a fundamentally educational diagnosis of contemporary problems, however, they had neither occasion nor ability to examine schools and other formal institutions in order to learn where and how they too might be made more effective for democratic ends. This was a task that John Dewey undertook in *Democracy and Education*. When it was published in 1916 it was in effect if not in intention a climactic statement of the progressive political philosophy.[18]

In the first instance the book was a treatise in educational method, and on these grounds alone it was a major achievement. Like the best examples of progressive scholarship it rested upon a functional analysis of the process it discussed. Given the nature of human beings, Dewey argued, a teacher's raw materials are not the subject matters or the disciplines that he is trying to communicate but the motives and attitudes students bring to learning, and his task is to enlist their purposive activity in the acquisition of knowledge. He cannot function properly if he is bound by a set of fixed goals to which he tries to lead them; both the objective and the proper method of education are growth, a continuous augmentation of the original core of activity and interest. Such growth is best defined by the quality of the relationships it promotes between an individual and his experience. The ideal is a capacity to deal intelligently with experience, to be able to extract its interconnections and extended meanings. It follows that the method of teaching must be one that provides situations in which such transactions are encouraged. Ultimately, moreover, any formal education must be related to the actual social milieu in which adult intelligence must operate. The school must therefore be immersed in society.[19]

Dewey's complicated analysis not only reoriented American educational theory but also incorporated a stringent criticism of the educational assumptions that most Americans, including all but a handful of progressives, took for granted. He repudiated the various common-sense theories of the past, for instance the belief that education is simply a preparation for life or for other external goals, that it disciplines latent faculties, or that it should recapitulate the experience of the race in capsule form, and he insisted that the need for constructive intelligence necessitates an entirely different attitude toward the function of the school. Men must understand that formal education is a preliminary and shaping experience in the active use of intelligence, which is to extend into all of life, and they can can no more rely on the lessons of the past than they can live in it. Their lifework is to master a unique present, and their achievements will be determined by the quality of intelligence— the developing ability to think perceptively and constructively about its special experience—that they bring to it. In the last analysis Dewey thought that this ability was identical with knowledge of the scientific method.[20]

At the same time, Dewey's reconstruction of educational theory also pressed him toward a reconstruction of democratic political theory. For one thing, it implied that democracy depends upon a universal capacity to think, and (more than that) a capacity to rethink answers to social problems as they arise; if effective education depends upon institutionalizing the experimental method, effective democracy requires a universal experimental attitude in politics. But Dewey visualized democratic education as more than the instrument of democratic politics; he also thought that it established the goals of democratic social achievement. In a complex modern society, he argued, education is the vehicle of whatever attitudes and values the people share, and in order to be democratic it must overcome every obstacle to the sharing of this culture. By the same token, if culture is finally nothing less than "the capacity for constantly expanding in range and accuracy one's perception of meanings," education in a democracy demands that all the social obstacles to experimental inquiry, to educational growth, and to the readjustment of experience itself must be eliminated. Common interests, mutual interests, and the power to readjust social institutions in keeping with them *are* democracy, he said, and he entered the schools of the democracy in the lists against the prevailing short-comings of democratic practice.[21]

Thus his theory of educational reform pressed Dewey toward a reform of democracy itself. Formal education was not a radical device; it could not be, and in any event Dewey insisted that all meaningful human aims must arise within the context of present actualities, that the future must be an extension from the present—not attempt to deny it. But his theory had radical overtones. It elevated democratic principle above every prejudicial social institution; it insisted upon liberating men from their conservative dogmas; it identified education with the acquisition of an experimental scientific outlook on public as well as private affairs. The techniques of progressive education, as expounded by Dewey, were intended to produce free men whose intelligences would engage in social reconstruction for democratic ends.

In these terms, formal education threatened to revolutionize American politics. The weapon that had seemed to nineteenth-century conservatives their best protection against deliberate social innovation had suddenly become its primary instrument. "The public school," wrote Dewey's young disciple, Randolph Bourne, in 1917, "is the most interesting and the most hopeful of our American social enterprises during these days of sluggishness for us and dreary horror for the rest of the world. It is becoming one of the few rational and one of the few democratic things we have, and science and hope are laying a foundation upon which a really self-conscious society could build almost anything it chose." [22] Dewey's philosophy had redefined the formal educational institutions of the country in such a fashion as to make them seem the best possible guarantee of progressive political achievement.

The fact was more than a coincidence. Dewey was a representative man of his times because education was still the representative American political device, and (for all its complexity and sophistication) his thought summed up the thought of the progressives. It carried forward the simple progressive faith in the direct confrontation of experience; it responded to the need that scholarly commentators felt to refine the techniques of confrontation in order to make democratic competence and responsibility real; it insisted that experiment and education and democracy are one. Not only did Dewey incorporate the political techniques that less philosophical thinkers had proposed into a new educational philosophy, but he subscribed to fundamental progressive values in all he wrote. Progressive democrats had geared politics to communication—discussion and deliberation, rooted in individual character, itself the product of growth. Dewey's definition of democracy by educational criteria insisted equally on communication, character, and growth. His educational philosophy explained the method.

Moreover, the outlines of Dewey's educational method recall in striking fashion the underlying loyalty most progressives gave to economic and social individualism. Indeed, his functional interpretation of education as the self-motivated acquisition of knowledge is reminiscent of John Locke—not of Locke's psychological theory but of his theory of property as the object with which one has mixed one's labor. The parallel is intensified by Dewey's emphasis on incentives to the acquisition of knowledge, by his regret over the passing of a simple social organization based upon handicraft production, even by his refusal to separate work from play in the educational process.

By the same token, Dewey's interpretation of learning as growth without end (without either terminus or destination) recalls the ceaseless activity of American entrepreneurs who have been unable to stop because, as Louis Hartz has pointed out, there was no distinct goal they could reach in American society, no way of lifting themselves out of the process and above the values of Lockean individualism. The fact that in an educational treatise Dewey again and again expressed indignation at obstacles to the universal acquisition of culture only lends more force to the analogy. His primary target was social class, understood in terms that almost any Jacksonian democrat would have appreciated: class is the arbitrary power that prejudices equal opportunity for endless growth, and it is also the selective enjoyment of universal goals. It is, in a word, aristocracy, the more culpable because grounded in the sanctions of the past, in defiance of the understandings of the present.

Finally, Dewey's interpretation of aims and values recalls the economic preoccupations of his most unphilosophical contemporaries. His pragmatic sense that "any aim is of value so far as it assists observation, choice, and planning in carrying on activity from moment to moment and hour to hour" was on one level an archetypal expression of the exploitative American concentration on present needs at the expense of ultimate values, the more so when he added that "if it gets in the way of the individual's own common sense (as it will surely do if imposed from without or accepted on authority) it does harm." [23] This was the kind of statement that led some angry critics in the postwar decade to charge that the instrumentalist doctrine underlying Dewey's educational method was no more than a justification for business ethics and an invitation to go and do likewise. But the charge is neither accurate nor relevant here. The point is not that Dewey justified business faults, but that his individualistic education-oriented philosophy epitomized the intellectual equipment with which his contemporaries approached the social problems of their era. His educational strategy called for reform from within, by intelligent persuasion; it added not new social theory but new methods for confronting social and economic problems within an established institutional framework. In this it was symptomatic of the age, which was more concerned with securing the methods of reform than with prescribing its results, and which assumed that (in Woodrow Wilson's phrase) liberating the vital energies of a free people was a sufficient political objective in itself.

THE PROGRESSIVE HERITAGE

Because Dewey's work dealt with schools and teaching methods, it continued to influence American thought well past the demise of political progressivism. (Like most of the progressive movement's changes in formal education, in fact, Dewey's innovations ramified during the 1920s and 1930s until "progressive education" dominated American educational theory.) In this respect Dewey suffered a happier fate than Croly and Lippmann, who were to discover that the generation of the 1920s subscribed to a different faith and was indifferent to progressive political education. We shall consider the political commitments of the 1920s in their proper place. What is important here is the fact that Croly and Lippmann, and in his political role John Dewey, were no more able than the least sophisticated progressives either to predict or to shape the outcome of the progressive movement.

Their political failure was implicit in their philosophy. They took reform for granted because it was going on when they wrote, but it was perhaps their place as philosophical critics to realize how insubstantial its foundations were, how short-lived its purposes might be. For all their incisive criticisms of progressive individualism, Croly and Lippmann virtually ignored vested interests and vested intelligence, and they were innocent of any social theory of politics that might at least have provided them with a sense of the necessary dynamics of political change. Meanwhile Dewey simply defined every social problem as a problem of education, and ignored the practical possibility that education however reformed might be powerless to overcome refractory social habits. To some extent Lippmann realized that the sources of deliberate social invention must lie in the direct experience of specific social groups rather than in the abstract good will and general information of the public mind, but even he anticipated, which is to say counted upon, an educational process of group interactions that would simply dissolve long-standing obstacles to social progress. Whatever the form of the hopes they expressed, these three commentators were like other progressives in that they put their trust in the authority of intelligence, and like other progressives too in that when intelligence failed them it left them not only defeated but also dismayed.

XVII. The Conservative Response,

Then and Now

PROGRESSIVE political principles dominated American thought during the first two decades of the twentieth century, but they also provoked a characteristic conservative reply. Conservative opponents of progressivism seldom attacked it where it was most vulnerable, however. Typically, their rebuttal took the form of a stubborn denial of every particular progressive reform in the name of constitutional precedent and representative institutions. The key principle underlying this response was a repudiation of the educational motives and devices that characterized progressive political thought. In effect, conservatives hoped to establish principles of constitutional interpretation that would make the informal education of the people unnecessary or unimportant. When they invoked popular education at all, therefore, they called upon a mechanism as restricted and as formal as their political principles.

Although standpat constitutionalism offered some protection to interest groups under attack by progressive social reformers, it was obviously only defensive. The Constitution might protect giant corporations against hasty or punitive legislation, but it could not justify their existence nor multiply their opportunities for political leadership. Therefore business spokesmen began during the progressive era to work out a political theory that would place the businessman rather than the people or their elected representatives in charge of public policy. They met with but slight success during the progressive era proper, but when business interests returned to power during the 1920s their political philosophy also triumphed. With it triumphed a theory of education that made it the most businesslike of American institutions. It is still with us today.[1]

THE CONSERVATIVE RESPONSE TO
PROGRESSIVE DEMOCRACY

The central theme of the conservative opposition to progressive political innovations was an assertion that it is impossible to obtain a valid popular judgment on public questions by direct means. "No large body of men can act *en masse* in the examination and determination of intricate and important questions," Henry M. Campbell declared in the *North American Review* in 1909. "Special investigation by qualified persons is indispensable." "It is scarcely conceivable," said conservative spokesmen for the National Economic League, "that the voters at large can, in the first place, possess the information required for a proper understanding of the merits of the measure to the same degree that was true of the legislators, and secondly they will lack the advantage of the legislative procedure." "The business of administering and legislating for a government is not an easy task," William Howard Taft wrote in 1913. "Men of experience in governmental affairs and special knowledge are certainly better able to carry it on than those who have neither." [2]

According to this view, the chief advantage of representative government was that it enlisted greater efficiency for the people's ends than the people could develop for themselves. "As government increases in its functions," Taft added, "—and the tendency of modern times is to increase the variety of the functions of government— the necessity for the employment of agents who have a specialized knowledge in carrying out such new governmental functions is much greater than where the office of government was limited . . . to a simple police system." At the same time, however, the representative principle also included a belief that the representative process will be superior to direct democracy almost irrespective of the talents it enlists. "Representative government," Elihu Root explained in 1913, "is something more than a device to enable the people to have their say when they are too numerous to get together and say it. It is something more than the employment of experts in legislation. Through legislative procedure a different kind of treatment for legislative questions is secured by concentration of responsibility, by discussion, and by opportunity to meet objection with amendment. For this reason the attempt to legislate by calling upon the people by popular vote to say yes or no to complicated statutes must prove unsatisfactory and on the whole injurious." [3]

Such conservative arguments would have been plausible had progressive democrats actually proposed to refer all public measures to the initiative and referendum. What was truly at issue between the two groups, however, was whether the electorate should possess the power of direct legislation where it was necessary to make democratic purposes effective against vested economic interests. But conservative spokesmen typically stated the difference between representation and direct legislation in dichotomous terms which had the effect of assigning the discussion of public questions exclusively to the representative body. "The choice must be made between experiment and experience," David Jayne Hill argued in *Americanism: What It Is* (1917), "between arbitrary decisions and fundamental principles; in a word, between political anarchy and constitutional government." [4] In other words, conservatives resolutely denied the possibility of democratic self-government as the progressives understood democracy, and they also denied the whole machinery of democratic political education that progressives had elaborated. They substituted representation for education.*

The extent to which conservatives substituted representation for education was apparent in their common argument that opinion which has not survived the processes of representative deliberation is not public opinion and is therefore of no account in a popular government. "The truth is," David Jayne Hill explained in a book that bore the title *The People's Government* (1915), "that, without specific discussion and reference to general principles, public opinion does not exist. Popular demonstrations of mere feeling, whether of sympathy or antipathy, do not constitute public opinion, no matter how extensive they may be, even though they include the participation of the entire population." Within this framework it was pos-

---

* Significantly, most outspoken opponents of progressive innovations made little use of sophisticated criticisms of direct democracy such as A. Lawrence Lowell introduced into *Public Opinion and Popular Government* (1913). Instead they portrayed an ideally rational political process, which they made grounds for denying greater authority to the electorate.

sible even to concede that representatives are not impeccable yet to defend their authority against urgent democratic reforms. "Representatives have and, being human, always will, from time to time fail in their duty," President Taft's Attorney-General said in 1911; "but in the long run, our representative bodies must and do give expression to precisely what the matured thought of the majority of the people demands. They may not yield at once to a spasmodic and artificially stimulated emotion induced by one particular class of society for its own ends as against all other classes. God forbid that they should! But they are inevitably controlled in the long run by the deliberate thought-out will of the people." [5]

Furthermore, conservative spokesmen often went beyond simple reverence for representative government to assert that true democracy is identical with constitutional institutions that check and control public opinion. "Our government is a democracy," Rome G. Brown wrote in the *Annals* of the American Academy in 1912, "but it is a *constitutional* democracy; and the very object of the constitutional feature is to place in the way of the sovereign people those limitations, checks and balances which, while not preventing enforcement of the will of the sovereign people, should insure the wise and deliberate exercise only of wise and deliberate, and therefore properly restrained, sovereign authority." Appropriately, therefore, conservatives finally appealed to the state and national constitutions as the chief embodiment of the popular will. Attacking the recall of judges, for example, J. Hampden Dougherty declared in the *Proceedings* of the New York Academy of Political Science: "The public will is presumably expressed in the constitution. The constitution must remain the supreme law until the people see fit to change it, and certainly in the states the power of amendment of the constitution is easily available. In New York state the constitution is, if anything, too readily amendable. The constitution thus represents the 'popular will' for the time being, and to attempt to substitute something else as an expression of the popular will by an unconstitutional method is in reality to subvert the popular will." [6]

Hence conservatives ended by identifying popular government with the decisions of the courts. Adamant opponents of progressive social legislation made no attempt to hide the tactical advantages of turning to the courts. "Indeed," a committee of the American Bar Association held in 1914, "as, through the initiative and referendum, the powers of state legislation become more and more under the direct arbitrary action of the electorate, it is necessary, for the proper protection of personal liberty and property rights, that the safeguards of the Federal Constitution should, more than ever, come within the direct jurisdiction of the Federal Supreme Court." Significantly, however, other conservative spokesmen described the courts in purely philosophical terms as the epitome of free institutions. "Legislature and executive are means given to allow the people to do what they please under certain constitutional forms," Arthur Twining Hadley argued. "The judiciary is a means given to prevent the people from doing what they please. How can we explain the fact that these judicial restrictions are the very essence of freedom? I answer, because the law of the United States as defined and administered by its courts, represents not only restraint, but self-restraint; and the kind of self-restraint which the nation must be prepared to exercise if it hopes permanently to enjoy the advantages of political freedom." [7]

None of these propositions in favor of a representative government guarded by an independent judiciary was new in American thought; they had been the standard elements of political belief, and especially of conservative belief, for many decades. But the political context in which they were put forward was new, and conservative constitutionalism stood in direct opposition to most progressive attempts to enhance democratic deliberations. Instead of seeking means to enlighten public opinion, conservatives assigned the ultimate responsibility for wise popular deliberation and thoughtful social experimentation to the courts, and they identified the wisdom of the electorate with external controls that would prevent them either from registering their opinion decisively or confronting its consequences experimentally. Yet conservatives also maintained that the courts were an epitome not only of liberty but also of self-government. They held this view, moreover, even when they recognized the need for experiments in social legislation. As Elihu Root told the New York State Bar Association in 1912, "Opinions must and will always differ as to the nature of changes which should be made and the extent to which they should go, and those differences must be settled in some way. . . . Ultimately, step by step through the ordinary processes of self-government, through investigation, education, the spread of true understanding of facts and full discussion, the process of readjustment is being worked out and will be worked out to conform to the mature, instructed, considerate judgment of the self-governing people of the country." The point of this temperate and encouraging statement, however, was a last-ditch defense of the courts against the judicial recall! Here, as in the argument for representative institutions generally, the conflict between democratic hopes and constitutional authority was extreme.[8]

In urging constitutional obstacles to the free action of the people's will, then, conservatives of the progressive era renounced most of the educational assumptions common to contemporary democratic theory. On the one hand, they simply neglected popular education as they went about grounding their defense of the status quo in constitutional precedents. In this context education could be no more than a perfunctory support for the established order, which conservatives proposed to defend primarily by noneducational means.[9] Hence they may remind us of the scholars in politics, who had gradually taken refuge in constitutionalism, but there was an important difference. Because of their economic liberalism the scholars had been political reformers, whereas (sometimes in spite of their tolerance for social reform) the new conservatives stood pat on the existing political structure. In addition, the scholars in politics had originally hoped to influence and not simply to foreclose popular deliberation, while the typical conservative opponent of progressive innovations debated most contemporary issues in terms of jurisprudence.

On the other hand, and to the extent that progressive reforms in the process of government were intended to expand the educational opportunities and influences of American politics, the conservatives' adamantly negative response to virtually every political innovation except perhaps the short ballot meant that with unerring accuracy they repudiated every major hope, every major device that might prepare the electorate to be more effective participants in the process of government. In this sense the conservative philosophy was really a radical departure from precedent. The progressives attempted to extend and develop and reorganize the traditional educational avenues of self-government in order to recover the democratic promise the Jacksonians had first imputed to universal public schooling. Conservatives replied by making the established institutions of the American government an obstacle, not only to willful democracy, but also to every attempt of democrats to cure their own willfulness. In place of informed self-government on either a traditional or a progressive model they upheld representative government and institutions.

THE THEORY OF BUSINESS LEADERSHIP: THE 1920s

For the most part, the political opponents of progressivism substituted traditional constitutional formulas for contemporary innovations in self-government. But there were a few conservative spokesmen who saw further than these recalcitrant traditionalists, and who countered progressive political theory with the argument that only expert management of the multiplying functions of government could achieve common social purposes. To some extent their argument harmonized with the contention of progressive scholars that popular government must learn how to use experts, but more characteristically they held that a business-oriented elite was necessary to shape public policy wisely. They tended to substitute the business expert for both the people and their elected representatives in the democratic process.

Perhaps the leading exponent of this theory was Arthur Twining Hadley, the president of Yale University and a prolific commentator on contemporary social questions. In 1910, for example, during an address at the University of California, Hadley acknowledged that the role of government in the control of the economy must be considerably extended, but he imposed significant conditions on this development. For he distinguished between two kinds of political problem, "problems of social order" and "problems of business administration," and while he thought that the people had shown they might become competent to judge the first he denied their competence as to the second. Significantly, he included in the second category most of the problems the progressive movement had defined, and he also cast doubt on the people's competence to judge all of those in the first category. "Even in dealing with our more fundamental problems of social order," he said, "we are brought face to face with the need of business administration and expert skill in enforcing the laws the people want." Meanwhile, in *Standards of Public Morality* (1907), he had also urged businessmen to assume a larger social responsibility as part of a tacit bargain for their political autonomy. In effect, he proposed that business disarm its political critics by improving its social efficiency.[10]

In making this recommendation Hadley was one of a small number of pioneer advocates of a new attitude in business that would in time deeply influence American thought. Not the government expert but the managerial specialist, alert to both economic needs and political pressures, would make the significant decisions for American society. Here, indeed, was the core of business social theory during the 1920s—a doctrine which had important educational ramifications, and to which we now turn. Hadley and others like him had only begun to explore the ideas of business efficiency and responsibility and service that were to become the most characteristic American contribution to the political theory of capitalism.[11]

During the 1920s leading spokesmen for American business asserted that business institutions infused with spiritual values would solve contemporary social problems. The ethical coloring business spokesmen gave to their social theory spoke volumes about its political meaning: in effect, they all but proclaimed their ability and their willingness to assume a sort of trusteeship over the lives and fortunes of the less well off. Their idea of trusteeship owed a good deal to the early social gospel, and their faith in business leadership had been adumbrated by Andrew Carnegie. Yet they also suggested a novel role for businessmen, one that deliberately embraced politics as well as economics. Whereas the traditional view of economic leadership had contemplated the exercise of business authority in a political vacuum, a vacuum deliberately maintained, the doctrine of the 1920s suggested that important functions of social control and determinations of public policy might and in fact should be absorbed by business statesmen. "Who are the managers of the United States in these days?" asked the old *Life* in 1925 in an editorial that *American Industries* pridefully reprinted, to add, "Are we approaching a millennium in which visible government will not be necessary and in which the job of running the world will slip away from obstructive politicians and be taken over by men trained in the shop?" In effect if not in intention, the theory of business leadership substituted the deliberations of businessmen for the deliberations of popular government.[12]

It is hardly surprising, therefore, that advocates of a business-led civilization paid but little attention to the political education of the electorate. Those who spoke of education at all tended to welcome it for the social and economic advantages formal training bestows, and to point with pride to the opportunities for personal advancement that the American school system provided, but their theory of leadership precluded any but the most elementary applications of popular education in politics. Having substituted economic trusteeship for democratic policy-making, their chief concern was to protect public authority against popular interference. Their theory of education followed from and lent support to their theory of extraordinary political responsibility.

Two aspects of their statements about formal education are especially noteworthy. In the first place, they put a special emphasis on the training of leaders. This meant that having accepted a social and economic elite they recommended that it be influenced by an appropriate education. In 1926 Herbert Hoover, delivering a commencement address at the University of Georgia, differentiated between the functions of common schools and those of universities. The schools, he said, train a people for representative government, but universities educate the potential leaders of society and determine the very principles that will be taught in the common schools. In *American Individualism*, on the other hand, Hoover ignored the universities, to suggest instead that chambers of commerce and other business associations constituted a significant educational influence in the United States. Either way, his statements indicated that education was to be an influence on public policy from the top down and not from the bottom up.[13]

In the second place, however, education also provided a technique for recruiting leaders. Spokesmen for the theory of business trusteeship urged that (apart from business itself) public education offered the surest guarantee of economic opportunity. Thomas Nixon Carver thought that it could be employed to equalize opportunity and income alike among different crafts and professions, and Hoover argued that it was, as he said in 1926, "the only door to equal opportunity." But, significantly, he thought in terms of an opportunity for leadership rather than merely of economic success. "Our leadership," he announced during his campaign for the presidency in 1928, "can be found and it will be sympathetic to our ideals if we maintain the decency and dignity of family life through a stable economic system; if we maintain free and universal education and thus provide them the open stair to leadership; if we maintain for every individual an equality of opportunity to attain that position in the community to which his character and his ability entitle him." Here, indeed, was the key to the business-oriented theory of education. Hoover and his colleagues offered the people of the United States an opportunity to participate in prosperity, but it was an opportunity to participate as dependents, except for extraordinary individuals who managed to qualify for a higher role by rising to the top. At that point education would have different meanings, including training in the ethical obligations of the prosperous citizen.[14]

The political education of the people that business spokesmen for the 1920s invoked, therefore, was precisely conservative: it was intended to train them to support a social and economic order over which they must attempt to exercise but slight control and in which they might expect to participate as beneficiaries but not as originators of public policy. On this point the standpat conservatism of such figures as Calvin Coolidge, who also called frequently for improved schools in much the same vein as his Secretary of Commerce, simply lent additional support to the benevolent trusteeship that men like Hoover praised.[15] Indeed, in the final analysis there was little to choose between them, for the one only articulated what the other in fact sanctioned. Gone were the hopes and the techniques of progressivism, and for them was substituted a vision of a business society in which an orthodox political education replaced the hopeful innovations of the progressive era just as the trusteeship of business statesmen replaced the universal deliberation of the people.

THE THEORY OF BUSINESS LEADERSHIP
SINCE 1929

The theory of business trusteeship faced a severe test during the 1930s and afterward. Both the depression itself and the inadequacies of business leaders in dealing with it threatened for a time to dissolve entirely the moral and political influence that businessmen had gained during the era of prosperity. Yet business spokesmen persevered, and after little more than two decades they succeeded in reasserting their social and political authority in terms highly reminiscent of the 1920s. The difference between the 1950s and the 1920s was that the later theory of business leadership was more sophisticated and more comprehensive than its antediluvian version.

Oddly enough, the depression itself stimulated a good part of this sophistication. In 1931, Owen D. Young and Gerard Swope (chairman of the board and president, respectively, of the General Electric Company) urged that American industries assume the responsibility for stabilizing employment, while the United States Chamber of Commerce proposed a national advisory economic council and a modification of the antitrust acts to legalize business collaboration. The business response to such proposals made clear that they were attractive because they promised to safeguard the sovereignty of business interests over the economy, and the coming of the New Deal simply reinforced businessmen's belief that they must assume an ever-broader range of social functions if they were to forestall further policy making by political agencies. "Industry itself ought to take the lead in solving problems of its own creation," a publicist for the National Association of Manufacturers wrote in 1941. "Private enterprise cannot survive . . . a policy of mere negation; it must take hold of its problems and work out solutions on its own initiative. If government aid is needed, this may then be enlisted before pressure for arbitrary government action becomes irresistible." Well before the country recovered from the depression, thoughtful business spokesmen had worked out a relatively systematic managerial theory based on the proposition that business leaders could minimize government intervention in the economy by assuming an unaccustomed responsibility for the welfare of their stockholders, their employees, and the public generally. Since the Second World War, moreover, that theory has dominated sophisticated business thought.[16]

One can hardly object to the fact that business spokesmen have preached a greater sense of responsibility in business enterprise, but their excursions into managerial theory have generally urged business leaders to absorb functions and powers that other spokesmen for democratic institutions believe should be left to the democratic political process. In the view of Edwin G. Nourse, for example, most managerial exhortations seem to echo an earlier age in which businessmen were the only arbiters of business policies. "At its best," he wrote in 1950, ". . . there is a fine baronial flavor generously tinctured with noblesse oblige. This is an aristocratic and ethical approach, quite different from the democratic and scientific one called for by the conditions of today and tomorrow. It really conceives of business as a vested interest and an end in itself rather than a means to an end." Another conservative economist has attacked even more vigorously the business-oriented view that the corporation must assume "the role of conscience-carrier of twentieth-century American society." Professor Ben W. Lewis told the American Economic Association in 1958: "It is not going to happen; if it did happen it would not work; and if it did work it would still be intolerable to free men. . . . If we are to have rulers, let them be men of good will; but above all, let us join in choosing our rulers—and in ruling them." Even the testimony of friends of business enterprise suggests that managerial theory substitutes business interests for democracy.[17]

Because of its undemocratic political implications, the new theory of business leadership led to a novel theory of popular education. During the 1920s it was possible for advocates of business leadership to rely upon orthodox devices of political education because constitutional precedents and the temper of the times conspired to support the hegemony of management. During the 1930s, however, the whole apparatus of business leadership threatened to collapse in the face of public resentment over its transparent failure. Consequently—in the United States—it was almost inevitable that business leaders should turn to the education of the people to reestablish their authority. Businessmen and their sympathizers responded to the New Deal with a deliberate campaign of informal popular education. Some of them sponsored a point-blank refutation of New Deal principles that duplicated the arguments of earlier opponents of progressivism: they sought to restore the true constitutional faith by formal exhortation. Yet the political disappointments businessmen suffered and the political difficulties they anticipated suggested that these traditional appeals would not work, and sophisticated spokesmen turned to more effective means of persuasion. They abandoned the attempt (as one of them later put it) to hypnotize the mass of the people through political advertising, and began instead to plot a course of industrial activities that would outmaneuver and thus disarm popular discontent with business leadership.[18]

Under these circumstances, the device of "public relations," which had undergone only a primitive development during the placid twenties, became the most prominent technique by which business spokesmen hoped to influence public opinion. According to Bronson Batchelor, one of its most articulate advocates, public relations was a technique for mediating between business and the public by interpreting each to the other on a mutual and reciprocal basis. "Into the atmosphere of tension and major difficulties that today beset industry," his *Profitable Public Relations* (1938) began, emphasizing the immediate political relevance of everything industry did, "an entirely new element has been injected. That factor, elusive and intangible, is *what the public thinks and why*. In other words, consideration of great national economic questions must now be based quite as much upon popular attitudes and reactions as upon a strictly economic approach to the problems themselves." Given this unprecedented necessity, Batchelor undertook to lay down a new strategy for management: "Three basic considerations underlie any formulation on the part of industry for its strategic plan. In the order of importance, these are: the integration of an authoritative leadership for the present loose agglomeration called 'American business,' the drawing up of a set of platform principles which places industry before the public in both a constructive and humanized light, and finally, the creation of new idea symbols for business which will emphasize vividly to the public, *service* rather than *profit* concepts." [19]

But deeds as well as words were essential to Batchelor's technique, and he also urged that public relations experts share in corporate policy decisions in order to prevent damaging discrepancies between them. Nor was Batchelor unique; it became a standard public relations criticism of industry that it often attempted to cover up with words what could be rectified only by deeds. The point was well taken, but it clearly implied that public relations would serve political as well as economic purposes. In 1939, in fact, in an enthusiastic article, *Fortune* defined public relations as "the name business gives to its recognition of itself as a political entity." The remark suggested that the primary emphasis of public relations, including both the deed and the publicity given the deed, was manipulative: direct advertising having failed to convert public opinion, subtler tactics would now prevail. In its highest reaches, indeed, public relations was the paramount political art: its techniques were available not simply to protect businessmen against foolish mistakes but also to give them scope for the independent exercise of their policy functions within a hostile environment by diverting opinion from its common targets. Significantly, Batchelor defined public relations as "a new kind of social and political engineering." [20] The corollary of trusteeship was or might be the deliberate manipulation of public opinion under the aegis of a new social science.*

* Presumably the economic crisis itself gave an additional impetus to the idea of manipulating public opinion. Insofar as business spokesmen came to believe that industrial recovery depended upon the creation of consumer demand through advertising, they had reason to attempt manipulation of popular thought. The same phenomenon may also help to explain the attraction managerial theories of society continue to hold during an era of prosperity. As J. K. Galbraith and others have pointed out, American prosperity depends more than ever upon the ceaseless creation of economic "wants" that would have seemed impossibly luxurious less than a generation ago.

Needless to say, Batchelor's words and those of his fellow-prac-
titioners did not always speak for the maturing tactics of business
management, if only because his book was (among other things) a
persuasive exercise in self-promotion. Yet his views were strikingly
adapted to the political situation in which businessmen found themselves, and they were paralleled in business spokesmen's exhortations
to American industry.[21] Moreover, the most common form for the
propaganda of the deed that these businessmen urged was itself
important in defining the political and educational implications of
managerialism. Where Batchelor and his kind hinted at the sophisticated management of a whole society, business spokesmen had long
since begun to explore new techniques in human management
within industry that also suggested how the body of the people
might be brought to acquiesce in business leadership.

In a sense the theory of sophisticated industrial management
originated with John D. Rockefeller Jr. and Ivy Lee, the pioneer
public relations counselor. In 1916 the younger Rockefeller, confronted by recurrent labor difficulties at his unprofitable Colorado
Fuel and Iron Company, made a tour of inspection of his property
there in the course of which he established a plan for the presenta-
tion of employee grievances to management through elected employee representatives. In the influential little book of speeches that
summarized his plan and his thinking about it, Rockefeller described
his consultative technique in industrial management as a way of
creating harmony between capital and labor by restoring the personal relationship modern industry had lost. Two aspects of Rockefeller's scheme particularly concern us here. One is that he introduced it in order to allay discontent—in order, in other words, to
disarm criticism and promote loyal cooperation of his employees
with their management. The other is that he introduced it on his
own terms: the employee-representation plan was (in less elegant
language) a company union. Neither of these phenomena con-
demns Rockefeller's pioneering effort, but together they suggest a
manipulative approach toward the industrial population.[22]

In its original version, the theory of improved industrial relations involved few political assumptions, but in the long run it held
significant implications for politics as well as industry. These were
spelled out with force and dignity by Elton Mayo of the Harvard

Business School. In *The Human Problems of an Industrial Civiliza-tion* (1933) Mayo described the extraordinary increase of produc-tivity that an expression of managerial interest in employees' work-ing conditions had brought about in the now-famous Hawthorne experiments of the Western Electric Company. The fact that such discoveries remained to be pointed out in 1933 was an eloquent comment on the state of sophistication of American business man-agement, but Mayo did not stop with their implications for indus-trial management as such. Instead he portrayed the sophisticated modern administrator as the only authority able to hold back so-cial disintegration through his knowledge of the techniques of personnel management. In *The Social Problems of an Industrial Civilization,* moreover, Mayo developed this larger theme in con-siderable detail. Again he looked to the practical administrator to save civilization. He implied that through skillful "communication" with the lower ranks of society, including therapeutic listening to their frequently arbitrary grievances, and through a general de-velopment of "social skills," such leaders might yet bring society through its age of crisis. It was clear that he had erected a theory of politics in the light of modern industrial problems, and that he prescribed social salvation on the model of skillful industrial rela-tions.[23]

Mayo was an influential writer, yet perhaps his far-ranging social theories extended beyond what even his acknowledged disciples might easily accept. What is important here, however, is the tendency of his thinking, which points up the tendency of less utopian theories of business management. There the concepts of manipulation are applied almost indiscriminately to an industrial plant and to the state. According to the president of the Pitney-Bowes postage meter company, for example, the modern business-man faces "the old problem of leadership in a democratic society . . . simply, how do we go about directing ever greater numbers of people in such a way that they will accept our direction and not undermine it." Similarly, *Fortune's* paean to the "American Proposi-tion" in 1951 defined the "full citizenship" of workers in terms of their loyalty to free enterprise, and suggested that labor must be reconciled to management by new industrial institutions. These

"citizenship" techniques, it made clear, included a facsimile partnership that would forestall a genuine share in management. "The
benefits, the profit-sharing systems, the incentive plans, and so forth,
are not really the point," it explained. "The important thing is the
underlying attitude. The American businessman is by no means
prepared to admit the worker as a literal partner, but he is increasingly aware that if the enterprise system is to persist, a *kind* of
partnership must be created." [24]

This was the ultimate outcome of the sophisticated business impulse to educate public opinion. Denying both the wisdom and the
legitimacy of popular attempts to control business policies, but recognizing popular power, business spokesmen turned to manipulation
rather than instruction to protect their traditional authority. In
doing so they renounced not only the extreme hopes of progressivism, not only the radical democratic doctrines of the nineteenth
century, but also the very framework of democratic education as
it had been understood since the age of Andrew Jackson. The information and education of the people, which had been the premise
of American democracy and the fundamental commitment of the
progressive movement, were to be subsumed so far as possible under the techniques of public relations. Businessmen rather than the
public were to heed events, to the end that by careful management
they might prevent public opinion and public actions uncongenial
to their wishes, and retain an actual if not a theoretical sovereignty.

Not all businessmen, not all conservatives have adopted these
special political devices; the greatest obstacle to managerial views
of business and society is the free-enterprise tradition to which
many businessmen still subscribe. (Significantly, the economists who
have criticized the managerial theory of business leadership advocate a market economics.) The theory is important not because
of the number of men who hold it but because it has survived
depression and war and because it seems to appeal to the most responsible figures in the business world. So long as we attempt to
maintain an enterprise society, their statements suggest, we must
recognize that informal popular education will be a means by which
business management must attempt to circumvent—not inform—
hostile democratic opinion.

THE APPEAL TO FORMAL EDUCATION

The managerial theory of leadership confronts two serious obstacles. On the one hand, it conflicts with the individualistic tradition that surrounds American capitalism, to which even the most
sophisticated business spokesman is likely to appeal from time to
time in order to justify the autonomy of business enterprise. On the
other hand, it must work if it is to survive, and there is as yet
slight evidence that business practice respects managerial theory
or that it would be effective if it did. If an economic crisis were to
develop, it seems probable that public opinion would compel the
government to impose remedial measures on the American economy.
Hence democracy understood as individualism and democracy understood as popular authority both stand in actual or potential opposition to business management of American society.

Nevertheless, the theory of business leadership also embraces a
vision of popular education that helps to identify it closely with
American democratic traditions. During the late nineteenth century, business spokesmen like Andrew Carnegie frequently expressed skepticism if not outright hostility toward formal education when it was carried beyond the common school. It was not that
they objected to higher education for those who could afford it, but
they cast doubt on its utility for those who wished to pursue business careers. During the twentieth century, on the other hand,
businessmen have become increasingly sympathetic to higher
education and even to higher education that cannot by any means
be thought to serve business interests. In effect, they have become
the advocates of universal public education carried to the highest
point that each student is qualified for. They have made generous
donations to private colleges and universities; they have contributed to scholarship funds intended to aid needy students; they
have established academic training programs within their own industries; and they have given job preference to men (and women)
who hold college and university degrees. Moreover, the most progressive corporations and business leaders have been most firmly
committed to these innovations; in a real sense enthusiastic support
for formal education is a corollary of managerial theory.[25]

At the same time, it is obvious that the American people generally share the enthusiasm for formal education; the history of the idea of education in American thought is a history of expanding provision for schools and colleges as well as developing tactics of informal education. Hence it seems legitimate to suggest that, quite without intending it, business spokesmen have succeeded in identifying managerial principles with fundamental popular beliefs. At the very least, their attempts to make higher education more accessible have suggested that they wish to make sure that individual merit is recognized in their economic system; contributions to scholarship funds are a way of overcoming admitted deficiencies in the social structure. Furthermore, the fact that major industries hire promising college and university students, and even give them opportunities to continue their formal education, suggests that they are developing a managerial equivalent for the competitive business system of the nineteenth century. What sophisticated business practice has accomplished, indeed, is to associate the competitive democratic values of Jacksonian and post-Jacksonian liberalism with the modern business system by improving educational opportunities for personal success within it and leading to it. In effect, progressive businessmen have transferred economic individualism from business to the schools and thus reconciled their innovations with traditional American values.

They can hardly be thought to have intended the result, but their commitment to education has undoubtedly helped to protect business enterprise against its democratic critics. Almost by chance, American business spokesmen have hit upon the one social measure that promises to serve the political ends they outlined during their controversy with the New Deal without at the same time antagonizing the electorate. Presumably not even universal higher education will protect the American economy against all the unsettling effects of world developments, but so long as that economy works reasonably well it seems legitimate to suppose that the businessmen's devotion to formal education will help to sanction a managerial theory of society and politics. If so, we may find that the American ideal of universal education increasingly supports as well as contradicts techniques of political management that defy the political traditions of the American democracy.

XVIII. Redefinitions of Democracy

AMERICAN business spokesmen have been free to develop a managerial theory of politics for two reasons. One is the reverence the American people feel toward conspicuous individual success. The other is the fact that Americans have become skeptical of the ideal of a rational electorate which lay at the bottom not only of progressivism but of all democratic theory. The implications of the American attitude toward success for the American definition of democratic education have already become apparent, but the development of a characteristic skepticism concerning the rationality and the educability of the electorate has not. After the First World War American political thought turned so completely against the hopes and techniques of progressivism that today the idea of an educated electorate shaping intelligent solutions to national problems has gone far toward becoming recognized as a national myth.

The events that have undermined our faith in democratic political education are extraordinarily complex, and they are still at work. Hence no one can discuss in anything like authoritative terms the uses to which contemporary political thought puts the idea of political education. Moreover, American thinking about politics, especially on the level of sophisticated political theory, has been profoundly influenced by European speculations as to the nature of man, society, and government; it is no longer feasible to identify American political thought solely with indigenous expressions of theory or belief. These two considerations militate against any very elaborate treatment of contemporary challenges to our traditional idea of an informed politics, but they do not preclude a tentative discussion of the apparent tendencies of recent thought. If (as seems certain) well-informed Americans no longer think of political education in the optimistic terms of progressive democracy, it is plausible to inquire how they have expressed some of their doubts and reservations.

THE CHALLENGES OF THE 1920s

Almost certainly one of the turning points in American political thought was the First World War, which occasioned a widespread disillusionment with the hopes of the prewar years. The major social and economic characteristics of this aftermath of the Great Crusade are too well known to need reiterating here, but the precise forms its political thinking took are perhaps less familiar. In effect, prominent popular writers of the postwar era repudiated the very premises on which progressive democracy had built.[1]

One of the chief spokesmen for the political attitudes of the 1920s was Frank R. Kent of the Baltimore *Sun*. In *The Great Game of Politics* (1923) Kent described American politics from the precinct up in resolutely empirical terms. He was almost cheerful in the way he explained the importance of the machine, the secret arrangement, money, and lobbying in politics, and he enthusiastically renounced the progressive ideal of an educational politics. "Political campaigns," he said, "—most of them—are inherently insincere. It is a game of 'frame-ups,' of hidden moves, of concealed and smothered convictions, of fake indignations and forced sympathies, of secret deals and, sometimes, sinister alliances, of sidestepping and evasion, of expediency and compromise. Try as he will, even the highest and best type of man who seeks votes for an elective office cannot wholly escape these things, either before or after his election." In *Political Behavior* (1928) Kent went even further, to blame the cynical manipulation of the electorate primarily on the voters themselves. "The voters," he wrote, "not only are not interested and would not understand a dispassionate discussion of public questions, free from cant, bunk and false pretense, but they would react resentfully against any candidate who held his campaign to those lines. None ever does." [2]

One of the reasons Kent was so sure that the people would always be manipulated was their demonstrated susceptibility to propaganda, which both he and other political commentators deplored.

During the first years after the war, for example, Will Irwin, former chief of foreign propaganda for the Creel Committee, wrote a number of magazine articles that described techniques by which public opinion at home and abroad had been and continued to be influenced by propaganda. With some show of authority, Irwin also insisted that the Germans had copied their propaganda methods from the slanted-news policies of American newspapers; in other words, he represented propaganda as a distortion inherent in the channels of public information. So did Walter Lippmann, in *Liberty and the News* (1920), which criticized the role of these same newspapers in misrepresenting the peace conference to the American people, while his *Public Opinion* (1922) elaborated on the human fallibilities and the social complexities that made propaganda feasible. Within a few years other writers, less subtle than Lippmann, had spelled out innumerable ways in which public opinion was shaped by skillful propagandists. By the late 1920s, indeed, the menace of propaganda was an accepted political datum, and references to it became increasingly prolific and increasingly destructive of democratic dogmas.[3]

According to a common diagnosis, moreover, the real power of propaganda lay not in its technical resources but in the intellectual inadequacies of the American people. Kent's brash assertion, "The truth is that in politics, if you are sufficiently solemn and have the right sort of propaganda and publicity set-up, you can fool so nearly all of the people all of the time that the ones not fooled are too few to count," rested finally on an assumption that the "more or less moronic" constitute a majority of the voters, an assumption which derived in large part from pseudo-scientific applications of the scores of army intelligence tests to American politics. The basic form of this application was deceptively simple: the people generally have "low intelligence" and are therefore incapable of governing effectively. The doctrine was often complicated by a racist and eugenicist theory, which held that low intelligence is the outcome of breeding inferior ethnic strains, but the fundamental belief was still more deeply grounded in an elitist theory of human nature. As such it appealed to iconoclasts like H. L. Mencken and reactionaries like Irving Babbitt, both of whom employed the intelligence quotient to substantiate their prewar prejudices against democracy, but it also influenced democratic political thinkers and helped to provide another discouraging explanation for the patterns of contemporary politics.[4]

Still another psychological doctrine of the postwar era served to undermine progressive assumptions. This was the idea of a "herd mind," borrowed originally from European sources, which received considerable attention from contemporary publicists. One of its early exponents was Everett D. Martin, director of the People's Institute at the Cooper Union, whose *The Behavior of Crowds* (1920) attempted to diagnose the psychic characteristics peculiar to men in the mass. Although Martin avoided either condemning democracy outright or anticipating its inevitable decline, his belief in democracy was not convincing, and the theoretical principles he most clearly developed were those of a "crowd mind" and its susceptibility to clever manipulation. This estimate was reinforced by *Liberty* (1930), in which Martin revived his criticisms of democracy in more desperate terms and in such a fashion that he could look only to aristocracy for the preservation of human freedom.[5]

Moreover, and although he did not develop it fully, Martin's attempt to understand the crowd mind in terms of psychic mechanisms was potentially even more threatening to democratic assumptions than any of the criticisms he worked out in detail. Even in a restricted treatment of the dynamics of psychological compensation and projection, Martin necessarily discounted rational motivations and suggested that there are irrational sources for the simplest human actions irrespective of the influence of the crowd. He was, in fact, on the verge of applying psychoanalytic theory to politics, and other popular writers went beyond his tentative beginnings with devastating results for democratic theory. One of them was Edward L. Bernays, a nephew of Sigmund Freud, who characteristically turned human irrationality into a working principle. "This general principle," he wrote in *Propaganda* (1928), "that men are very largely actuated by motives which they conceal from themselves, is as true of mass as of individual psychology. It is evident that the successful propagandist must understand the true motives and not be content to accept the reasons which men give for what they do." [6]

All of these doctrines so served to discredit the educational aspirations of progressive democracy that H. L. Mencken was able to set up as political theorist for the 1920s. His *Notes on Democracy* (1926) was a catalogue of the ways in which democratic pretensions had been proved false by the innate incompetence of the majority of the people, who are swayed by primal urges and silly delusions and gulled by scheming politicians—"rival rogues" competing for mob approval.[7] On the other hand, democracy was not without its defenders during this age of disillusionment. Yet their most noticeable characteristic was the lengths to which many of them would go to rectify the errors of government by democratic opinion. They did not concede that the forms of democracy were entirely hopeless, but they hedged them about with all sorts of alien safeguards.

Among them the most interesting was Walter Lippmann, who deliberated throughout the 1920s on the difficulties inherent in creating an informed public opinion. In *Liberty and the News* he argued that the effective meaning of liberty of the press in a complex society is not freedom from restraint but the comprehensiveness and accuracy of the public's sources of information. Hence he exhorted professional news gatherers and publishers to better observe the standards of truth, and he also hinted that government might have to penalize deliberate inaccuracies, or itself provide objective information to counteract the flood of half-truth and propaganda. In *Public Opinion* he departed even further from precedent. Part of the book was a devastating analysis of the intellectual habits of the mass of the people, whose opinion on public questions is conditioned by arbitrary symbols and stereotypes. Now Lippmann's remedy was improvement of the mechanisms that report the real environment to the decision-making elements in society—which he took not to include the people as a whole. Their role in a democracy, instead, was to ensure that decisions were made by their representatives after proper investigation and according to objective facts. For, as Lippmann explained, the traditional techniques of democracy do not work. Ordinary men will not recognize their own best interests, and an occasional plebiscite is not a sufficiently delicate mechanism for settling public questions.[8]

Nor was this Lippmann's most critical analysis of democracy. In *The Phantom Public* (1925) he extended his definition of democratic failings to the point of arguing that universal popular education cannot possibly inform public opinion nor improve popular deliberation; all it can do is teach the people the criteria they should insist upon in their leaders' policy-making. In addition, Lippmann denounced the nineteenth-century idea that governments could discern or legislate a common good, and he suggested that the exercise of political authority must be juridical rather than purposive in that it must elevate the rule of law over the rule of will in the conduct of public affairs. By concerning himself with the inadequacies of public opinion, indeed, he reached a position reminiscent in many ways of that adopted by the conservative advocates of representative government, who had emphasized rule by law rather than by men and who had relied upon a formal self-denying education of the people to achieve it. The public, Lippmann said invidiously, is not a dispenser of law or morals, but "a reserve force that may be mobilized on behalf of the method and spirit of law and morals." [9]

Lippmann's renunciation of progressive principles was perhaps the most striking phenomenon of its kind, but other writers who felt some loyalty to democratic institutions also expressed significant reservations about them. Recognizing the influence of party shibboleths and empty symbols over the public mind, for example, and urging that plural voting and the better education of the electorate be employed to combat it, Harry Elmer Barnes conceded in 1924 that there was little hope the people could ever become truly intelligent. "The majority of the voters," he said, "will always be likely to react fundamentally on an emotional plane, and education is most effective with those who consider public, as well as other problems, in a rational light." In such statements there was little hope for that "liberation of intelligence" that James Harvey Robinson had looked forward to in *The Mind in the Making* (1921)—

and even Robinson had suggested that the people would be reluctant to give up their prejudices and formula-ridden habits of
thought.[10]

Moreover, it was noteworthy that one of the more hopeful psychological doctrines of the era, John B. Watson's behaviorism, also
severely modified traditional belief in a self-determining democratic
intelligence. As a psychological theory, behaviorism held that the
primary determinant of human behavior is the conditioning influence of the environment on the child and the adult. H. L. Mencken
characteristically appropriated its argument that there are fundamental instinctual drives that may be modified by proper conditioning to prove that ordinary men lack virtue, but more typically
the doctrine gave rise to a theory that by use of the conditioned
reflex it would be possible to train human beings to achieve progressive social purposes. Yet this was a doubtful prop for a self-governing democracy, depending as it did on a manipulation of the environment by a scientific elite, and perhaps the most appropriate
comment on the liberal hopes it aroused was that after being fired
by the Johns Hopkins University for his psychological heresies
Watson became the president of an advertising agency.[11]

In the context of contemporary political and psychological belief,
therefore, any idea of achieving a more effective democracy through
democratic education was bound to seem either optimistic or
hortatory. This was evident in T. V. Smith's *The Democratic Way of
Life* (1926), a Whitmanesque attempt to extend the American definition of democracy to include social and economic fraternity,
which described comprehensive popular education as "the measure
through which men dare to press from democratic government to
the democratic way of life." But it was also evident in Charles E.
Merriam's scholarly summary of *New Aspects of Politics* (1925),
which assumed that all the new techniques of social analysis—psychology, social psychology, anthropology, the empirical study of
political processes—would have a liberating rather than a destructive
effect on democracy. On the one hand his urbane little volume anticipated later developments in empirical political science, which were,
however, to fail to support his hopes. On the other hand it insisted
again and again that it is necessary to enlarge public intelligence

about political affairs by expanding popular education. Indeed, Merriam thought that an enlarged public intelligence was the very condition of effective democracy, and so failed to deal convincingly with whether it was in truth feasible.[12]

Furthermore, both Smith and Merriam looked mainly to innovations in formal education to achieve democratic political ends; the fact suggested that even in their eyes the democratic political process seemed unlikely to educate the electorate in ways the progressives had hoped. During the 1920s, indeed, John Dewey was one of few thinkers who continued to visualize politics itself as an educational process, and—significantly—his chief essay in political theory rested heavily upon theoretical rather than empirical arguments. In *The Public and Its Problems* (1927) he defined community in terms of the felt consequences of individual and group activities, public in terms of a common recognition of these shared consequences, political action as a conscious attempt to shape them constructively. Having developed these instrumentalist formulas he attributed the inability of the contemporary community to deal with social and economic problems to men's inability to identify themselves as a public, and he insisted that the first problem of democracy is one of communication and hence ultimately of education in the method of intelligence. Like Smith and Merriam he tended to state the necessary conditions of democracy in such a fashion as to ignore its practices, and to resolve the difficulties this method of analysis created by calling for a more effective formal education.[13]

Given the attitudes and the social patterns of the 1920s, in fact, the best that Dewey and others like him could hope for *was* improvements in formal education, which might ultimately encourage American citizens to be more intelligent about politics, and which would serve desirable social and cultural purposes better meanwhile. As Dewey subsequently acknowledged in *Individualism, Old and New* (1930), however, formal education in an unprogressive social order was more likely to support than to challenge the values of that order.[14] If informal political education no longer seemed a truly promising vehicle of social progress, formal education was all too clearly an instrument of the status quo. The experience of the war years and common reactions to it had made the political education of the people seem implausible, and democracy itself an act of faith.

THE CHALLENGE OF THE 1930s

In many ways the experience of the 1930s reinforced the discouraging lessons of the 1920s. Although there was much in the spectacle of a popular government dealing with a severe economic crisis to confound both skeptics and outright critics of democracy, the success of the New Deal in preserving both the domestic economy and the domestic political system also posed a difficult challenge to the belief that an informed people is the basis of democracy. Popular government survived at a heavy cost to the democratic theory of educated politics.

The cost was no accident. The depression emergency precluded leisurely popular deliberation such as had characterized the progressive movement, and Franklin D. Roosevelt tended to employ the educational resources of the presidency pragmatically to preserve the freedom of action of his administration rather than to illuminate public opinion. During his first campaign for the presidency, indeed, Roosevelt outlined an educational philosophy of politics that stood comparison with the best progressive statements. "Government," he told the Commonwealth Club of San Francisco, "includes the art of formulating a policy, and using the political technique to attain so much of that policy as will receive general support; persuading, leading, sacrificing, teaching always, because the greatest duty of a statesman is to educate." But he also went on to warn his audience that "we are learning rapidly, in a severe school"; even before he won office he apparently anticipated that there would seldom be time to wait for public opinion to rally to the support of necessary measures, and he was to conduct the presidency on this assumption. As Edgar Kemler, a vigorous supporter, wrote in 1941:

President Roosevelt has prided himself on the amount of discussion that he has provoked and on the thorough grounding in political and economic fundamentals that he has given the voters in the pursuance of his program. And yet he is palpably more interested in having them con-

sent to and participate in his *faits accomplis* than in having them share
in the preliminary deliberations. As an educator, he has disseminated
the facts, because the facts have been mainly on his side. On the other
hand, he is no more interested in stimulating strategic thought among
the citizens than the General Staff of the U. S. Army is interested in
stimulating strategic thought among the soldiers.[15]

It was characteristic of the age, moreover, that Kemler should
present his evaluation of Roosevelt's presidency in the form of an
"ethical guide for New Dealers" that praised the New Deal for
abandoning progressive principles. Perhaps it should be said that
Kemler's views were influenced by the international crisis, which
seemed to him to necessitate quasi-military leadership in place of
democratic inefficiency, but his basic theory had to do with domestic
achievements, which he imputed to the substitution of progressive
social engineering for democratic pieties. "As a result," he explained,
"the progressive cause has found purpose at the cost of its spiritual
content." Above all Kemler paid his respects to the discipline that
Roosevelt maintained over his party and his nation by fair means
and foul, and he even praised the president's uncanny ability as
hero of a national cult to offset his gradual loss of rational authority. Kemler as well as Roosevelt believed in leadership, that is to
say, but in a special kind of leadership and in the kind of political
education that followed from it. "We no longer care," he argued,
"to develop the individual as a unique contributor to a democratic
form. We want him as a private in an army, cooperating with all
the other privates. The old Jeffersonian emphasis on schools for
citizenship and on self-government has changed to a Rooseveltian
emphasis on response to a heroic leadership." "I do not think that
this change in educational policy is anything to glory in," he added.
"Yet it is essential. If it seems to undermine the dignity of the common man, it is because his dignity has already been undermined." [16]

Making much the same assumption, Thurman Arnold developed
a theory of social reform that drew on Walter Lippmann's concept
of symbols and stereotypes but went far beyond it to discredit the
whole intellectual apparatus with which even informed men nor-
mally seek to understand the social environment. Arnold was in
the first instance a penetrating critic of die-hard conservative op-

position to the pragmatic social experiments that the New Deal had introduced, and he evidenced a genuine concern that human needs should take precedence over scholarly rationalism, but his thinking effectively deprecated all forms of popular participation in government. In *The Symbols of Government* (1935) he argued that good government consists of assigning skilled administrators almost unlimited power to reshape economic institutions, and he implied that the electorate is not only technically incompetent to guide such tasks but also disqualified by its inheritance of legal and economic symbols. Hence he left little room for their future education, whether by formal or informal means. Indeed, his first impulse, in a chapter intended to deal with the political problems his method of reform confronted, was to identify the good society with an insane asylum in which the people are the patients. "The concept of government as an insane asylum," he wrote, "liberates us from the notion that wise men think up principles and schemes of government for their duller fellows to learn and follow, and that thus social change is accomplished. It frees us from the notion that 'thinking men' decide between the relative merits of communism and capitalism, and choose the better form. Finally, the theory is based on a humanitarian ideal which seems to be indestructible in the march of society—the ideal that it is a good thing to make people comfortable if the means exist by which it can be done." [17]

The analogy of the insane asylum proved inexact, and Arnold finally rejected it because it was incompatible with other human values, yet he was unable to suggest a convincing alternative. Moreover, in *The Folklore of Capitalism* (1937), he still further extended his destructive attack on democratic politics. There he argued that for all practical purposes the country's industrial centers had previously constituted the government of the United States, suggested that a new *de facto* political leadership was necessary because industrial leaders had failed, and described the political resources of the new leadership in obviously manipulative terms. This time his model was not the attendant in an insane asylum but the psychiatrist, and he was even clearer than before that political therapy was not to be confused with the traditional images of self-government. "The notion that legislation becomes more expert because of prolonged public discussions of proposed measures," he said, "is an illusion which follows the notion that public debate is addressed to a thinking man through whose decisions organizations have group free will. All prolonged public discussions of any measure can do is to reconcile conflicts and get people used to the general ideal which the measure represents." In effect, Arnold domesticated in the reform movement he championed both the political skepticism and the manipulative political attitudes that had been expressed by disillusioned progressives and advocates of business leadership during the 1920s and 1930s.[18]

Other New Dealers were far from caustic about democratic ideals, but their statements tended characteristically to be unconvincing. In *New Frontiers* (1934), for example, Henry Wallace rested the case for democracy on vague optimism about the nature of the political process together with generalized exhortation to bring the people more directly into it. On the other hand, in *The New Democracy* (1934), Harold Ickes invoked an informed public opinion as the basis of democracy but defined the relationship between government and education in terms of expert planning, democratic opportunities for advancement, and public opinion hostile to the arguments of economic royalists. Both books cast doubt on the educational definition of American politics by the way in which they employed it.[19]

Even when New Deal theorists visualized making positive political use of established group interests and group experiences, moreover, they offered little more than a pious hope that some sort of educational process would be possible within the necessary framework of reform. David Lilienthal was the chief spokesman for this hope. In *TVA: Democracy on the March* (1944) he urged that regional political authorities, and only such authorities, could bring together the technical knowledge of experts with the hopes and attitudes of the people in such a fashion that each might stimulate and inform the other. But for a number of reasons the example of the TVA was not entirely convincing; it was in any event unique; and other New Dealers who combined democracy and social planning were less able than Lilienthal to reconcile popular opinion with the needs of reform. Among them, Rexford G. Tugwell called for so great a reorientation of the contemporary social and economic system in his *The Industrial Discipline and the Governmental Arts* (1933) that his hope labor and management might collaborate in planning a new society seemed utopian, while in proposing an industrial equivalent of the Agricultural Adjustment Administration, Mordecai Ezekiel betrayed obvious practical and theoretical limitations to popular participation in the government of the economy. It was almost a foregone conclusion that those who concerned themselves with the practical problems of recovery, or even with the practical problems of long-range planning, would be unable to visualize democracy in anything like its traditional educational terms.[20]

Hence the most nearly systematic statements of an educational theory of politics during the 1930s came from the opposition on the Right and Left, which, relieved of the immediate necessity of dealing with the practical problems the New Deal confronted, could project both a rationally ordered society and a comprehensive technique of political education to reach it. There was a body of such writers on the non-Marxian Left, advocates of a more deliberate use of intelligence in developing a new social order, who appealed to the people to support necessary changes because the government had failed to plan intelligently. Few of them agreed with each other on the precise measures that were necessary to consummate reform, but in their view differences in tactics were insignificant because they could be resolved by intelligence and experience. Their primary task, instead, was to exercise an educative leadership, and they were confident that continued experience of the New Deal's fitful measures of recovery and reform would inevitably consolidate public opinion on their side. "This is the opportunity for liberal and radical thought," wrote John T. Flynn in *Common Sense* in May, 1934. "It affords time for education which is its only weapon. And this very languor in the business machine will tend to increase the questioning of those who have been fooled with promises for the last year. Those who are interested in a better economic world for the great masses of our people should be ready with the answers to those questions." [21]

This does not mean that all advocates of a greater rationality in reform automatically appealed to the more effective education of the people. In *Insurgent America* (1935), for example, Alfred M. Bingham suggested that nonrational or only seemingly rational techniques of persuasion might be necessary to convert middle-class opinion in America to the support of a planned and ordered system of distribution, if only because the middle classes were unlikely to learn effectively from brute experience. Further to the Left, in *It Is Later Than You Think* (1939), Max Lerner exhorted the people of the United States to achieve "democratic collectivism" by means vaguely identified with "violence," presumably under the leadership of a radical elite. And certainly less superficial social theorists, for example George Soule, put such a heavy emphasis on the practical complexities of social reorganization as to imply that most of the major decisions must be reserved to an administrative elite. Even so, and for all their irrationalism, both Bingham and Lerner appealed as well to an informed public conscience to support their innovations, while Soule thought, in *The Coming American Revolution* (1934), that the failure of liberal reform must "educate" the people to understand the need for sounder social planning. Indeed, this was an age in which George S. Counts, an educator become social theorist, could ask seriously "Dare the School Build a New Social Order?" So long as a new social order seemed to be the primary issue in contemporary politics the appeal to education was almost inevitable.[22]

At the same time, conservative opponents of the New Deal also appealed to popular education to build a better social order, albeit a social order modeled on nineteenth-century precedents rather than twentieth-century doctrines. No more than the commentators of the Left could those of the Right rely exclusively upon the education of the people, yet it was one of their characteristic political values.

One of the arguments conservatives employed against the New Deal was an insistent constitutionalism, which was augmented by Supreme Court decisions adverse to many of the major innovations of the first Roosevelt administration. Although conservative spokesmen sometimes appealed to constitutional precedent for merely tactical or partisan reasons, their views also represented a deeply felt criticism of the New Deal for its pragmatic tendency to substitute temporary expedients for what had once seemed irreducible principles of free government. Whether conservatives sympathized with the restoration of business trusteeship or with the restoration of a traditionally free economy—and some opted for both—they frequently asserted that a return to constitutional principles would also revive the economy, and every encroachment on constitutional precedents simply confirmed their belief that they faced what the vice president of the Liberty League described in 1936 as "Democratic Despotism." They were fighting a battle against political innovation that conservatives of the progressive era had begun, and their only weapons were formal incantations and prophecies of doom.[23]

In other moods, however, conservative spokesmen conceded the necessity for some expansion of government activities but opposed the New Deal for its unprincipled attack on the integrity of the democratic process. The Constitution and the Court were useful bulwarks even here, but they were less important than the image of an electorate passing informed judgment on its representatives and guiding public policy according to right reason. In effect, conservatives in this mood appealed to the political principles that had once moved progressive liberals—scrupulous political leadership, political candor, a tendency to wait for and cultivate the best judgment of the people—and charged that the New Deal had deliberately abandoned these criteria of politics for partisan reasons. Nor was it only a question of candor and good judgment; in the last analysis, these conservative thinkers urged, the New Deal threatened to corrupt the electorate itself—not through bought votes alone but through calculated appeals to selfish material prejudices against the best interests of the nation as a whole.[24]

Such objections to New Deal politics made an easy bridge by which former progressives might cross over to the conservative position, and so many made the journey that at times they seemed to be the leading figures in the opposition. It also made an easy bridge for disillusioned New Dealers, who became almost as numerous as the ex-progressives. There were of course fugitives from the New Deal who adopted none of these historic political attitudes, but it is nevertheless striking how often their maturing views approximated the education-oriented liberalism of the progressive era. During the 1930s even Frank Kent, *enfant terrible* of the debunking twenties, and a long-time Democrat, repudiated President Roosevelt on the ground that he had broken too many political promises! "It is not always fair to quote a man's words against him after a long lapse of time," he explained in 1935. "Often, on the spur of the moment, or in the heat of a fight, men say or write things for which they should not be held to too strict accountability. Conditions change and men change with them. No one should be condemned for changing his mind if he has a sound reason to change." "Nevertheless," he added in defiance of these considerations, "men who hope to become President of the United States are expected to weigh their words well and mean what they say. Consistency and steadfastness in the White House are vital to the welfare of the nation. If the people cannot depend upon the promises of their President they are in a bad way. When a President or a candidate for the Presidency, in a prepared speech to the country, makes a solemn pledge and takes a definite and unequivocal stand, the obligation to live up to his words is far heavier than on the ordinary man." [25]

Obviously conservatives like Kent shared few social purposes with left-wing critics of the New Deal, yet the political doctrine they expressed had in common with radical theory a belief that democratic leaders must deal with issues in public policy by rationalizing public opinion. They also had in common that they were ignored. Even if these opinions had not been discredited by the company they kept they would inevitably have been left behind by the achievements of the Roosevelt years. The New Deal won not by principle but by practice.

POLITICAL SCIENCE AS POLITICAL THEORY

The New Deal not only won elections; it also hastened the reformulation of academic political theory along empirical lines. Systematic exploration of the American political process dated from Arthur F. Bentley's *The Process of Government* (1908) but reached maturity only after the depression years had given political scientists invaluable opportunities for watching democratic government and politics at work. Not surprisingly, empirical research provided one more challenge to democratic belief in an educational politics.

Some of the implications of sophisticated political science became apparent even during the 1920s, when academic commentators blended contemporary criticisms of democratic government and institutions into systematic statements about American politics. Employing themes familiar to readers of H. L. Mencken, for example, William B. Munro gathered loosely together in *The Invisible Government* (1928) a number of skeptical reflections on the traditional mythology of democracy. Among these myths he included the ideas of public opinion, popular sovereignty, and thoughtful public deliberation. Similarly, in *The American Public Mind* (1930), Peter H. Odegard systematically described nonrational influences in American politics, among them group-mindedness, conditioned reflexes, popular slogans, the mass media, and party loyalties. Neither Munro nor Odegard subscribed to exaggerated fears that free government was lost because of the phenomena he described, but in its methodical way their level-headed empiricism was even more destructive of democratic ideals than the most dramatic journalistic exposés of popular incompetence. Odegard's catalogue of nonrational influences mustered so many illogical sources of political belief and practice as to cast doubt on the role of intelligence in politics, while in attempting to discern basic patterns in American politics Munro simply threw overboard political free will and independent judgment.[26]

Even so, these early excursions into realistic political science tended to assume that the faith in public deliberation should be modified rather than that it should be abandoned entirely, and for all his concern with ineluctable patterns Munro also expressed sympathy with reforms like the short ballot that might in fact work to make popular participation in government more effective. Harold D. Lasswell presented a far more fundamental challenge to the idea of meaningful popular deliberation, however, in his *Psychopathology and Politics* (1930), which attempted to apply a moderately sophisticated understanding of psychic mechanisms to political motives and belief. In *Propaganda Technique in the World*

War (1927) Lasswell had implied that politics might be held to a rational standard even if rationality is difficult to maintain. Now he deprecated thinking itself, and argued that formal political activities reflect the displacement of deep libidinal drives into only seemingly rational motives and behavior. Although his whole argument was couched in therapeutic terms, as an appeal to political leaders and administrators to recognize the irrational sources of their behavior, his contribution to the theory of politics could only challenge the rationalistic basis of democratic thought.[27]

While the psychoanalytic theory of personality worked to broaden the scope of political science at the expense of rationalistic beliefs, the main lines of academic political thinking lay elsewhere. Lasswell himself indicated some of them in his *Politics: Who Gets What, When, How* (1936), a sociological treatment of the tactics and achievements of political elites. He was rather narrowly concerned with the elite as a primary explanation of politics, however, and it remained to more catholic scholars to state the characteristic modern interpretation of democracy. According to their view, democracy is simply a process of continuous interaction among political leaders, interest groups, and the electorate, all of whom are pragmatically disinclined to pursue objective inquiries into contemporary social issues. Instead they operate within certain specified limits to achieve personal goals through their power to shape the activities of government.[28]

This pragmatic definition of democracy originated in empirical studies of American political activities. In *Pressure Politics* (1928), for example, Peter H. Odegard dispassionately analyzed the tough-minded but effective political tactics the Anti-Saloon League had employed in imposing Prohibition on the United States. His study was especially significant in that Prohibition had once been understood as a great progressive reform, one that rested in turn upon woman suffrage—itself a progressive innovation in government. But it was not necessary for every empirical study to contradict progressive ideals directly in order to challenge them. In *Group Representation before Congress* (1929), Pendleton Herring argued that organized lobbying not only made the expression of public opinion possible on specific matters of policy but also served as a vehicle of popular deliberation, and Harwood L. Childs developed a similar view in *Labor and Capital in National Politics* (1930), which depicted the often contradictory pressures of two major interest groups on the federal government. In spite of the rational behavior such studies attributed to given agencies in the political process, they inevitably denied the existence of comprehensive public deliberation on issues of public policy.[29]

Furthermore, the concept of competing interests broadened as empirical studies accumulated. On the one hand, empirical interest in lobbying and similar activities developed into a more general interest in political behavior at every level of the governmental process from voting to the decisions of the Supreme Court. The assumption that there is a group basis to American politics remained powerful, but it blended into an increasingly intricate sense of how governmental decisions are reached and enforced. The very intricacy of the process made it clear that the will of the people was neither coherent nor effective nor educable in the sense that progressive theorists had assumed, and cast doubt not only on progressive assumptions but on all of the rationalist assumptions of liberal democracy. On the other hand, in addition to depicting an extraordinarily complicated political process, modern political scientists also came increasingly to attach democratic values to it. According to their view, the most important characteristic of the American political system was that it worked—which is to say that it generated decisions that agencies of government were able to enforce because the electorate accepted their legitimacy. On this basis, the competence of the voters was not doubtful so much as irrelevant to a viable politics, which reduced to the peaceful resolution of conflicts. In effect, political science substituted the political process for education as the key principle in American democratic theory.[30]

Inevitably, therefore, sophisticated political scientists also came to treat the democratic ideals of a rational electorate and an educative politics as mere ideology. "Treated frankly as a social myth," Pendleton Herring wrote in *The Politics of Democracy* (1940), "public opinion holds implications highly significant for our political process. . . . As with all symbols, meaning is not to be found in the thing itself as a logical concept but rather in its effectiveness for evoking loyalties and sanctioning rule. A symbol may appear irrational, mystical, even fantastic, yet it may nonetheless give meaning and form to life for those who accept it." "Faith in the idea of self-government," V. O. Key Jr. contended in *Politics, Parties, and Pressure Groups* (1942), another of the major syntheses in the field, "has a profound political effect in that a general belief in such a doctrine creates throughout the masses of people a sense of security, of satisfaction with the established order, and of hope of eventual improvement of their lot by the exertion of their own strength." Even the philosophical advocates of democracy could not escape the idea that rational democracy is a myth. In *Liberal Democracy: Its Merits and Prospects* (1950), J. Roland Pennock asserted that the democratic process displays an elementary rationality in dealing with important issues, but he also observed that because the liberal democratic myth had been challenged by such writers as Tarde, Le Bon, Sorel, and Freud it was less able than it had been to attract men's loyalties or influence their actions.[31]

As Pennock's argument suggests, moreover, political scientists who assumed a degree of rationality in the electorate were generally unwilling to visualize American politics in educational terms. Significantly, in *The New Image of the Common Man* (1950), a wise and persuasive reaffirmation of democracy as it actually is, Carl J. Friedrich identified the ideal of an educated politics with a mistaken attempt to universalize the rational qualities of an aristocracy. Similarly, in *An Introduction to Democratic Theory* (1960), H. B. Mayo argued that democratic government would be impossible if it had to meet the standards of popular competence and informed deliberation that traditional liberal theory assumed; fortunately, he explained, it need not. By the same token, political scientists who continued to visualize American politics chiefly in terms of competing interests also denied the rationality of group-based politics even when they assumed the basic rationality of the groups themselves. Robert A. Dahl's *A Preface to Democratic Theory* (1956) is a case in point. Restating the theory of American constitutionalism to accommodate the realities of American politics, Dahl argued that only certain segments of any society can possess sufficient opportunities to become informed about questions of public policy, and he insisted that "the making of governmental decisions is not a majestic march of great majorities united upon certain matters of basic policy. It is the steady appeasement of relatively small groups." The fact that Dahl praised the democratic process for protecting minorities did not alter his sense that it might well be nonrational in other respects.[32]

If the idea of popular education survived in sophisticated political thought, therefore, it derived most of its strength from modern attempts to treat the electorate as if they were knowledgeable consumers of economic goods. According to this general view, which was most clearly stated by Joseph Schumpeter in *Capitalism, Socialism, and Democracy* (1942), democracy is best understood as a process of competition for office among a few major producers of political goods, and legislation in the public interest is a by-product of their struggle to acquire and keep office. Like most economic theory, this doctrine implied a basic rationality among the electorate and some willingness on their part to acquire sufficient information to choose between competing politicians. Nevertheless, Schumpeter also argued that citizens can not and will not act as rationally in politics as they can and will in economic matters, and he pointed out that political advertising is even more likely than commercial advertising to deprecate reason and mislead intelligence. Hence he concluded that democracy can work only if certain minimal qualities of intelligence and self-control characterize both the electorate and competing political entrepreneurs. To this extent he may be said to have described the possibilities of democratic politics in terms of reason and education, but it is clear that he awarded each only a minor supporting role in the political process. In developing a full-fledged economic theory of democracy from Schumpeter's premises, moreover, Anthony Downs pointed to a great many circumstances that may make it uneconomical and thus "irrational" for voters to seek political information before they vote. The economic model of the political process offered scant room for popular political education even under ideal conditions.[33]

In this context, any scholarly attempt to restate the political theory of democracy in terms of public opinion and education was likely to seem obsolete or irrelevant. In 1939, for example, Charles W. Smith Jr. described the politics of democracy in terms of the functioning and malfunctioning of public opinion. His *Public Opinion in a Democracy* assumed the will of the people, discussed various kinds of influences on it, and opened and concluded with apostrophes to democracy as the embodiment of government by public opinion. His essay was a useful study of its kind, but it failed to deal conclusively with far greater challenges to the ideal of government by informed opinion than propaganda and demagogues and censorship because, in effect, it failed to recognize their existence.[34]

Nor should Smith's judicious discussion of the problem be singled out as an example of wishful scholarship; the fact is that almost any attempt of its kind would have seemed implausible or hortatory. In *On the Agenda of Democracy* (1941), for example, Charles E. Merriam recognized the influence of pressure groups and lobbies in American politics but avoided discussing their ultimate political significance. Instead, he defined the immediate agenda of democracy in terms of better soliciting and focusing and defining public opinion on major public issues. Similarly, Harold D. Lasswell incorporated into *Democracy through Public Opinion* (1941) many of his earlier assertions about the nonrational sources of democratic politics, only to argue that democracy may be revived by introducing various mechanisms for improving the scope, point, and rationality of public opinion. Some of Lasswell's mechanisms were ingenious in a fashion reminiscent of Walter Lippmann in *Public Opinion,* but they were also less convincing than Lippmann's in that they were more hopeful. Finally, in *Political Campaigning: Problems in Creating an Informed Electorate* (1960), Stanley Kelley Jr. depicted the failure of both major parties to debate crucial issues in the presidential election of 1956 and described various laws and practices that had worked with only mixed success in the past to raise the level of popular political discussion. On this basis he argued that although the problems of creating an informed electorate are difficult they are not insoluble.[35]

The hortatory quality of such analyses of the political process suggests that the idea of informing public opinion served ideological rather than scientific purposes. At any rate, it is easier to understand the renewed respect paid democratic doctrines in terms of extraneous influences brought to bear on American political science than to accede to it as a reflection of changing political reality. This is not to say that empirical scholarship consistently made good its criticisms of democratic ideals; it turned out, for example, that propaganda is not all-powerful, if only because there is so much of it, and even irrational political men could be seen to have behaved with a certain narrow rationality part of the time. But these second thoughts alone were not enough to account for the democratic renaissance that took place after 1940. It seems quite clear, instead, that the world crisis and the relationship of the United States to it explain the revival of traditional belief and the tenacity with which experienced scholars like Merriam and Lasswell held to it. The ideal of a competent electorate enabled somehow to function effectively in the determination of public policies acquired new luster as the rest of the world adopted strange gods, and the idea of an educative political process served to identify and distinguish what was still thought of as the American experiment.

Yet on a longer view there was slight reason to accept reviving claims for the political education of the people, and (as this discussion has suggested) sophisticated investigators denied them almost as vigorously after the war as they had before it. Political scientists could find little empirical evidence for an educational definition of American politics even if the postwar world provided many motives for adopting it as a creed.

Conclusion

THE twentieth century has dealt harshly with liberal democratic theories, and above all with the American belief in universal suffrage made competent through education. Sensitive to the shortcomings of populist democracy but committed to its hopes, the progressive generation gathered together most of the doctrines of nineteenth-century liberalism for one final assault on national evils. A popular reaction was inevitable, and when it came it took the form of disillusionment with both democracy and democratic education. Not the dogmatic conservatives who opposed progressive innovations from the start, but former progressives themselves, led the way. Thoughtful commentators like Walter Lippmann had suggested even before the First World War that a people can be neither rational nor educable in the classic American sense, but their enthusiasm for what their generation had accomplished momentarily overcame their doubts. After experiencing the war and its disappointments they had less reason for enthusiasm, and they turned to a skeptical and often destructive reexamination of democratic belief.

Empirical political scientists reinforced postwar skepticism, and by 1929 informed American citizens were as inclined to scoff at progressive political values as their predecessors had been to praise them. They doubted the rationality and the educability of the electorate, and they accepted the manipulation of public opinion as a fundamental fact of democratic politics. Although a decade of depression then challenged the theory of business leadership to which many Americans turned in reaction against egalitarian democracy, it did not challenge their sense that effective conduct of public affairs depends more upon the wisdom of political leaders than upon the wisdom of the people. The extent to which the American democracy turned away from its historic educational criteria was dramatically illustrated when the liberal and rationalist tenets of progressivism became terms of reproach to the leadership of Franklin D. Roosevelt—who succeeded, after all, because he acted like a disciple of the early Lippmann. Furthermore, even the revival of political and business-oriented conservatism during and after the Second World War could not restore traditional democratic values either to American society or to American politics, and the continuing world crisis has simply reinforced the American people's loyalty to the established order, not caused them to demand that their politics be made educational.

Yet the progressive synthesis of democracy and education has not disappeared so much as been transformed; the idea of universal democratic education shaping our social and political institutions has been fragmented into separate and sometimes contradictory parts. On the one hand, Americans have become openly skeptical of political education, and especially of informal political education through popular deliberation and discussion of public issues. To this extent they simply deny the importance of popular education to democracy, although they also insist that their schools must inculcate democratic lessons. Because of their devotion to citizenship training, indeed, it may be argued that Americans today carry forward the nineteenth-century belief in the power of education to safeguard democratic politics. But when their concern for the political content of formal education has not been simply ritualistic it has often been restrictive and apprehensive, rather than flexible and confident like the best progressive model. In effect, in their rejection of characteristic progressive ideals, the American people have adopted attitudes toward formal political training that complement their skepticism toward informal political education.

On the other hand, Americans have made great strides in extending formal education both vertically and horizontally to take care of new social and economic needs. The progressive generation initiated this development, which has gone on with increasing vigor in every succeeding decade. The 1920s witnessed a rapid increase in high-school education and widespread improvements in public education generally. The 1930s further strengthened existing educational institutions, and they also introduced new pressures to equalize formal educational opportunity and to provide new kinds of education for different social groups. Thanks in part to the G.I. Bill, the 1940s saw more than twice as many students enter college as had entered high school during the 1900s (these figures are in proportion to population), and the 1950s witnessed a vigorous attempt to educate Negroes equally with whites. The Americans are almost universally committed to educating their children as long as education promises to help them achieve a better life economically. What they have questioned is not every form of education but the fundamental progressive belief that democracy depends upon an educational definition of politics as well as a formal educational establishment. They are sure that democracy requires universal educational opportunity.

In other words, while they no longer visualize politics in educational terms Americans remain deeply committed to the idea that they can achieve important social purposes by means of improvements in formal education. The strength of their commitment suggests that their belief is not merely one of the values they hold but a basic social doctrine that has survived the disappearance of most of the influences that originally gave rise to it. During the early nineteenth century Jacksonian democrats and liberal Whigs joined in making universal liberty and universal education the basic tenets of American democratic politics. Confronted by serious social problems after the Civil War, their descendants extended the original ideal of liberty and schools, but without seriously threatening its individualistic and rationalistic premises. If they sometimes advocated legislation to correct social evils, they more frequently turned to informal political agitation to achieve its ends without infringing on personal liberty, and they commonly assumed that the development of additional educational resources of one kind or another would overcome contemporary problems. Hence as late as the progressive era most Americans were still prone to think of reform in terms of individual rights and popular education despite the fact that many of the problems they hoped to deal with were not amenable to these classic prescriptions. They responded to the weaknesses of liberal democracy by attempting to strengthen it, not by doubting it.

With the development and consolidation of large-scale industry, however, the social basis of the liberal ideal disappeared. Not only did disappointed progressives, empirical political scientists, and advocates of business trusteeship repudiate political progressivism; social organization itself made progressive economic values obsolete. (Like traditional liberal doctrine, progressive theory assumed that a competitive economy would provide effectively for most of the needs of society.) Hence progressives typically attempted to revive free competition and to protect economic individualism, and they turned to legislation chiefly to safeguard competition and only incidentally to control its social results. By contrast, modern social theory recognizes that economic competition in the classic sense is seldom effective in an economy that is very largely dominated by oligopolistic combinations of capital and labor, and it holds that even where competition is effective it must be carefully shaped and limited by positive legislation if it is to achieve desirable social ends. Certainly a candid observer would be hard put today to describe our economy in terms of the individual competition progressives generally assumed.

Nevertheless, although the American people commonly accept the economic revolution of the twentieth century, they continue to press for formal education as if it would serve their traditional liberal values. Put to the test, perhaps, they do not really believe that universal education will solve contemporary social problems, any more than they believe that the democratic political process is always wise or that it always responds to wise leadership. Yet they obviously place great faith in the power of their schools and colleges to overcome the defects of their social order by a clearly individualistic method. They have grown skeptical of purely economic competition for success only to substitute educational competition for the rewards that economic competition used to promise. To this extent, at least, they continue to identify democracy with education, and equal rights to education with social and economic democracy.

The fact suggests that, much of the time, the American belief in education serves to explain and also to justify a social order that bears few resemblances to the social order that nineteenth-century democrats postulated. From the Jacksonians through the progressives, American reformers sought to establish an egalitarian competitive society. Modern American society is obviously hierarchically divided and stratified, but the idea of individual competition for economic advancement through education helps to make it acceptable in traditional liberal terms. Indeed, it is not too much to suggest that the American social and economic order today assumes a form which closely parallels the hierarchical structure that characterized colonial and republican society, but that whereas hierarchy was recognized and in fact insisted upon by colonial and republican social theorists it is disguised today by the egalitarian hopes that the idea of democratic education preserves in American thought.

There is a paradox implicit in the Americans' attitudes toward formal education, however. Progressive individualism extended not only to economics but also to politics: progressives generally assumed that when social legislation was necessary to protect disadvantaged social groups it would be arrived at through the rational deliberation of individual citizens led by a process of political and economic education to prescribe cures for the evils they witnessed or experienced. Hence they thought both formal and informal political education were indispensable tools of social progress, supplementing the practical training that supported economic individualism. Yet while the American people today retain a large measure of the competitive economic orientation that characterized the progressive generation, they have repudiated progressive political doctrines that were based upon much the same individualistic assumptions. Although unsophisticated commentators often describe democratic politics as an exercise in popular education, and although professional political leaders publicly invoke the wisdom of the electorate to help resolve major policy issues, modern American thought commonly denies the individual political competence even when it seeks to ensure his economic competence through formal education.

Logically it is possible to dissociate political from economic assumptions; what makes contemporary American attitudes toward individualism and education paradoxical is not their logical incompatibilities but the fact that until recently our democratic theory demanded both individualism and education simultaneously in both political and economic life. Moreover, the terms in which the modern theory of the political process is stated heighten the paradox. The defect of liberal economic theory lay in the fact that the free competition of individuals often failed to serve the general welfare, and sophisticated commentators today characteristically believe that government must deliberately shape a nation's economic life to achieve necessary public ends. Nevertheless, these same observers, who commonly identify democracy with group interactions, also assume that the interplay of group interests and pressures in politics will produce the nearest equivalent of the public welfare that we can hope to attain by political means. Rightly or wrongly, they profess to be satisfied with the outcome of political competition even though they voice dissatisfaction with the outcome of economic competition. Having denied both the rationality and the educability of the electorate they may have no alternative, but it would seem that they have not redeemed democratic theory from the errors the progressives made so much as repeated the progressives' economic error in a different and more culpable fashion.

Indeed, contemporary American attitudes toward democracy and democratic education suggest that our social thought may have gained sophistication without gaining wisdom. Granted, our time-honored theory of democracy had no warrant for assuming that atomistic individuals would reach viable collective decisions through a deliberative political process. Granted, further, that American democratic theory was in error in assuming that popular education could overcome all of the deficiencies in public opinion either by formal training in the schools or by informal training via the processes of politics. Nevertheless, these outmoded theories of democracy also had the advantage of treating intelligence as the only tool men have with which to confront unanticipated contingencies in their lives as social beings as well as in their lives as individuals. Significantly, a commitment to intelligence was common to a transcendentalist like George Bancroft, a common-sense rationalist like Horace Mann, an evolutionary philosopher like Lester Frank Ward, and a pragmatic political commentator like

Walter Lippmann. Although they defined human intelligence in different philosophical terms, all agreed that it is the distinctive weapon men possess for coping with their experience, and all assumed that education is indispensable in a democracy because only widespread intelligence will solve democratic problems.

By contrast, modern theories of democracy seem to deprecate not only the rationality and the educability of the electorate but also the value of intelligence as a technique for reaching political decisions on public issues. Having grown skeptical of individual reason in the political process, most contemporary political theorists take little or no interest in the possibility of rationalizing the political pressures generated by a group-based electorate. Yet the attempt would not be incompatible with their theory of group interaction. Discarding political individualism and deprecating individual political education, they might still hold group participation in politics to a standard of intelligent deliberation, which they might consider enhancing by means of education. Instead, they abandon the attempt to equate democracy with intelligence and substitute an invisible hand for rational deliberation as the definition of democratic politics.*

They abandon the attempt to rationalize popular deliberation; but they also impute educational influences to interest groups competing for public attention and support. On one level, the idea that

---

* The attraction the theory of group competition holds was most strikingly demonstrated in J. K. Galbraith's *American Capitalism: The Concept of Countervailing Power* (1952). Significantly, Galbraith wrote from the left wing of professional economics; his book was neither an apology for business management nor an appeal for business autonomy. He argued, however, that within certain limits the interplay of big business and big labor and big consumers would achieve social and economic goals that progressive reformers had once thought to achieve through deliberate legislation. In effect, Galbraith substituted group competition for deliberation as the substance of modern democratic institutions.

In *The Affluent Society* (1958) Galbraith has recognized some of the defects of a society in which the interaction of major economic groups shapes public policy, and he has undertaken to compensate for them by appealing to a different order of values, largely aesthetic and intellectual. That is, he proceeds by means of a predominantly economic analysis to depict the weaknesses of the society, but behind the practical economic criteria lurks a noneconomic definition of the public welfare. Significantly, Galbraith invokes both "social balance" (a term that may echo his original image of the ideal society as one in which all major groups balance each other) and "a rational social order" (a term that suggests another kind of criterion entirely).

interest groups vie with each other in shaping public opinion may
be no more than an honorific device to dignify public relations and
kindred techniques with the traditional sanctions of democracy.
On another level, however, sophisticated observers who deny that
the processes of politics can be truly deliberative none the less assume that in a group-based society any assertion of a special interest is likely to confront the counterassertion of another interest,
and that if the interplay of conflicting ideas cannot educate public
opinion it will at least set intellectual limits on political manipulation and misrepresentation. In other words, some of the critics of
traditional democratic ideals deny that intelligence can be a criterion of democratic politics yet also assume that it will be a by-
product.

The only major contemporary doctrine that directly confronts the
question of political intelligence is the theory that democratic politics are best understood in terms of political leadership. This is a
point of view that makes both the rationality and the educability of
the electorate incidental to the rationality and the educability of
public officials. Nevertheless, any attempt to ground a theory of
democracy in the intelligence of political elites confronts almost
insurmountable difficulties, for the following reasons. Every theory
of democracy assumes that the electorate will regularly be offered
a choice of public officials and, through them, some choice among
major public policies. (In addition, of course, it assumes that members of the electorate will have access to public officials between
elections; but this assumption is not peculiar to the theory of leadership and is not adequate as a theory of democracy.) Moreover,
no democratic theory can deny a priori that the choice an electorate
exercises may be significant, although various commentators have
pointed out that in a two-party system the most significant choices
are likely to be reached in preliminary stages of the electoral process and not in the final election itself. Yet if a choice may be significant, it obviously invites intelligent deliberation, and the fact
that a democratic electoral process gives sanction and viability to
the choice the voters ultimately make is not in itself a proof that
the choice will in practice be intelligent. Hence the question must

arise whether leadership politics alone are a sufficient guarantee that public policy will follow intelligent paths.

On this point the theory of leadership is no more satisfactory than the theory that group interactions will serve the public welfare. If it asserts that all leaders will behave intelligently it makes choice among them indifferent and thereby denies one of its premises; in addition, it confronts obvious instances of unintelligent leadership. If it asserts that the process of political competition among rival leaders and their parties will produce intelligent public policies apart from the qualifications and motives of the leaders, it simply translates the faith in group competition into leadership terms without solving its characteristic problems. If it asserts that political leaders who differ on issues of public policy can sway public opinion to support the wisest of several alternatives, it both denies the reality of the electorate's choice (which is by definition a matter of political manipulation) and also assumes that the leader who urges the wisest policy will always be most effective in manipulating public opinion. Furthermore, any theory of political leadership almost inevitably involves some recognition of the group as the original source of a political leader's strength and of group interaction as the vehicle of his rise to prominence. Hence it adds the nonrational qualities of the group theory of politics to its own inherent weaknesses as a theory of democracy.

If modern political thought is to convince us that it offers us an adequate theory of democracy, therefore, it may be forced to reconsider the role of popular intelligence and hence of popular education in making democratic politics work. Consensus and peaceful adaptation to change are not the only tests of a viable political order and not the only indispensable conditions of democracy; the intelligence with which a society meets its problems will also affect its health and may even affect its survival. That is, if the decisions reached through our politics are to answer to our needs and to deal with them in ways that promise to secure our long-term welfare as well as serve our immediate purposes, we must concern ourselves some of the time with the quality of the alternatives the public tolerates and with the choices it registers in the political process. Hence we may recognize the group basis of our national life, acknowledge the irrationality and weaknesses of a democratic electorate, and accept the necessity of political leadership, yet insist at the same time that some kinds of popular education are indispensable to a democracy because some kinds of popular intelligence are necessary. In short, we might do well to imitate the progressives in their willingness to explore techniques of popular political education as a corollary of their belief in democracy. If they had reason to apply new forms of education to overcome the defects of populist democracy, we have equal reason to apply it to overcome the defects of contemporary politics.

Nevertheless, to argue that popular political education remains indispensable to an effective democracy is not to support any of the educational formulas with which Americans have been wont to define their political and economic life. This volume has been a history of educational innovations that have not worked for the purposes and in the ways in which they were intended to, and it should caution us against most of the educational ideas that are current in American thought. Clearly, an indiscriminate assertion that democracy consists simply of bigger and better political education of the people will be inadequate. Not every form of political persuasion is conducive to popular intelligence; not every vehicle of informal political "education" is effective in reaching real public issues. Equally clearly, an indiscriminate belief in the values and serviceability of career-oriented education will also be inadequate. Technical education however defined will not overcome abiding social problems and will not develop the range of political intelligence that democratic deliberation requires. Yet no attempt to correct the shortcomings of our politics by inculcating democratic principles in the schools is any more likely to equip the rising generation to deal effectively with a rapidly changing world. Whether the pedagogical techniques employed are to be "progressive" or "conservative" they seem likely to eventuate in democratic pieties, and democratic pieties are hardly a solution for democratic problems. The idea of education is powerful in the United States today without being persuasive, and it will require an extraordinary talent to restate it so that it is both democratic and significant.

Here we face the ultimate paradox of the American people's belief in education. Not only is their idea of formal schooling likely to help disguise an hierarchical social order by appealing to individualistic economic values their society has outmoded; not only is the idea of informal political education likely to help dignify the calculated manipulation of public opinion by labeling it free competition in ideas; but any reaffirmation of the belief in education is likely to sanction unintelligent methods of dealing with national problems by making it seem that our only need is to do the job we have always tried to do, but better. The preservation of American democratic institutions depends upon the reality, not the mythology, of democratic education.

Notes

PART ONE: EARLY PRECEDENTS
AND POLICIES

The quotations are from Clews, ed., *Educational Legislation and Administration*, pp. 355–56, 83–84.

CHAPTER I. COLONIAL PRECEDENTS FOR
DEMOCRATIC EDUCATION

1. The literature on colonial education is endless and uneven. I would have been spared a good deal of relatively fruitless reading had Bernard Bailyn's *Education in the Forming of American Society* been available before 1960. In general I have found the following comprehensive treatments of colonial theory and practice in education most useful for my purposes: Monroe, *Founding of the American Public School System*, Vol. I, chs. 1–7; Edwards and Richey, *The School in the American Social Order*, chs. 1–5; Butts and Cremin, *A History of Education in American Culture*, chs. 2–5; Wright, *Cultural Life of the American Colonies*, ch. 5; Knight, *Public Education in the South*, chs. 2–3; Bridenbaugh, *Myths and Realities*; Jernegan, *Laboring and Dependent Classes in Colonial America*; Curti, *Social Ideas of American Educators*, ch. 1; and Beale, *History of Freedom of Teaching*, ch. 1.

I have also relied heavily upon the following more specialized studies of colonial history: Bridenbaugh, *Cities in the Wilderness*, and also his *Cities in Revolt*; Small, *Early New England Schools*; Morison, *The Puritan Pronaos*; Seybolt, *Apprenticeship & Apprenticeship Education*, chs. 1–4; Ensign, *Compulsory School Attendance*, ch. 2; Kemp, *Support of Schools in Colonial New York*; Wickersham, *History of Education in Pennsylvania*, chs. 1–9; Mulhern, *History of Secondary Education in Pennsylvania*, chs. 1–5; Woody, *Early Quaker Education in Pennsylvania*; Woody, *Quaker Education in the Colony and State of New Jersey*, passim; Wells, *Parish Education in Virginia*; and Virginius Dabney, *Liberalism in the South*, ch. 3.

In addition, there are valuable collections of primary sources in Clews, ed., *Educational Legislation and Administration*; Knight, ed., *Documentary History of Education in the South*, Vol. I; and in the second volume, published in microfilm, of Monroe, *Founding of the American Public School System.*

2. As found in Miller and Johnson, eds., *The Puritans,* p. 701.

3. Clews, ed., *Educational Legislation and Administration,* pp. 59, 72 ff.

4. Samuel Eliot Morison depicts a waning interest in higher education as early as the 1650s, in *Harvard College in the Seventeenth Century,* I, 329–34. Thomas J. Wertenbaker describes the reaction of the New England ministry to their declining schools in chapter 5 of *The Puritan Oligarchy: The Founding of American Civilization* (New York: Scribner's, 1947).

5. See in particular William H. Kilpatrick, *The Dutch Schools of New Netherland and Colonial New York,* Bureau of Education, Bulletin No. 12, 1912 (Washington: Government Printing Office, 1912); also Flick, ed., *History of New York,* II, 3–27, 393, and Clews, ed., *Educational Legislation and Administration,* pp. 198 ff.

6. In addition to Kemp, *Support of Schools in Colonial New York,* see Flick, ed., *History of New York,* III, 49–56 and 70–76.

7. Clews, ed., *Educational Legislation and Administration,* p. 278.

8. In addition to Wickersham, *History of Education in Pennsylvania,* pp. 53–57, and Mulhern, *History of Secondary Education in Pennsylvania,* pp. 12–20 *et passim,* see Dunaway, *History of Pennsylvania,* p. 300.

9. It is probably legitimate to attribute much the same uneven quality to colonial schooling in Rhode Island, and for much the same reasons. Education in Rhode Island depended upon the initiative of the churches, whose variety and stubborn independence virtually precluded *common* schools. See Samuel G. Arnold, *History of the State of Rhode Island* (2 vols.; New York, 1859–60), *passim.*

Preoccupation with religious differences seems also to have inhibited education in both New Jersey and Maryland. Jersey Quakers were restless under the government of New York, while Maryland's Protestants were almost constantly engaged in controversy with that colony's Catholic leaders.

10. Clews, ed., *Educational Legislation and Administration,* p. 359.

11. See Knight, *Public Education in the South,* pp. 36–58, and Wells, *Parish Education in Virginia,* chs. 4–5.

12. As a result of the plantation system, the most efficient way for the wealthy to arrange an education for their children was to hire a private tutor. The existence of such a tutorial system made good schoolmasters even harder to find in Virginia than in Massachusetts, where it was a common practice for college students to teach in the town schools.

13. See Bridenbaugh, *Myths and Realities,* pp. 185–89.

14. In recent years a number of scholars have called theories of colonial

stratification into question. Obviously they are justified insofar as the American colonies could not duplicate European social institutions. But there were significant social distinctions even in the colonies, and—what is more important—colonial authorities were often concerned to maintain whatever distinctions existed. Hence the traditional view, while exaggerated, still has merit. See in particular Labaree, *Conservatism in Early American History*, chs. 1–2; Bridenbaugh, *Cities in the Wilderness, passim*, and *Cities in Revolt, passim*; Bernard Bailyn, "Politics and Social Structure in Virginia," and William H. Seiler, "The Anglican Parish in Virginia," both in James M. Smith, ed., *Seventeenth-Century America*; and Rossiter, *Seedtime of the Republic*, chs. 4–5.

15. See in particular Samuel Eliot Morison, *The Founding of Harvard College* (Cambridge: Harvard University Press, 1935), p. 150.

16. As found in Small, *Early New England Schools*, p. 12.

17. Miller and Johnson, eds., *The Puritans*, p. 19.

18. For the shift in authority in Massachusetts, see Bernard Bailyn, *The New England Merchants in the Seventeenth Century* (Cambridge: Harvard University Press, 1955).

19. Labaree, *Conservatism in Early American History*, ch. 4; Beale, *History of Freedom of Teaching*, ch. 1; and Curti, *Social Ideas of American Educators*, ch. 1, are particularly suggestive on this point.

CHAPTER II. REPUBLICAN INNOVATIONS IN
THEORY AND PRACTICE

1. Many of the general works cited in Chapter I remain pertinent here, especially Monroe, *Founding of the American Public School System*, Vol. I, ch. 8; Edwards and Richey, *The School in the American Social Order*, chs. 6–7; Butts and Cremin, *A History of Education in American Culture*, chs. 6–8; Knight, *Public Education in the South*, chs. 4–5; Curti, *Social Ideas of American Educators*, chs. 1–2; and Beale, *History of Freedom of Teaching*, ch. 2; while Vols. II and III of Knight, ed., *Documentary History of Education in the South*, and Vol. II of Monroe, *Founding of the American Public School System*, bring together valuable source materials.

Certain other works are especially relevant for the republican era: Plaehn, "Early American Political Theory of Public Education" (Unpublished master's thesis, State University of Iowa, 1933); Hansen, *Liberalism and American Education*; Randall, *History of the Common School System*, pp. 1–77; Finegan, *Free Schools*, chs. 2–3; Wickersham, *History of Education in Pennsylvania*, chs. 13–14; Heath, *Constructive Liberalism*, pp. 336–50; and "Constitutional Provisions in Regard to Education in the Several States of the American Union," *Circulars of Information of the Bureau of Education*, 1875, No. 7.

2. The Constitution of Massachusetts (1780), Chapter V, Section II, and see "Constitutional Provisions in Regard to Education."

3. Lincoln, ed., *State of New York. Messages from the Governors*, II, 512, 528; Randall, *History of the Common School System*, pp. 9–11.

4. See Honeywell, *Educational Work of Thomas Jefferson*.

5. Coon, ed., *Beginnings of Public Education in North Carolina*, I, 43 *et passim*.

6. As found in William MacDonald, ed., *Select Documents Illustrative of the History of the United States, 1776–1861* (New York: Macmillan, 1919), p. 27; Richardson, ed., *Messages and Papers of the Presidents*, I, 220.

7. Hansen, *Liberalism and American Education*, pp. 48–62, 110–38, *et passim*.

8. Richardson, ed., *Messages and Papers of the Presidents*, I, 202, 485; Rush, "Plan of a Federal University," as found in Good, *Benjamin Rush*, p. 212.

9. At the Constitutional Convention in Philadelphia, Madison sought an explicit authorization for Congress to establish a national university, and C. C. Pinckney's draft constitution included the authority. But it was eliminated from the final version, partly at least because some delegates felt a specific grant of power for such an obvious purpose was unnecessary. See Wesley, *Proposed: The University of the United States*, pp. 4–5 *et passim;* also Knight, ed., *Documentary History of Education in the South*, II, 8–40.

10. See especially Monroe, *Founding of the American Public School System*, I, 185–221, 296–307, and the accompanying documents in Vol. II; Virginius Dabney, *Liberalism in the South*, ch. 3; and Knight, ed., *Documentary History of Education in the South*, Vols. II and III *passim*.

11. As found in Good, *Benjamin Rush*, p. 202; and see Hansen, *Liberalism and American Education*, *passim*.

12. Statement for use without attribution of source, in a letter to Uriah Forrest, December 31, 1787. See Jefferson, *Papers*, XII, 442n and 478. On contemporary disputes over public policy see in particular Dorfman, *Economic Mind in American Civilization*, Vol. I, chs. 12–18.

13. Jefferson to Cabell, November 28, 1820, in Jefferson, *Writings*, X, 167.

14. Morison, "William Manning's *The Key of Libberty*," *William and Mary Quarterly* (3d ser.), XIII, No. 2 (April, 1956), 202–54, 221.

15. Most of the works cited in note 1 remain indispensable here. I have also relied heavily on Cremin, *The American Common School*,

pp. 28–82 *passim;* Cubberley, *Public Education,* chs. 5–6; Ensign, *Compulsory School Attendance,* ch. 3; and on the more specialized works cited in notes 16 through 21 below.

16. Lincoln, ed., *Messages from the Governors,* II, 1100; *ibid.,* III, 114. See also Fitzpatrick, *The Educational Views and Influence of De Witt Clinton,* and Randall, *History of the Common School System,* pp. 13–23.

17. *Journal of the Twenty-first House of Representatives of the Commonwealth of Pennsylvania* (Lancaster, 1810), pp. 108–14, 109; and see McCadden, *Education in Pennsylvania,* pp. 1–20, 38–44.

18. Handlin and Handlin, *Commonwealth,* p. 249; Farnam, *Chapters in the History of Social Legislation,* pp. 255–56; *A Report of the Debates and Proceedings of the Convention of the State of New-York, 1821,* p. 178.

19. Daveis, "An Address Delivered on the Commemoration at Fryeburg, May 19, 1825," pp. 49–50.

20. *Weekly Register,* X, No. 3 (March 16, 1816), 34–36; XIII, No. 10 (November 1, 1817), 145–47; XIV, No. 10 (May 2, 1818), *Supplement,* 173–75; XXIII, No. 4 (September 28, 1822), 53; XXIII, No. 24 (February 15, 1823), 375–78.

21. Mercer, "A Discourse on Popular Education." On Mercer see Charles W. Dabney, *Universal Education in the South,* I, 36–40. For developments in southern education see not only Dabney but Knight, *Public Education in the South,* chs. 4–6; Virginius Dabney, *Liberalism in the South,* ch. 3; Maddox, *The Free School Idea in Virginia,* chs. 2–7; Heath, *Constructive Liberalism,* pp. 345–50; and Knight, ed., *Documentary History of Education in the South,* Vol. II *passim.*

22. As quoted by Knight, *Public Education in the South,* pp. 130–31.

23. The works cited in note 10 are relevant here, as is Ensign, *Compulsory School Attendance,* ch. 3.

24. See especially Cremin, *The American Common School,* pp. 151–75.

25. Carter, *Essays upon Popular Education,* p. 21; and see Cremin, *The American Common School,* pp. 139–42.

26. See in particular Kenyon, "Conceptions of Human Nature in American Political Thought, 1630–1826" (Unpublished doctoral dissertation, Radcliffe College, 1949).

27. Jefferson, *Writings,* X, 396.

28. In England in 1847 Catholic groups were given a share of public funds, but in New York all religious education under state auspices was barred when the Catholic vote became powerful. On English developments see in particular chapter 11 of J. L. and Barbara Hammond, *The Age of the Chartists;* also E. L. Woodward, *The Age of Reform,*

1815–1870 (Oxford: Clarendon Press, 1938), *passim;* G. D. H. Cole and Raymond Postgate, *The British Common People, 1746–1938* (New York: Knopf, 1939), *passim;* and Raymond G. Cowherd, *The Politics of English Dissent* (New York: New York University Press, 1956), ch. 9.

29. [James Mill], "Education of the Poor," *Edinburgh Review,* XXI, No. 41 (February, 1813), 207–19; Graham Wallas, *The Life of Francis Place, 1771–1854* (rev. ed.; London: George Allen & Unwin, 1925), ch. 4; [Place], "Education," *Westminster Review,* I, No. 1 (January, 1824), 43–79, 79. See also Elie Halévy, *The Growth of Philosophic Radicalism,* trans. Mary Morris (Boston: Beacon, 1955), pp. 282–96, and Thistlethwaite, *The Anglo-American Connection,* ch. 5.

30. Jefferson to Yancey, January 6, 1816, *Writings,* X, 4. Lowe's remark is a staple of British social history; his actual words were "I believe it will be absolutely necessary that you should prevail on our future masters to learn their letters." (*Oxford Dictionary of Quotations* [London: Oxford University Press, 1941], p. 572.)

PART TWO: THE THRUST OF JACKSONIAN LIBERALISM

The quotations are from J. Orville Taylor, ed., *Lord Brougham on Education* (New York, 1839), p. 36, and Thomas Carlyle, Inaugural Address as Rector of the University of Edinburgh, *Critical and Miscellaneous Essays* (5 vols.; New York, 1899–1901), IV, 477.

CHAPTER III. PRELIMINARY DEFINITIONS OF
DEMOCRATIC EDUCATION: THE WORKINGMEN

1. This chapter draws heavily on a few major works. Although somewhat out of date, Vol. I of John R. Commons and others' *History of Labour in the United States* and the primary sources gathered in Vols. V and VI of their *Documentary History of American Industrial Society* were indispensable. Other especially useful works include Pessen, "The Workingmen's Movement of the Jacksonian Era," *Mississippi Valley Historical Review,* XLIII, No. 3 (December, 1956), 428–43; Berrian, "A Brief Sketch of the Origin and Rise of the Workingmen's Party in the City of New York" (a contemporary account); Hugins, *Jacksonian Democracy and the Working Class;* Sullivan, *The Industrial Worker in Pennsylvania;* and Arky, "The Mechanics' Union of Trade Associations and the Formation of the Philadelphia Workingmen's Movement," *Pennsylvania Magazine of History and Biography,* LXXVI, No. 2 (April, 1952), 142–76. Foner, *History of the Labor Movement,* Vol. I, chs. 7–12, is tendentious and uneven but reflects extensive familiarity with the primary sources. Other works that deal primarily with the party affiliations of the work-

ingmen's movement are listed in note 14, below, while works dealing with their educational views are cited in note 3.

2. As quoted by Commons, *History of Labour*, I, 192.

3. As quoted by Commons, *History of Labour*, I, 283, from the *Working Man's Advocate* for September 18, 1830; resolutions adopted at a meeting of "Working Men, Mechanics, and others friendly to their interests," Commons, ed., *Documentary History*, V, 188. The most complete studies of the workingmen's views of education are to be found in Jackson, *America's Struggle for Free Schools*, chs. 15–17; Curoe, *Educational Attitudes and Policies of Organized Labor*, pp. 8–47; and Carlton, *Economic Influences upon Educational Progress*, pp. 72–83. Jackson also traces the evolution of these views in "Labor, Education, and Politics in the 1830's," *Pennsylvania Magazine of History and Biography*, LXVI, No. 3 (July, 1942), 279–93.

4. "Report of the Joint Committees of the City and County of Philadelphia," Commons, ed., *Documentary History*, V, 98, 98–99; Hugins, *Jacksonian Democracy and the Working Class*, pp. 132–34; and see "Address and Resolutions of the Conference Committee of the Wards," Commons, ed., *Documentary History*, V, 158.

5. As quoted by Commons, *History of Labour*, I, 186, from *Mechanics' Free Press*, June 21, 1828.

6. See in particular the "Circular to the Working Men of the City and County of Philadelphia," as quoted by Commons, *History of Labour*, I, 227–28; "Address of the Working Men's Political Association of the Northern Liberties" (June 30, 1829), as quoted *ibid.*, I, 192; and the discussion in *ibid.*, I, 227–332 *passim*.

7. See especially Commons, *History of Labour*, I, 169–332 *passim* and the works cited in note 3.

8. Luther, "An Address to the Workingmen of New England, on the State of Education, and on the Condition of the Producing Classes in Europe and America." Louis Hartz has analyzed Luther's political convictions in "Seth Luther: The Story of a Working-Class Rebel," *New England Quarterly*, XIII, No. 3 (September, 1940), 401–18.

9. Wright, "Address on the State of the Public Mind, and the Measures Which It Calls For," p. 16. See also her "To the Intelligent among the Working Classes," *Popular Tracts*, No. 3, p. 5, and "A Lecture on Existing Evils and Their Remedy," p. 12.

10. New York *Daily Sentinel*, May 29, 1830, as found in Paul Monroe, ed., *Readings in the Founding of the American Public School System* (Vol. II, in microfilm, of his *Founding of the American Public School System*), p. 878; and see Richard W. Leopold, *Robert Dale Owen: A Biography* (Cambridge: Harvard University Press, 1940), pp. 1–102.

11. See Commons, *History of Labour*, I, 245–60. Leopold suggests

(*Robert Dale Owen,* pp. 94–98) that the schism was a product of conservatives' efforts to take over the workingmen's movement, but it seems
unlikely that the Owenite scheme was truly acceptable even to bona
fide workingmen. Compare Cremin, *The American Common School,*
pp. 37–44.

12. Skidmore, *The Rights of Man to Property!* p. 369; Wright, "Parting Address," p. 15.

13. [Brown], *The Radical: And Advocate of Equality,* pp. 10, 127.

14. The shifting focus of the labor movement is depicted in Commons,
History of Labour, I, 335–453. Recent studies show that in Pennsylvania
and to a lesser extent in Boston workingmen affiliated themselves with
the National Republican party after Jackson's attack on the Second Bank
of the United States, although New York workingmen apparently
joined the Democratic party and later the Locofoco party. Nevertheless,
these studies are conclusive only so far as they can trace the activities
of organized workingmen's parties through the careers of their leaders,
or measure the vote for and against Jackson in wards and districts known
to have been occupied by poor people. Although they have cast doubt
on the thesis advanced by Arthur M. Schlesinger Jr., that Jacksonian
Democracy was fundamentally a movement of the urban producing
classes, they have not shown that craftsmen and mechanics who were
disturbed by the rapid development of industrialism and industrial
competition repudiated the liberal democratic principles the Democratic
party ultimately espoused. See Schlesinger, *The Age of Jackson,* chs.
10–16; Sullivan, *The Industrial Worker in Pennsylvania,* pp. 168–207,
and "Did Labor Support Andrew Jackson?" *Political Science Quarterly,*
LXII, No. 4 (December, 1947), 569–80; Pessen, "Did Labor Support
Jackson? The Boston Story," *ibid.,* LXIV, No. 2 (June, 1949), 262–74;
and compare Hugins, *Jacksonian Democracy and the Working Class,* chs.
1–3, 8–10.

15. Evans as quoted by Hugins, *Jacksonian Democracy and the Working Class,* p. 134; and see Commons, *History of Labour,* I, 424–37 *passim,*
and Commons, ed., *Documentary History,* VI, 201, 205–7, 215–16, 247,
255–56.

16. "Address to the Working Men of the District," Commons, ed.,
Documentary History, VI, 118; Massachusetts, *House Documents,* 1842,
No. 4, as quoted by Handlin and Handlin, *Commonwealth,* p. 249; and
see Commons, *History of Labour,* I, 302–25; Commons, ed., *Docu-
mentary History,* V, 192–99; and Persons, "The Early History of Factory
Legislation in Massachusetts," in Kingsbury, ed., *Labor Laws and Their
Enforcement,* pp. 9–26.

17. As quoted in Kingsbury, ed., *Labor Laws and Their Enforcement,*
p. 26.

18. See especially Byrdsall, *History of the Loco-Foco or Equal Rights Party, passim;* also Hugins, *Jacksonian Democracy and the Working Class,* chs. 8–9, and Jabez D. Hammond, *History of Political Parties,* Vol. II, ch. 41.

19. Adam Smith, *An Inquiry into the Nature and Causes of the Wealth of Nations,* ed. Edwin Cannan (New York: Modern Library, 1937), pp. 716–40.

20. See Hovell, *The Chartist Movement, passim,* especially pp. 52–63, 68–69, 200–207; A. E. Dobbs, *Education & Social Movements, 1700– 1850* (London: Longmans, Green, 1919), chs. 5–8; and Thistlethwaite, *The Anglo-American Connection,* pp. 134–40; also R. K. Webb, *The British Working Class Reader, 1790–1848: Literacy and Social Tension* (London: Allen & Unwin, 1955).

CHAPTER IV. THE BROADENING OF DEMOCRATIC
DOCTRINE: THE DEMOCRATIC PARTY OF
THE 1830s AND 1840s

1. Schlesinger, *The Age of Jackson,* remains the best single treatment of the rise of a liberal Democratic party during the 1830s and 1840s; it has the peculiar merit of providing sufficient information to enable its readers to quarrel with its interpretation of disputed points. I have also relied heavily on Darling, *Political Changes in Massachusetts,* and "Jacksonian Democracy in Massachusetts, 1824–1848," *American Historical Review,* XXIX, No. 2 (January, 1924), 271–87; Jabez D. Hammond, *History of Political Parties,* Vols. II and III; Alexander, *A Political History of the State of New York,* Vols. I and II; Klein, *Pennsylvania Politics;* Snyder, *The Jacksonian Heritage;* Hubbart, *The Older Middle West,* ch. 1; and Holt, *Party Politics in Ohio.* Meyers, *The Jacksonian Persuasion,* and Joseph L. Blau's introduction to *Social Theories of Jacksonian Democracy* help to identify lasting Democratic commitments, while Leonard D. White, *The Jacksonians,* discusses a wide range of national policies the party sponsored. Unfortunately, Lee Benson's *The Concept of Jacksonian Democracy: New York as a Test Case* (Princeton: Princeton University Press, 1961) appeared too late to influence my interpretation of the politics of the period; in general, I think it would have changed my vocabulary and some of my perspectives but not the basic thesis.

2. Lincoln, ed., *State of New York. Messages from the Governors,* III, 414–19, 459–76, 507–9, 516–22, 554–59, 564–65, 608–11, 625–33, 647–67.

3. *Ibid.,* III, 420–22, 454–57, 498–99, 536–37, 612.

4. *Ibid.,* III, 454, 611, 454–55.

5. See Cremin, *The American Common School*, pp. 94–103; Randall, *History of the Common School System*, pp. 78–96, 139–97; Jabez D. Hammond, *History of Political Parties*, II, 453, 457–58; Jabez D. Hammond, *Political History of New York*, pp. 379–80, 431–32, 525–26; Lincoln, ed., *Messages from the Governors*, IV, 265–69.

6. Darling, *Political Changes in Massachusetts*, pp. 188–89, 202–11, 260–67, 284–90; "Address of His Excellency Marcus Morton, 1840," *Documents Printed by Order of the House of Representatives of the Commonwealth of Massachusetts*, 1840, No. 9.

7. Massachusetts, *House Documents*, 1840, No. 9, pp. 29–31; *ibid.*, No. 49; and see Cremin, *The American Common School*, pp. 128–45.

8. *Acts and Resolves Passed by the Legislature of Massachusetts in the Year 1843*, pp. 115–29, 120, 117.

9. Rantoul, "Oration at Scituate," *Memoirs, Speeches and Writings*, p. 283; "The Education of a Free People," *ibid.*, p. 115. See also Meyers, *The Jacksonian Persuasion*, ch. 10.

10. See in particular Cremin, *The American Common School*, pp. 104–10; Wickersham, *History of Education in Pennsylvania*, chs. 15–17; Hartz, *Economic Policy and Democratic Thought*, pp. 187–91; and Dunaway, *History of Pennsylvania*, pp. 652–55.

11. Bancroft, "Oration Delivered before the Democracy of Springfield," pp. 31, 10; "The Office of the People in Art, Government, and Religion," *Literary and Historical Miscellanies*, pp. 408 ff.

12. Bancroft, *Literary and Historical Miscellanies*, pp. 422, 428, 430; "Oration Delivered before the Democracy of Springfield," p. 24.

13. Bancroft, "Address at Hartford," p. 13.

14. Leggett, *Writings*, I, 281; and see Nevins, *The Evening Post*, pp. 124–53; Godwin, *A Biography of William Cullen Bryant*, Vol. I, chs. 13, 15, 17–18, 20; Leggett, *Writings*, I, 171–78 *et passim;* Hofstadter, "William Leggett, Spokesman of Jacksonian Democracy," *Political Science Quarterly*, LVIII, No. 4 (December, 1943), 581–94; and Meyers, *The Jacksonian Persuasion*, ch. 9.

15. Whitman, *The Gathering of the Forces*, I, 39, and see *ibid.*, pp. 121–47 *et passim.* As I have already indicated in discussing the liberalism of the workingmen, I propose to deal with the question of internal improvements during the course of a general analysis of democratic theory, which appears in Chapter VII.

16. "Introduction. The Democratic Principle," *United States Magazine and Democratic Review*, I, No. 1 (October–December, 1837), 1–15, 4, 4–5.

17. "France—Its King, Court, and Government. By an American," *Democratic Review*, VII, No. 28 (April, 1840), 357n; "On the Elevation of the Laboring Portion of the Community," *ibid.*, VIII, No. 31 (July,

1840), 57–62; "Of the Intelligence of the People," *ibid.*, VIII, No. 34 (October, 1840), 360–65, 365.

18. Brownson, "The Laboring Classes," *Boston Quarterly Review,* III, No. 11 (July, 1840), 365. See also *ibid.*, I, No. 2 (April, 1838), 229, and IV, No. 15 (July, 1841), 265–90; also Schlesinger, *Orestes A. Brownson,* ch. 3.

CHAPTER V. THE CONSERVATIVE RESPONSE TO DEMOCRATIC THOUGHT: NATIONAL REPUBLICANS AND LIBERAL WHIGS

1. Glyndon Van Deusen characterizes conservative reactions to Jacksonian liberalism in "Some Aspects of Whig Thought and Theory in the Jacksonian Period," *American Historical Review,* LXIII, No. 2 (January, 1958), 305–22. The works cited in note 1 to the previous chapter are also indispensable to an understanding of the evolution of Whig liberalism, and see E. Malcolm Carroll, *Origins of the Whig Party,* and Mueller, *The Whig Party in Pennsylvania.*

2. Story, "Discourse Pronounced before the Phi Beta Kappa Society," pp. 30, 31, 4.

3. Story, "The Science of Government," in American Institute of Instruction, *Introductory Discourse and Lectures, August 1834,* pp. 249–75; Parsons, "Address delivered before the Phi Beta Kappa Society of Harvard University, 27 August 1835," pp. 10, 28.

4. Bushnell, "An Oration, Pronounced before the Society of Phi Beta Kappa, at New Haven, on the Principles of National Greatness, August 15, 1837," in Northup, ed., *Representative Phi Beta Kappa Orations* (2d ed.), pp. 5, 2, 21. Both this Northup collection and its companion volume (second series) illustrate the tenor of Phi Beta Kappa orations.

5. Everett, *Orations and Speeches* (1836 ed.), pp. 378–412, 382. See also "A Discourse on the Importance to Practical Men of Scientific Knowledge" (1827), *ibid.*, pp. 231–64.

6. Everett, "Address of His Excellency, 1836," Massachusetts, *House Documents,* 1836, No. 6, pp. 11, 4, 5–6. See also "Education Favorable to Liberty, Knowledge and Morals" (1835), *Orations and Speeches* (2d ed.), I, 599–633.

7. Everett, "Address of His Excellency, 1836," pp. 11–22; "Address of His Excellency, 1837," Massachusetts, *Senate Documents,* 1837, No. 1, p. 7; Everett, "Superior and Popular Education" (1837), *Orations and Speeches* (2d ed.), II, 206–34, 212, 224.

8. [Channing], "The Abuses of Political Discourse," *North American Review,* IV, No. 11 (January, 1817), 193–201; [Sparks], "Appropriation of Public Lands for Schools," *ibid.*, XIII, No. 33 (October, 1821),

336–38; [Ticknor], "Free Schools of New England," *ibid.*, XIX, No. 45 (October, 1824), 448–57; [Sewall], "Suggestions on Education," *ibid.*, XXX, No. 67 (April, 1830), 323.

9. [Dewey], "Popular Education," *ibid.*, XXIII, No. 52 (July, 1826), 49–67; "Improvement of Common Schools," *ibid.*, XXIV, No. 54 (January, 1827), 156–69; and "Popular Education," *ibid.*, XXXVI, No. 78 (January, 1833), 73–99.

10. *Ibid.*, XXXVI, 73, 74, 78–79.

11. *Ibid.*, p. 81.

12. *Ibid.*, pp. 81, 86, 92, 83, 84.

13. [Rantoul], "Common School Education," *ibid.*, XLVII, No. 101 (October, 1838), 273–318.

14. "American Education," *ibid.*, XLVIII, No. 102 (January, 1839), 310.

15. *Journal of Debates and Proceedings in the Convention of Delegates, Chosen to Revise the Constitution of Massachusetts*, p. 315.

16. Lincoln, ed., *State of New York. Messages from the Governors*, III, 729–38, 801–16, 853–55, 806.

17. *Ibid.*, III, 713–26, 772–76, 881–82. See also Alexander, *A Political History of the State of New York*, II, 15–35.

18. Seward, "Internal Improvements and Education," *Works*, III, 133; Lincoln, ed., *Messages from the Governors*, III, 729–34, 743–44, 727, 817–19.

19. Seward, "Discourse on Education," pp. 5–9, 5, 8; Address at a Sunday-school celebration, July 4, 1839, *Works*, II, 210. Significantly, Seward's *Works* (1853) omits the apprehensive paragraphs that originally introduced the discourse at Westfield Academy. (*Works*, III, 133.)

20. Seward, *Works*, III, 213; "Discourse on Education," pp. 9, 18.

21. See Cremin, *The American Common School*, pp. 165–74, and Shea, *History of the Catholic Church in the United States*, III, 524–32.

22. Lincoln, ed., *Messages from the Governors*, III, 728–29, 882–87, 886, 887; Seward to Birdsall, June 30, 1841, *Works*, III, 489.

23. Stevens's speech will be found in Thomas E. Finegan's *Free Schools*, pp. 59–66; see also Report of the Joint Committee upon Education, *Journal of the Forty-fourth House of Representatives of the Commonwealth of Pennsylvania* (2 vols.; Harrisburg, 1833–34), II, 566–616, which is egalitarian and individualistic in tone, stressing the economic opportunities public education offers. (See especially II, 567, 573.) Sumner's eulogy is quoted in Cubberley, *Public Education*, p. 196n. On developments in Vermont see Ludlum, *Social Ferment in Vermont*, ch. 7. For other Whig views see Jackson, *America's Struggle for Free Schools*, chs. 2–7 *passim*, where, however, the emphasis is on class prejudice and class motivation.

CHAPTER VI. EDUCATIONAL REFORM AND DEMOCRATIC LIBERALISM

1. Part II of Edward A. Fitzpatrick's *The Educational Views and Influence of De Witt Clinton* includes a discussion of his pedagogical principles, while Allen O. Hansen's *Liberalism and American Education* represents the pedagogical as well as the other views of early advocates of systematic public education. The views of other early innovators are described *passim* in the works cited in Chapter II, note 2.

2. Seward's perspective is most apparent in his "Discourse on Education." Everett's views are most clearly reflected in his "Discourse on the Importance to Practical Men of Scientific Knowledge," *Orations and Speeches* (1836 ed.), pp. 231–64; in his Yale Phi Beta Kappa address (1833), *ibid.*, pp. 378–412; in "Superior and Popular Education," *Orations and Speeches* (2d ed.), II, 206–34; and in "Normal Schools" (1839), *ibid.*, II, 335–62.

3. Nye, *George Bancroft*, ch. 3; Whitman, *The Gathering of the Forces*, I, 121–47.

4. The political orientation of professional educators and advocates of education is discussed in Curti, *Social Ideas of American Educators*, ch. 2, and in Jackson, *America's Struggle for Free Schools*, chs. 8–9. The political orientation of leading clergymen is discussed in Cole, *The Social Ideas of the Northern Evangelists*, in May, *Protestant Churches and Industrial America*, chs. 1–2, and in Griffin, "Religious Benevolence as Social Control, 1815–1860," *Mississippi Valley Historical Review*, XLIV, No. 3 (December, 1957), 423–44. Lyman Beecher's *Autobiography* is a classic portrait of a clergyman who sought to restore clerical influence to a society in which the power of the church was decaying.

5. See Hansen, *Early Educational Leadership in the Ohio Valley*; W. H. Venable, *Beginnings of Literary Culture in the Ohio Valley: Historical and Biographical Sketches* (Cincinnati, 1891), especially pp. 409–34; Western Literary Institute, *Transactions*, 1834–1840; and Mosier, *Making the American Mind*.

The Institute was not invariably orthodox in theological matters, for it attracted the support of such a heterodox figure as Alexander Campbell, a founder of the Disciples of Christ, and even Lyman Beecher had to stand trial for heresy in the Presbyterian Church. But the heterodoxy its members displayed did not often extend to political and social matters, and even their theology did not challenge so much as restate Calvinism.

6. Wayland, *The Elements of Political Economy*, pp. 106–65, 326–57, 452–65. See also Wilson Smith, *Professors & Public Ethics*, ch. 7; Dorfman, *Economic Mind in American Civilization*, II, 758–67; and O'Connor, *Origins of Academic Economics*, pp. 172–89.

7. Wayland, *Thoughts on the Present Collegiate System in the United States,* especially pp. 12–37, 53–59, 62–75, 91–99.

8. Wayland to his son, ca. 1861–65, as quoted by Francis and H. L. Wayland, *A Memoir of the Life and Labors of Francis Wayland . . . Including Selections from His Personal Reminiscences and Correspondence* (2 vols.; New York, 1867), II, 294. See also Wayland, "The Education demanded by the People of the U. States."

9. Channing, "Spiritual Freedom. Discourse Preached at the Annual Election, May 26, 1830," *Works,* IV, 67–103.

10. Channing, "Remarks on the Associations Formed by the Working Classes"; "Lectures on the Elevation of the Laboring Portion of the Community," *Works,* V, 223.

11. See Channing, "Remarks on Associations" (1829), *Works,* I, 281–332.

12. Channing, "Remarks on the Associations Formed by the Working Classes," pp. 36–39; "Remarks on Education" (1833), *Works,* I, 369–87, 380, 381; *ibid.,* V, 184.

13. Henry Steele Commager's *Theodore Parker* portrays New England reformers well; see especially pp. 151–53.

14. Parker, "The Mercantile Classes," *Social Classes in a Republic,* p. 23; "The Education of the Laboring Classes," *ibid.,* p. 94; *ibid.,* p. 14. See also Commager, *Theodore Parker,* pp. 161–93, and Aaron, *Men of Good Hope,* ch. 2.

15. Parker, *Social Classes in a Republic,* pp. 17, 18, 18–19; "The Education of the Laboring Classes," *ibid.,* pp. 72–102.

16. *Ibid.,* pp. 87, 88; see also "The Laboring Classes," *ibid.,* pp. 57–71; "Education of the People," *Sins and Safeguards of Society,* pp. 139–77; "The Public Education of the People," *ibid.,* pp. 91–138; and *Lessons from the World of Matter and the World of Man,* pp. 201–3, 206–8, 214, 252.

17. Emerson, entry for September 14, 1839, *Journals of Ralph Waldo Emerson,* ed. Edward W. Emerson and Waldo E. Forbes (Boston: Houghton Mifflin, 1909–14), V, 250.

18. Mann, "Report for 1845," *Life and Works,* IV, 1–104, 37. Mann's social and educational philosophy are ably discussed in Curti, *Social Ideas of American Educators,* ch. 3.

19. Mann, "Report for 1848," *Life and Works,* IV, 287, 292.

20. Mann, "Report for 1843," *ibid.,* III, 287–379, especially pp. 335–44, 365–69, 372–79.

21. *Ibid.,* III, 402–17.

22. Mann, "Report for 1848," *ibid.,* IV, 245–67, 246, 250–51.

23. *Ibid.,* IV, 251–65.

24. Like Mann during the 1840s, Barnard responded to the charge

by stating that either the diffusion of knowledge in Prussia must change the form and spirit of the Prussian government or the government must change the schools. He added that it was impossible for the government to destroy the intelligence that had already been disseminated among the people. Barnard's social and educational philosophy is discussed in Curti, *Social Ideas of American Educators*, ch. 4; and see John S. Brubacher, ed., *Henry Barnard on Education* (New York: McGraw-Hill, 1931), especially pp. 74–75.

25. [Peabody], "The District School Library," *North American Review*, L, No. 107 (April, 1840), 507–8.

CHAPTER VII. RECOGNITION OF THE COMMON PRINCIPLE

1. Lawrence A. Cremin describes some of the controversies that typically surrounded public schooling in *The American Common School*, pp. 83–175 *passim*. Among older works, both Cubberley, *Public Education*, pp. 120–245, and Carlton, *Economic Influences upon Educational Progress*, pp. 45–71, stress resistances.

2. See especially Carlton, *Economic Influences upon Educational Progress*, pp. 45 ff., and Ensign, *Compulsory School Attendance*, chs. 3–7 *passim*.

3. Cubberley, *Public Education*, pp. 315–22, and Monroe, *Founding of the American Public School System*, I, 212–14, 274–93, discuss the district school and its impact, while Edwards and Richey, *The School in the American Social Order*, pp. 421–31, evaluate popular attitudes toward the educational awakening generally. Cubberley, *Public Education*, p. 201, shows the distribution of votes by county in the New York State common school referendum of 1850, while the following works are especially useful in portraying currents of opinion in the Middle West: Buley, *The Old Northwest*, Vol. II, especially pp. 348–69; Hubbart, *The Older Middle West*, pp. 37–39; McAlpine, "The Origin of Public Education in Ohio," *Ohio Archaeological and Historical Quarterly*, XXXVIII, No. 3 (July, 1929), 409–45; and Esarey, *A History of Indiana*, II, 679–707.

4. J. J. Janeway, *Report to the Synod of New Jersey on the Subject of Parochial Schools*, as quoted by Sherrill, *Presbyterian Parochial Schools*, p. 14, which see *passim*; Culver, *Horace Mann and Religion in the Schools*, chs. 5–6.

The issue between Packard and Mann arose in the first place because Mann was authorized to recommend books for district school libraries. Technically, therefore, the controversy that ensued over sectarian teaching in the schools was irrelevant. The Massachusetts legislature had banned sectarian textbooks from the common schools long before the

Board of Education came into being, and in any event Packard was a resident of Pennsylvania whose interest in Massachusetts stemmed from the fact that the American Sunday School Union wished to force its unsalable library upon an indifferent New England. But the very way in which a major controversy built up in spite of these circumstances indicates how important it was to the success of the common school awakening that the alignments and emotions it generated find some common ground.

5. Culver, *Horace Mann and Religion in the Schools,* pp. 105–9.

6. See especially chapters 4–7 and 11 of Billington, *The Protestant Crusade,* which stresses the religious aspect of nativist hostility to immigrants.

7. Cremin, *The American Common School,* pp. 172–75; Beale, *History of Freedom of Teaching,* pp. 93–104.

8. Beecher, *A Plea for the West,* pp. 42, 12.

9. The convention declaration as quoted by Beale, *History of Freedom of Teaching,* p. 101; [Anspach], *The Sons of the Sires,* p. 50.

10. Bushnell, "Common Schools," p. 5. See also Aydelott, "Our Country's Evils and Their Remedy," pp. 35–38; Ely, "American Liberty, Its Sources,—Its Dangers,—and the Means of Its Preservation," especially pp. 15, 18, 21; Porter, *The Educational Systems of the Puritans and Jesuits Compared, passim;* Anna Carroll, *The Great American Battle,* p. 104; and Carroll, *The Star of the West,* p. 476.

11. The activities of the state constitutional conventions are analyzed in Bayrd Still's comprehensive "State Constitutional Developments in the United States, 1829–1851" (Unpublished doctoral dissertation, University of Wisconsin, 1933). In addition to Still, and to the records of conventions themselves, I have found the following works particularly helpful: Jabez D. Hammond, *History of Political Parties,* Vol. II, ch. 27; Hammond, *Political History of New York,* ch. 21; Akagi, "The Pennsylvania Constitution of 1838," *Pennsylvania Magazine of History and Biography,* XLVIII, No. 192 (October, 1924), 301–33; and Arthur C. Cole's introduction to his edition of *The Constitutional Debates of 1847* (Illinois). Moreover, although they do not focus directly on the constitutional conventions, Goodrich, "The Revulsion against Internal Improvements," *Journal of Economic History,* X, No. 2 (November, 1950), 145–69, and Hartz, *Economic Policy and Democratic Thought,* are invaluable for an understanding of the tendencies of contemporary thought.

I am reserving discussion of southern developments and therefore postpone citations to the appropriate sources.

12. In addition to the sources cited in note 11, see Chilton Williamson, *American Suffrage from Property to Democracy, 1760–1860* (Princeton: Princeton University Press, 1960), chs. 10–11, 13.

13. See especially Akagi, "The Pennsylvania Constitution of 1838," *Pennsylvania Magazine of History and Biography*, XLVIII, No. 192 (October, 1924), 301–33, and Snyder, *The Jacksonian Heritage*, chs. 4–6.

14. Dunaway, *History of Pennsylvania*, p. 655; *Proceedings and Debates of the Convention of the Commonwealth of Pennsylvania, 1837*, V, 186, 217, 246, 338, *et passim*. For the delegates' political affiliations, see Snyder, *The Jacksonian Heritage*, Hartz, *Economic Policy and Democratic Thought*, and Sister M. Theophane Geary, *A History of Third Parties in Pennsylvania, 1840–1860* (Washington: Catholic University Press, 1938).

15. See in particular *Proceedings and Debates*, V, 187–88, 194–97, 204–8, 253–61, 294–95, 300, 306–9, 346, 402–6.

16. Snyder, *The Jacksonian Heritage*, p. 109; *Proceedings and Debates*, V, 197, 201, 207–8, 217, 294–95, 301–4, 308–9, 346, 383–84. The quotation is from *ibid.*, V, 294.

17. *Report of the Debates and Proceedings of the Convention for the Revision of the Constitution of the State of New York* (1846), pp. 388 ff., 1022 ff., and 1074 ff.; and see Cremin, *The American Common School*, pp. 99–101, and Finegan, *Free Schools*, chs. 5–10.

18. Arthur C. Cole, ed., *The Constitutional Debates of 1847*, pp. 171–87, 238–49, 898–927, and biographical appendix. Acting in committee of the whole, the convention reduced its committee's elaborate constitutional provisions to a requirement that common school funds be safely invested and a grant of authority to establish a state superintendency. At this point men like Campbell apparently decided not to settle for half measures, and in the end the convention tabled the amended committee report by a vote of 73 to 58 although it was clear that a majority of its members favored some kind of constitutional provision for public education.

19. *Report of the Debates and Proceedings of the Convention for the Revision of the Constitution of the State of Ohio, 1850–1851*, I, 693–94; II, 10–20, 698–711, and biographical data at I, 3 ff.

20. *Ibid.*, II, 15.

21. [Hazewell], "Agrarianism," *Atlantic Monthly*, III, No. 18 (April, 1859), 396.

22. See especially Butts and Cremin, *A History of Education in American Culture*, pp. 165, 177–79; Brubacher, *A History of the Problems of Education*, pp. 135–43; and Grund, *The Americans, in Their Moral, Social, and Political Relations*, ch. 7.

23. Wyllie, *The Self-made Man in America*, pp. 35–37. See also "The Absolute Equality of Mind," *United States Magazine and Democratic Review*, XXIV, No. 127 (January, 1849), 24–33.

24. *First Annual Report of the State Superintendent of Schools,* as quoted by Ludlum, *Social Ferment in Vermont,* p. 237. See also "American Political Ideas," *North American Review,* CI, No. 209 (October, 1865), 550–66.

Representative George W. Julian of Indiana, one of the country's leading advocates of homestead legislation, also testified to the common faith in terms reminiscent of Thomas Skidmore and Orestes Brownson. "The country has been flooded with discourses and essays on the subject of education," he told the House in 1851. "Statistics have been published in the United States, in Great Britain, and in other countries, showing the proportion of the population who are uneducated, and tracing the prevalence of crime to that source. This is all well enough, and no effort certainly should be spared by Governments to educate the masses; but their first and great want is *homes,* and *bread.* Without these, education, and temperance, and preaching, and praying, will fail in the purpose. They will be palliatives at best." (January 29, 1851, *Congressional Globe,* 31st Congress, 2d Session, *Appendix,* p. 137.)

25. Cremin, *The American Common School,* Part III, analyzes educational achievements up to 1850 by reference to developments in Massachusetts, New York, Pennsylvania, Virginia, and Ohio. Monroe, *Founding of the American Public School System,* Vol. I, chs. 9–11, and Cubberley, *Public Education,* chs. 6–9, are still valuable surveys.

26. On Carey see in particular A. D. H. Kaplan, *Henry Charles Carey, a Study in American Economic Thought* (Baltimore:The Johns Hopkins University Press, 1931), pp. 30–36; Arnold W. Green, *Henry Charles Carey, Nineteenth-Century Sociologist* (Philadelphia: University of Pennsylvania Press, 1951), p. 152; Dorfman, *Economic Mind in American Civilization,* II, 789–805; and Carey, *Principles of Political Economy,* especially Vol. I, ch. 21; Vol. II, pp. 182–207 and ch. 16; Vol. III, Part Three, ch. 8, and Part Four, ch. 9. On Lieber, see Bernard E. Brown, *American Conservatives,* pp. 72–100; Lieber, *On Civil Liberty and Self Government, passim,* and *Manual of Political Ethics,* II, 108–38. The quotation is from *On Civil Liberty,* I, 324.

27. Camp, *Democracy, passim;* Grimké, *Considerations upon the Nature and Tendency of Free Institutions,* pp. 56–57.

28. Lieber, *On Civil Liberty,* I, 323–24; *Manual of Political Ethics,* II, 108–38; Camp, *Democracy* (1859 ed.), p. 244; Grimké, *Considerations upon the Nature and Tendency of Free Institutions,* pp. 260–62.

29. Grimké, *Considerations upon the Nature and Tendency of Free Institutions,* p. 265; Carey, *Principles of Political Economy,* II, 199.

30. Emerson, "Education," *Complete Works,* X, 134.

CHAPTER VIII. IRRECONCILABLE DISSENT
FROM ANARCHY

1. *Proceedings and Debates of the Virginia State Convention of 1829–1830*, p. 319.

2. Kent, "An Address Delivered at New Haven before the Phi Beta Kappa Society, September 13, 1831," p. 16; John T. Horton, *James Kent: A Study in Conservatism* (New York: Appleton-Century, 1939), pp. 285–86, 321n.

3. Brownson, "Catholicity Necessary to Sustain Popular Liberty," *Works*, X, 5, 8, 12; and see "Native Americanism," *ibid.*, pp. 31–38.

4. Brownson, "The Church and the Republic," *Works*, XII, 13–14.

5. Brownson, "Schools and Education" (1854), *Works*, X, 564–84; "Public and Parochial Schools" (1859), *ibid.*, XII, 205; *ibid.*, X, 584; *ibid.*, XII, 200–201. On Catholic attitudes toward the school question see Shea, *History of the Catholic Church in the United States*, III, 524 ff., and IV, 108 ff.

6. Knight, *Public Education in the South*, chs. 5–7, and Knight, ed., *Documentary History of Education in the South*, Vol. II *passim;* Charles W. Dabney, *Universal Education in the South*, Vol. I, chs. 2–3; Eaton, *Freedom of Thought in the Old South*, ch. 3; Virginius Dabney, *Liberalism in the South*, ch. 8; Sydnor, *The Development of Southern Sectionalism*, pp. 57–64; Maddox, *The Free School Idea in Virginia*, pp. 97–104; Cremin, *The American Common School*, pp. 110–18. Sydnor discusses county government, *The Development of Southern Sectionalism*, pp. 281–89.

7. Superintendent James Brown Jr. to county commissioners, 1829, as quoted by Maddox, *The Free School Idea in Virginia*, p. 101. In addition to the works cited above, see Green, *Constitutional Development in the South Atlantic States*, especially ch. 4, and Ambler, *Sectionalism in Virginia*, especially ch. 9.

8. See especially Sydnor, *The Development of Southern Sectionalism*, pp. 283–306; Eaton, *Freedom of Thought in the Old South*, ch. 3 *passim;* and *Proceedings and Debates of the Virginia State Convention*, pp. 37–38, 101–2, 104–7, 351–53, 359, 390, 400. Elkins and McKitrick, "A Meaning for Turner's Frontier," *Political Science Quarterly*, LXIX, No. 4 (December, 1954), especially pp. 565–83, also cast light on the meaning of southern democracy.

9. Craven, *The Growth of Southern Nationalism*, pp. 167–270 *passim;* Cremin, *The American Common School*, pp. 179–81. It seems to me that when Frank L. Owsley challenges this point of view, in *Plain Folk of the Old South* (Baton Rouge: Louisiana State University Press, 1949), pp. 146–48, he actually proves what he intends to disprove.

10. I have drawn upon Jenkins, *Pro-Slavery Thought in the Old South;* Lloyd, *The Slavery Controversy,* chs. 4 and 7; and Hartz, *The Liberal Tradition in America,* chs. 6–7, for a general view of proslavery theory. Ralph E. Morrow shows, in "The Proslavery Argument Revisited," *Mississippi Valley Historical Review,* XLVIII, No. 1 (June, 1961), 76–94, that the proslavery argument was directed to a southern rather than a northern audience; what is important here, however, is that it was intended to supersede liberal democratic theory.

11. March 4, 1858, *Congressional Globe,* 35th Congress, 1st Session, *Appendix,* p. 71.

12. January 26, 1842, *Congressional Globe,* 27th Congress, 2d Session, p. 173; MS Executive Minutes of the State of Georgia as quoted by Eaton, *Freedom of Thought in the Old South,* p. 74.

13. February 1, 1836, *Register of Debates in Congress,* 24th Congress, 1st Session, Vol. XII, Part 2, p. 2460.

14. Harper, "Anniversary Oration," pp. 11, 19–21, and see Hammond, "Slavery in the Light of Political Science" (1845), in Elliott, ed., *Cotton Is King,* especially pp. 638–39.

15. Estes, *A Defence of Negro Slavery,* p. 144; Harper, "Slavery in the Light of Social Ethics," in Elliott, ed., *Cotton Is King,* p. 577. See also "Religious Instruction of Slaves," *Southern Quarterly Review,* XIV, No. 27 (July, 1848), 170–83, and "Is Southern Civilization Worth Preserving?" *ibid.* (n.s.), III, No. 5 (January, 1851), 217–23.

16. "Instruction in Schools and Colleges," *Southern Quarterly Review* (n.s.), VI, No. 12 (October, 1852), 460–78, 467, 467–68. See also James Hammond, "The North and the South," *ibid.,* XV, No. 30 (July, 1849), 273–311, especially p. 292; "Free School System in South-Carolina," *ibid.,* XVI, No. 31 (October, 1849), especially pp. 31–33; Archibald Roane, "Common Schools and Universities, North and South," *Commercial Review of the South and West,* XVIII, No. 4 (April, 1855), 552–55; and "The States' Duties in Regard to Popular Education," *ibid.,* XX, No. 2 (February, 1856), 143–56. In general, it should be said, De Bow's *Commercial Review* supported public education; see, for example, IV, No. 4 (December, 1847), 436–50; V, No. 3 (March, 1848), 231–35; XVIII, No. 3 (March, 1855), 409–32; and XXV, No. 4 (October, 1858), 417–30.

17. Harper, "Anniversary Oration," p. 12.

18. D. K. Whitaker, "System of Common Schools," *Southern Quarterly Review,* VI, No. 12 (October, 1844), 453–82; Whitaker, "Education in Europe," *ibid.,* VII, No. 13 (January, 1845), 1–74; "Popular Education," *ibid.* (n.s.), IV, No. 8 (October, 1851), 480–90; "Free School System of South Carolina," *ibid.* (n. s.), II, No. 1 (November, 1856), 125–60; and see Eaton, *Freedom of Thought in the Old South,* pp. 73–74 and

248–60, and Virginius Dabney, *Liberalism in the South,* ch. 8 *passim.*
19. Fitzhugh, *Sociology for the South,* p. 170.
20. Brownson, "Liberal Studies" (1853), *Works,* XIX, 431–33.
21. Fitzhugh, "The Revolutions of 1776 and 1861 Contrasted," *Southern Literary Messenger,* XXXVII, No. 11 & 12 (November and December, 1863), 723.
22. Morse, *Imminent Dangers to the Free Institutions of the United States through Foreign Immigration,* pp. 20–21; "An Argument on the Ethical Position of Slavery in the Social System, and Its Relation to the Politics of the Day," *Papers from the Society for the Diffusion of Political Knowledge,* No. 12, pp. 5–7, 7.

PART THREE: CONFLICT AND CONSENSUS AFTER THE CIVIL WAR

The quotations are from Rutherford B. Hayes's diary, as quoted by Charles R. Williams, *The Life of Rutherford Birchard Hayes* (2 vols.; Columbus: Ohio State Archaeological and Historical Society, 1928), II, 382, and Brooks, *The Social Unrest,* pp. 136–37.

CHAPTER IX. NATIONAL RECONSTRUCTION THROUGH FORMAL EDUCATION

1. Paul Buck, *The Road to Reunion,* p. 23; *Christian Index,* August 4, 1866, as quoted by Coulter, *The South during Reconstruction,* p. 80. See also Buck, *The Road to Reunion,* chs. 1, 3; Coulter, *The South during Reconstruction,* chs. 2–4 *passim;* Fleming, *The Sequel of Appomattox,* pp. 208–9 *et passim;* Fleming, ed., *Documentary History of Reconstruction,* II, 165–74; and Swint, *The Northern Teacher in the South, passim.*
2. Wayland as found in Fleming, ed., *Documentary History of Reconstruction,* II, 172; July 27, 1882, *Congressional Record,* 47th Congress, 1st Session, *Appendix,* p. 588; March 18, 1884, *ibid.,* 48th Congress, 1st Session, p. 1999. See also Curtis, "Political Infidelity" (1864), *Orations and Addresses,* I, 125–48.
3. February 24, 1873, *Congressional Globe,* 42d Congress, 3d Session, p. 1710; Richardson, ed., *Messages and Papers of the Presidents,* VII, 602–3; March 18, 1884, *Congressional Record,* 48th Congress, 1st Session, p. 1999; June 13, 1882, *ibid.,* 47th Congress, 1st Session, p. 4831.
4. *Freedman's Record,* September, 1866, as quoted by Swint, *The Northern Teacher in the South,* p. 84; February 8, 1871, *Congressional Globe,* 41st Congress, 3d Session, p. 1073; January 25, 1872, *ibid.,* 42d Congress, 2d Session, p. 591; February 24, 1883, *Congressional Record,*

47th Congress, 2d Session, p. 3254; and see Du Bois, *Black Reconstruction*, pp. 642–45.

It should be said that some advocates of Negro education apparently intended it to punish southern whites, in that they insisted that the federal government require racially integrated schools. Although various forms of their proposal continued to influence congressional debate after 1876, it was mainly a by-product of Radical Reconstruction. See Kelly, "The Congressional Controversy over School Segregation, 1867–1876," *American Historical Review*, LXIV, No. 3 (April, 1959), 537–63.

5. March 25, 1884, *Congressional Record*, 48th Congress, 1st Session, p. 2244; Washington, *Up from Slavery*, p. 30. See also Du Bois, *Black Reconstruction*, pp. 123, 637–38; Henderson H. Donald, *The Negro Freedman: Life Conditions of the American Negro in the Early Years after Emancipation* (New York: Schuman, 1953), pp. 98–100; Fleming, ed., *Documentary History of Reconstruction*, II, 182–83, 207–28; and Herbert Aptheker, ed., *A Documentary History of the Negro People in the United States* (New York: Citadel, 1951), p. 429.

6. In all likelihood, southern white resistance to education of the freedmen, and especially to academic education of the freedmen, helped to confirm the Negroes' commitment to it. In harassing northern schoolteachers, moreover, southern whites put a premium on academic training just as before the war they had put a premium upon literacy by denying it to Negroes. See especially Jones, "Some Theories Regarding the Education of the Negro," *Journal of Negro Education*, IX, No. 1 (January, 1940), 39–43; also Fleming, *The Sequel of Appomattox*, pp. 211–12, and Simkins and Woody, *South Carolina during Reconstruction*, p. 426.

7. February, 1886, *Congressional Record*, 49th Congress, 1st Session, p. 1482; National Colored Labor Convention, Platform and Memorial to Congress, in Commons, ed., *Documentary History*, IX, 248; and see Fleming, *The Sequel of Appomattox*, pp. 154 ff., 216, and Simkins and Woody, *South Carolina during Reconstruction*, p. 437. Du Bois argues, in *Black Reconstruction*, that in the state constitutional conventions Negroes usually demanded integrated schools. In other respects his book supports my interpretation; see pp. 396–98, 437, 468–69, 491–92, 500, 529–30, 542–43, 576, and ch. 15.

8. Donald, *The Negro Freedman*, pp. 100 ff.; Elsie M. Lewis, "The Political Mind of the Negro, 1865–1900," *Journal of Southern History*, XXI, No. 2 (May, 1955), 195; Fleming, *The Sequel of Appomattox*, pp. 218–20; Coulter, *The South during Reconstruction*, ch. 16; Franklin, *From Slavery to Freedom*, ch. 18.

9. Woodward, *Origins of the New South*, passim.

10. Richardson, ed., *Messages and Papers of the Presidents*, VII, 444;

ibid., VII, 602; James A. Garfield (1881), *ibid.*, VIII, 8–9; Chester A. Arthur (1881), *ibid.*, VIII, 58; (1882), VIII, 143–44; (1883), VIII, 184; Benjamin Harrison (1889), *ibid.*, IX, 54–55. See also Logan, *The Negro in American Life and Thought, passim.*

11. In 1873 the trustees of the Fund used all their influence in Congress to eliminate from a pending civil-rights bill a clause requiring integrated schools in the South. Their principal reason, Barnas Sears explained, was that integration "would overthrow the State systems of free schools, and leave both the blacks and the poor whites, who are now provided for by the rich chiefly, destitute of schools altogether, as private schools would be substituted for public schools." Their judgment was undoubtedly correct, at least in its main outlines, but what is significant here is that the trustees of the Fund proposed to advance public education at the price of ignoring pressing social issues. Moreover, under Sears's direction the Fund made no grants to integrated schools even where they had already been successfully established. See Curry, *George Peabody*, p. 64 *et passim;* also Rubin, ed., *Teach the Freeman*, especially the introduction, Bond, *The Education of the Negro*, ch. 7, and Franklin, *From Slavery to Freedom*, ch. 21.

12. Mayo, "National Aid to Education," p. 11.

13. Washington, *Selected Speeches*, pp. 35–36. See also Curti, *Social Ideas of American Educators*, ch. 7, and Samuel R. Spencer, *Booker T. Washington and the Negro's Place in American Life* (Boston: Little, Brown, 1955). In private, as August Meier and others have pointed out, Washington worked to defeat segregation and disfranchisement of his race, but his public statements emphasized accommodation to existing circumstances and practical education. See Meier, "Toward a Reinterpretation of Booker T. Washington," *Journal of Southern History*, XXIII, No. 2 (May, 1957), 220–27.

14. Washington, *Selected Speeches*, pp. 32–33 *et passim;* and see his address to the National Educational Association (1884), *ibid.*, pp. 1–11; also Bond, *The Education of the Negro*, ch. 6.

15. Fortune, *Black and White*, p. 65 *et passim;* and compare his testimony before the Senate Committee on Education and Labor, *Report of the Committee of the Senate upon the Relations between Labor and Capital*, 48th Congress, 1st Session, II, 527. On Du Bois, see Chaffee, "William E. B. Du Bois' Concept of the Racial Problem in the United States," *Journal of Negro History*, XLI, No. 3 (July, 1956), 241–58, and Francis L. Broderick, *W. E. B. Du Bois: Negro Leader in a Time of Crisis* (Stanford: Stanford University Press, 1959), ch. 3. Other Negro spokesmen also testified in favor of national aid to education: see *Report on Labor and Capital*, Vol. IV *passim.*

16. It also seems plausible that the very vigor with which southern

whites circumscribed Negro education after 1876 helped to preserve the Negroes' belief that education would serve their political and social ends. See in particular Bond, *The Education of the Negro*, ch. 5. Significantly, even in 1935 W. E. B. Du Bois concluded his discussion of achievements in Negro education between 1860 and 1880 by saying: "Had it not been for the Negro school and college, the Negro would, to all intents and purposes, have been driven back to slavery. . . . But already, through establishing public schools and private colleges, and by organizing the Negro church, the Negro had acquired enough leadership and knowledge to thwart the worst designs of the new slave drivers." (Du Bois, *Black Reconstruction*, p. 667.)

17. Part of the interest northern congressmen took in extending federal aid to education according to illiteracy undoubtedly stemmed from their wish to share federal funds that would otherwise have gone exclusively to the South. Nevertheless, they generally agreed upon a distribution of funds according to illiteracy rather than population, although it would have favored the South, whereas a distribution according to population would have favored the North. At any rate, what is most important here is the terms in which northern spokesmen advocated federal appropriations, not the sectional interest that may have motivated them.

18. *Congressional Record*, 48th Congress, 1st Session, p. 2008. Lee, *The Struggle for Federal Aid*, and Going, "The South and the Blair Education Bill," *Mississippi Valley Historical Review*, XLIV, No. 2 (September, 1957), 267–90, describe the agitation.

19. May 29, 1876, *Congressional Record*, 44th Congress, 1st Session, p. 3370; July 27, 1882, *ibid.*, 47th Congress, 1st Session, *Appendix*, p. 588; June 13, 1882, *ibid.*, pp. 4822, 4823. See also Senator Pugh's remarks, December 16, 1880, *ibid.*, 46th Congress, 3d Session, pp. 181–82, and Senator Logan's, March 16, 1882, *ibid.*, 47th Congress, 1st Session, pp. 1955–56.

20. *Proceedings of the Department of Superintendence of the National Educational Association* (Salem, Ohio, 1881), pp. 68–77, 69.

21. Richardson, ed., *Messages and Papers of the Presidents*, VIII, 9; February 16, 1886, *Congressional Record*, 49th Congress, 1st Session, p. 1475; February 2, 1888, *ibid.*, 50th Congresss, 1st Session, p. 908.

The arguments Patterson and others employed were clearly intended to overcome constitutional scruples against appropriating federal funds to so novel a purpose as education, as well as to outmaneuver critics who charged that the whole idea of national aid was intended only to justify a high tariff by spending the government's surplus revenue. (Blair's bill called originally for an appropriation of $105,000,000 over a ten-year period, and subsequently for an appropriation of $67,000,000 over an eight-year period.) Although some of the arguments advanced in favor of federal aid were circumstantial, no one who reads the debates—and especially the debates of the 1880s—can ignore their essentially conservative and even reactionary character.

22. June 13, 1882, *Congressional Record*, 47th Congress, 1st Session, pp. 4824–29; January 17, 1888, *ibid.*, 50th Congress, 1st Session, p. 511; January 17, 1888, *ibid.*, p. 514.

23. December 15, 1880, *Congressional Record*, 46th Congress, 3d Session, pp. 148–49; and compare the statement by Representative Willis of Kentucky, July 26, 1882, *ibid.*, 47th Congress, 1st Session, pp. 6574–75.

In demanding the education of illiterate voters in northern cities, advocates of national aid to common schools both responded to and gave additional force to contemporary pressures to impose a literacy test on prospective voters and prospective immigrants. Connecticut and Massachusetts had established the first literacy tests for the suffrage in 1855 and 1857, and other northern states followed suit after the Civil War. During the 1890s, moreover, conservative leaders like Senator Henry Cabot Lodge mounted a full-fledged campaign to restrict immigration by means of a literacy test. See Kirk H. Porter, *A History of Suffrage in the United States* (Chicago: University of Chicago Press, 1918), pp. 116–19, 229–32, 240–46, and Higham, *Strangers in the Land*, pp. 101–5.

24. See Ross, *Democracy's College*, ch. 9.

25. April 26, 1876, *Congressional Record*, 44th Congress, 1st Session, p. 2762.

26. January 14, 1873, *Congressional Globe*, 42d Congress, 3d Session, p. 566; Atherton, "The Relation of the General Government to Education," NEA, *Addresses and Proceedings*, 1873, p. 68; Andrew D. White, "Scientific and Industrial Education in the United States," p. 19.

27. June 13, 1882, *Congressional Record*, 47th Congress, 1st Session, p. 4831; March 18, 1884, *ibid.*, 48th Congress, 1st Session, p. 2001.

28. Arthur M. Schlesinger describes educational developments before 1900 in *The Rise of the City, 1878–1898* (New York: Macmillan, 1933), pp. 160–72, whereas most histories of education discuss a much longer period. The statistics on high-school attendance are those used by I. L. Kandel in *American Education in the Twentieth Century*, p. 144. Edgar W. Knight indicates the improvements that remained to be achieved in *Fifty Years of American Education, passim*, while Lawrence A. Cremin sketches both the educational strengths and the weaknesses that gave rise to the progressive movement in American education in Part I of *The Transformation of the School*.

29. Curti, *Social Ideas of American Educators*, chs. 6, 10, 12; NEA,

Addresses and Proceedings, passim; [Doty and Harris], *A Statement of the Theory of Education,* especially pp. 11–12. See also McKenna, "Policy Evolution in the National Education Association" (Unpublished doctoral dissertation, Harvard University School of Education, 1954); Wesley, *NEA: The First Hundred Years,* especially ch. 5; and a typical statement of the 1880s, Thomas W. Bicknell's presidential address, NEA, *Addresses and Proceedings,* 1884, pp. 32–75.

30. "How Can Our Schools Best Prepare Law-abiding and Law-respecting Citizens?" NEA, *Addresses and Proceedings,* 1888, pp. 102–26, 115, 123; *ibid.,* 1892, p. 248; *ibid.,* 1895, p. 32. The political perspectives of the industrial education movement were stated as early as 1879; see Proceedings of the Industrial Department, *ibid.,* 1879, pp. 203–14.

31. Angell, "The Development of State Universities," p. 19.

CHAPTER X. THE FARMERS: "ORGANIZATION AND EDUCATION"

1. I have relied mainly upon Shannon, *The Farmer's Last Frontier,* for an understanding of the economic plight of the farmers, although Shannon's interpretation of railroad rates and banking has been sharply challenged by Edward C. Kirkland in *Industry Comes of Age,* chs. 2–4.

2. *Journal of Proceedings of the National Grange of the Patrons of Husbandry,* XIII (1879), 25. Solon J. Buck, *The Granger Movement,* remains the most useful interpretation of the subject.

3. Solon J. Buck, *The Granger Movement,* pp. 103–4, 290–93; Saloutos, *Farmer Movements in the South,* pp. 40–43; *Journal of Proceedings,* XIII (1879), 111–12; XVI (1882), 71; XXV (1891), 182–86; Kansas State Grange, "Education and Industry"; and Report of the Committee on Education, *Proceedings of the Minnesota State Grange,* XXII (1890), 25–26.

4. *Journal of Proceedings,* XVII (1883), 83; and see *ibid.,* X (1876), 106–8; XI (1877), 127–28; XIII (1879), 112–14; XV (1881), 23; XVI (1882), 106–7; XVII (1883), 119–20; XIX (1885), 132; XXIX (1895), 155–59; XXX (1896), 141–46.

5. *Ibid.,* VII (1874), 58; *ibid.,* XIX (1885), 20; and see *ibid.,* XVI (1882), 107–9; XVII (1883), 15, 119–20; XX (1886), 140–41; XXII (1888), 14, 132–36; XXVI (1892), 88–91.

6. Whitehead, "The Origin and Progress of the Grange," p. 7 (unpaged); and see Solon J. Buck, *The Granger Movement,* pp. 279–87; Foster, "The Grange and the Co-op Enterprises in New England," *Annals of the American Academy of Political and Social Science,* IV, No. 5 (March, 1894), 104; and *Journal of Proceedings,* XXIII (1889), 155–56; XXIV (1890), 19; XXVII (1893), 35–36; XXVIII (1894), 30, 186–89; XXIX (1895), 151–55.

7. *Journal of Proceedings,* IX (1875), 6; *ibid.,* XII (1878), 102; D. Wyatt Aiken, "The Grange: Its Origin, Progress, and Educational Purpose," Department of Agriculture, *Special Report* No. 55 (Washington, 1883), p. 3; John W. McArthur, *New Developments: Including the Grange, Anti-Monopoly, Farmers' Alliance, Co-operative Fire Insurance, and the Economic Barn, to Which Is Added An Account of Artificial Butter* (Oneonta, N.Y., 1886), ch. 8; *Journal of Proceedings,* XXVII (1893), 20; Walker, "The Farmer's Movement," *Annals,* IV, No. 5 (March, 1894), 97.

8. For the political activities of the farmers see Haynes, *Third Party Movements,* chs. 6–7; Solon J. Buck, *The Granger Movement,* ch. 3; Solon J. Buck, *The Agrarian Crusade,* pp. 29–59; and Nye, *Midwestern Progressive Politics,* pp. 40–53.

9. *Journal of Proceedings,* IX (1875), 6; Foster, "The Grange and the Co-op Enterprises in New England," *Annals,* IV, No. 5, 105–15; and see *Journal of Proceedings,* XI (1877), 24–25; XII (1878), 72; XIII (1879), 10–11; XIV (1880), 24, 90 ff.; XV (1881), 10–23.

10. *Journal of Proceedings,* XI (1877), 41; *ibid.,* XIV (1880), 24; and see *ibid.,* XII (1878), 72, 101–2, 108; XIV (1880), 109–10; XV (1881), 83; XX (1886), 85–88; XXIX (1895), 155–59.

11. *Proceedings of the Minnesota State Grange,* XXII (1890), 12; *Journal of Proceedings,* XXVIII (1894), 10; and see *ibid.,* XX (1886), 85–88, and *Proceedings of the Minnesota State Grange,* XXIV (1892), 16–20.

12. *Journal of Proceedings,* XXVII (1893), 144–48; *ibid.,* XXIX (1895), 160.

13. *Ibid.,* XXVIII (1894), 185.

14. I have drawn largely on Hicks, *The Populist Revolt,* for an understanding of the Populist movement. Saloutos, *Farmer Movements in the South,* chs. 5–9; Nye, *Midwestern Progressive Politics,* pp. 56–78; and Morgan, *History of the Wheel and Alliance,* are also valuable.

15. The case for understanding the Populist movement as an educational crusade appears in the following paragraphs. In general I accept Richard Hofstadter's interpretation of Bryan and of the campaign of 1896; see Hofstadter, *The American Political Tradition,* pp. 183–90, and *The Age of Reform,* ch. 2.

16. Hicks, *The Populist Revolt,* pp. 128–30; Saloutos, *Farmer Movements in the South,* p. 86; Shannon, *The Farmer's Last Frontier,* pp. 276–80; the declaration as quoted by Morgan, *History of the Wheel and Alliance,* p. 327. See also *National Economist,* I, No. 23 (August 24, 1889), 353, and V, No. 1 (March 21, 1891), 6–7; Allen, *The Life and Services of Weaver,* pp. 388–89, 523; and Morgan, *History of the Wheel and Alliance,* pp. 74, 94, 150, 279, 334.

17. Hicks, *The Populist Revolt*, pp. 128–32; Saloutos, *Farmer Movements in the South*, p. 75; and see *National Economist*, I, No. 3 (April 6, 1889), 38; I, No. 23 (August 24, 1889), 353; *et passim* 1889–92.

18. *National Economist*, II, No. 8 (November 9, 1889), 113; Ashby, *The Riddle of the Sphinx*, especially Part II, ch. 7; Peffer, *The Farmer's Side*, especially Part III, ch. 5.

19. As quoted by Allen, *The Life and Services of Weaver*, p. 401; as quoted by Morgan, *History of the Wheel and Alliance*, p. 92; *National Economist*, V, No. 15 (June 27, 1891), 227. See also Morgan, *History of the Wheel and Alliance*, pp. 14, 279, 327, and Fred E. Haynes, *James Baird Weaver* (Iowa City: State Historical Society of Iowa, 1919), pp. 340–41.

20. *National Economist*, V, No. 1 (March 21, 1891), 7; Vincent Bros. Publishing Company, *Populist Hand-Book for Kansas*, p. 3; and see Morgan, *History of the Wheel and Alliance*, p. 753.

21. *National Economist*, V, No. 25 (September 5, 1891), 385; and compare *ibid.*, V, No. 8 (May 9, 1891), 117–19.

22. *Ibid.*, VII, No. 16 (July 2, 1892), and following numbers.

23. Morgan, *History of the Wheel and Alliance*, especially pp. 1–39; Watson, *Not a Revolt*, chs. 16–17; Howard, *The American Plutocracy*, p. 29; and see Allen, *The Life and Services of Weaver*, p. 380, and Haynes, *Weaver*, chs. 15–16.

24. *National Economist*, I, No. 5 (April 20, 1889), 76; Vincent Bros., *Populist Hand-Book for Kansas*, p. 3; and see *National Economist*, V, No. 13 (June 13, 1891), 198–99.

25. C. B. Hoffman in *Agora*, April, 1895, as quoted by Mott, *A History of American Magazines*, IV, 177; and see Hubbard, *The Coming Climax in the Destinies of America*, *passim*.

26. Howard, *The American Plutocracy*, p. 103; Bryan, *The First Battle*, p. 277.

Significantly, one of the reasons the Populists postponed their convention until after the Democrats had nominated their presidential candidate was the belief that no silver candidate could overcome the money interests and the party bosses entrenched in the Democratic party. Hence Bryan's dramatic victory at the Democratic convention seemed a striking evidence of the success of the farmers' methods.

It should be added that there was an additional powerful reason for accepting Bryan: southern whites were reluctant to abandon the Democratic party lest they undermine white supremacy. But by 1896 thoroughgoing Populists were deeply alienated from the Democratic party, not eager to find grounds of collaboration.

27. Lloyd to [Richard T. Ely], October 10, 1896, as quoted by Caro Lloyd, *Henry Demarest Lloyd, 1847–1903: A Biography* (2 vols.; New York: Putnam's, 1912), I, 264.

28. Shannon, *The Farmer's Last Frontier*, pp. 275–76; Cremin, *The Transformation of the School*, pp. 43 (note 5) and 43 ff.

CHAPTER XI. THE LABOR MOVEMENT: ACCOMMODATION
AND EDUCATION

1. I have depended heavily on a few major works for an understanding of divergent tendencies within the postbellum labor movement. Vol. II of John R. Commons and others' *History of Labour in the United States* and Vol. IX of their *A Documentary History of American Industrial Society* are indispensable although limited in scope and perspective. Ware, *The Labor Movement*, rectifies many of the oversights in the Commons volumes, while Curoe, *Educational Attitudes and Policies of Organized Labor*, pp. 70–92 and 101–88, is a useful special study. Foner, *History of the Labor Movement*, Vol. I, chs. 17–25, and Vol. II, is anecdotal and highly colored. Probably the best single work on the ideological tensions of the period is Gerald N. Grob, *Workers and Utopia: A Study of Ideological Conflict in the American Labor Movement, 1865–1900* (Evanston, Ill.: Northwestern University Press, 1961), which appeared too late to guide my own research although parts of it had appeared in articles.

2. In addition to Commons, *History of Labour*, II, 3–194, *Documentary History*, Vol. IX, and Ware, *The Labor Movement*, ch. 1, see the contemporary treatment in McNeill and others, *The Labor Movement*, ch. 5.

3. Sylvis, *Life of Sylvis*, especially pp. 96–127; Commons, *History of Labour*, II, 132n; and see *ibid.*, II, 86–134; Jonathan Grossman, *William Sylvis, Pioneer of American Labor: A Study of the Labor Movement during the Era of the Civil War* (New York: Columbia University Press, 1945), chs. 10–11; and Grob, "Reform Unionism: The National Labor Union," *Journal of Economic History*, XIV, No. 2 (Spring, 1954), 126–42, on Sylvis and the National Labor Union.

4. Sylvis, *Life of Sylvis*, pp. 124, 444.

5. Steward, "The Meaning of the Eight Hour Movement," especially pp. 5–6; see also "A Reduction of Hours an Increase of Wages" in Commons, ed., *Documentary History*, IX, 284–301, especially p. 297, and McNeill, *The Labor Movement*, chs. 5–6 *passim*.

6. Steward, "The Meaning of the Eight Hour Movement," p. 11; resolutions as quoted by Commons, *History of Labour*, II, 89.

7. Commons, *History of Labour*, II, 86–101, 124–46; Ware, *The Labor Movement*, pp. 6–19.

8. Phillips, "The Labor Question," *Speeches, Lectures and Letters*, p. 171; "Remarks of Wendell Phillips, at the Mass Meeting of Working-

men in Faneuil Hall, November 2, 1865," p. 15; *Speeches, Lectures, and Letters*, p. 176.

9. See in particular Ware, *The Labor Movement*, chs. 2–5, 7; Commons, *History of Labour*, II, 332–55; and Powderly, *Thirty Years of Labor, passim*.

10. *Report of the Committee of the Senate upon the Relations between Labor and Capital*, 48th Congress, 1st Session, I, 37–38, 11.

11. *Ibid.*, III, 543; Ware, *The Labor Movement*, pp. 80–91, 302–3; Powderly, *Thirty Years of Labor*, pp. 157–58; Knights of Labor, *Record of Proceedings*, II (1879), 62; and see Foner, *History of the Labor Movement*, II, 75–76, 81.

12. *Journal of United Labor*, V, No. 7 (August 10, 1884), 763; Goodhue, "Educational, Industrial, and Political Functions of the K. of L.: Address Delivered at Aurora, Ills., December 15 . . . ," *Knights of Labor* (Chicago), I, No. 38 (December 23, 1886), 2; *Report on Labor and Capital*, I, 38; Powderly, *Thirty Years of Labor*, pp. 279–81.

13. Curoe, *Educational Attitudes and Policies of Organized Labor*, pp. 80–92; Powderly, *Thirty Years of Labor*, p. 159; Knights of Labor, *Record of Proceedings*, I (1878), 29.

14. Knights of Labor, *Record of Proceedings*, X (1886), 41.

15. Commons, *History of Labour*, II, 301–31, 357–429; Ware, *The Labor Movement*, chs. 8–12.

16. *Report on Labor and Capital*, I, 460, and see Reed, *The Labor Philosophy of Samuel Gompers*.

17. Curoe, *Educational Attitudes and Policies of Organized Labor*, pp. 102 ff., and see AFL, *Proceedings, 1881 . . . 1888*, 1881, p. 3; 1882, p. 3; 1885, p. 3; *Proceedings, 1889 . . . 1892*, 1889, p. 37; 1891, p. 32; *Proceedings, 1893 . . . 1896*, 1895, p. 60; Gompers, editorial, *American Federationist*, XVIII, No. 4 (April, 1911), 300; and Gompers, *Labor and the Common Welfare*, pp. 101–7.

18. *Report on Labor and Capital*, I, 449, 456–57, 459–60.

19. AFL, *Proceedings, 1893 . . . 1896*, 1894, p. 30; AFL, *Report of Proceedings*, 1898, p. 6.

20. *Report of the Industrial Commission*, VII, 620; *ibid.*, p. 718. See also AFL, *Proceedings, 1881 . . . 1888*, 1887, p. 30, and *Proceedings, 1889 . . . 1892*, 1891, p. 32, where the Committee on Resolutions urged compulsory elementary schooling in terms reminiscent of the Jacksonian workingmen. During the first decade of the twentieth century, moreover, the *American Federationist* published a number of articles enthusiastically demanding universal education as a vehicle of social and economic liberation. (See *American Federationist*, IX, No. 10 [October, 1902], 691; X, No. 4 [April, 1903], 262; X, No. 10 [October, 1903], 1031–33; XIII, No. 12 [December, 1906], 968–69.)

21. See American Federation of Labor, "Labor and Education: A

Brief Outline of the Resolutions and Pronouncements of the American Federation of Labor . . . , 1881–1938" (n.p.: American Federation of Labor, n.d.).

22. Farmers found a political equivalent for collective bargaining after the turn of the century in the deliberate organization of a farm-bloc pressure group. In effect, while they refused to revive their campaign of popular education, they sought to use political organization to compel the economy to yield them a greater return on their labor. Their activities were political, but in a wholly new sense that earlier farm spokesmen would have repudiated, as both Grant McConnell and Richard Hofstadter have pointed out.

CHAPTER XII. MIDDLE-CLASS LIBERALISM AFTER
THE CIVIL WAR: POPULAR EDUCATION AND
CIVIL SERVICE REFORM

1. Middle-class liberalism after the Civil War has seldom been studied for its own sake. Probably the best single treatment is that of Alan P. Grimes in *American Political Thought*, pp. 295–309, which draws on his *The Political Liberalism of the New York Nation, 1865–1932*. I have also found the following works useful or suggestive: Merriam, *American Political Ideas*, ch. 10; Cochran and Miller, *The Age of Enterprise*, ch. 8; Fine, *Laissez Faire and the General-Welfare State*, chs. 3–4; Kirkland, *Business in the Gilded Age*, and *Dream and Thought in the Business Community*, especially ch. 5; Nevins, *The Evening Post*, pp. 444–502; Mott, *A History of American Magazines*, Vols. III and IV; and Ross, *The Liberal Republican Movement*. Irvin G. Wyllie shows, in *The Self-made Man in America*, ch. 5, that business spokesmen often looked askance at Social Darwinism but not that they abandoned economic individualism.

2. Curtis, "The Good Fight," *Orations and Addresses*, I, 151–77, 152, 156, 164. See also *Proceedings of the National Civil-Service Reform League*, 1883, p. 27 (Curtis); 1893, pp. 31–32 (Carl Schurz); and 1894, p. 107 (William Dudley Foulke).

3. Godkin, "Aristocratic Opinions of Democracy," *Problems of Modern Democracy*, pp. 1–67; Lowell, "Democracy," *Literary and Political Addresses*, pp. 7–37; Eliot, "The Working of the American Democracy," *American Contributions to Civilization*, pp. 71–102.

4. Eliot, *American Contributions to Civilization*, p. 87; Atkinson, "How Society Reforms Itself," *Forum*, VII, No. 1 (March, 1889), 18–29, 29; and see Eliot, "Some Reasons Why the American Republic May Endure" (1894), *American Contributions to Civilization*, especially pp. 49–50, and "Five American Contributions to Civilization" (1896), *ibid.*, especially pp. 23–25.

5. Godkin, "The Democratic View of Democracy," *North American*

Review, CI, No. 208 (July, 1865), especially pp. 114–18; Lowell, "The Place of the Independent in Politics," *Literary and Political Addresses,* p. 195; Atkinson, "How Society Reforms Itself," *Forum,* VII, No. 1, 18–29; Eliot, *American Contributions to Civilization,* pp. 79–80.

6. Eliot, "The Function of Education in a Democratic Society," *Educational Reform,* pp. 401–18, 413; Curtis, "The Public Duty of Educated Men," *Orations and Addresses,* I, 264. Eliot also invoked the expert in "One Remedy for Municipal Misgovernment" (1891), *American Contributions to Civilization,* pp. 173–202, while William Watts Folwell, president of the University of Minnesota, repeatedly urged scholarly training of public servants. (See his *University Addresses* [Minneapolis: Wilson, 1909].) But "scholars in politics" typically advocated little more than a liberal education. (See Northup, ed., *Representative Phi Beta Kappa Orations* and *Representative Phi Beta Kappa Orations* [2d ser.], *passim;* also Thomas Le Duc, *Piety and Intellect at Amherst College, 1865–1912* [New York: Columbia University Press, 1946].)

7. Bullock, "Intellectual Leadership in American History," Northup, ed., *Representative Phi Beta Kappa Orations* (2d ed.), pp. 128–51, 150; Schurz, Address before the Harvard Phi Beta Kappa, pp. 78–79. See also Curtis, "The American Doctrine of Liberty" (Harvard Phi Beta Kappa address, 1862), *Orations and Addresses,* I, especially pp. 110–11; "The Spirit and Influence of Higher Education" (1884), *ibid.,* I, 339–66; *ibid.,* I, 281–82; Godkin, "Role of the Universities in Politics" (1876?), *Reflections and Comments,* pp. 155–62; Eliot, *American Contributions to Civilization,* pp. 24–27; *Educational Reform,* pp. 417–18; Emory Washburne, "The College as an Element of the State" (Yale Phi Beta Kappa address, 1869), Northup, ed., *Representative Phi Beta Kappa Orations* (2d ser.), especially pp. 164–80; James W. Patterson, "The Relations of Education to Public Questions" (Dartmouth Phi Beta Kappa address, 1875), *ibid.,* 185–206; Charles W. Baird, "The Scholar's Duty and Opportunity" (University of the City of New York Phi Beta Kappa address, 1886), *ibid.,* especially p. 259.

8. Schurz, Address before the Harvard Phi Beta Kappa, p. 4; Lowell, Harvard Anniversary Address, *Literary and Political Addresses,* pp. 158–59; and see Northup, ed., *Representative Phi Beta Kappa Orations* (2d ed.), pp. 139–43, and *ibid.* (2d ser.), pp. 163, 205–6.

9. [Godkin], " 'Educated Men' in Centennial Politics," *Nation,* XXIII, No. 1 (July 6, 1876), 6; Curtis, "The Leadership of Educated Men," *Orations and Addresses,* I, 331–32; Godkin, "The Duty of Educated Men in a Democracy," *Forum,* XVII, No. 1 (March, 1894), 39–51.

10. Schurz, Address before the Harvard Phi Beta Kappa, p. 47; Northup, ed., *Representative Phi Beta Kappa Orations* (2d ed.), p. 150.

11. As quoted by Nevins, *The Evening Post,* p. 543.

12. Curtis, "Education and Local Patriotism," *Orations and Addresses,* I, 478, and compare Mill's rectorial address at St. Andrews in 1867 as quoted by Charles F. Thwing, *A History of Education in the United States since the Civil War* (Boston: Houghton Mifflin, 1910), p. 52.

13. The case for this admittedly uncomplimentary view is made in the paragraphs that follow. For data on the reform movement, in addition to the works cited in note 1 see Stewart, *The National Civil Service Reform League,* chs. 1–3; also Leonard D. White, *The Republican Era,* ch. 13, and Matthew Josephson, *The Politicos, 1865–1896* (New York: Harcourt, Brace, 1938), *passim.*

14. *Proceedings of the National Civil-Service Reform League,* 1886, p. 22.

15. Lowell, "The Place of the Independent in Politics," *Literary and Political Addresses,* p. 210; *Proceedings of the National Civil-Service Reform League,* 1893, pp. 26, 16; and see Schurz, *ibid.,* 1894, pp. 10–12.

16. In addition to Ross, *The Liberal Republican Movement,* see Haynes, *Third Party Movements,* chs. 2–5.

17. Curtis, *Orations and Addresses,* I, 280; Lowell, *Literary and Political Addresses,* pp. 212–13; Adams, "Individuality in Politics," p. 13; and see Godkin, "Legislation and Social Science" (A paper read before the American Social Science Association, March 18, 1870) (n.p., n.d.), and *Nation,* XXIII, No. 1, 5–6.

18. Adams, "Individuality in Politics," p. 15.

19. Eaton, *Civil Service in Great Britain,* chs. 17, 28; *ibid.,* p. iii; *Proceedings of the National Civil-Service Reform League,* 1883, pp. 25–26; and see Schurz, *ibid.,* 1893, p. 15.

20. Eaton, *Civil Service in Great Britain,* p. 381, ch. 29; *Proceedings of the National Civil-Service Reform League,* 1890, pp. 12–13.

21. *Proceedings of the National Civil-Service Reform League,* 1890, pp. 50–51; *ibid.,* 1888, p. 24.

22. Eaton, "The 'Spoils' System and Civil Service Reform in New York," pp. 84–85; *Proceedings of the National Civil-Service Reform League,* 1889, p. 43; *ibid.,* 1890, p. 46; Stewart, *The National Civil Service Reform League,* p. 16 *et passim.*

23. *North American Review,* CI, No. 208, 117–20; Grimes, *The Political Liberalism of the Nation,* ch. 1.

24. Godkin, "Idleness and Immorality," *Problems of Modern Democracy,* pp. 197, 198.

25. Godkin, *Unforeseen Tendencies of Democracy,* pp. 31–47, 76–79, 90–95, 132–44, 209–22.

26. Phillips, "The Scholar in a Republic," *Speeches, Lectures, and Letters,* p. 344. Significantly, Phillips appended a footnote to his oration in which he criticized Curtis for demanding merit examinations for the

civil service. Phillips proposed to substitute local elections of postmasters and other officials. (*Ibid.*, p. 363n.)

27. Curoe, *Educational Attitudes and Policies of Organized Labor,* pp. 91–92.

28. See particularly J. L. M. Curry, "Citizenship and Education," NEA, *Addresses and Proceedings,* 1884, pp. 4–16, 13.

29. James H. Smart, Inaugural Address, *ibid.,* 1881, p. 12.

30. *Ibid.,* 1892, p. 575.

31. *Report of the Committee of the Senate upon the Relations between Labor and Capital,* 48th Congress, 1st Session, III, 351; *ibid.,* I, 1089–90; *ibid.,* III, 329–32.

CHAPTER XIII. KEEPERS OF THE MIDDLE-CLASS CONSCIENCE

1. Gladden, *Tools and the Man,* ch. 5; Bascom, *Sociology,* pp. 229–30.

The social gospel is discussed with great insight in Hopkins, *The Rise of the Social Gospel,* chs. 1–3 *passim,* and in May, *Protestant Churches and Industrial America,* pp. 91–234. I have also found useful Abell, *The Urban Impact on American Protestantism,* Mann, *Yankee Reformers in the Urban Age,* ch. 4, Fine, *Laissez Faire and the General-Welfare State,* ch. 6, and Dombrowski, *The Early Days of Christian Socialism,* ch. 1.

2. Abbott, *Christianity and Social Problems,* pp. 186, 124–25, and compare Gladden, *Tools and the Man,* chs. 3–4. Abbott's social thought is capably discussed in Brown, *Lyman Abbott,* pp. 79–112.

3. Gladden, *Applied Christianity,* p. 100 and ch. 3 *passim;* Abbott, *Christianity and Social Problems,* p. 125 and pp. 66 ff., 179 ff., and 223 ff.; and see Gladden, *Tools and the Man,* chs. 1, 10, and Hopkins, *The Rise of the Social Gospel,* pp. 67–76.

4. Gladden, *Applied Christianity,* pp. 18, 19, 17–18, and ch. 1 *passim.* See also Gladden, *Tools and the Man,* ch. 7; *Social Facts and Forces, passim;* Abbott, *Christianity and Social Problems,* pp. 115–24, 203–23; Newton, *Social Studies,* pp. 51–79; Bascom, *Sociology,* ch. 8; and the discussions in May, *Protestant Churches and Industrial America,* pp. 169–82; Hopkins, *The Rise of the Social Gospel,* pp. 79–102; Abell, *The Urban Impact on American Protestantism,* pp. 70–76; Mann, *Yankee Reformers in the Urban Age,* ch. 4; Fine, *Laissez Faire and the General-Welfare State,* pp. 179–88; and Brown, *Lyman Abbott,* pp. 104–9.

5. See especially Gladden, *Applied Christianity,* chs. 1, 2, and 4; *Tools and the Man,* chs. 1, 5, and 8; Abbott, *Christianity and Social*

Problems, pp. 194–203, 351–70; Nicholas Paine Gilman, *Profit-Sharing between Employer and Employee: A Study in the Evolution of the Wages System* (Boston, 1889); Newton, *Social Studies,* pp. 363–65; and Brown, *Lyman Abbott,* pp. 97–104.

6. See especially Abell, *The Urban Impact on American Protestantism,* pp. 81–116; Gladden, *Applied Christianity,* chs. 5 and 7; *Social Facts and Forces, passim;* Bascom, *Sociology;* and C. R. Henderson, *The Social Spirit in America* (Meadville, Pa., 1897).

One of the products of ethical concern over contemporary social evils was the settlement house, which was also the source of a good deal of the raw material that went into Christian sociology. See Bremner, *From the Depths,* pp. 60–66, and the testimony of witnesses before the United States Industrial Commission (*Report of the Industrial Commission,* XIV, 78–95, 114–28, 197–204).

7. Gladden, *Applied Christianity,* pp. 166–67; *Report of the Industrial Commission,* XIV, 2.

8. *Report of the Industrial Commission,* XIV, 11; Newton, *Social Studies,* p. 365; and see May, *Protestant Churches and Industrial America,* pp. 26–36, 125–30, and Mann, "British Social Thought and American Reformers of the Progressive Era," *Mississippi Valley Historical Review,* XLII, No. 4 (March, 1956), 672–92.

9. Newton, "Old-Time Guilds and Modern Commercial Associations," *Social Studies,* pp. 153–71; Gilman, *Socialism and the American Spirit,* p. 299; Gladden, *Applied Christianity,* p. 22. See also Abbott, *Christianity and Social Problems,* pp. 203 ff., and Newton, *Social Studies,* pp. 29–41.

10. Gladden, *Social Salvation,* ch. 1; *Social Facts and Forces,* p. 39. It is true that in *Tools and the Man* Gladden spoke favorably of increasing the political power of municipalities on the grounds that "I am not at all sure that a considerable extension of the functions of government would not arouse our people, as nothing else has done, to attend to their political duties. At any rate I am quite ready to see the experiment tried." (*Tools and the Man,* p. 285.) Nevertheless, the very phrasing of his statement suggests that he hoped political power would rouse chiefly the better classes, and in any event this is a rare instance in his writings of locating education in actual political experience.

11. Newton, *Social Studies,* pp. 364–65; Gladden, *Social Salvation,* p. 192 and ch. 6 *passim; Applied Christianity,* ch. 8. See also Newton, *Social Studies,* pp. 22–26, 199–212, 215–57, and his chapter on industrial education in McNeill and others, *The Labor Movement;* also Abbott, *Christianity and Social Problems,* pp. 186 ff.; Brown, *Lyman Abbott,* pp. 102–4; and Rev. Charles Francis Donovan, S.J., "Education in American Social Thought, 1865–1900: Educational Ideas of Social

Scientists and Social-Minded Clergymen" (Unpublished doctoral dissertation in education, Yale University, 1948), ch. 5.

12. My judgment of George and Bellamy has been very largely shaped by William H. Brubeck's unpublished doctoral dissertation, "The American as Radical, 1870–1900" (Harvard University, 1952), pp. 9–182, but it also draws upon Aaron, *Men of Good Hope*, chs. 3–4; Dombrowski, *The Early Days of Christian Socialism*, chs. 3 and 8; and Morgan, *Edward Bellamy*.

13. George, *Social Problems*, pp. 25–29, 49–54; *Progress and Poverty*, pp. 273–79, 277, 277–78.

14. *Report of the Committee of the Senate upon the Relations between Labor and Capital*, 48th Congress, 1st Session, I, 514. After the Civil War as well as before it, the idea of public ownership of indispensable means of transportation and communication was compatible with extreme economic individualism in other realms.

15. *Report on Labor and Capital*, I, 514; George, *Progress and Poverty*, pp. 477–78; *Social Problems*, pp. 20, 327.

16. *Report on Labor and Capital*, I, 512.

17. George, *Social Problems*, p. 331; *Progress and Poverty*, p. 423.

18. Nevertheless, it is significant that in his testimony before the Senate Committee on Education and Labor, George remarked that he had not given any thought to formal measures of intellectual or industrial education. (*Report on Labor and Capital*, I, 515.) Like other middle-class reformers, and in contradistinction to spokesmen for the farmers and organized labor, he was interested only in the educational processes that directly supported his reforms.

19. Bellamy, *Equality*, pp. 269, 340.

20. *Ibid.*, pp. 207–10, 305–7, 307, 330, 331.

21. *Ibid.*, pp. 336, 324–30, 330.

22. Ely, *The Labor Movement in America*, especially pp. 120, 303n, 309–12; *Social Aspects of Christianity*, p. 122. Ely is discussed in chapter 3 of John R. Everett's *Religion in Economics;* in Sidney Fine's essay "Richard T. Ely, Forerunner of Progressivism, 1880–1901," *Mississippi Valley Historical Review*, XXXVII, No. 4 (March, 1951), 599–624; in Dombrowski, *The Early Days of Christian Socialism*, ch. 4; and in Noble, *The Paradox of Progressive Thought*, ch. 7. Commons is discussed in Dorfman, *Economic Mind in American Civilization*, III, 276–94.

23. Commons, *Social Reform and the Church*, pp. 51, 96.

24. William H. Brubeck's doctoral dissertation, "The American as Radical," pp. 183–264, has very largely affected my thinking about Lloyd as about George and Bellamy, but I have also found helpful Aaron, *Men of Good Hope*, ch. 5, Dombrowski, *The Early Days of Christian Socialism*, ch. 12, and Noble, *The Paradox of Progressive Thought*, ch. 6. Chester M.

Destler points out, in chapter 7 of *American Radicalism,* that Lloyd intended *Wealth against Commonwealth* as an essay in popular education.

25. See in particular Lloyd, *Man, the Social Creator,* chs. 1, 5–8, and 11, and "The Scholar in Contemporary Practical Questions" (1895), *Mazzini and Other Essays,* pp. 147–89.

26. Brooks, *The Social Unrest, passim;* Rauschenbusch, *Christianity and the Social Crisis,* p. 409 *et passim.* See also Brooks, *Labor's Challenge to the Social Order: Democracy Its Own Critic and Educator* (New York: Macmillan, 1920); Rauschenbusch, *Christianizing the Social Order* (New York: Macmillan, 1912); and the discussions of Rauschenbusch in Noble, *The Paradox of Progressive Thought,* ch. 10, and in Hopkins, *The Rise of the Social Gospel,* pp. 131–34.

CHAPTER XIV. DEMOCRATIC EDUCATION IN
AN EVOLUTIONARY SOCIETY

1. Like everyone who explores the impact of evolutionary theory, I am heavily indebted to Richard Hofstadter's *Social Darwinism in American Thought,* and to Stow Persons, ed., *Evolutionary Thought in America.* I have also found McCloskey, *American Conservatism in the Age of Enterprise,* and Fine, *Laissez Faire and the General-Welfare State,* chs. 2–3, suggestive.

2. Sumner, "The Challenge of Facts," *The Challenge of Facts,* p. 37. See also Hofstadter, *Social Darwinism,* ch. 3, and Gabriel, *The Course of American Democratic Thought,* ch. 19.

3. Fine, *Laissez Faire and the General-Welfare State,* pp. 32–46; Harris E. Starr, *William Graham Sumner* (New York: Holt, 1925), pp. 195 ff.; Hofstadter, *Social Darwinism,* p. 47.

In *What Social Classes Owe to Each Other* (1883), it is true, Sumner criticized universal education at public expense even when it was urged for reasons of political safety, but it is clear from the context that he wished chiefly to attack those who claimed education and other advantages as rights against the "Forgotten Man" who had to pay for them. When he recognized political dangers he was more tolerant of tax-supported schools.

4. Sumner, "Purposes and Consequences," *Earth-Hunger,* pp. 72–74; "Protectionism, the -ism Which Teaches That Waste Makes Wealth," *The Forgotten Man,* p. 38; and see "The First Steps toward a Millennium," *Earth-Hunger,* pp. 98–101.

5. Sumner, "The Teacher's Unconscious Success," *Earth-Hunger,* pp. 10–11; see also "Liberty and Responsibility," *ibid.,* pp. 170, 177–78; "Integrity in Education," *The Forgotten Man,* pp. 409–15; "Discipline," *ibid.,* pp. 423–38.

6. Ward, *Dynamic Sociology*, II, 17 *et passim*, especially I, 30–39, 71–81, 480–699, and II, 1–17. Hofstadter, *Social Darwinism*, ch. 4, Gabriel, *The Course of American Democratic Thought*, pp. 204–9, and Fine, *Laissez Faire and the General-Welfare State*, pp. 253–64, have useful discussions of Ward's thought, but the most pertinent study for my purpose is chapters 4 and 5 of Kimball, *Sociology and Education*.

7. Ward, *Dynamic Sociology*, I, 21; *ibid.*, II, 468; and see *ibid.*, I, 71–81, and II, 95–103, 161–252.

8. *Ibid.*, II, 591, 107–9, 597; and see *ibid.*, II, 400–633.

9. Ward, *The Psychic Factors of Civilization*, p. 301; *Dynamic Sociology*, II, 235; and see *ibid.*, I, 18–25, and II, 156–57, 211, 227, 359–66, 410–19, 534–39, 578–79, and 593–97.

10. There are thoughtful evaluations of Carnegie in Gabriel, *The Course of American Democratic Thought*, ch. 13, and in McCloskey, *American Conservatism in the Age of Enterprise*, ch. 6. In addition to the works cited hereafter, see Carnegie, "Popular Illusions about Trusts," *The Gospel of Wealth*, pp. 85–103, and *Problems of To-day*, *passim*.

11. Carnegie, *Triumphant Democracy*, pp. 101, 135; "The Advantages of Poverty," *The Gospel of Wealth*, pp. 69–70; and see "Democracy in England" (1886), *ibid.*, pp. 211–12.

12. Carnegie, *The Gospel of Wealth*, pp. 29, 30–31; and see "The Common Interest of Labour and Capital" (1889), *The Empire of Business*, pp. 71–99.

13. See particularly Sumner, "Theory and Practice of Elections" and "Presidential Elections and Civil-Service Reform," *Collected Essays*, pp. 98–139 and 140–59, and "Republican Government" and "Democracy and Responsible Government," *The Challenge of Facts*, pp. 223–40 and 243–86.

14. Sumner, *The Challenge of Facts*, p. 37; "Laissez-faire," *Essays of William Graham Sumner*, II, 469, 476–77.

15. As quoted by Starr, *William Graham Sumner*, p. 222.

16. Ward, *The Psychic Factors of Civilization*, p. 315; *Dynamic Sociology*, II, 398; *ibid.*, II, 251–52. See also "True and False Civil Service Reform," *Glimpses of the Cosmos*, IV, 105–13.

17. Ward, *Dynamic Sociology*, I, 37–44, 137–38, 359; II, 227–52; *The Psychic Factors of Civilization*, pp. 301–12, 307.

18. Ward, *The Psychic Factors of Civilization*, p. 309.

19. Jordan, "The Scholar in the Community" (1893), *The Care and Culture of Men*, p. 93.

20. Gilman, *Socialism and the American Spirit*, p. 340; and see Dorfman, *Economic Mind in American Civilization*, III, 104, 131, 263, and Nye, *Midwestern Progressive Politics*, p. 26.

PART FOUR: TWENTIETH-CENTURY INNOVATIONS

The quotations are from Croly, *Progressive Democracy*, p. 423, and David E. Lilienthal, "Science and the Spirit of Man" (February 6, 1949), as found in Avery Craven and others, eds., *A Documentary History of the American People* (Boston: Ginn, 1951), pp. 863–64.

CHAPTER XV. THE PROGRESSIVE SYNTHESIS

1. A great deal of literature dealing with progressivism has accumulated in recent years, but it has usually been biographical and genetic rather than ideological in approach. Hence my treatment of the phenomenon draws heavily on earlier interpretations, especially Filler, *Crusaders for American Liberalism*, Chamberlain, *Farewell to Reform*, and De Witt, *The Progressive Movement*. I have also been guided by Merriam, *American Political Ideas, passim*; Hofstadter, *The American Political Tradition*, chs. 9–10, and *The Age of Reform*, chs. 4–6; Goldman, *Rendezvous with Destiny*, chs. 8–10; Nye, *Midwestern Progressive Politics*, chs. 4–6; Edward R. Lewis, *A History of American Political Thought*, chs. 8 and 12; and Mowry, *The Era of Theodore Roosevelt, passim*.

2. National Economic League, *The Initiative and Referendum*, p. 48; Wilcox, *Government by All the People*, p. 95; and see Abbott, "The Rights of Man," *Outlook*, LXVIII, No. 7 (June 15, 1901), 396–401, and Schafer, "Oregon as a Political Experiment Station," *Review of Reviews*, XXXIV, No. 2 (August, 1906), 175.

The direct-government movement is analyzed in some detail in Edward R. Lewis, *A History of American Political Thought*, ch. 12, and in De Witt, *The Progressive Movement*, chs. 10–11. Perhaps the best means of gaining perspective on the whole development, however, is the numerous compilations of excerpts from contemporary articles on proposed reforms that the H. W. Wilson Company published. See in particular Edith M. Phelps, comp., *Selected Articles on the Initiative and Referendum* (Minneapolis, 1909); Phelps, comp., *Selected Articles on the Recall, Including the Recall of Judges and Judicial Decisions* (2d ed., rev. and enl.; New York, 1915); C. E. Fanning, comp., *Selected Articles on the Election of United States Senators* (2d ed., rev.; Minneapolis, 1912); and Fanning, comp., *Selected Articles on Direct Primaries* (4th ed., rev.; New York, 1918).

3. Haynes, *The Election of Senators*, p. 268; National Economic League, *The Initiative and Referendum*, p. 16; Lobingier, "Direct Popular Legislation: The Chief Objections Examined," *Arena*, XXXIV, No. 3

(September, 1905), 237; and see Fox, "Popular Election of United States Senators," *Arena*, XXVII, No. 5 (May, 1902), 455–67; also "Results in Oregon of Direct Legislation," *American Federationist*, XVIII, No. 3 (March, 1911), 225–26.

4. "Direct Legislation Movement," *Independent*, LXIV, No. 3093 (March 12, 1908), 596; Academy of Political Science, *The Revision of the State Constitution*, I, 18; and see Senator Jonathan Bourne Jr., "Functions of the Initiative, Referendum and Recall," *Annals of the American Academy of Political and Social Science*, XLIII, No. 132 (September, 1912), 3–16, and Mackenzie, "Direct-Vote System," *Arena*, XXXIX, No. 2 (February, 1908), 140.

5. Academy of Political Science, *The Revision of the State Constitution*, I, 18, 19, 18.

6. Mackenzie, "Direct-Vote System," *Arena*, XXXIX, 140; Wilcox, *Government by All the People*, pp. 278–79; and see Theodore Roosevelt, "The Meaning of Free Government" (1912), *Works*, XVII, 173–74.

7. Roosevelt, "A Charter of Democracy," *Works*, XVII, 122–23; Roe, "Recall of Judges," *Proceedings of the Academy of Political Science*, III, No. 2 (January, 1913), 142; and see Overton, "Democracy and the Recall," *Forum*, XLVII, No. 2 (February, 1912), 164–65.

8. Roosevelt to E. A. Van Valkenberg, as quoted in Joseph B. Bishop, *Theodore Roosevelt and His Time* (2 vols.; New York: Scribner's, 1920), II, 414; Ross, *Changing America*, p. 106; and see Roosevelt, "The Right of the People to Rule" (1912), *Works*, XVII, 170, and "The Meaning of Free Government," *ibid.*, XVII, 174.

9. Wilson, *The New Freedom*, ch. 6, pp. 115–16, 123–25. See also Wilson, *A Crossroads of Freedom*, pp. 82–85, 102–3, 121, 145–47, 181, 195, 241, 247–56, 317–18, 470; and compare Wilson, *Congressional Government: A Study in American Politics* (Boston, 1885), ch. 6; "Character of Democracy in the United States" (1889), *An Old Master, and Other Political Essays* (New York, 1893), pp. 99–138; "Democracy and Efficiency" (1901), *College and State* (Vols. I and II of *Public Papers*), I, 396–410; and *Constitutional Government in the United States* (New York: Columbia University Press, 1908), ch. 8. See also Hofstadter, *The American Political Tradition*, ch. 10, and Younger, "Woodrow Wilson— the Making of a Leader," *Virginia Magazine of History and Biography*, LXIV, No. 4 (October, 1956), 387–401; and Howard J. McMurray, "American Politics in Transition," in Bruce Bliven, ed., *Twentieth Century Unlimited, from the Vantage Point of the First Fifty Years* (Philadelphia: Lippincott, 1950), p. 136.

10. Wilson, *The New Freedom*, p. 225 and ch. 10 *passim;* and see *A Crossroads of Freedom*, pp. 84, 147.

11. La Follette, *Autobiography, passim;* and see Chamberlain, *Farewell to Reform,* pp. 237–56.

12. La Follette, *Autobiography,* pp. 240–41; *ibid.,* pp. 64–70, 224–40, 302–3, 388–89, and see Torelle, ed., *The Political Philosophy of La Follette,* pp. 13–59 *passim.*

13. La Follette, *Autobiography,* pp. 388–89; *ibid.,* pp. 40–52, 64–70; and see Torelle, ed., *The Political Philosophy of La Follette,* p. 53, Owen, "The Progressive and Government," *La Follette's Weekly Magazine,* IV, No. 34 (August 24, 1912), 512, and Johnson, *My Story, passim.*

14. See, for example, Beard, *American City Government: A Survey of Newer Tendencies* (New York: Century, 1912); Goodnow, *Politics and Administration: A Study in Government* (New York: Macmillan, 1900) and *Social Reform and the Constitution* (New York: Macmillan, 1911); Ford, *The Rise and Growth of American Politics: A Sketch of Constitutional Development* (New York, 1898) and "Direct Legislation and the Recall," *Annals,* XLIII, No. 132, 65–77; Commons and John B. Andrews, *Principles of Labor Legislation* (New York: Harper, 1916). Criticisms of progressive scholarship multiply; see particularly White, *Social Thought in America, passim;* Hartz, *The Liberal Tradition in America,* ch. 9; and Crick, *The American Science of Politics, passim.*

15. C. C. Regier's *The Era of the Muckrakers* describes the journalistic effort in considerable detail. Steffens's views are developed in *The Shame of the Cities,* especially pp. 3–15, and in *The Struggle for Self-Government, passim.* See also *The Autobiography of Lincoln Steffens* (New York: Harcourt, Brace, 1931), especially pp. 374–449.

16. Baker as quoted by Bremner, *From the Depths,* p. 140; Flower, *Progressive Men, Women, and Movements of the Past Twenty-five Years* (Boston: New Arena, 1914), p. 151.

17. Ross, *Sin and Society,* pp. 40, vii.

18. Ross, *Changing America,* preface.

19. Lawrence A. Cremin touches on the fundamental similarities in *The Transformation of the School, passim.*

20. La Follette, *Autobiography,* pp. 26–32, 102–4, 203, 359–60; Torelle, ed., *The Political Philosophy of La Follette,* pp. 55, 65–66, 289–308; and see Maxwell, *La Follette and the Rise of the Progressives in Wisconsin,* ch. 9, and Van Hise, "The Place of the University in a Democracy" (Address before the NEA in 1916), *School and Society,* IV, No. 81 (July 15, 1916), 81–86.

21. McCarthy, *The Wisconsin Idea,* p. 138 and pp. 16–18, 21–23, 67–69, 124–53, 172–78, 185–232, and 287.

22. Howe, *Wisconsin: An Experiment in Democracy,* pp. 39, 189, xi. See also Ross, *Changing America,* ch. 10, and Lincoln Steffens's descrip-

tion of the Wisconsin idea (1909) as quoted by Cremin, *The Transformation of the School*, pp. 167–68.

23. Educational developments are best seen in the perspective of short-term histories of recent developments, for example Kandel, ed., *Twenty-five Years of American Education;* Knight, *Fifty Years of American Education, passim;* Charles H. Judd, "Education," in *Recent Social Trends* (Report of the President's Research Committee on Social Trends) (2 vols.; New York: McGraw-Hill, 1933), Vol. I, ch. 7; Kandel, *American Education in the Twentieth Century;* and Cremin, *The Transformation of the School.* Theodore Saloutos and John D. Hicks point out that even in 1910 only the University of Wisconsin among state universities really served farmers' needs as businessmen (*Agricultural Discontent in the Middle West, 1900–1939* [Madison: University of Wisconsin Press, 1951], pp. 67–68).

24. Figures on high-school attendance are difficult to interpret because it is impossible to determine what age group should be used as a base in measuring prospective attendance. A recent government tabulation indicates that 8.4% of the population aged 14 through 17 was in public secondary day schools in 1900; 12.7% in 1910; 23.9% in 1920; 44.3% in 1930; and 59.8% in 1938. An older tabulation shows 9% of the population aged 16 through 19 enrolled in 1900; 13% in 1910; 29% in 1920; and 50% in 1928. Furthermore, another recent tabulation shows that 6.4% of the population aged 17 had graduated from high school in 1900; 8.8% in 1910; 16.8% in 1920; 29.0% in 1930; and 50.8% in 1940. The older tabulation also shows that in 1908 only 30.9% of first-year high-school students had reached the fourth year, whereas 44.3% had reached it in 1916 and 53.5% had reached it in 1928. See Office of Education, *Statistics of Public Secondary Day Schools, 1951–1952* as quoted by Kandel, *American Education in the Twentieth Century*, p. 144; Office of Education, *Biennial Survey of Education, 1926–1928* (Washington: Government Printing Office, 1930), p. 958; Bureau of the Census, *Historical Statistics of the United States: Colonial Times to 1957* (Washington: Department of Commerce, 1960), p. 207; and *Biennial Survey of Education, 1926–1928*, p. 976.

25. See note 23.

26. Gladden, *Recollections* (Boston: Houghton Mifflin, 1909), pp. 430–31.

27. For acute if somewhat tendentious estimates of progressive social theory see Hartz, *The Liberal Tradition in America*, ch. 9, and Hofstadter, *The Age of Reform*, chs. 5–6. Andrew M. Scott has justifiably taken Hofstadter to task for some of his exaggerations, in "The Progressive Era in Perspective," *Journal of Politics*, XX, No. 4 (November, 1959), 685–

701, but he has not proved that the progressives anticipated the philosophy of the New Deal.

28. See, for example, Ross, *Changing America*, ch. 1; Roosevelt, "The New Nationalism," *Works*, XVII, 3–22; and *American Federationist*, XVIII, No. 3 (March, 1911), 198–200, and XIX, Nos. 8–12 (August–December, 1912), 618–22, 694–98, 840–43, 926–31, 1021–26.

29. Filler, *Crusaders for American Liberalism*, p. 341.

CHAPTER XVI. THE PROGRESSIVE PHILOSOPHY

1. Croly, *The Promise of American Life*, p. 278; also chs. 6, 9; and see Kaplan, "Social Engineers as Saviors: Effects of World War I on Some American Liberals," *Journal of the History of Ideas*, XVII, No. 3 (June, 1956), 351–56, which discusses Croly's elitist tendencies. Charles Forcey provides a useful summary of Croly's career in *The Crossroads of Liberalism, passim*.

2. Croly, *The Promise of American Life*, p. 269 and ch. 11.

3. *Ibid.*, pp. 196, 199, and ch. 7 *passim*.

4. *Ibid.*, pp. 402, 404, and ch. 13 *passim*. David W. Noble examines the utopianism of Croly's thought in chapter 3 of *The Paradox of Progressive Thought*, where I think he lays too much stress on its apocalyptic overtones and too little on the educational theories that related Croly's hopes to reality.

5. Croly, *Progressive Democracy*, especially chs. 1–3, 7, 10, and 13.

6. *Ibid.*, pp. 38, 279.

7. *Ibid.*, chs. 5, 9.

8. *Ibid.*, pp. 210, 210–11, and see chs. 8 and 19.

9. Arthur M. Schlesinger Jr. has discussed Lippmann perceptively in Marquis Childs, ed., *Walter Lippmann and His Times*, ch. 11, while Stow Persons has stressed his intellectual roots in *American Minds*, ch. 22. Forcey, *The Crossroads of Liberalism*, has useful material on Lippmann as well as Croly.

10. Lippmann, *A Preface to Politics*, especially chs. 1 and 6.

11. *Ibid.*, ch. 4, pp. 106, 107. Sidney Kaplan discusses Lippmann's elitism in *Journal of the History of Ideas*, XVII, No. 3, 356–59.

12. Lippmann, *A Preface to Politics*, p. 147 and ch. 7.

13. *Ibid.*, pp. 250, 306–7.

14. *Ibid.*, pp. 307, 305.

15. Lippmann, *Drift and Mastery*, p. 169 and chs. 2, 5, and 8.

16. *Ibid.*, ch. 9, pp. 179–80, 189.

17. *Ibid.*, ch. 14, pp. 273, 276, 272, 277.

18. The discussion that follows is based exclusively upon *Democracy*

and Education, inasmuch as my purpose is neither to trace the development of Dewey's philosophy nor to account for it, but to examine this major work in educational philosophy in the context of the progressive era. I have found Sidney Hook's *John Dewey: An Intellectual Portrait* (New York: John Day, 1939) useful in outlining the major dimensions and issues of Dewey's thought in a nontechnical fashion.

19. Dewey, *Democracy and Education,* especially chs. 1–4, 11–12, 14.

20. *Ibid.,* chs. 5, 8, 24.

21. *Ibid.,* chs. 7–9; p. 145; and see Curti, *Social Ideas of American Educators,* ch. 15.

22. Bourne, *Education and Living,* p. v.

23. Dewey, *Democracy and Education,* p. 125.

CHAPTER XVII. THE CONSERVATIVE RESPONSE, THEN AND NOW

1. These are admittedly strong words, but I think that the evidence to follow will bear them out. In my approach to systematic conservatism during the progressive era I have depended heavily on Merriam, *American Political Ideas, passim,* and to a lesser extent on Edward R. Lewis, *A History of American Political Thought,* ch. 9. For the period after 1920 I have depended equally heavily upon Prothro, *The Dollar Decade,* and Sutton and others, *The American Business Creed.*

2. Campbell, "Representative Government *versus* the Initiative and Primary Nominations," *North American Review,* CXC, No. 2 (August, 1909), 225; National Economic League, *The Initiative and Referendum,* p. 34; Taft, *Popular Government,* p. 25. The compilations of excerpts from contemporary articles cited in note 2 of Chapter XV also provide an admirable guide to conservative opinion of direct-government proposals.

3. Taft, *Popular Government,* p. 25; Root, "Experiments in Government," in *Addresses on Government and Citizenship,* p. 95.

4. Hill, *Americanism,* p. 78. See also Lodge, "The Constitution and Its Makers" (1911), *The Democracy of the Constitution,* pp. 32–87; Hill, *The People's Government, passim;* Butler, *Why Should We Change Our Form of Government?,* especially the preface and the title essay (1911); and Guthrie, "Nominating Conventions" (1915), *Magna Carta, and Other Addresses,* pp. 219–46.

5. Hill, *The People's Government,* pp. 212–13; Wickersham, "College Men and Public Questions," *The Changing Order,* p. 35.

6. Brown, "The Judicial Recall—a Fallacy Repugnant to Constitutional Government," *Annals of the American Academy of Political and Social Science,* XLIII, No. 132 (September, 1912), 246; Dougherty, "Substi-

tutes for the Recall of Judges," *Proceedings of the Academy of Political Science*, III, No. 2 (January, 1913), 150.

7. *Report of the Thirty-seventh Annual Meeting of the American Bar Association* (Baltimore: American Bar Association, 1914), p. 611; Hadley as quoted by Judson, *The Judiciary and the People*, p. 169; and see Root, "Essentials of the Constitution" (1913), in *Addresses on Government and Citizenship*, pp. 98–117; Lodge, "The Constitution and the Bill of Rights" (1912), *The Democracy of the Constitution*, pp. 106–21; and Guthrie, "Constitutional Morality" (1912), *Magna Carta, and Other Addresses*, pp. 42–85.

8. Root, "Judicial Decisions and Public Feeling," *Proceedings of the New York State Bar Association*, 1912, p. 153. Root's argument was especially striking in view of the fact that the eminent constitutional lawyer James Bradley Thayer had deplored the diseducational effects of judicial legislation on public opinion in his biography of John Marshall. "Great and, indeed, inestimable as are the advantages in a popular government of this conservative influence,—the power of the judiciary to disregard unconstitutional legislation,—it should be remembered," he wrote, "that the exercise of it, even when unavoidable, is always attended with a serious evil, namely, that the correction of legislative mistakes comes from the outside, and the people thus lose the political experience, and the moral education and stimulus that come from fighting the question out in the ordinary way, and correcting their own errors." (Thayer, *John Marshall* [Boston: Houghton Mifflin, 1901], p. 106.)

9. For an illustration of conservative appeals to formal education, see Samuel W. McCall, "Representative Legislation" (1911), in Munro, ed., *The Initiative Referendum and Recall*, p. 192.

10. Hadley, "An Educated Democracy," *University of California Chronicle*, XII, No. 3 (July, 1910), 208, 209; *Standards of Public Morality*, especially ch. 3; and see "Government by Public Opinion" (1901?), *The Education of the American Citizen*, p. 33; "The Development of Public Spirit" (1901), *Baccalaureate Addresses*, pp. 184, 188 ff.; and *Undercurrents in American Politics* (1915), especially pp. 90–93.

11. Nicholas Murray Butler also adopted much the same view in *Is America Worth Saving? passim;* and see Charles M. Hollingsworth, "The So-called Progressive Movement: Its Real Nature, Causes and Significance," *Annals*, XLIII, No. 132, 32–48, and Frank, *The Politics of Industry*, especially the foreword and pp. 152–59. Morrell Heald describes other origins of managerial theory in "Management's Responsibility to Society: The Growth of an Idea," *Business History Review*, XXXI, No. 4 (Winter, 1957), 375–84.

To the extent that Theodore Roosevelt's agitation of public opinion was intended chiefly to scare the malefactors of great wealth into behaving better and only incidentally to enlighten the public mind, he also belonged with these far-sighted conservatives. The question of Roosevelt's perspective can hardly be settled within the limits of this essay, however.

12. "The Nation's Industry through Editorial Eyes," *American Industries*, May, 1925, as quoted by Prothro, *The Dollar Decade*, pp. 94–95. See also Prothro, *The Dollar Decade, passim;* Brady, *Business as a System of Power*, chs. 6 and 8 *passim;* Crecraft, *Government and Business, passim;* Heermance, *The Ethics of Business, passim;* and the following statements of principle: Feiker, "The Profession of Commerce in the Making," *Annals*, CI (May, 1922), 203–7; Hoover, *American Individualism*, especially pp. 25, 31–47; Filene, *The Way Out*, especially pp. 43–47, but see also pp. 145, 161–62, and 170–71 on the industrial democracy of the future; and Owen D. Young, "Humanizing Modern Production," in J. George Frederick, ed., *A Philosophy of Production: A Symposium* (New York: Business Bourse, 1930), pp. 3–28. The *Independent* directly criticized the political assumptions of business spokesmen in 1923; see "The Curse of Propaganda," *Independent*, CX, No. 3833 (January 6, 1923), 4–5.

13. Hoover, "Higher Education and the State Government" (Address at University of Georgia Commencement, June 16, 1926), pp. 8–11; *American Individualism*, pp. 41–43; and see "Education as a National Asset" (Address to the NEA, 1926), and Frank, "State Universities in State Politics," *Century*, CX, No. 1 (May, 1925), 121–24.

14. Carver, *The Present Economic Revolution in the United States*, pp. 183, 247–50, *et passim*, also *Essays in Social Justice* (Cambridge: Harvard University Press, 1915), ch. 14; Hoover, *The New Day*, pp. 85–86.

15. Coolidge, *America's Need for Education, passim*, including the introduction by Henry Suzzallo, president of the University of Washington.

16. Frederick, ed., *The Swope Plan, passim;* Haan, "American Planning in the Words of Its Promoters," *passim;* Howard Coonley, *Making Democracy Work*, as quoted by Jenkin, "Reactions of Major Groups to Positive Government in the United States, 1930–1940: A Study in Contemporary Political Thought," *University of California Publications in Political Science*, I, No. 3 (1945), 313. See also Jenkin, *passim;* Brady, *Business as a System of Power*, chs. 6 and 8; Sutton, *The American Business Creed*, chs. 2–3, 8–9, 12; Bowen, *Social Responsibilities of the Businessman, passim;* Alpheus T. Mason, "Welfare Capitalism: Opportunity or Delusion?" *Virginia Quarterly Review*, XXVI, No. 4 (Autumn, 1950), 530–43; and the following statements of principle: Batchelor, ed., *The*

New Outlook in Business; Editorial, "Business-and-Government," *Fortune,* XXI, No. 3 (March, 1940), 38–39; Wood, "The Corporation Goes into Politics," *Harvard Business Review,* XXI, No. 1 (Autumn, 1942), 60–70; Editors of *Fortune* and Russell W. Davenport, *U.S.A.: The Permanent Revolution.* Robert V. Eagly traces institutional and historical reasons for the shift in business policy apart from the economic crisis in "American Capitalism: A Transformation?" *Business History Review,* XXXIII, No. 4 (Winter, 1959), 549–68.

17. Nourse, "From the Point of View of the Economist," in Chase, ed., *The Social Responsibility of Management,* p. 54; Lewis, "Economics by Admonition," *American Economic Review,* XLIX, No. 2 (May, 1959), *Supplement,* p. 395. (Lewis referred to a statement by A. A. Berle Jr. in *The 20th Century Capitalist Revolution,* p. 182.) For similar criticisms see Latham, "Anthropomorphic Corporations, Elites, and Monopoly Power," *American Economic Review,* XLVII, No. 2 (May, 1957), 303–10; Edward S. Mason, "The Apologetics of Managerialism," *Journal of Business,* XXXI, No. 1 (January, 1958), 1–11; and Carl Kaysen, "The Corporation: How Much Power? What Scope?" in Edward S. Mason, ed., *The Corporation in Modern Society,* pp. 85–105.

18. See in particular Walker and Sklar, "Business Finds Its Voice," *Harper's,* CLXXVI, Nos. 2–4 (January–March, 1938), 113–23, 317–29, 428–40. It was the vice president of an advertising agency who criticized attempts at "mass hypnotism" (*ibid.,* p. 429).

19. Batchelor, *Profitable Public Relations,* pp. ix, 91. I use Batchelor rather than Edward L. Bernays as the chief spokesman for the theory of public relations because he developed its political implications most succinctly, although Bernays anticipated most of his arguments as early as the 1920s and continued to employ them during the 1930s and 1940s. In one important respect, indeed, Bernays outdid even Batchelor in assigning public relations a political role: unlike Batchelor, he rewrote the theory of democracy itself in terms of public relations techniques. See Bernays, "The Engineering of Consent," *Annals,* CCL (March, 1947), 113–20; and for a description of evolving techniques of corporate public relations see Gras, "Shifts in Public Relations," *Bulletin of the Business Historical Society,* XIX, No. 4 (October, 1945), 97–148, and Goldman, *Two-Way Street.*

20. "The Public Is Not Damned," *Fortune,* XIX, No. 3 (March, 1939), 86; Batchelor, *Profitable Public Relations,* p. 30.

21. See, for example, Batchelor's own compilation, *The New Outlook in Business,* and Merrill, ed., *The Responsibilities of Business Leadership,* especially the foreword.

22. Rockefeller, *The Personal Relation in Industry, passim.*

Rockefeller was by no means the first American industrialist to establish a company union, but he was one of the first to do so on the advice of a public relations specialist, and his example was important.

23. Mayo, *The Human Problems of an Industrial Civilization, passim,* and *The Social Problems of an Industrial Civilization,* especially chs. 1, 4, and 6. Mayo's thought is tellingly analyzed in C. Wright Mills, "The Contribution of Sociology to Studies of Industrial Relations," *Proceedings of the First Annual Meeting, Industrial Relations Research Association,* 1948, ed. Milton Derber, pp. 207–18, and in Bendix and Fisher, "The Perspectives of Elton Mayo," *Review of Economics and Statistics,* XXXI, No. 4 (November, 1949), 312–19.

24. As quoted by Whyte, *Is Anybody Listening?* p. 43; Editors of *Fortune, U.S.A.: The Permanent Revolution,* pp. 197–98.

25. Shifting business views of education are described in Wyllie, *The Self-made Man in America,* ch. 6, and in Kirkland, *Dream and Thought in the Business Community,* ch. 4. Twentieth-century managerial attitudes are described, albeit tendentiously, in Whyte, *The Organization Man,* while the generosity modern corporations display toward higher education is touched on in Knight, *Fifty Years of American Education,* pp. 413–18.

CHAPTER XVIII. REDEFINITIONS OF DEMOCRACY

1. Henry F. May has shown, in *The End of American Innocence,* that postwar skepticism and relativism had roots in prewar thought, while Arthur S. Link argues, in "What Happened to the Progressive Movement in the 1920's?" *American Historical Review,* LXIV, No. 4 (July, 1959), 833–51, that progressivism was far from dead after the war. Despite these continuities, however, the characteristic style and assumptions of American political thought shifted drastically between the 1910s and the 1920s. In addition to the works cited below, see Francis G. Wilson, *The American Political Mind,* ch. 15, and Coker, *Recent Political Thought,* ch. 11, which I have used extensively in drafting this chapter.

2. Kent, *The Great Game of Politics,* pp. 267–68; *Political Behavior,* p. 80.

3. Irwin, "An Age of Lies. How the Propagandist Attacks the Foundation of Public Opinion," *Sunset, the Pacific Monthly,* XLIII, No. 6 (December, 1919), 23 ff.; "If You See It in the Paper, It's ——?" *Collier's,* August 18, 1923, pp. 11 ff.; "You Have a Sixth Sense for Truth," *ibid.,* August 25, 1923, pp. 13 ff.; Lippmann, *Liberty and the News, passim,* and *Public Opinion,* Parts II and III; Garrett, "A Primer of Propaganda," *Saturday Evening Post,* CXCIX, No. 29 (January 15, 1927), 3 ff.; Ber-

nays, *Propaganda, passim,* and "The Minority Rules," *Bookman,* LXV, No. 2 (April, 1927), 150–55; Angoff, "When Truth Goes to War," *American Mercury,* XIII, No. 51 (March, 1928), 355–64; and see Frederick E. Lumley, *The Propaganda Menace* (New York: Century, 1933), *passim.*

I am indebted to Dr. Barry Marks for permission to see and use his University of Minnesota doctoral dissertation on the idea of propaganda in American thought. Dr. Marks describes not only the democratic dismay of the 1920s and early 1930s but also a tentative reassertion of democratic principles against excessive fears occasioned by the discovery of propaganda. This phenomenon will be touched on in later pages of this chapter.

4. Kent, *Political Behavior,* p. 305; Carl C. Brigham, *A Study of American Intelligence* (Princeton: Princeton University Press, 1923); Cannon, "American Misgivings," *Atlantic,* CXXIX, No. 2 (February, 1922), 145–57; Mencken, *Notes on Democracy, passim;* Babbitt, *Democracy and Leadership,* p. 264 *et passim;* and McDougall, *Is America Safe for Democracy?* chs. 2–3, 6.

5. Martin, *The Behavior of Crowds, passim;* and see McDougall, *Is America Safe for Democracy?* ch. 4, and Hoover, *American Individualism,* p. 31.

6. Bernays, *Propaganda,* p. 52; and see Bernays, *Crystallizing Public Opinion, passim,* and McDougall, *Is America Safe for Democracy?* ch. 5.

7. Mencken, *Notes on Democracy,* especially chs. 1–2.

8. Lippmann, *Liberty and the News,* especially pp. 7–15, 62–68; *Public Opinion,* especially chs. 1, 6–9, 20, 26–27.

9. Lippmann, *The Phantom Public,* p. 106 *et passim.*

10. Barnes, "The Political Party in Democracy," *History and Social Intelligence,* p. 448, and compare "The Election of 1924 and the Future of Democracy," *ibid.,* pp. 452–53; Robinson, *The Mind in the Making,* Part I.

11. See Birnbaum, "Behaviorism in the 1920's," *American Quarterly,* VII, No. 1 (Spring, 1955), 15–30; and Watson, "Practical and Theoretical Problems in Instinct and Habits," in Jennings and others, *Suggestions of Modern Science Concerning Education,* pp. 53–99.

12. Smith, *The Democratic Way of Life,* p. 79; Merriam, *New Aspects of Politics, passim.*

13. Dewey, *The Public and Its Problems, passim,* and see *Characters and Events,* Vol. II *passim.*

14. Dewey, *Individualism, Old and New,* ch. 7, and see Lindeman, *The Meaning of Adult Education, passim.*

15. Franklin D. Roosevelt, *Public Papers and Addresses,* I, 756; Kemler, *The Deflation of American Ideals,* p. 109. I have been very largely

guided in my interpretation of the New Deal era by Hofstadter, *The Age of Reform*, ch. 7, and by Goldman, *Rendezvous with Destiny*, chs. 14–15. Arthur M. Schlesinger Jr. gives Roosevelt great credit for educational leadership in chapter 34 of *The Coming of the New Deal*.

16. Kemler, *The Deflation of American Ideals*, pp. 45, 109.

17. Arnold, *The Symbols of Government*, p. 235 *et passim*.

18. Arnold, *The Folklore of Capitalism*, p. 380 *et passim*.

19. Wallace, *New Frontiers*, Part IV; Ickes, *The New Democracy*, *passim*, especially pp. viii–ix, 68–69, 145–50.

20. Lilienthal, *TVA: Democracy on the March*, *passim*; Tugwell, *The Industrial Discipline and the Governmental Arts*, especially ch. 1; Ezekiel, *$2500 a Year*, *passim*, and *Jobs for All through Industrial Expansion*, *passim*.

21. Flynn, "Big Business and the NRA," as found in Bingham and Rodman, eds., *Challenge to the New Deal*, p. 122, and compare *ibid.*, *passim*, and Schlesinger, *The Politics of Upheaval*, ch. 10.

22. Bingham, *Insurgent America*, Part IV; Lerner, *It Is Later Than You Think*, *passim*; Soule, *A Planned Society*, *passim*, and *The Coming American Revolution*, especially p. 281; and Counts, "Dare the School Build a New Social Order?" *The John Day Pamphlets*, No. 9.

23. See, for example, David Lawrence, *Nine Honest Men* (New York: Appleton, 1936), and Raoul E. Desvernine, *Democratic Despotism* (New York: Dodd, Mead, 1936).

24. Walter Lippmann gave voice to most of these convictions both in his newspaper columns and in *An Inquiry into the Principles of the Good Society* (1937). Two aspects of that work are particularly significant here: Lippmann deliberately employed Adam Smith's *Wealth of Nations* as a source book for progressive liberalism, and he appealed once again to the rational criteria of politics that had always influenced his thought even when he was most pragmatic about political institutions.

25. Kent as quoted by Warburg, *Hell Bent for Election*, pp. 32–33.

26. Munro, *The Invisible Government*, *passim*; Odegard, *The American Public Mind*, *passim*.

27. Munro, *The Invisible Government*, ch. 1; Lasswell, *Propaganda Technique in the World War*, *passim*; *Psychopathology and Politics*, especially ch. 10.

28. Waldo, *Political Science in the United States of America*, summarizes contemporary developments in masterful fashion, while Latham's "Group Basis of Politics: Notes for a Theory," *American Political Science Review*, XLVI, No. 2 (June, 1952), 379–97, concentrates on theories of group interaction. See also W. J. M. Mackenzie, "Pressure Groups: The 'Conceptual Framework,'" *Political Studies*, III, No. 3 (October, 1955), 247–55.

29. Odegard, *Pressure Politics, passim;* Herring, *Group Representation before Congress,* especially ch. 14; Childs, *Labor and Capital in National Politics,* especially ch. 9.

30. The best example of the comprehensive empirical approach to American politics is probably David B. Truman's *The Governmental Process* (1951), which in some measure returns to the "transactional" theory of politics Arthur F. Bentley developed but his successors more or less ignored in their emphasis on group politics. (See Taylor, "Arthur F. Bentley's Political Science," *Western Political Quarterly,* V, No. 2 [June, 1952], 214–30.)

31. Herring, *The Politics of Democracy,* p. 307; Key, *Politics, Parties, and Pressure Groups,* p. 5; Pennock, *Liberal Democracy,* chs. 7 and 11.

32. Friedrich, *The New Image of the Common Man,* pp. 271–74; Mayo, *An Introduction to Democratic Theory,* pp. 62, 111–13, *et passim;* Dahl, *A Preface to Democratic Theory,* p. 146 and chs. 3 and 5 *passim.*

33. Schumpeter, *Capitalism, Socialism, and Democracy,* chs. 21–23; Downs, *An Economic Theory of Democracy,* ch. 13. Schumpeter also pointed out that even economists had generally been forced to abandon their traditional assumption that human behavior is rational.

34. Charles W. Smith Jr., *Public Opinion in a Democracy, passim.*

35. Merriam, *On the Agenda of Democracy, passim;* Lasswell, *Democracy through Public Opinion, passim;* Kelley, *Political Campaigning, passim.*

Bibliography

WORKS HAVING RELEVANCE FOR PART ONE

PRIMARY

Adams, John. *The Works of John Adams, Second President of the United States: With a Life of the Author, Notes and Illustrations.* Edited by Charles Francis Adams. 10 vols. Boston, 1850–56.

Carey, Mathew. "Reflections on the Proposed Plan for Establishing a College in Philadelphia, in Which English Literature, the Sciences, and the Liberal Arts Shall Be Taught: And for Admission into Which No Prerequisite of Having Learned the Latin or Greek Shall Be Necessary." 3d ed., improved. With a reply to Mr. Sanderson's remarks. Philadelphia, 1826.

Carter, James G. *Essays upon Popular Education, Containing a Particular Examination of the Schools of Massachusetts, and an Outline of an Institution for the Education of Teachers.* Boston, 1826.

Clews, Elsie W., ed. *Educational Legislation and Administration of the Colonial Governments.* New York, 1899.

Clinton, De Witt. *The Life and Writings of De Witt Clinton.* Edited by William W. Campbell. New York, 1849.

"Constitutional Provisions in Regard to Education in the Several States of the American Union." Circulars of Information of the Bureau of Education, No. 7, 1875. Washington, 1875.

Coon, Charles L., ed. *The Beginnings of Public Education in North Carolina: A Documentary History, 1790–1840.* 2 vols. Raleigh: Publications of the North Carolina Historical Commission, 1908.

Cooper, Thomas. *Lectures on the Elements of Political Economy.* Columbia, S.C., 1826.

—— *A Manual of Political Economy.* Washington, 1834.

Daveis, Charles S. "An Address Delivered on the Commemoration at Fryeburg, May 19, 1825." Portland, Maine, 1825.

Dyott, T. W. "An Exposition of the System of Moral and Mental Labor, Established at the Glass Factory of Dyottville, in the County of Philadelphia . . . with the Report of the Committee Chosen to Investigate the Internal Regulations of the Place." Philadelphia, 1833.

Finegan, Thomas E. *Free Schools: A Documentary History of the Free School Movement in New York State.* Fifteenth Annual Report of the New York State Education Department, 1917–18. Vol. I. Albany: University of the State of New York, 1921.

Jefferson, Thomas. *The Papers of Thomas Jefferson.* Edited by Julian P. Boyd. Princeton: Princeton University Press, 1950–

—— *The Writings of Thomas Jefferson.* Edited by Paul L. Ford. 10 vols. New York, 1892–99.

Knight, Edgar W., ed. *A Documentary History of Education in the South before 1860.* 5 vols. Chapel Hill: University of North Carolina Press, 1949–54.

Lincoln, Charles Z., ed. *State of New York. Messages from the Governors, Comprising Executive Communications to the Legislature and Other Papers Relating to Legislation from the Organization of the First Colonial Assembly in 1683 to and Including the Year 1906, with Notes.* 11 vols. Albany: Published by authority of the state, 1909.

Manning, William. *See* Morison.

Marsh, James. "An Address Delivered in Burlington, upon the Inauguration of the Author to the Office of President of the University of Vermont, November 28, 1826." Burlington, Vt., 1826.

Massachusetts. *Journal of Debates and Proceedings in the Convention of Delegates, Chosen to Revise the Constitution of Massachusetts, Begun and Holden at Boston, November 15, 1820 and Continued by Adjournment to January 9, 1821.* Reported for the Boston *Daily Advertiser.* New ed., rev. and corr. Boston, 1853.

Mercer, Charles F. "A Discourse on Popular Education; Delivered in the Church at Princeton, the Evening before the Annual Commencement of the College of New Jersey, September 26, 1826." Princeton, 1826.

[Mill, James.] "Education of the Poor," *Edinburgh Review,* XXI, No. 41 (February, 1813), 207–19.

Miller, Perry, and Thomas H. Johnson, eds. *The Puritans.* New York: American Book Co., 1938.

Morison, Samuel Eliot, ed. "William Manning's *The Key of Libberty,*" *William and Mary Quarterly* (3d ser.), XIII, No. 2 (April, 1956), 202–54.

New York. *A Report of the Debates and Proceedings of the Convention of the State of New-York: Held at the Capitol, in the City of Albany, on the 28th Day of August, 1821.* By L. H. Clarke. New York, 1821.

Niles' Weekly Register, Containing Political, Geographical, Scientifical, Statistical, Economical, and Biographical Documents, Essays and Facts; Together with Notices of the Arts and Manufactures, and a Record of the Events of the Times. Baltimore [etc.], 1811–49.

North American Review. Vols. I–LXXXIV. Boston, 1815–61.

Northup, Clark S., ed. *Representative Phi Beta Kappa Orations*. 2d ed. New York: Elisha Parmele, 1930.

—— *Representative Phi Beta Kappa Orations*. 2d ser. New York: Elisha Parmele, 1927.

Pennsylvania. Report of the Committee on Education of the House of Representatives of Pennsylvania, December 17, 1810. *Journal of the Twenty-first House of Representatives of the Commonwealth of Pennsylvania*. . . . Lancaster, 1810.

[Place, Francis.] "Education," *Westminster Review*, I, No. 1 (January, 1824), 43–79.

Richardson, James D., ed. *A Compilation of the Messages and Papers of the Presidents, 1789–1902*. 11 vols. New York: Bureau of National Literature and Art, 1907.

Thorpe, Francis N., ed. *The Federal and State Constitutions, Colonial Charters, and Other Organic Laws of the States, Territories, and Colonies Now or Heretofore Forming the United States of America*. Compiled and edited under the Act of Congress of June 30, 1906. Washington: Government Printing Office, 1909.

Woody, Thomas, ed. *Educational Views of Benjamin Franklin*. New York: Macmillan, 1931.

SECONDARY

Bailyn, Bernard. *Education in the Forming of American Society: Needs and Opportunities for Study*. Published for the Institute of Early American History and Culture at Williamsburg, Virginia. Chapel Hill: University of North Carolina Press, 1960.

Beale, Howard K. *A History of Freedom of Teaching in American Schools*. Report of the Commission on the Social Studies, American Historical Association. Part XVI. New York: Scribner's, 1941.

Bridenbaugh, Carl. *Cities in Revolt: Urban Life in America, 1743–1776*. New York: Knopf, 1955.

—— *Cities in the Wilderness: The First Century of Urban Life in America, 1625–1742*. New York: Ronald, 1938.

—— *Myths and Realities: Societies of the Colonial South*. Baton Rouge: Louisiana State University Press, 1952.

Brinton, C. Crane. *English Political Thought in the Nineteenth Century*. The Library of European Political Thought. London: E. Benn, 1933.

Brubacher, John S. *A History of the Problems of Education*. New York: McGraw-Hill, 1947.

Butts, R. Freeman, and Lawrence A. Cremin. *A History of Education in American Culture*. New York: Holt, 1953.

Cremin, Lawrence A. *The American Common School: An Historic Con-*

ception. Teachers College Studies in Education. New York: Teachers College, 1951.

Cubberley, Ellwood P. *Public Education in the United States: A Study and Interpretation of American Educational History*. Rev. and enl. ed. Boston: Houghton Mifflin, 1934.

Curti, Merle. *The Growth of American Thought*. New York: Harper, 1943.

—— "Human Nature in American Thought: The Age of Reason and Morality, 1750–1860," *Political Science Quarterly*, LXVIII, No. 3 (September, 1953), 354–75.

—— *The Social Ideas of American Educators*. Report of the Commission on the Social Studies, American Historical Association. Part X. New York: Scribner's, 1935.

Dabney, Charles W. *Universal Education in the South*. 2 vols. Chapel Hill: University of North Carolina Press, 1936.

Dabney, Virginius. *Liberalism in the South*. Chapel Hill: University of North Carolina Press, 1932.

Dorfman, Joseph. *The Economic Mind in American Civilization, 1606–1918*. 3 vols. New York: Viking, 1946–49.

Dunaway, Wayland F. *A History of Pennsylvania*. 2d ed. New York: Prentice-Hall, 1948.

Edwards, Newton, and Herman G. Richey. *The School in the American Social Order: The Dynamics of American Education*. Boston: Houghton Mifflin, 1947.

Ensign, Forest C. *Compulsory School Attendance and Child Labor*. New York, 1921.

Farnam, Henry W. *Chapters in the History of Social Legislation in the United States to 1860*. Washington: Carnegie Institution, 1938.

Fitzpatrick, Edward A. *The Educational Views and Influence of De Witt Clinton*. Teachers College Contributions to Education, No. 44. New York: Teachers College, 1911.

Flick, Alexander C., ed. *History of the State of New York*. 10 vols. New York: Columbia University Press, 1933–37.

Fox, Dixon R. *The Decline of Aristocracy in the Politics of New York*. Columbia University Studies in History, Economics and Public Law, Vol. LXXXVI, No. 198. New York: Columbia University Press, 1919.

Good, Harry G. *Benjamin Rush and His Services to American Education*. Berne, Ind.: Witness Press, 1918.

Grimes, Alan P. *American Political Thought*. New York: Holt, 1955.

Handlin, Oscar, and Mary Flug Handlin. *Commonwealth; a Study of the Role of Government in the American Economy: Massachusetts, 1774–1861*. New York: New York University Press, 1947.

Hansen, Allen O. *Liberalism and American Education in the Eighteenth Century.* New York: Macmillan, 1926.

Hartz, Louis. *Economic Policy and Democratic Thought: Pennsylvania, 1776–1860.* Cambridge: Harvard University Press, 1948.

—— *The Liberal Tradition in America: An Interpretation of American Political Thought since the Revolution.* New York: Harcourt, Brace, 1955.

Heath, Milton S. *Constructive Liberalism: The Role of the State in Economic Development in Georgia to 1860.* Cambridge: Harvard University Press, 1954.

Honeywell, Roy J. *The Educational Work of Thomas Jefferson.* Cambridge: Harvard University Press, 1931.

Jernegan, Marcus W. *Laboring and Dependent Classes in Colonial America, 1607–1783: Studies of the Economic, Educational, and Social Significance of Slaves, Servants, Apprentices, and Poor Folk.* Chicago: University of Chicago Press, 1931.

Kemp, William W. *The Support of Schools in Colonial New York by the Society for the Propagation of the Gospel in Foreign Parts.* Teachers College Contributions to Education, No. 56. New York: Teachers College, 1913.

Kenyon, Cecelia M. "Conceptions of Human Nature in American Political Thought, 1630–1826." Unpublished doctoral dissertation, Radcliffe College, 1949.

Knight, Edgar W. *Public Education in the South.* Boston: Ginn, 1922.

Labaree, Leonard W. *Conservatism in Early American History.* New York: New York University Press, 1948.

McCadden, Joseph J. *Education in Pennsylvania 1801–1835 and Its Debt to Roberts Vaux.* Philadelphia: University of Pennsylvania Press, 1937.

Maddox, William A. *The Free School Idea in Virginia before the Civil War: A Phase of Political and Social Evolution.* Teachers College Contributions to Education, No. 93. New York: Teachers College, 1918.

Merriam, Charles E. *A History of American Political Theories.* New York: Macmillan, 1903.

Miller, Perry. "Religion and Society in the Early Literature: The Religious Impulse in the Founding of Virginia," *William and Mary Quarterly* (3d ser.), VI, No. 1 (January, 1949), 24–41.

Monroe, Paul. *Founding of the American Public School System: A History of Education in the United States, from the Early Settlements to the Close of the Civil War Period.* 2 vols., the second in microfilm. New York: Macmillan, 1940.

Morison, Samuel Eliot. *Harvard College in the Seventeenth Century.* 2 vols. Cambridge: Harvard University Press, 1936.

Morison, Samuel Eliot. *The Puritan Pronaos: Studies in the Intellectual Life of New England in the Seventeenth Century.* New York: New York University Press, 1936.

Mulhern, James. *A History of Secondary Education in Pennsylvania.* Philadelphia: Privately printed, 1933.

Nye, Russel B. *The Cultural Life of the New Nation, 1776–1830.* The New American Nation Series. New York: Harper, 1960.

Persons, Stow. *American Minds: A History of Ideas.* New York: Holt, 1958.

Plaehn, Erma B. "Early American Political Theory of Public Education." Unpublished master's thesis, State University of Iowa, 1933.

Randall, S. S. *History of the Common School System of the State of New York, from Its Origin in 1795, to the Present Time: Including the Various City and Other Special Organizations, and the Religious Controversies of 1821, 1822, and 1840.* New York, 1871.

Rossiter, Clinton. *Seedtime of the Republic: The Origin of the American Tradition of Political Liberty.* New York: Harcourt, Brace, 1953.

Seybolt, Robert F. *Apprenticeship & Apprenticeship Education in Colonial New England & New York.* Teachers College Contributions to Education, No. 85. New York: Teachers College, 1917.

Small, Walter H. *Early New England Schools.* Boston: Ginn, 1914.

Smith, James M., ed. *Seventeenth-Century America: Essays in Colonial History.* Published for the Institute of Early American History and Culture at Williamsburg, Virginia. Chapel Hill: University of North Carolina Press, 1959.

Wells, Guy F. *Parish Education in Colonial Virginia.* Teachers College Contributions to Education, No. 138. New York: Teachers College, 1923.

Wesley, Edgar B. *Proposed: The University of the United States.* Minneapolis: University of Minnesota Press, 1936.

White, Leonard D. *The Federalists: A Study in Administrative History.* New York: Macmillan, 1948.

—— *The Jeffersonians: A Study in Administrative History, 1801–1829.* New York: Macmillan, 1951.

Wickersham, James P. *A History of Education in Pennsylvania, Private and Public, Elementary and Higher. From the Time the Swedes Settled on the Delaware to the Present Day.* Lancaster, Pennsylvania, 1886.

Wilson, Francis G. *The American Political Mind: A Textbook in Political Theory.* New York: McGraw-Hill, 1949.

Woody, Thomas. *Early Quaker Education in Pennsylvania.* Teachers College Contributions to Education, No. 105. New York: Teachers College, 1920.

—— *Quaker Education in the Colony and State of New Jersey: A Source Book.* Philadelphia: By the author, 1923.

Wright, Louis B. *The Cultural Life of the American Colonies, 1607–1763.* The New American Nation Series. New York: Harper, 1957.

WORKS HAVING RELEVANCE FOR PART TWO

PRIMARY

Adams, John Quincy. "A Discourse on Education. Delivered at Braintree, Thursday, Oct. 24, 1839." Boston, 1840.

—— *The Selected Writings of John and John Quincy Adams.* Edited by Adrienne Koch and William Peden. New York: Knopf, 1946.

American Institute of Instruction. *The Introductory Discourse and the Lectures Delivered before the American Institute of Instruction, 1834–1850.* Boston, 1835–51.

[Anspach, Frederick L.] *The Sons of the Sires: A History of the Rise, Progress, and Destiny of the American Party and Its Probable Influence on the Next Presidential Election: To Which Is Added a Review of the Letter of the Hon. Henry A. Wise, against the Know-Nothings.* By an American. Philadelphia, 1855.

Atwater, Caleb. *An Essay on Education.* Cincinnati, 1841.

Aydelott, B. P. "Our Country's Evils and Their Remedy." Cincinnati, 1843.

Bancroft, George. "Address at Hartford, before the Delegates to the Democratic Convention of the Young Men of Connecticut on the Evening of February 18, 1840." Published in conformity to a vote of the convention. N.p., n.d.

—— *Literary and Historical Miscellanies.* New York, 1855.

—— "Oration Delivered before the Democracy of Springfield and Neighboring Towns, July 4, 1836." Springfield, Mass., 1836.

Beecher, Lyman. *Autobiography, Correspondence, etc. of Lyman Beecher, D.D.* Edited by Charles Beecher. 2 vols. New York, 1864–65.

—— *Lectures on Political Atheism and Kindred Subjects . . . Dedicated to the Workingmen of the United States.* Boston, 1852.

—— *A Plea for the West.* 2d ed. Cincinnati and New York, 1835.

Berrian, Hobart. "A Brief Sketch of the Origin and Rise of the Workingmen's Party in the City of New York." Washington, 1840?

Blau, Joseph L., ed. *Social Theories of Jacksonian Democracy: Representative Writings of the Period 1825–1850.* New York: Liberal Arts, 1954.

Boston Quarterly Review. Vols. I–V. Boston, 1838–42.

[Brown, Paul.] *The Radical: And Advocate of Equality: Presenting a Series of Expostulatory Animadversions on the Present State of Practical Politics and Morals; with a View to an Access of Improvement. Addressed to the People of the United States*. Albany, 1834.

Brownson, Orestes. *The Works of Orestes A. Brownson*. Collected and arranged by Henry F. Brownson. 20 vols. Detroit: T. Nourse, 1882–1907.

Bushnell, Horace. "Common Schools: A Discourse on the Modifications Demanded by the Roman Catholics, Delivered in the North Church, Hartford, March 25, 1853." Hartford, 1853.

Byrdsall, Fitzwilliam. *The History of the Loco-Foco, or Equal Rights Party: Its Movements, Conventions and Proceedings*. New York, 1842.

Camp, George S. *Democracy*. New York, 1841.

Carey, Henry C. *Principles of Political Economy*. 3 vols. Philadelphia, 1837–40.

Carroll, Anna. *The Great American Battle; or, The Contest between Christianity and Political Romanism*. New York and Auburn, 1856.

—— *The Star of the West; or, National Men and National Measures*. 3d ed., rev. and enl. New York, 1857.

Channing, William E. "Remarks on the Associations Formed by the Working Classes of America. . . ." London, 1833.

—— *The Works of William Ellery Channing*. 8th complete ed. 6 vols. Boston and New York, 1848.

Cole, Arthur C., ed. *The Constitutional Debates of 1847*. Collections of the Illinois State Historical Society, Vol. XIV. Springfield: Illinois State Historical Library, 1919.

Commercial Review of the South and West: Agricultural, Commercial, Industrial Progress & Resources (De Bow's Review). Vols. I–XXX. New Orleans, 1846–61.

Commons, John R., *et al.*, eds. *A Documentary History of American Industrial Society*. Prepared under the auspices of the American Bureau of Industrial Research, with the cooperation of the Carnegie Institution of Washington. 10 vols. Cleveland: A. H. Clark, 1910–11.

"Constitutional Provisions in Regard to Education in the Several States of the American Union." Circulars of Information of the Bureau of Education, No. 7, 1875. Washington, 1875.

Elliott, E. N., ed. *Cotton Is King, and Pro-Slavery Arguments: Comprising the Writings of Hammond, Harper, Christy, Stringfellow, Hodge, Bledsoe, and Cartwright, on this Important Subject . . . with an Essay on Slavery in the Light of International Law, by the Author*. Augusta, Ga., 1860.

Ely, Alfred B. "American Liberty, Its Sources,—Its Dangers,—and the Means of Its Preservation: An Oration, Delivered at the Broadway Tabernacle, in New-York, before the Order of United Americans, on the 22nd of February, A.D. 1850, Being the 118th Anniversary of the Birthday of Washington." New York, 1850.

Emerson, Ralph Waldo. *The Complete Works of Ralph Waldo Emerson.* Edited by Edward W. Emerson. Centenary ed. 12 vols. Cambridge: Riverside Press, 1903–4.

Estes, Matthew. *A Defence of Negro Slavery, as It Exists in the United States.* Montgomery, Ala., 1846.

Everett, Edward. "Address of His Excellency Edward Everett, to the Two Branches of the Legislature, on the Organization of the Government, for the Political Year . . . 1836." *Documents Printed by Order of the House of Representatives of the Commonwealth of Massachusetts,* 1836, No. 6. Boston, 1836.

—— "Address of His Excellency Edward Everett, to the Two Branches of the Legislature, on the Organization of the Government, for the Political Year . . . 1837." *Documents Printed by Order of the Senate of the Commonwealth of Massachusetts,* 1837, No. 1. Boston, 1837.

—— "Address of His Excellency Edward Everett, to the Two Branches of the Legislature, on the Organization of the Government, for the Political Year . . . 1838." *Documents Printed by . . . the House of Representatives . . . of Massachusetts,* 1838, No. 3. Boston, 1838.

—— "Address of His Excellency Edward Everett, to the Two Branches of the Legislature, on the Organization of the Government, for the Political Year . . . 1839." *Documents Printed by . . . the Senate . . . of Massachusetts,* 1839, No. 1. Boston, 1839.

—— *Orations and Speeches on Various Occasions.* Boston, 1836.

—— *Orations and Speeches on Various Occasions.* 2d ed. 4 vols. Boston, 1850–68.

Finegan, Thomas E. *Free Schools: A Documentary History of the Free School Movement in New York State.* Fifteenth Annual Report of the New York State Education Department, 1917–18. Vol. I. Albany: University of the State of New York, 1921.

Fitzhugh, George. *Cannibals All! or, Slaves without Masters.* Richmond, 1857.

—— *Sociology for the South; or, The Failure of Free Society.* Richmond, 1854.

Greeley, Horace. *Hints toward Reforms, in Lectures, Addresses, and Other Writings.* New York, 1850.

Grimké, Frederick. *Considerations upon the Nature and Tendency of Free Institutions.* Cincinnati, 1848.

Hammond, James H. *Selections from the Letters and Speeches of the Hon. James H. Hammond, of South Carolina.* New York, 1866.

Harper, William. "Anniversary Oration; Delivered . . . in the Representative Hall, on the 9th of December, 1835." The South Carolina Society for the Advancement of Learning, Publication No. 2. Columbia, S.C., 1836.

[Hazewell, C. C.] "Agrarianism," *Atlantic Monthly*, III, No. 18 (April, 1859), 393–402.

Kent, James. "An Address Delivered at New Haven before the Phi Beta Kappa Society, September 13, 1831." New Haven, 1831.

Knight, Edgar W., ed. *A Documentary History of Education in the South before 1860.* 5 vols. Chapel Hill: University of North Carolina Press, 1949–54.

—— *Reports on European Education.* New York: McGraw-Hill, 1930.

Leggett, William. *A Collection of the Political Writings of William Leggett.* Selected and arranged with a Preface by Theodore Sedgwick. 2 vols. New York, 1840.

Lieber, Francis. *Manual of Political Ethics, Designed Chiefly for the Use of Colleges and Students at Law.* Edited by Theodore D. Woolsey. 2d ed. 2 vols. Philadelphia, 1875. [Originally published in 1838–39.]

—— *On Civil Liberty and Self-Government.* 2 vols. Philadelphia, 1853.

Lincoln, Charles Z., ed. *State of New York. Messages from the Governors, Comprising Executive Communications to the Legislature and Other Papers Relating to Legislation from the Organization of the First Colonial Assembly in 1683 to and Including the Year 1906, with Notes.* 11 vols. Albany: Published by authority of the state, 1909.

Lovett, William. *Life and Struggles of William Lovett in His Pursuit of Bread, Knowledge, and Freedom. With Some Short Account of the Different Associations He Belonged To and of the Opinions He Entertained.* With an Introduction by R. H. Tawney. 2 vols. London: G. Bell and Sons, 1920.

Luther, Seth. "An Address to the Workingmen of New England, on the State of Education, and on the Condition of the Producing Classes in Europe and America: With Particular Reference to the Effect of Manufacturing (as Now Conducted) on the Health and Happiness of the Poor, and on the Safety of Our Republic." New York, 1833.

Mann, Horace. *Life and Works of Horace Mann.* 5 vols. Boston and New York, 1891.

Morse, Samuel F. B. "An Argument on the Ethical Position of Slavery in the Social System, and Its Relation to the Politics of the Day." *Papers from the Society for the Diffusion of Political Knowledge*, No. 12. New York, 1863.

—— *Foreign Conspiracy against the Liberties of the United States: The Numbers under the Signature of Brutus, Originally Published in the New York Observer.* 7th ed. New York, 1855. [Originally published in 1835.]

—— *Imminent Dangers to the Free Institutions of the United States through Foreign Immigration, and the Present State of the Naturaliza-tion Laws: A Series of Numbers, Originally Published in the New-York Journal of Commerce.* By an American. Rev. and corr., with additions. New York, 1835.

Morton, Marcus. "Address of His Excellency Marcus Morton, to the Two Branches of the Legislature, on the Organization of the Government, for the Political Year . . . 1840." *Documents Printed by Order of the House of Representatives of the Commonwealth of Massachusetts,* 1840, No. 9. Boston, 1840.

—— "Address of His Excellency Marcus Morton, to the Two Branches of the Legislature, on the Organization of the Government, for the Political Year . . . 1843." *Acts and Resolves Passed by the Legislature of Massachusetts in the Year 1843,* pp. 115–29. Boston, 1843.

Moses, Myer. *Full Annals of the Revolution in France, 1830, to Which Is Added, A Full Account of the Celebration of Said Revolution in the City of New-York, on the 25th November 1830. . . .* New York, 1830.

New York. *Journal of the Convention of the State of New-York, Begun and Held at the Capitol in the City of Albany, on the First Day of June, 1846.* Albany, 1846.

—— *Report of the Debates and Proceedings of the Convention for the Revision of the Constitution of the State of New York.* Reported by William G. Bishop and William H. Attree. Albany, 1846.

North American Review. Vols. I–LXXXIV. Boston, 1815–61.

Northup, Clark S., ed. *Representative Phi Beta Kappa Orations.* 2d ed. New York: Elisha Parmele, 1930.

—— *Representative Phi Beta Kappa Orations.* 2d ser. New York: Elisha Parmele, 1927.

Ohio. *Report of the Debates and Proceedings of the Convention for the Revision of the Constitution of the State of Ohio, 1850–1851.* J. V. Smith, official reporter to the Convention. 2 vols. Columbus, 1851.

[Packard, Frederick.] "Thoughts on the Condition and Prospects of Popular Education in the United States. By a Citizen of Pennsylvania. . . ." Philadelphia, 1836.

Parker, Theodore. *Lessons from the World of Matter and the World of Man.* Edited by Rufus Leighton. *Works of Theodore Parker,* Centenary ed., Vol. V. Boston: American Unitarian Association, 1908.

—— *Sins and Safeguards of Society.* Edited by Samuel B. Stewart. *Works of Theodore Parker,* Centenary ed. Boston: American Unitarian Association, n.d.

—— *Social Classes in a Republic.* Edited by Samuel A. Eliot. *Works of Theodore Parker,* Centenary ed., Vol. XIX. Boston: American Unitarian Association, n.d.

Parsons, Theophilus. "Address Delivered before the Phi Beta Kappa

Society of Harvard University, 27 August 1835, on the Duties of Educated Men in a Republic." Boston, 1835.

Pennsylvania. *Proceedings and Debates of the Convention of the Commonwealth of Pennsylvania, to Propose Amendments to the Constitution, Commenced . . . at Harrisburg, on the Second Day of May, 1837.* Reported by John Agg, stenographer to the Convention. 14 vols. Harrisburg, 1837–39.

Porter, Noah. *The Educational Systems of the Puritans and Jesuits Compared. A Premium Essay, Written for "The Society for the Promotion of Collegiate and Theological Education at the West."* New York, 1851.

The Pro-Slavery Argument. Charleston, S.C., 1852.

Rantoul, Robert, Jr. *Memoirs, Speeches and Writings of Robert Rantoul, Jr.* Edited by Luther Hamilton. Boston, 1854.

Richardson, James D., ed. *A Compilation of the Messages and Papers of the Presidents, 1789–1902.* 11 vols. New York: Bureau of National Literature and Art, 1907.

Seward, William H. "The Destiny of America: Speech of William H. Seward at the Dedication of Capital University, at Columbus, Ohio, September 14, 1853." Albany, 1853.

—— "Discourse on Education, Delivered at Westfield, July 26, 1837." Albany, 1837.

—— *The Works of William H. Seward.* Edited by George E. Baker. 3 vols. New York, 1853.

Simpson, Stephen. *The Working Man's Manual: A New Theory of Political Economy, on the Principle of Production the Source of Wealth.* Philadelphia, 1831.

Skidmore, Thomas. *The Rights of Man to Property! Being a Proposition to Make It Equal among the Adults of the Present Generation: And to Provide for Its Equal Transmission to Every Individual of Each Succeeding Generation on Arriving at the Age of Maturity.* New York, 1829.

Southern Literary Messenger. Vols. I–XXXVIII. Richmond, 1835–64.

Southern Quarterly Review. Vols. I–XXX. New Orleans [etc.], 1842–57.

Story, Joseph. "Discourse Pronounced before the Phi Beta Kappa Society at the Anniversary Celebration, on the Thirty-first Day of August, 1826." Boston, 1826.

Thorpe, Francis N., ed. *The Federal and State Constitutions, Colonial Charters, and Other Organic Laws of the States, Territories, and Colonies Now or Heretofore Forming the United States of America.* Compiled and edited under the Act of Congress of June 30, 1906. Washington: Government Printing Office, 1909.

United States Magazine and Democratic Review. Vols. I–XLIII. Washington and New York, 1837–59.

Virginia. *Proceedings and Debates of the Virginia State Convention of 1829–1830. To Which Are Subjoined, the New Constitution of Virginia, and the Votes of the People.* . . . Richmond, 1830.

Wayland, Francis. "The Education Demanded by the People of the U. States: A Discourse Delivered at Union College, Schenectady, July 25, 1854, on the Occasion of the Fiftieth Anniversary of the Presidency of Eliphalet Nott." Boston, 1855.

—— *The Elements of Political Economy.* New York, 1837.

—— *Thoughts on the Present Collegiate System in the United States.* Boston, 1842.

Webster, Daniel. *The Writings and Speeches of Daniel Webster.* National ed. 18 vols. Boston: Little, Brown, 1903.

Western Literary Institute. *Transactions of the . . . Annual Meeting of the Western Literary Institute and College of Professional Teachers Held in Cincinnati, 1834–40.* Cincinnati, 1835–41.

Whitman, Walt. *The Gathering of the Forces: Editorials, Literary and Dramatic Reviews and Other Material Written by Walt Whitman as Editor of the Brooklyn Daily Eagle in 1846 and 1847.* Edited by Cleveland Rodgers and John Black. 2 vols. New York: Putnam, 1920.

Woodbury, Levi. *Writings of Levi Woodbury LL.D. Political, Judicial and Literary: Now First Selected and Arranged.* 3 vols. Boston, 1852.

Wright, Frances. "Address on the State of the Public Mind, and the Measures Which It Calls For. . . ." New York, 1829.

—— "A Lecture on Existing Evils and Their Remedy. . . ." New York, 1829.

—— "Parting Address. . . ." New York, 1830.

—— "To the Intelligent among the Working Classes," *Popular Tracts,* No. 3. New York, 1830.

Young, Samuel. "Lecture on Civilization, Delivered before the Young Men's Association of Saratoga Springs, March 5th, 1841." Saratoga Springs, N.Y., 1841.

—— "Oration Delivered at the Democratic Republican Celebration of the Sixty-fourth Anniversary of the Independence of the United States, July Fourth, 1840, in the City of New-York." New York, 1840.

SECONDARY

Aaron, Daniel. *Men of Good Hope: A Story of American Progressivism.* New York: Oxford, 1951.

Akagi, Roy H. "The Pennsylvania Constitution of 1838," *Pennsylvania Magazine of History and Biography,* XLVIII, No. 192 (October, 1924), 301–33.

Alexander, De Alva S. *A Political History of the State of New York*. 2 vols. New York: Holt, 1906.

Ambler, Charles H. *Sectionalism in Virginia from 1776 to 1851*. Chicago: University of Chicago Press, 1910.

Arky, Louis H. "The Mechanics' Union of Trade Associations and the Formation of the Philadelphia Workingmen's Movement," *Pennsylvania Magazine of History and Biography*, LXXVI, No. 2 (April, 1952), 142–76.

Beale, Howard K. *A History of Freedom of Teaching in American Schools*. Report of the Commission on the Social Studies, American Historical Association. Part XVI. New York: Scribner's, 1941.

Billington, Ray A. *The Protestant Crusade, 1800–1860: A Study of the Origins of American Nativism*. New York: Macmillan, 1938.

Bode, Carl. *The American Lyceum: Town Meeting of the Mind*. New York: Oxford, 1956.

Brinton, C. Crane. *English Political Thought in the Nineteenth Century*. The Library of European Political Thought. London: E. Benn, 1933.

Brown, Bernard E. *American Conservatives: The Political Thought of Francis Lieber and John W. Burgess*. Columbia University Studies in History, Economics, and Public Law, No. 565. New York: Columbia University Press, 1954.

Brubacher, John S. *A History of the Problems of Education*. New York: McGraw-Hill, 1947.

Buley, R. C. *The Old Northwest: Pioneer Period, 1814–1840*. 2 vols. Indianapolis: Indiana Historical Society, 1950.

Butts, R. Freeman, and Lawrence A. Cremin. *A History of Education in American Culture*. New York: Holt, 1953.

Carlton, Frank T. *Economic Influences upon Educational Progress in the United States, 1820–1850*. Reprinted from the Bulletin of the University of Wisconsin, Economics and Political Science Series, IV, No. 1, 1–135. Madison, 1908.

—— "The Workingmen's Party of New York City, 1829–1831," *Political Science Quarterly*, XXII, No. 3 (September, 1907), 401–15.

Carroll, E. Malcolm. *Origins of the Whig Party*. Durham, N.C.: Duke University Press, 1925.

Cochran, Thomas C., and William Miller. *The Age of Enterprise: A Social History of Industrial America*. New York: Macmillan, 1942.

Cole, Charles C., Jr. *The Social Ideas of the Northern Evangelists, 1826–1860*. Columbia Studies in the Social Sciences, No. 580. New York: Columbia University Press, 1954.

Commager, Henry Steele. *Theodore Parker*. Boston: Little, Brown, 1936.

Commons, John R., et al. *History of Labour in the United States*. 2 vols. New York: Macmillan, 1918–21.

Craven, Avery. *The Growth of Southern Nationalism, 1848–1861.* A History of the South, Vol. VI. Baton Rouge: Louisiana State University Press, 1953.

Cremin, Lawrence A. *The American Common School: An Historic Conception.* Teachers College Studies in Education. New York: Teachers College, 1951.

Cubberley, Ellwood P. *Public Education in the United States: A Study and Interpretation of American Educational History.* Rev. and enl. ed. Boston: Houghton Mifflin, 1934.

Culver, Raymond B. *Horace Mann and Religion in the Massachusetts Public Schools.* Yale Studies in the History and Theory of Religious Education, Vol. III. New Haven: Yale University Press, 1929.

Curoe, Philip R. V. *Educational Attitudes and Policies of Organized Labor in the United States.* Teachers College Contributions to Education, No. 201. New York: Teachers College, 1926.

Curti, Merle. *The Growth of American Thought.* New York: Harper, 1943.

—— *The Social Ideas of American Educators.* Report of the Commission on the Social Studies, American Historical Association. Part X. New York: Scribner's, 1935.

Dabney, Charles W. *Universal Education in the South.* 2 vols. Chapel Hill: University of North Carolina Press, 1936.

Dabney, Virginius. *Liberalism in the South.* Chapel Hill: University of North Carolina Press, 1932.

Darling, Arthur B. "Jacksonian Democracy in Massachusetts 1824–1848," *American Historical Review,* XXIX, No. 2 (January, 1924), 271–87.

—— *Political Changes in Massachusetts, 1824–1848.* New Haven: Yale University Press, 1925.

—— "The Workingmen's Party in Massachusetts, 1833–1834," *American Historical Review,* XXIX, No. 1 (October, 1923), 81–86.

Ditzion, Sidney. *Arsenals of a Democratic Culture: A Social History of the American Public Library Movement in New England and the Middle States from 1850 to 1900.* Chicago: American Library Association, 1947.

Dorfman, Joseph. *The Economic Mind in American Civilization, 1606–1918.* 3 vols. New York: Viking, 1946–49.

Dunaway, Wayland F. *A History of Pennsylvania.* 2d ed. New York: Prentice-Hall, 1948.

Eaton, Clement. "Class Differences in the Old South," *Virginia Quarterly Review,* XXX, No. 3 (Summer, 1957), 357–70.

—— *Freedom of Thought in the Old South.* Durham: Duke University Press, 1940.

Edwards, Newton, and Herman G. Richey. *The School in the American*

Social Order: The Dynamics of American Education. Boston: Houghton Mifflin, 1947.

Ekirch, Arthur A., Jr. *The Idea of Progress in America, 1815–1860.* Columbia University Studies in History, Economics, and Public Law, No. 511. New York: Columbia University Press, 1944.

Elkins, Stanley, and Eric McKitrick. "Institutions and the Law of Slavery: The Dynamics of Unopposed Capitalism," *American Quarterly Review,* IX, No. 1 (Spring, 1957), 3–21.

—— "A Meaning for Turner's Frontier," *Political Science Quarterly,* LXIX, No. 3–4 (September–December, 1954), 321–53 and 565–602.

Ensign, Forest C. *Compulsory School Attendance and Child Labor.* New York, 1921.

Esarey, Logan. *A History of Indiana from Its Exploration to 1850.* 2 vols. Indianapolis: W. K. Stewart, 1915.

Farnam, Henry W. *Chapters in the History of Social Legislation in the United States to 1860.* Washington: Carnegie Institution, 1938.

Flick, Alexander C., ed. *History of the State of New York.* 10 vols. New York: Columbia University Press, 1933–37.

Foner, Philip. *History of the Labor Movement in the United States.* 2 vols. New York: International Publishers, 1947–55.

Fox, Dixon Ryan. "The Protestant Counter-Reformation in America," *New York History,* XVI, No. 1 (January, 1935), 19–35.

Gabriel, Ralph. *The Course of American Democratic Thought: An Intellectual History since 1815.* New York: Ronald, 1940.

Godwin, Parke. *A Biography of William Cullen Bryant, with Extracts from His Private Correspondence.* 2 vols. New York, 1883.

Goodrich, Carter. "The Revulsion against Internal Improvements," *Journal of Economic History,* X, No. 2 (November, 1950), 145–69.

—— "The Virginia System of Mixed Enterprise," *Political Science Quarterly,* LXIV, No. 3 (September, 1949), 355–87.

Green, Fletcher M. *Constitutional Development in the South Atlantic States, 1776–1860: A Study in the Evolution of Democracy.* Chapel Hill: University of North Carolina Press, 1930.

Griffin, Clifford S. "Religious Benevolence as Social Control, 1815–1860," *Mississippi Valley Historical Review,* XLIV, No. 3 (December, 1957), 423–44.

Grimes, Alan P. *American Political Thought.* New York: Holt, 1955.

Grund, Francis J. *The Americans, in Their Moral, Social, and Political Relations.* 2 vols. in one. Boston, 1837.

Hammond, J. L., and Barbara Hammond. *The Age of the Chartists, 1832–1854: A Study of Discontent.* London: Longmans, Green, 1930.

Hammond, Jabez D. *The History of Political Parties in the State of New-York.* 3d ed., rev. 2 vols. Cooperstown, N.Y., 1845.

—— *Political History of the State of New York, from Jan. 1, 1841, to Jan. 1, 1847: Including the Life of Silas Wright*. Syracuse, 1852.

Handlin, Oscar, and Mary Flug Handlin. *Commonwealth; a Study of the Role of Government in the American Economy: Massachusetts, 1774–1861*. New York: New York University Press, 1947.

Hansen, Allen O. *Early Educational Leadership in the Ohio Valley: A Study of Educational Reconstruction through the Western Literary Institute and College of Professional Teachers. Journal of Educational Research Monographs*, No. 5, 1923. Bloomington, Ill.: Public School Publishing Company, 1923.

Hartz, Louis. *Economic Policy and Democratic Thought: Pennsylvania, 1776–1860*. Cambridge: Harvard University Press, 1948.

—— *The Liberal Tradition in America: An Interpretation of American Political Thought since the Revolution*. New York: Harcourt, Brace, 1955.

—— "Seth Luther: The Story of a Working-Class Rebel," *New England Quarterly*, XIII, No. 3 (September, 1940), 401–18.

Heath, Milton S. *Constructive Liberalism: The Role of the State in Economic Development in Georgia to 1860*. Cambridge: Harvard University Press, 1954.

Hofstadter, Richard. *The American Political Tradition, and the Men Who Made It*. New York: Knopf, 1948.

—— "William Leggett, Spokesman of Jacksonian Democracy," *Political Science Quarterly*, XLVIII, No. 4 (December, 1943), 581–94.

Holt, Edgar A. *Party Politics in Ohio, 1840–1850*. Columbus: F. J. Heer, 1931.

Hovell, Mark. *The Chartist Movement*. Manchester and London: Manchester University Press and Longmans, Green, 1918.

Hubbart, Henry C. *The Older Middle West, 1840–1880: Its Social, Economic and Political Life and Sectional Tendencies Before, During and After the Civil War*. New York: Appleton–Century, 1936.

Hugins, Walter. *Jacksonian Democracy and the Working Class: A Study of the New York Workingmen's Movement, 1829–1837*. Stanford: Stanford University Press, 1960.

Hurst, James W. *Law and the Conditions of Freedom in the Nineteenth-Century United States*. Madison: University of Wisconsin Press, 1956.

Jackson, Sidney L. *America's Struggle for Free Schools: Social Tension and Education in New England and New York, 1827–1842*. Washington: American Council on Public Affairs, 1941.

—— "Labor, Education, and Politics in the 1830's," *Pennsylvania Magazine of History and Biography*, LXVI, No. 3 (July, 1942), 279–93.

Jenkins, William S. *Pro-Slavery Thought in the Old South*. Chapel Hill: University of North Carolina Press, 1935.

Klein, Philip S. *Pennsylvania Politics, 1817–1832: A Game without Rules.* Philadelphia: Historical Society of Pennsylvania, 1940.

Knight, Edgar W. *Public Education in the South.* Boston: Ginn, 1922.

Ladu, Arthur I. "Emerson: Whig or Democrat," *New England Quarterly,* XIII, No. 3 (September, 1940), 419–41.

Lively, Robert A. "The American System: A Review Article," *Business History Review,* XXIX, No. 1 (March, 1955), 81–95.

Lloyd, Arthur Y. *The Slavery Controversy, 1831–1860.* Chapel Hill: University of North Carolina Press, 1939.

Ludlum, David M. *Social Ferment in Vermont, 1791–1850.* New York: Columbia University Press, 1939.

McAlpine, William. "The Origin of Public Education in Ohio," *Ohio Archaeological and Historical Quarterly,* XXXVIII, No. 3 (July, 1929), 409–45.

Maddox, William A. *The Free School Idea in Virginia before the Civil War: A Phase of Political and Social Evolution.* Teachers College Contributions to Education, No. 93. New York: Teachers College, 1918.

May, Henry F. *Protestant Churches and Industrial America.* New York: Harper, 1949.

Merriam, Charles E. *A History of American Political Theories.* New York: Macmillan, 1903.

Meyers, Marvin. *The Jacksonian Persuasion: Politics and Belief.* Stanford: Stanford University Press, 1957.

Monroe, Paul. *Founding of the American Public School System: A History of Education in the United States, from the Early Settlements to the Close of the Civil War Period.* 2 vols., the second in microfilm. New York: Macmillan, 1940.

Morris, Richard B. Review of Oscar and Mary Flug Handlin, *Commonwealth . . . Massachusetts, 1774–1861,* in *Political Science Quarterly,* LXII, No. 4 (December, 1947), 581–87

Mosier, Richard D. *Making the American Mind: Social and Moral Ideas in the McGuffey Readers.* New York: King's Crown, 1947.

Mott, Frank L. *A History of American Magazines.* 4 vols. Cambridge: Harvard University Press, 1938–57.

Mueller, Henry R. *The Whig Party in Pennsylvania.* Columbia University Studies in History, Economics and Public Law, No. 230. New York: Columbia University Press, 1922.

Mulhern, James. *A History of Secondary Education in Pennsylvania.* Philadelphia: Privately printed, 1933.

Nevins, Allan. *The Evening Post: A Century of Journalism.* New York: Boni & Liveright, 1922.

Nye, Russel B. *George Bancroft: Brahmin Rebel.* New York: Knopf, 1944.

O'Connor, Michael J. L. *Origins of Academic Economics in the United States.* New York: Columbia University Press, 1944.

Osterweis, Rollin G. *Romanticism and Nationalism in the Old South.* New Haven: Yale University Press, 1949.

Persons, Charles E. "The Early History of Factory Legislation in Massachusetts," in Susan M. Kingsbury, ed., *Labor Laws and Their Enforcement: With Special Reference to Massachusetts.* New York: Longmans, Green, 1911.

Persons, Stow. *American Minds: A History of Ideas.* New York: Holt, 1958.

Pessen, Edward. "Did Labor Support Jackson? The Boston Story," *Political Science Quarterly,* LXIV, No. 2 (June, 1949), 262–74.

—— "The Workingmen's Movement of the Jacksonian Era," *Mississippi Valley Historical Review,* XLIII, No. 3 (December, 1956), 428–43.

Peterson, Merrill D. "The Jefferson Image in the American Mind, 1826–1861." Unpublished doctoral dissertation, Harvard University, 1950.

Power, Richard L. "A Crusade to Extend Yankee Culture, 1820–1865," *New England Quarterly,* XIII, No. 4 (December, 1940), 638–53.

Primm, James N. *Economic Policy in the Development of a Western State: Missouri 1820–1860.* Cambridge: Harvard University Press, 1954.

Randall, S. S. *History of the Common School System of the State of New York, from Its Origin in 1795, to the Present Time: Including the Various City and Other Special Organizations, and the Religious Controversies of 1821, 1822, and 1840.* New York, 1871.

Schlesinger, Arthur M., Jr. *The Age of Jackson.* Boston: Little, Brown, 1945.

—— *Orestes A. Brownson: A Pilgrim's Progress.* Boston: Little, Brown, 1939.

Shea, John G. *History of the Catholic Church in the United States.* 4 vols. New York, 1886–92.

Sherrill, Lewis J. *Presbyterian Parochial Schools, 1846–1870.* New Haven: Yale University Press, 1932.

Smith, Wilson. *Professors & Public Ethics: Studies of Northern Moral Philosophers before the Civil War.* Ithaca: Published for the American Historical Association [by] Cornell University Press, 1956.

Snyder, Charles M. *The Jacksonian Heritage: Pennsylvania Politics, 1833–1848.* Harrisburg: Pennsylvania Historical and Museum Commission, 1958.

Spengler, Joseph. "Laissez Faire and Intervention: A Potential Source of Historical Error," *Journal of Political Economy,* LVII, No. 5 (October, 1949), 438–41.

Stephenson, George M. "Nativism in the Forties and Fifties, with Special

Reference to the Mississippi Valley," *Mississippi Valley Historical Review*, IX, No. 3 (December, 1922), 185–202.

Still, Bayrd. "State Constitutional Development in the United States, 1829–1851. . . ." Unpublished doctoral dissertation, University of Wisconsin, 1933.

Sullivan, William A. "Did Labor Support Andrew Jackson?" *Political Science Quarterly*, LXII, No. 4 (December, 1947), 569–80.

—— *The Industrial Worker in Pennsylvania, 1800–1840.* Harrisburg: Pennsylvania Historical and Museum Commission, 1955.

—— "Philadelphia Labor during the Jackson Era," *Pennsylvania History*, XV, No. 4 (October, 1948), 305–20.

Sydnor, Charles. *The Development of Southern Sectionalism, 1819–1848.* A History of the South, Vol. V. Baton Rouge: Louisiana State University Press, 1948.

Taylor, George R. *The Transportation Revolution, 1815–1860.* The Economic History of the United States, Vol. V. New York: Rinehart, 1951.

Thistlethwaite, Frank. *The Anglo-American Connection in the Early Nineteenth Century.* Philadelphia: University of Pennsylvania Press, 1959.

Tocqueville, Alexis de. *Democracy in America.* Retranslated and edited by Phillips Bradley. 2 vols. New York: Knopf, 1945.

Trimble, William J. "The Social Philosophy of the Locofoco Democracy," *American Journal of Sociology*, XXVI, No. 6 (May, 1921), 705–15.

Van Deusen, Glyndon. *The Jacksonian Era, 1828–1848.* The New American Nation Series. New York: Harper, 1959.

—— "Some Aspects of Whig Thought and Theory in the Jacksonian Period," *American Historical Review*, LXIII, No. 2 (January, 1958), 305–22.

Ware, Norman. *The Industrial Worker, 1840–1860: The Reaction of American Industrial Society to the Advance of the Industrial Revolution.* Boston: Houghton Mifflin, 1924.

White, Leonard D. *The Jacksonians: A Study in Administrative History, 1829–1861.* New York: Macmillan, 1954.

Wickersham, James P. *A History of Education in Pennsylvania, Private and Public, Elementary and Higher. From the Time the Swedes Settled on the Delaware to the Present Day.* Lancaster, Pa., 1886.

Wilson, Francis G. *The American Political Mind: A Textbook in Political Theory.* New York: McGraw-Hill, 1949.

Wright, Louis B. *Culture on the Moving Frontier.* Bloomington: Indiana University Press, 1955.

Wyllie, Irvin G. *The Self-made Man in America: The Myth of Rags to Riches.* New Brunswick: Rutgers University Press, 1954.

WORKS HAVING RELEVANCE FOR PART THREE

PRIMARY

Abbott, Lyman. *Christianity and Social Problems*. Boston, 1896.

Adams, Charles Francis. "Individuality in Politics," *Independent Republican Campaign Documents*, No. 2. New York, 1880.

Allen, E. A. *The Life and Public Services of James Baird Weaver, . . . to Which Is Added the Life and Public Services of James G. Field, with a Series of Articles Showing the Development and Achievements of the National People's Party. . . .* N.p., 1892.

Altgeld, John P. *Live Questions: Including Our Penal Machinery and Its Victims*. Chicago, 1890.

American Federation of Labor. *Proceedings of the American Federation of Labor, 1881* [through] *1888*. Bloomington, Ill.: Pantagraph Printing & Stationery Co., 1905.

—— *Proceedings of the American Federation of Labor, 1889* [through] *1892*. Bloomington, Ill.: Pantagraph Printing & Stationery Co., n.d.

—— *Proceedings of the American Federation of Labor, 1893* [through] *1896*. Bloomington, Ill.: Pantagraph Printing & Stationery Co., 1905.

—— *Report of the Proceedings of the 18th Annual Convention of the American Federation of Labor . . . 1898*. N.p., n.d.

American Federationist: Official Magazine of the American Federation of Labor. Vols. I–XXI. New York [etc.], 1894–1914.

Angell, James B. "The Development of State Universities." Address at the University of Kansas, 1891. N.p., n.d.

—— "The Higher Education: A Plea for Making It Accessible to All." An address delivered at the annual commencement of the University of Michigan, June 26, 1879. Ann Arbor, 1879.

Ashby, N. B. *The Riddle of the Sphinx: A Discussion of the Economic Questions Relating to Agriculture, Land, Transportation, Money, Taxation and Cost of Interchange. . . .* Des Moines, 1890.

Bascom, John. *Sociology*. New York, 1887.

Bellamy, Edward. *Equality*. New York, 1897.

—— *Looking Backward, 2000–1887*. Boston, 1888.

Brooks, John Graham. *The Social Unrest: Studies in Labor and Socialist Movements*. New York: Macmillan, 1903.

Bryan, William J. *The First Battle: A Story of the Campaign of 1896 . . . Together with a Collection of His Speeches and a Biographical Sketch by His Wife*. Chicago, 1897.

Carnegie, Andrew. *The Empire of Business.* New York: Doubleday, 1902.
—— *The Gospel of Wealth, and Other Timely Essays.* New York: Century, 1900.
—— *Problems of To-day: Wealth—Labor—Socialism.* New York: Doubleday, 1908.
—— *Triumphant Democracy; or, Fifty Years' March of the Republic.* New York, 1886.
Commons, John R. *Myself.* New York: Macmillan, 1934.
—— *Social Reform and the Church.* New York, 1894.
Commons, John R., *et al.*, eds. *A Documentary History of American Industrial Society.* Prepared under the auspices of the American Bureau of Industrial Research, with the cooperation of the Carnegie Institution of Washington. 10 vols. Cleveland: A. H. Clark, 1910–11.
Curtis, George W. *Orations and Addresses of George William Curtis.* Edited by Charles Eliot Norton. 3 vols. New York, 1894.
[Doty, Duane, and W. T. Harris.] *A Statement of the Theory of Education in the United States of America, as Approved by Many Leading Educators.* Washington, 1874.
Dunning, Nelson A., comp. *People's Party Campaign Book of Reference. National Watchman Economic Quarterly,* I, No. 1 (July 1, 1894). Washington and Alexandria, n.d.
Eaton, Dorman. *Civil Service in Great Britain: A History of Abuses and Reforms and Their Bearing upon American Politics.* New York, 1880.
—— "The 'Spoils' System and Civil Service Reform in New York," *Publications of the Civil Service Reform Association,* No. 3. New York, 1882.
Eliot, Charles W. *American Contributions to Civilization and Other Essays.* New York, 1897.
—— *The Conflict between Individualism and Collectivism in a Democracy.* New York: Scribner's, 1910.
—— *Educational Reform: Essays and Addresses.* New York, 1898.
Ely, Richard T. *An Introduction to Political Economy.* Chautauqua Literary and Scientific Circle, Studies for 1889–1890, No. 1. New York, 1889.
—— *The Labor Movement in America.* New York, 1886.
—— *Social Aspects of Christianity and Other Essays.* New York, 1889.
Fleming, Walter L., ed. *Documentary History of Reconstruction: Political, Military, Social, Religious, Educational & Industrial, 1865 to the Present Time.* 2 vols. Cleveland: Arthur H. Clark, 1906.
Fortune, T. Thomas. *Black and White: Land, Labor, and Politics in the South.* New York, 1885.
Forum. Vols. I–XXII. New York, 1886–96.
Foster, Florence J. "The Grange and the Co-op Enterprises in New Eng-

land," *Annals of the American Academy of Political and Social Science,* IV, No. 5 (March, 1894), 102–9.

George, Henry. *The Condition of Labor: An Open Letter to Pope Leo XIII.* New York, 1891.

—— *Progress and Poverty: An Inquiry into the Cause of Industrial Depressions and of Increase of Want with Increase of Wealth. The Remedy.* New York, 1892. [First published in 1879.]

—— *Social Problems.* Chicago, 1883.

Gilman, Nicholas P. *Socialism and the American Spirit.* Boston, 1893.

Gladden, Washington. *Applied Christianity: Moral Aspects of Social Questions.* Boston, 1886.

—— *Recollections.* Boston: Houghton Mifflin, 1909.

—— *Social Facts and Forces: The Factory, the Labor Union, the Corporation, the Railway, the City, the Church.* New York, 1897.

—— *Social Salvation.* Boston: Houghton Mifflin, 1902.

—— *Tools and the Man: Property and Industry under the Christian Law.* Boston, 1893.

Godkin, E. L. "The Civil Service Reform Controversy," *North American Review,* CXXXIV, No. 305 (April, 1882), 379–94.

—— "The Dangers of an Office-holding Aristocracy," *Publications of the Civil-Service Reform Association,* No. 7. New York, 1883.

—— "The Democratic View of Democracy," *North American Review,* CI, No. 208 (July, 1865), 103–46.

—— " 'Educated Men' in Centennial Politics," *Nation,* XXIII, No. 1 (July 6, 1876), 5–6.

—— *Problems of Modern Democracy: Political and Economic Essays.* New York, 1896.

—— *Reflections and Comments, 1865–1895.* New York, 1895.

—— *Unforeseen Tendencies of Democracy.* Boston, 1898.

Gompers, Samuel. *Labor and the Common Welfare.* Edited by Hayes Robbins. New York: Dutton, 1919.

Gronlund, Laurence. *The Co-operative Commonwealth: An Exposition of Socialism.* Rev. and enl. ed. Boston and New York, 1890.

Harris, George. *Inequality and Progress.* Boston, 1897.

Hill, Thomas E. *Money Found: Recovered from Its Hiding-Places, and Put into Circulation through Confidence in Government Banks.* Chicago, 1894.

Howard, M. W. *The American Plutocracy.* New York, 1895.

Hubbard, Lester C. *The Coming Climax in the Destinies of America.* Chicago, 1892 [copyright 1891].

Jarvis, Edward. *The Value of Common School Education to Common Labor Together with Illustrations of the Same as Shown by the Answers to Inquiries Addressed to Employers, Workmen, and Observers.* Circulars of Information, Bureau of Education, No. 3, 1879. Washington, 1879.

Jordan, David Starr. *The Care and Culture of Men: A Series of Addresses on the Higher Education.* San Francisco, 1896.

Journal of United Labor. Peace and Prosperity to the Faithful. Vols. I–VII. Washington, 1880–87.

Kansas State Grange. "Education and Industry. A Report of the Course of Education Adapted to the Wants of Common Schools, Made by the Educational Committee of the Kansas State Grange . . . at the Annual Meeting . . . December 13th, 1879." Topeka, 1877.

Knights of Labor. Vol. I. Chicago, 1886.

Knights of Labor. *Record of Proceedings of the General Assembly of the [Knights of Labor].* Vols. I–XIII. Reading, Pa. [etc.], 1878–89.

Lloyd, Henry D. *Lords of Industry.* New York: Putnam, 1910.

—— *Man, the Social Creator.* New York: Doubleday, 1906.

—— *Mazzini and Other Essays.* New York: Putnam, 1910.

—— *Men, the Workers.* New York: Doubleday, 1909.

—— *Wealth against Commonwealth.* New York, 1894.

Lowell, James Russell. *Literary and Political Addresses. The Writings of James Russell Lowell,* Vol. VI. Boston, 1890.

McNeill, George E., et al. *The Labor Movement: The Problem of To-day. The History, Purpose and Possibilities of Labor Organizations in Europe and America.* Boston and New York, 1887.

Mayo, A. D. "American Brains in American Hands." Annual Address at the Kansas Agricultural College, Commencement, 1885. Manhattan, Kansas, 1885.

—— "National Aid to Education." An Address before the American Social Science Association, 1882. Boston, 1883.

Minnesota State Grange. *Proceedings of the Minnesota State Grange.* Vols. XXII, XXIV. Minneapolis, 1891, 1893.

Morgan, W. Scott. *History of the Wheel and Alliance and the Impending Revolution.* Hardy, Ark., 1889.

National Civil-Service Reform League. *Proceedings at the Annual Meeting of the National Civil-Service Reform League,* 1882–1900. New York, 1882–1900.

National Economist: Official Organ of the Farmers Alliance, Agricultural Wheel, and Farmers Union. Devoted to Social, Financial, and Political Economy. Vols. I–VIII. Washington, 1889–93.

National Educational Association. *The Addresses and Journal of Proceedings of the National Educational Association,* 1871–1900.

National Grange of the Patrons of Husbandry. *Journal of Proceedings of the National Grange of the Patrons of Husbandry.* Vols. VII–XXXI. New York [etc.], 1874–97.

Newton, R. Heber. *Social Studies*. New York, 1887.

Northup, Clark S., ed. *Representative Phi Beta Kappa Orations*. 2d ed. New York: Elisha Parmele, 1930.

—— *Representative Phi Beta Kappa Orations*. 2d ser. New York: Elisha Parmele, 1927.

Patrons of Husbandry. *See* National Grange.

Patterson, James W. "Influence of Education upon Labor." Lecture delivered before the American Institute of Instruction, at Lewiston, Maine, August 14, 1872. Springfield, Mass., 1873.

Peffer, William A. *The Farmer's Side: His Troubles and Their Remedy*. New York, 1891.

Phillips, Wendell. "Remarks of Wendell Phillips, at the Mass Meeting of Workingmen in Faneuil Hall, November 2, 1865." Boston, 1865.

—— *Speeches, Lectures, and Letters*. 2d ser. Boston, 1891.

Powderly, Terence V. *The Path I Trod: The Autobiography of Terence V. Powderly*. Edited by Harry J. Carman, Henry David, and Paul N. Guthrie. New York: Columbia University Press, 1940.

—— "The Plea for Eight Hours," *North American Review*, CL, No. 401 (April, 1890), 464–69.

—— *Thirty Years of Labor, 1859 to 1889, in Which the History of the Attempts to Form Organizations of Workingmen for the Discussion of Political, Social, and Economic Questions Is Traced. . . .* Columbus, Ohio, 1890.

—— *Thirty Years of Labor, 1859 to 1889. . . .* Rev. and corr., 1890. Philadelphia, 1890.

Rauschenbusch, Walter. *Christianity and the Social Crisis*. New York: Macmillan, 1907.

Richardson, James D., ed. *A Compilation of the Messages and Papers of the Presidents, 1789–1902*. 11 vols. New York: Bureau of National Literature and Art, 1907.

Rubin, Louis D., Jr., ed. *Teach the Freeman: The Correspondence of Rutherford B. Hayes and the Slater Fund for Negro Education, 1881–1887*. 2 vols. Baton Rouge: Louisiana State University Press, 1959.

Schurz, Carl. Address before the Phi Beta Kappa, Harvard College, June 29, 1882. MS, Harvard College Library.

—— *Speeches, Correspondence and Political Papers of Carl Schurz*. Selected and edited by Frederick Bancroft on behalf of the Carl Schurz Memorial Committee. 6 vols. New York: Putnam, 1913.

Steward, Ira. "The Meaning of the Eight Hour Movement." Boston, 1868.

Stickney, Albert. *The Political Problem*. New York, 1890.

Sumner, William Graham. *The Challenge of Facts and Other Essays*. Edited by Albert G. Keller. New Haven: Yale University Press, 1914.

—— *Collected Essays in Political and Social Science*. New York, 1885.

Sumner, William Graham. *Earth-Hunger and Other Essays.* Edited by Albert G. Keller. New Haven: Yale University Press, 1913.

—— *Essays of William Graham Sumner.* Edited by Albert G. Keller and Maurice R. Davie. New Haven: Yale University Press, 1934.

—— *The Forgotten Man and Other Essays.* Edited by Albert G. Keller. New Haven: Yale University Press, 1918.

—— *War, and Other Essays.* Edited by Albert G. Keller. New Haven: Yale University Press, 1911.

—— *What Social Classes Owe to Each Other.* New York, 1883.

Sylvis, James C. *The Life, Speeches, Labors and Essays of William H. Sylvis, Late President of the Iron-Moulders' International Union; and Also of the National Labor Union.* Philadelphia, 1872.

Tilden Commission. "Report of the Tilden Commission; to Devise a Plan for the Government of Cities in the State of New York," *Municipal Affairs,* III, No. 3 (September, 1899), 434–54.

United States. 48th Congress, 1st Session. *Report of the Committee of the Senate upon the Relations between Labor and Capital, and Testimony Taken by the Committee.* 4 vols. Washington, 1885.

—— Industrial Commission. *Report of the Industrial Commission on the Relations and Conditions of Capital and Labor, Employed in Manufactures and General Business.* Vols. VII and XIV of the Reports of the Commission. Washington, 1901.

Vincent, John H. *The Chautauqua Movement.* Boston, 1886.

Vincent Brothers. *Populist Hand-Book for Kansas: A Compilation from Official Sources of Some Facts for Use in Succeeding Political Campaigns.* Indianapolis, 1891.

Walker, C. S. "The Farmer's Movement," *Annals of the American Academy of Political and Social Science,* IV, No. 5 (March, 1894), 94–102.

Ward, Lester F. *Dynamic Sociology, or Applied Social Science, as Based upon Statical Sociology and the Less Complex Sciences.* 2 vols. New York, 1883.

—— *Glimpses of the Cosmos.* 6 vols. New York: Putnam, 1913–18.

—— *The Psychic Factors of Civilization.* Boston, 1897. [Copyright 1892.]

Washington, Booker T. *Selected Speeches of Booker T. Washington.* Edited by E. D. Washington. Garden City: Doubleday, Doran, 1932.

—— *Up from Slavery: An Autobiography.* Garden City: Doubleday, 1947.

Watkins, Albert. "Radicalism, East and West," *Arena,* XXIII, No. 2 (February, 1900), 149–56.

Watson, Thomas E. *Not a Revolt; It Is a Revolution. The People's Party Campaign Book, 1892.* Washington, 1892.

Weaver, James B. *A Call to Action: An Interpretation of the Great Uprising, Its Source and Causes.* Des Moines, 1892.

White, Andrew D. "Scientific and Industrial Education in the United States. An Address Delivered before the New-York State Agricultural Society." New York, 1874.

Whitehead, Mortimer. "The Origin, and Progress of the Grange, Containing 'Declaration of Purposes,' P. of H." Brooklyn, 1888.

SECONDARY

Aaron, Daniel. *Men of Good Hope: A Story of American Progressivism.* New York: Oxford, 1951.

Abell, Aaron I. *The Urban Impact on American Protestantism, 1865–1900.* Cambridge: Harvard University Press, 1943.

Barker, Charles A. *Henry George.* New York: Oxford, 1955.

Beale, Howard K. *A History of Freedom of Teaching in American Schools.* Report of the Commission on the Social Studies, American Historical Association. Part XVI. New York: Scribner's, 1941.

Bond, Horace M. *The Education of the Negro in the American Social Order.* New York: Prentice-Hall, 1934.

Bremner, Robert H. *From the Depths: The Discovery of Poverty in the United States.* New York: New York University Press, 1956.

Brown, Ira V. *Lyman Abbott, Christian Evolutionist: A Study in Religious Liberalism.* Cambridge: Harvard University Press, 1953.

Brubacher, John S. *A History of the Problems of Education.* New York: McGraw-Hill, 1947.

Brubeck, William H. "The American as Radical, 1870–1900." Unpublished doctoral dissertation, Harvard University, 1952.

Buck, Paul. *The Road to Reunion, 1865–1900.* Boston: Little, Brown, 1937.

Buck, Solon J. *The Agrarian Crusade: A Chronicle of the Farmer in Politics.* The Chronicles of America, Vol. 45. New Haven: Yale University Press, 1920.

—— *The Granger Movement: A Study of Agricultural Organization and Its Political, Economic and Social Manifestations, 1870–1880.* Cambridge: Harvard University Press, 1913.

Butts, R. Freeman, and Lawrence A. Cremin. *A History of Education in American Culture.* New York: Holt, 1953.

Chaffee, Mary Law. "William E. Du Bois' Concept of the Racial Problem in the United States," *Journal of Negro History,* XLI, No. 3 (July, 1956), 249–58.

Cochran, Thomas C., and William Miller. *The Age of Enterprise: A Social History of Industrial America.* New York: Macmillan, 1942.

Commons, John R., *et al. History of Labour in the United States.* 2 vols. New York: Macmillan, 1918–21.

Coulter, E. M. *The South during Reconstruction, 1865–1877.* A History of the South, Vol. VIII. Baton Rouge: Louisiana State University Press, 1947.

Cremin, Lawrence A. *The Transformation of the School: Progressivism in American Education, 1876–1957.* New York: Knopf, 1961.

Cubberley, Ellwood P. *Public Education in the United States: A Study and Interpretation of American Educational History.* Rev. and enl. ed. Boston: Houghton Mifflin, 1934.

Curoe, Philip R. V. *Educational Attitudes and Policies of Organized Labor in the United States.* Teachers College Contributions to Education, No. 201. New York: Teachers College, 1926.

Curry, J. L. M. *A Brief Sketch of George Peabody, and a History of the Peabody Education Fund.* Cambridge, 1898.

Curti, Merle. *The Growth of American Thought.* New York: Harper, 1943.

—— *The Social Ideas of American Educators.* Report of the Commission on the Social Studies, American Historical Association. Part X. New York: Scribner's, 1935.

Dabney, Charles W. *Universal Education in the South.* 2 vols. Chapel Hill: University of North Carolina Press, 1936.

Destler, Chester M. *American Radicalism, 1865–1901: Essays and Documents.* New London: Connecticut College, 1946.

Ditzion, Sidney. *Arsenals of a Democratic Culture: A Social History of the American Public Library Movement in New England and the Middle States from 1850 to 1900.* Chicago: American Library Association, 1947.

Dombrowski, James. *The Early Days of Christian Socialism in America.* New York: Columbia University Press, 1936.

Dorfman, Joseph. *The Economic Mind in American Civilization, 1606–1918.* 3 vols. New York: Viking, 1946–49.

Du Bois, W. E. B. *Black Reconstruction: An Essay toward a History of the Part Which Black Folk Played in the Attempt to Reconstruct Democracy in America, 1860–1880.* New York: Harcourt, Brace, 1935.

Edwards, Newton, and Herman G. Richey. *The School in the American Social Order: The Dynamics of American Education.* Boston: Houghton Mifflin, 1947.

Everett, John R. *Religion in Economics: A Study of John Bates Clark, Richard T. Ely* [and] *Simon N. Patten.* New York: King's Crown, 1946.

Fine, Sidney. *Laissez Faire and the General-Welfare State: A Study of Conflict in American Thought, 1865–1901.* Ann Arbor: University of Michigan Press, 1956.

—— "Richard T. Ely, Forerunner of Progressivism, 1880–1901," *Mississippi Valley Historical Review*, XXXVII, No. 4 (March, 1951), 599–624.

Fleming, Walter L. *The Sequel of Appomattox: A Chronicle of the Re-union of the United States.* The Chronicles of America, Vol. 32. New Haven: Yale University Press, 1919.

Foner, Philip. *History of the Labor Movement in the United States.* 2 vols. New York: International Publishers, 1947–55.

Franklin, John Hope. *From Slavery to Freedom: A History of American Negroes.* New York: Knopf, 1947.

Gabriel, Ralph. *The Course of American Democratic Thought: An Intellectual History since 1815.* New York: Ronald, 1940.

Geiger, George R. *The Philosophy of Henry George.* New York: Macmillan, 1933.

Going, Allen J. "The South and the Blair Education Bill," *Mississippi Valley Historical Review,* XLIV, No. 2 (September, 1957), 267–90.

Goldman, Eric. *Rendezvous with Destiny: A History of Modern American Reform.* New York: Knopf, 1952.

Grimes, Alan P. *American Political Thought.* New York: Holt, 1955.

—— *The Political Liberalism of the New York Nation, 1865–1932.* The James Sprunt Studies in History and Political Science. Chapel Hill: University of North Carolina Press, 1953.

Grob, Gerald N. "The Knights of Labor and the Trade Unions, 1878–1886," *Journal of Economic History,* XVIII, No. 2 (June, 1958), 176–92.

—— "The Knights of Labor, Politics, and Populism," *Mid-America,* XL, No. 1 (January, 1958), 3–21.

—— "Reform Unionism: The National Labor Union," *Journal of Economic History,* XIV, No. 2 (Spring, 1954), 126–42.

Haynes, Fred E. *Third Party Movements since the Civil War, with Special Reference to Iowa: A Study in Social Politics.* Iowa City: The State Historical Society of Iowa, 1916.

Hicks, John D. *The Populist Revolt: A History of the Farmers' Alliance and the People's Party.* Minneapolis: University of Minnesota Press, 1931.

Higham, John. *Strangers in the Land: Patterns of American Nativism, 1860–1925.* New Brunswick: Rutgers University Press, 1955.

Hofstadter, Richard. *The Age of Reform: From Bryan to F.D.R.* New York: Knopf, 1955.

—— *The American Political Tradition, and the Men Who Made It.* New York: Knopf, 1948.

—— *Social Darwinism in American Thought, 1860–1915.* Philadelphia: University of Pennsylvania Press, 1945.

Hopkins, Charles H. *The Rise of the Social Gospel in American Protestantism, 1865–1915.* Yale Studies in Religious Education, Vol. XIV. New Haven: Yale University Press, 1940.

Jones, William H. "Some Theories Regarding the Education of the Negro," *Journal of Negro Education*, IX, No. 1 (January, 1940), 39–43.

Kelly, Alfred H. "The Congressional Controversy over School Segregation, 1867–1876," *American Historical Review*, LXIV, No. 3 (April, 1959), 537–63.

Kimball, Elsa P. *Sociology and Education: An Analysis of the Theories of Spencer and Ward*. Columbia University Studies in History, Economics and Public Law, No. 369. New York: Columbia University Press, 1932.

Kirkland, Edward C. *Business in the Gilded Age: The Conservatives' Balance Sheet*. Madison: University of Wisconsin Press, 1952.

—— *Dream and Thought in the Business Community, 1860–1900*. Ithaca: Cornell University Press, 1956.

—— *Industry Comes of Age: Business, Labor, and Public Policy, 1860–1897*. The Economic History of the United States, Vol. VI. New York: Holt, Rinehart and Winston, 1961.

Knight, Edgar W. *Public Education in the South*. Boston: Ginn, 1922.

LeDuc, Thomas. *Piety and Intellect at Amherst College, 1865–1912*. Columbia Studies in American Culture, No. 16. New York: Columbia University Press, 1946.

Lee, Gordon C. *The Struggle for Federal Aid, First Phase: A History of the Attempts to Obtain Federal Aid for the Common Schools, 1870–1890*. Teachers College Contributions to Education, No. 957. New York: Teachers College, 1949.

Lewis, Edward R. *A History of American Political Thought from the Civil War to the World War*. New York: Macmillan, 1937.

Lewis, Elsie M. "The Political Mind of the Negro, 1865–1900," *Journal of Southern History*, XXI, No. 2 (May, 1955), 189–202.

Logan, Rayford W. *The Negro in American Life and Thought: The Nadir, 1877–1901*. New York: Dial, 1954.

McCloskey, Robert G. *American Conservatism in the Age of Enterprise: A Study of William Graham Sumner, Stephen J. Field, and Andrew Carnegie*. Cambridge: Harvard University Press, 1951.

McConnell, Grant. *The Decline of Agrarian Democracy*. Berkeley: University of California Press, 1953.

McKenna, F. Raymond. "Policy Evolution in the National Education Association." Unpublished doctoral dissertation in education, Harvard University, 1954.

Mann, Arthur. "British Social Thought and American Reformers of the Progressive Era," *Mississippi Valley Historical Review*, XLII, No. 4 (March, 1956), 672–92.

—— *Yankee Reformers in the Urban Age*. Cambridge: Harvard University Press, 1954.

May, Henry F. *Protestant Churches and Industrial America*. New York: Harper, 1949.

Meier, August. "Toward a Reinterpretation of Booker T. Washington," *Journal of Southern History*, XXIII, No. 2 (May, 1957), 220–27.

Merriam, Charles E. *American Political Ideas: Studies in the Development of American Political Thought, 1865–1917*. New York: Macmillan, 1929.

Morgan, Arthur E. *Edward Bellamy*. New York: Columbia University Press, 1944.

Mott, Frank L. *A History of American Magazines*. 4 vols. Cambridge: Harvard University Press, 1938–57.

Nevins, Allan. *The Evening Post: A Century of Journalism*. New York: Boni & Liveright, 1922.

Noble, David W. *The Paradox of Progressive Thought*. Minneapolis: University of Minnesota Press, 1958.

Nye, Russel B. *Midwestern Progressive Politics: A Historical Study of Its Origins and Development, 1870–1950*. East Lansing: Michigan State College Press, 1951.

Persons, Stow. *American Minds: A History of Ideas*. New York: Holt, 1958.

Persons, Stow, ed. *Evolutionary Thought in America*. New Haven: Yale University Press, 1950.

Reed, Louis. *The Labor Philosophy of Samuel Gompers*. Columbia University Studies in History, Economics and Public Law, No. 327. New York: Columbia University Press, 1930.

Ross, Earle D. *Democracy's College: The Land-Grant Movement in the Formative Period*. Ames, Iowa: Iowa State College Press, 1942.

—— *The Liberal Republican Movement*. New York: Holt, 1919.

Saloutos, Theodore. *Farmer Movements in the South, 1865–1933*. University of California Publications in History, Vol. LXIV. Berkeley and Los Angeles: University of California Press, 1960.

Shannon, Fred A. *The Farmer's Last Frontier: Agriculture, 1860–1897*. The Economic History of the United States, Vol. V. New York: Rinehart, 1945.

Simkins, Francis B., and Robert H. Woody, *South Carolina during Reconstruction*. Chapel Hill: University of North Carolina Press, 1932.

Stewart, Frank M. *The National Civil Service Reform League: History, Activities, and Problems*. Austin: University of Texas Press, 1929.

Swint, Henry L. *The Northern Teacher in the South, 1862–1870*. Nashville: Vanderbilt University Press, 1941.

Ware, Norman J. *The Labor Movement in the United States, 1860–1895: A Study in Democracy*. New York: Appleton, 1929.

Wesley, Edgar B. *NEA: The First Hundred Years. The Building of the Teaching Profession.* New York: Harper, 1957.

White, Leonard D., with the assistance of Jean Schneider. *The Republican Era, 1869–1901: A Study in Administrative History.* New York: Macmillan, 1958.

Wilson, Francis G. *The American Political Mind: A Textbook in Political Theory.* New York: McGraw-Hill, 1949.

Woodward, C. Vann. *Origins of the New South, 1877–1913.* A History of the South, Vol. IX. Baton Rouge: Louisiana State University Press, 1951.

Wyllie, Irvin G. *The Self-made Man in America: The Myth of Rags to Riches.* New Brunswick: Rutgers University Press, 1954.

WORKS HAVING RELEVANCE FOR PART FOUR

PRIMARY

Abbott, Lyman. "The Rights of Man," *Outlook*, LXVIII, No. 7 (June 15, 1901), 396–401.

Academy of Political Science, New York. *The Revision of the State Constitution: A Collection of Papers, Addresses and Discussions Presented at the Annual Meeting of the Academy of Political Science in the City of New York, November 19 and 20, 1914. . . .* Albany: New York State Constitutional Convention Commission, 1915.

Allen, William H. *Efficient Democracy.* New York: Dodd, Mead, 1907.

American Academy of Political and Social Science. *The Initiative, Referendum and Recall. Annals,* XLIII, No. 132 (September, 1912).

American Federationist: Official Magazine of the American Federation of Labor. Vols. I–XXI. New York [etc.], 1894–1914.

Angoff, Charles. "When Truth Goes to War," *American Mercury*, XIII, No. 51 (March, 1928), 355–64.

Arnold, Thurman. *The Folklore of Capitalism.* New Haven: Yale University Press, 1937.

—— *The Symbols of Government.* New Haven: Yale University Press, 1935.

Babbitt, Irving. *Democracy and Leadership.* Boston: Houghton Mifflin, 1927. [Copyright 1924.]

Bagley, William C. "Educational Determinism; or, Democracy and the I.Q.," *School and Society*, XV, No. 380 (April 8, 1922), 373–84.

Barnes, Harry Elmer. *History and Social Intelligence.* New York: Knopf, 1926.

Batchelor, Bronson. *Profitable Public Relations.* New York: Harper, 1938.

Batchelor, Bronson, ed. *The New Outlook in Business*. New York: Harper, 1940.

Beard, Charles, ed. *America Faces the Future*. Boston: Houghton Mifflin, 1932.

Beck, James M. *The Passing of the New Freedom*. New York: Doran, 1920.

Bentley, Arthur F. *The Process of Government: A Study of Social Pressures*. Bloomington, Ind.: Principia, 1949. [Copyright 1908.]

Berle, A. A., Jr. *The 20th Century Capitalist Revolution*. New York: Harcourt, Brace, 1954.

Bernays, Edward L. *Crystallizing Public Opinion*. New York: Boni & Liveright, 1923.

—— "The Engineering of Consent," *Annals of the American Academy of Political and Social Science*, CCL (March, 1947), 113–20.

—— "The Minority Rules," *Bookman*, LXV, No. 2 (April, 1927), 150–55.

—— *Propaganda*. New York: Liveright, 1928.

Bingham, Alfred M. *Insurgent America: Revolt of the Middle Classes*. New York: Harper, 1935.

Bingham, Alfred M., and Selden Rodman, eds. *Challenge to the New Deal*. New York: Falcon, 1934.

Bourne, Randolph. *Education and Living*. New York: Century, 1917.

—— "Twilight of Idols," in *Untimely Papers*. New York: Huebsch, 1919.

Bowen, Howard R. *Social Responsibilities of the Businessman; with a Commentary by F. Ernest Johnson*. New York: Harper, 1953.

Brady, Robert A. *Business as a System of Power*. New York: Columbia University Press, 1943.

Bryan, William Jennings. *Speeches of William Jennings Bryan*. Revised and arranged by himself, with a biographical introduction by Mary Baird Bryan. 2 vols. New York: Funk and Wagnalls, 1911–13.

Butler, Nicholas Murray. "The Education of Public Opinion: An Address Delivered at the Annual Commencement of the University of Michigan." June 22, 1899. Ann Arbor, 1899.

—— *Is America Worth Saving? Addresses on National Problems and Party Policies*. New York: Scribner's, 1920.

—— *The Meaning of Education, and Other Essays and Addresses*. New York: Macmillan, 1903.

—— *Why Should We Change Our Form of Government? Studies in Practical Politics*. New York: Scribner's, 1912.

Calkins, Earnest Elmo. *Business, the Civilizer*. Boston: Little, Brown, 1928.

Campbell, Henry M. "Representative Government *versus* the Initiative and Primary Nominations," *North American Review*, CXC, No. 2 (August, 1909), 222–30.

Cannon, Cornelia J. "American Misgivings," *Atlantic Monthly,* CXXIX (February, 1922), 145–57.

Carver, Thomas N. *The Present Economic Revolution in the United States.* Boston: Little, Brown, 1926. [Copyright 1925.]

Chamberlain, John. *The American Stakes.* New York: Carrick & Evans, 1940.

Chase, Stuart, *et al. The Social Responsibility of Management.* New York: New York University School of Commerce, Accounts, and Finance, 1950.

Childs, Harwood L. *Labor and Capital in National Politics.* Columbus: Ohio State University Press, 1930.

Cohen, Morris. "Democracy Inspected," in *The Faith of a Liberal: Selected Essays.* New York: Holt, 1946.

Conant, James B. *Education in a Divided World: The Function of the Public Schools in Our Unique Society.* Cambridge: Harvard University Press, 1948.

Coolidge, Calvin. *America's Need for Education, and Other Educational Addresses.* Riverside Educational Monographs. Boston: Houghton Mifflin, 1925.

—— *The Price of Freedom: Speeches and Addresses.* New York: Scribner's, 1924.

Counts, George S. "Dare the School Build a New Social Order?" *John Day Pamphlets,* No. 11. New York: John Day, 1932.

—— *The Prospects of American Democracy.* New York: John Day, 1938.

Crecraft, Earl W. *Government and Business: A Study in the Economic Aspects of Government and the Public Aspects of Business.* Yonkers-on-Hudson and Chicago: World Book Co., 1928.

Creel, George. *How We Advertised America: The First Telling of the Amazing Story of the Committee on Public Information That Carried the Gospel of Americanism to Every Corner of the Globe.* New York: Harper, 1920.

Croly, Herbert. *Progressive Democracy.* New York: Macmillan, 1914.

—— *The Promise of American Life.* New York: Macmillan, 1909.

"The Curse of Propaganda," *Independent,* CX, No. 3833 (January 6, 1923), 4–5.

Dahl, Robert A. *A Preface to Democratic Theory.* Chicago: University of Chicago Press, 1956.

De Grazia, Sebastian. *The Political Community: A Study of Anomie.* Chicago: University of Chicago Press, 1948.

Dewey, John. *Characters and Events: Popular Essays in Social and Political Philosophy.* Edited by Joseph Ratner. 2 vols. New York: Holt, 1929.

—— *Democracy and Education: An Introduction to the Philosophy of Education*. New York: Macmillan, 1916.

—— *Individualism, Old and New*. New York: Minton, Balch, 1930.

—— *Liberalism and Social Action*. New York: Putnam, 1935.

—— *The Public and Its Problems*. New York: Holt, 1927.

De Witt, Benjamin P. *The Progressive Movement: A Non-partisan, Comprehensive Discussion of Current Tendencies in American Politics*. The Citizen's Library of Economics, Politics, and Sociology, New Series, ed. Richard T. Ely. New York: Macmillan, 1915.

"Direct Legislation Movement," *Independent*, XLIV, No. 3093 (March 12, 1908), 595–96.

Dougherty, J. Hampden. "Substitutes for the Recall of Judges," *Proceedings of the Academy of Political Science*, III, No. 2 (January, 1913), 99–108.

Downs, Anthony. *An Economic Theory of Democracy*. New York: Harper, 1957.

Eddy, Arthur J. *The New Competition: An Examination of the Conditions Underlying the Radical Change That Is Taking Place in the Commercial and Industrial World—the Change from a Competitive to a Coöperative Basis*. New York: Appleton, 1912.

Elliott, William Y. *The Pragmatic Revolt in Politics: Syndicalism, Fascism, and the Constitutional State*. New York: Macmillan, 1928.

Ezekiel, Mordecai. *Jobs for All through Industrial Expansion*. New York: Knopf, 1939.

—— *$2500 a Year: From Scarcity to Abundance*. New York: Harcourt, Brace, 1936.

Feiker, F. M. "The Profession of Commerce in the Making," *Annals of the American Academy of Political and Social Science*, CI (May, 1922), 203–7.

Filene, Edward A. *The Way Out: A Forecast of Coming Changes in American Business and Industry*. Garden City: Doubleday, 1924.

Follett, M. P. *The New State: Group Organization in the Solution of Popular Government*. New York: Longmans, Green, 1918.

Ford, Henry Jones, and David Jayne Hill. "Addresses Delivered before the Lawyers Club of New York on the Subject of Representative Government, by Professor Henry Jones Ford and Doctor David Jayne Hill, Saturday, January 13th, 1917." N.p., n.d.

Fortune, editors of. "Business-and-Government," *Fortune*, XXI, No. 3 (March, 1940), 38–39.

—— "The Public Is Not Damned," *Fortune*, XIX, No. 3 (March, 1939), 83–88, 109 ff.

Fortune, editors of, and Russell W. Davenport. *U.S.A.: The Permanent Revolution*. New York: Prentice-Hall, 1951.

Fox, Charles James. "Popular Election of United States Senators," *Arena*, XXVII, No. 5 (May, 1902), 455–67.

Frank, Glenn. *The Politics of Industry: A Footnote to the Social Unrest.* New York: Century, 1919.

—— "State Universities in State Politics," *Century*, CX, No. 1 (May, 1925), 121–24.

Frederick, J. George, ed. *A Philosophy of Production: A Symposium.* New York: Business Bourse, 1930.

—— *The Swope Plan: Details, Criticisms, Analysis.* New York: Business Bourse, 1931.

Friedrich, Carl J. *The New Image of the Common Man.* Boston: Beacon, 1950.

Galbraith, J. K. *The Affluent Society.* Boston: Houghton Mifflin, 1958.

—— *American Capitalism: The Concept of Countervailing Power.* Boston: Houghton Mifflin, 1952.

Garceau, Oliver. "Research in the Political Process," *American Political Science Review*, XLV, No. 1 (March, 1951), 69–85.

Garrett, Garet. "A Primer of Propaganda," *Saturday Evening Post*, CXCI, No. 29 (January 15, 1927), 3–5.

Gary, Elbert H. "Ethics in Business." Address at Northwestern University, June 17, 1922. N.p., n.d.

Ghent, William J. *Our Benevolent Feudalism.* New York: Macmillan, 1902.

Guthrie, William D. *Magna Carta, and Other Addresses.* New York: Columbia University Press, 1916.

Haan, Hugo. "American Planning in the Words of Its Promoters: A Bird's-Eye Survey Expressed in Quotations. . . ." Philadelphia: American Academy of Political and Social Science, 1932.

Hadley, Arthur T. *Baccalaureate Addresses, and Other Talks on Kindred Themes.* New York: Scribner's, 1907.

—— *Economic Problems of Democracy.* New York: Macmillan, 1923.

—— "An Educated Democracy," *University of California Chronicle*, XII, No. 5 (July, 1910), 207–22.

—— *The Education of the American Citizen.* New York: Scribner's, 1902.

—— *Standards of Public Morality.* American Social Progress Series, No. 2. New York: Macmillan, 1907.

—— *Undercurrents in American Politics.* New Haven: Yale University Press, 1915.

Haynes, George H. *The Election of Senators.* New York: Holt, 1906.

Heermance, Edgar L. *The Ethics of Business: A Study of Current Standards.* New York: Harper, 1926.

Herring, Edward Pendleton. *Group Representation before Congress.* Baltimore: The Johns Hopkins University Press, 1929.

—— *The Politics of Democracy: American Parties in Action*. New York: Norton, 1940.

Hill, David Jayne. *Americanism: What It Is*. New York: Appleton, 1917.

—— *The People's Government*. New York: Appleton, 1915.

Hoover, Herbert. *Addresses upon the American Road, 1933–1938*. New York: Scribner's, 1938.

—— *American Individualism*. Garden City: Doubleday, 1922.

—— *The Challenge to Liberty*. New York: Scribner's, 1934.

—— "Education as a National Asset," in National Education Association, *Proceedings of the Sixty-fourth Annual Meeting*, 1926, pp. 728–33.

—— "Higher Education and the State Government." Address at Commencement, University of Georgia, June 16, 1926. N.p., n.d.

—— *The New Day: Campaign Speeches of Herbert Hoover*. Stanford: Stanford University Press, 1928.

—— *The State Papers and Other Public Writings of Herbert Hoover*. Edited by William Starr Myers. 2 vols. Garden City: Doubleday, 1934.

Howe, Frederic C. *The City: The Hope of Democracy*. New York: Scribner's, 1905.

—— *The Confessions of a Reformer*. New York: Scribner's, 1925.

—— *Revolution and Democracy*. New York: Huebsch, 1921.

—— *Wisconsin: An Experiment in Democracy*. New York: Scribner's, 1912.

Ickes, Harold. *The New Democracy*. New York: Norton, 1934.

Irwin, Will. "An Age of Lies. How the Propagandist Attacks the Foundation of Public Opinion," *Sunset, the Pacific Monthly*, XLIII, No. 6 (December, 1919), 23–25, 54.

—— "If You See It in the Paper, It's ——?" *Collier's*, LXXII (August 18, 1923), 11–12.

—— "You Have a Sixth Sense for Truth," *Collier's*, LXXII (August 25, 1923), 13–14.

Jenks, Jeremiah H. *Business and the Government*. Modern Business Series of Alexander Hamilton Institute. New York: Alexander Hamilton Institute, 1917.

Johnson, Tom L. *My Story*. Edited by Elizabeth J. Hansen. New York: Huebsch, 1911.

Judson, Frederick N. *The Judiciary and the People*. New Haven: Yale University Press, 1913.

Kales, Albert M. *Unpopular Government in the United States*. Chicago: University of Chicago Press, 1914.

Kallen, Horace M. *The Education of Free Men: An Essay toward a Philosophy of Education for Americans*. New York: Farrar, Straus, 1949.

Kelley, Stanley, Jr. *Political Campaigning: Problems in Creating an Informed Electorate*. Washington: Brookings Institution, 1960.

Kemler, Edgar. *The Deflation of American Ideals: An Ethical Guide for New Dealers.* Washington: American Council on Public Affairs, 1941.

Kennedy, Gail. "The Process of Evaluation in a Democratic Community," *Journal of Philosophy,* LVI, No. 6 (March 12, 1959), 253–63.

Kent, Frank R. *The Great Game of Politics: An Effort to Present the Elementary Human Facts about Politics, Politicians, and Political Machines, Candidates and Their Ways, for the Benefit of the Average Citizen.* Garden City: Doubleday, 1923.

—— *Political Behavior: The Heretofore Unwritten Laws, Customs and Principles of Politics as Practiced in the United States.* New York: Morrow, 1928.

Kent, William. "Democracy and Efficiency." An Address at Harvard University, March 29, 1912. 63d Congress, 1st Session. Senate Document No. 302. Washington: Government Printing Office, 1913.

Key, V. O., Jr. *Politics, Parties, and Pressure Groups.* New York: Crowell, 1942.

Kilpatrick, William H., ed. *The Educational Frontier.* New York: Century, 1933.

La Follette, Robert M. *La Follette's Autobiography: A Personal Narrative of Political Experiences.* Madison, Wis.: La Follette Co., 1913.

Landon, Alfred M. *America at the Crossroads: Alfred M. Landon's Program for American Government. His Interpretation of the Political, Economic and Social Principles of the Republican Party.* With an introduction by Senator Arthur Capper. New York: Dodge, 1936.

Lasswell, Harold D. *Democracy through Public Opinion.* [Menasha, Wis.]: George Banta, 1941.

—— *Politics: Who Gets What, When, How.* New York: Whittlesey House, 1936.

—— *Propaganda Technique in the World War.* New York: Knopf, 1927.

—— *Psychopathology and Politics.* Chicago: University of Chicago Press, 1930.

Latham, Earl. "Anthropomorphic Corporations, Elites, and Monopoly Power," *American Economic Review,* XLVII, No. 2 (May, 1957), *Supplement,* pp. 303–10.

—— "Group Basis of Politics: Notes for a Theory," *American Political Science Review,* XLVI, No. 2 (June, 1952), 379–97.

Lee, Ivy L. *Publicity: Some of the Things It Is and Is Not. . . .* New York: Industries Publishing Company, 1925.

Lerner, Max, *It Is Later Than You Think: The Need for a Militant Democracy.* New York: Viking, 1938.

Lewis, Ben. "Economics by Admonition," *American Economic Review,* XLI, No. 2 (May, 1959), *Supplement,* pp. 384–98.

Lilienthal, David E. *Big Business: A New Era.* New York: Harper, 1953.

—— *TVA: Democracy on the March*. New York: Harper, 1944.

Lindeman, Eduard C. *The Meaning of Adult Education*. New York: New Republic, Inc., 1926.

Lindley, Ernest K. *Half Way with Roosevelt*. New York: Viking, 1936.

Lippmann, Walter. *Drift and Mastery: An Attempt to Diagnose the Current Unrest*. New York: Kennerly, 1914.

—— *Essays in the Public Philosophy*. Boston: Little, Brown, 1955.

—— *An Inquiry into the Principles of the Good Society*. Boston: Little, Brown, 1937.

—— *Liberty and the News*. New York: Harcourt, Brace, 1920.

—— *The Method of Freedom*. New York: Macmillan, 1934.

—— *The New Imperative*. New York: Macmillan, 1935.

—— *The Phantom Public*. New York: Harcourt, Brace, 1925.

—— *A Preface to Politics*. New York: Kennerly, 1914.

—— *Public Opinion*. New York: Harcourt, Brace, 1922.

Lobingier, Charles S. "Direct Popular Legislation: The Chief Objections Examined," *Arena*, XXXIV, No. 3 (September, 1905), 234–40.

Lodge, Henry Cabot. *The Democracy of the Constitution, and Other Addresses and Essays*. New York: Scribner's, 1915.

Lowell, A. Lawrence. *Public Opinion and Popular Government*. New ed. New York: Longmans, Green, 1914. [Copyright 1913.]

—— *Public Opinion in War and Peace*. Cambridge: Harvard University Press, 1923.

McCarthy, Charles. *The Wisconsin Idea*. New York: Macmillan, 1912.

McDougall, William. *The Indestructible Union: Rudiments of Political Science for the American Citizen*. Boston: Little, Brown, 1925.

—— *Is America Safe for Democracy? Six Lectures Given at the Lowell Institution of Boston under the Title "Anthropology and History, or the Influence of Anthropologic Constitution on the Destinies of Nations."* New York: Scribner's, 1921.

McGrath, Earl J. *Education, the Wellspring of Democracy*. University, Ala.: University of Alabama Press, 1951.

Mackenzie, William D. "Direct-Vote System," *Arena*, XXXIX, No. 2 (February, 1908), 131–41.

Martin, Everett D. *The Behavior of Crowds: A Psychological Study*. New York: Harper, 1920.

—— *Liberty*. New York: Norton, 1930.

Mason, Alpheus T. "Welfare Capitalism: Opportunity or Delusion?" *Virginia Quarterly Review*, XXVI, No. 4 (October, 1950), 530–43.

Mason, Edward S. "The Apologetics of Managerialism," *Journal of Business*, XXXI, No. 1 (January, 1958), 1–11.

Mason, Edward S., ed. *The Corporation in Modern Society*. Cambridge: Harvard University Press, 1959.

Mayo, Elton. *The Human Problems of an Industrial Civilization.* New York: Macmillan, 1933.

—— "The Political Problems of Industrial Civilization." Boston: Harvard University Graduate School of Business Administration, 1947.

—— *The Social Problems of an Industrial Civilization.* Boston: Harvard University Graduate School of Business Administration, 1945.

Mayo, H. B. *An Introduction to Democratic Theory.* New York: Oxford, 1960.

Mencken, H. L. *Notes on Democracy.* New York: Knopf, 1926.

Merriam, Charles E. *New Aspects of Politics.* Chicago: University of Chicago Press, 1925.

—— *On the Agenda of Democracy.* The Godkin Lectures, 1940–41. Cambridge: Harvard University Press, 1941.

Merrill, Harwood F., ed. *The Responsibilities of Business Leadership: Speeches at the 18th Annual Conference of Harvard Business School Alumni, 1948.* Cambridge: Harvard University Press, 1948.

Mills, Ogden L. *Liberalism Fights On.* New York: Macmillan, 1936.

—— *What of Tomorrow?* New York: Macmillan, 1935.

Moley, Raymond. *How to Keep Our Liberty: A Program for Political Action.* New York: Knopf, 1952.

Munro, William B. *The Invisible Government.* The Jacob H. Schiff Foundation Lectures Delivered at Cornell University, 1926. New York: Macmillan, 1928.

Munro, William B., ed. *The Initiative Referendum and Recall.* New York: Appleton, 1913.

National Association of Manufacturers. *Pamphlets,* Nos. 1–28, 1909–12.

National Economic League. *The Initiative and Referendum: Arguments Pro and Con by a Special Committee of the National Economic League.* Boston: National Economic League, 1912.

National Education Association. Committee on Social Economic Goals of America. "Implications of Social-Economic Goals for Education." Washington: National Education Association, 1937.

—— Educational Policies Commission. *The Unique Function of Education in American Democracy.* Washington: Educational Policies Commission and the Department of Superintendence, 1937.

Oberholtzer, Ellis P. *The Referendum in America: Together with Some Chapters on the Initiative and the Recall.* New ed., with supplement covering the years from 1900 to 1911. New York: Scribner's, 1911.

Odegard, Peter. *The American Public Mind.* New York: Columbia University Press, 1930.

—— *Pressure Politics: The Story of the Anti-Saloon League.* New York: Columbia University Press, 1928.

Overton, Gwendolen. "Democracy and the Recall," *Forum,* XLVII, No. 2 (February, 1912), 157–68.

Owen, Walter C. "The Progressive and Government," *La Follette's Weekly Magazine,* IV, No. 34 (August 24, 1912), 8 ff.

Pennock, J. Roland. *Liberal Democracy: Its Merits and Prospects.* New York: Rinehart, 1950.

[The President's Commission on Higher Education.] *Higher Education for American Democracy: A Report.* 6 vols. in one. New York: Harper, 1948.

Robinson, James Harvey. *The Mind in the Making: The Relation of Intelligence to Social Reform.* New York: Harper, 1921.

Rockefeller, John D., Jr. *The Personal Relation in Industry.* New York: Boni & Liveright, 1923.

Roe, Gilbert E. "Recall of Judges," *Proceedings of the Academy of Political Science,* III, No. 2 (January, 1913), 93–98.

Roosevelt, Franklin D. *The Public Papers and Addresses of Franklin D. Roosevelt.* Edited by Samuel I. Rosenman. 13 vols. New York: Random House/Harper, 1938–50.

Roosevelt, Theodore. *Progressive Principles: Selections from Addresses Made during the Presidential Campaign of 1912.* Edited by Elmer H. Youngman. New York: Progressive National Service, 1912.

—— *The Works of Theodore Roosevelt.* Edited by Herman Hagedorn. National ed. 20 vols. New York: Scribner's, 1926.

Root, Elihu. *Addresses on Government and Citizenship.* Edited by Robert Bacon and James B. Scott. Cambridge: Harvard University Press, 1916.

Ross, Edward A. *Changing America: Studies in Contemporary Society.* New York: Century, 1912.

—— *Sin and Society: An Analysis of Latter-Day Iniquity.* Boston: Houghton Mifflin, 1907.

—— *Social Psychology: An Outline and Source Book.* New York: Macmillan, 1908.

Schafer, Joseph. "Oregon as a Political Experiment Station," *Review of Reviews,* XXXIV, No. 2 (August, 1906), 172–76.

Schumpeter, Joseph. *Capitalism, Socialism, and Democracy.* 3d ed. New York: Harper, 1950. [Original copyright 1942.]

Sedgwick, Arthur G. *The Democratic Mistake: Godkin Lectures of 1910 Delivered at Harvard University.* New York: Scribner's, 1912.

Smith, Charles W., Jr. *Public Opinion in a Democracy: A Study in American Politics.* New York: Prentice-Hall, 1939.

Smith, J. Allen. *The Spirit of American Government: A Study of the Constitution: Its Origins, Influence and Relation to Democracy.* New York: Macmillan, 1907.

Smith, T. V. *The Democratic Way of Life*. Chicago: University of Chicago Press, 1926.

Soule, George. *The Coming American Revolution*. New York: Macmillan, 1934.

—— *A Planned Society*. New York: Macmillan, 1932.

Steffens, Lincoln. *The Shame of the Cities*. New York: McClure, Phillips, 1904.

—— *The Struggle for Self-Government: Being an Attempt to Trace American Political Corruption to Its Sources in Six States of the United States, with a Dedication to the Czar*. New York: McClure, Phillips, 1906.

Taft, William Howard. *Liberty under Law: An Interpretation of the Principles of Our Constitutional Government*. New Haven: Published for the University of Rochester by the Yale University Press, 1922.

—— *Popular Government: Its Essence, Its Permanence and Its Perils*. New Haven: Yale University Press, 1913.

[Thompson, Dorothy.] *Dorothy Thompson's Political Guide: A Study of American Liberalism and Its Relationship to Modern Totalitarian States*. New York: Stackpole, 1938.

Torelle, Ellen, ed. *The Political Philosophy of Robert M. La Follette as Revealed in His Speeches and Writings*. Madison, Wis.: La Follette Co., 1920.

Truman, David B. *The Governmental Process: Political Interests and Public Opinion*. New York: Knopf, 1951.

Tugwell, Rexford G. *The Battle for Democracy*. New York: Columbia University Press, 1935.

—— *The Industrial Discipline and the Governmental Arts*. New York: Columbia University Press, 1933.

Van Hise, Charles R. "The Place of the University in a Democracy," *School and Society*, IV, No. 81 (July 15, 1916), 81–86.

Veblen, Thorstein. *The Engineers and the Price System*. New York: Huebsch, 1921.

Wallace, Henry A. *New Frontiers*. New York: Reynal and Hitchcock, 1934.

Wallas, Graham. *Human Nature in Politics*. 3d ed. London: Constable, 1920. [Original copyright 1908.]

Warburg, James P. *Hell Bent for Election*. Garden City: Doubleday, Doran, 1935.

Ward, Paul W. *Intelligence in Politics: An Approach to Social Problems*. Chapel Hill: University of North Carolina Press, 1931.

Watson, John B. "Practical and Theoretical Problems in Instinct and Habits," in Herbert S. Jennings *et al.*, *Suggestions of Modern Science Concerning Education*. New York: Macmillan, 1917.

Weyl, Walter E. *The New Democracy: An Essay on Certain Political and Economic Tendencies in the United States.* New York: Macmillan, 1912.

—— "Tired Radicals," in *Tired Radicals, and Other Papers.* New York: Huebsch, 1921.

Whipple, Guy M. "The Intelligence Testing Program and Its Objectors— Conscientious and Otherwise," *School and Society,* XVII, No. 439 (May 26, 1923), 561–68, and XVII, No. 440 (June 2, 1923), 596–604.

White, William Allen. "Introduction" to Fremont Older, *My Own Story.* New York: Macmillan, 1926.

—— *The Old Order Changeth: A View of American Democracy.* New York: Macmillan, 1910.

Whitehead, T. N. *Leadership in a Free Society: A Study in Human Relations Based on an Analysis of Present-Day Industrial Civilization.* Cambridge: Harvard University Press, 1936.

Whyte, William H., Jr. *Is Anybody Listening? How and Why U.S. Business Fumbles When It Talks with Human Beings.* New York: Simon and Schuster, 1952.

—— *The Organization Man.* New York: Simon and Schuster, 1956.

Wickersham, George W. *The Changing Order: Essays on Government, Monopoly, and Education, Written during a Period of Readjustment.* New York: Putnam, 1914.

Wilcox, Delos F. *Government by All the People; or, The Initiative, the Referendum and the Recall as Instruments of Democracy.* New York: Macmillan, 1912.

Wilson, Woodrow. *A Crossroads of Freedom: The 1912 Campaign Speeches.* Edited by John Wells Davidson. With a Preface by Charles Seymour. New Haven: Published for the Woodrow Wilson Foundation by Yale University Press, 1956.

—— *The New Freedom: A Call for the Emancipation of the Generous Energies of a People.* New York: Doubleday, 1913.

—— *The Public Papers of Woodrow Wilson.* Edited by Ray S. Baker and William E. Dodd. Authorized ed. 6 vols. New York: Harper, 1925–27.

Wood, Richardson. "The Corporation Goes into Politics," *Harvard Business Review,* XXI, No. 1 (Autumn, 1942), 60–70.

SECONDARY

Aaron, Daniel. *Men of Good Hope: A Story of American Progressivism.* New York: Oxford, 1951.

Beale, Howard K. *A History of Freedom of Teaching in American*

Schools. Report of the Commission on the Social Studies, American Historical Association. Part XVI. New York: Scribner's, 1941.

Bendix, Reinhard, and Lloyd H. Fisher. "The Perspectives of Elton Mayo," *Review of Economics and Statistics,* XXXI, No. 4 (November, 1949), 312–19.

Birnbaum, Lucille C. "Behaviorism in the 1920's," *American Quarterly,* VII, No. 1 (Spring, 1955), 15–30.

Bremner, Robert H. *From the Depths: The Discovery of Poverty in the United States.* New York: New York University Press, 1956.

Butts, R. Freeman, and Lawrence A. Cremin. *A History of Education in American Culture.* New York: Holt, 1953.

Chamberlain, John. *Farewell to Reform: Being a History of the Rise, Life and Decay of the Progressive Mind in America.* New York: Liveright, 1932.

Childs, Marquis, ed. *Walter Lippmann and His Times.* New York: Harcourt, Brace, 1959.

Cochran, Thomas C., and William Miller. *The Age of Enterprise: A Social History of Industrial America.* New York: Macmillan, 1942.

Coker, Francis W. *Recent Political Thought.* New York: Appleton–Century, 1934.

Commager, Henry Steele. *The American Mind: An Interpretation of American Thought and Character since the 1880's.* New Haven: Yale University Press, 1950.

Cremin, Lawrence A. *The Transformation of the School: Progressivism in American Education, 1876–1957.* New York: Knopf, 1961.

Crick, Bernard. *The American Science of Politics: Its Origins and Conditions.* Berkeley and Los Angeles: University of California Press, 1959.

Cubberley, Ellwood P. *Public Education in the United States: A Study and Interpretation of American Educational History.* Rev. and enl. ed. Boston: Houghton Mifflin, 1934.

Curoe, Philip R. V. *Educational Attitudes and Policies of Organized Labor in the United States.* Teachers College Contributions to Education, No. 201. New York: Teachers College, 1926.

Curti, Merle. *The Growth of American Thought.* New York: Harper, 1943.

—— *The Social Ideas of American Educators.* Report of the Commission on the Social Studies, American Historical Association. Part X. New York: Scribner's, 1935.

Dabney, Charles W. *Universal Education in the South.* 2 vols. Chapel Hill: University of North Carolina Press, 1936.

Eagly, Robert V. "American Capitalism: A Transformation?" *Business History Review,* XXXIII, No. 4 (Winter, 1959), 549–68.

Edwards, Newton, and Herman G. Richey. *The School in the American*

Social Order: The Dynamics of American Education. Boston: Houghton Mifflin, 1947.

Filler, Louis. *Crusaders for American Liberalism.* New York: Harcourt, Brace, 1939.

Forcey, Charles. *The Crossroads of Liberalism: Croly, Weyl, Lippmann and the Progressive Era, 1900–1925.* New York: Oxford University Press, 1961.

Gabriel, Ralph. *The Course of American Democratic Thought: An Intellectual History since 1815.* New York: Ronald, 1940.

Glover, J. D. *The Attack on Big Business.* Boston: Graduate School of Business Administration, Harvard University, 1954.

Goldman, Eric. *Rendezvous with Destiny: A History of Modern American Reform.* New York: Knopf, 1952.

—— *Two-Way Street: The Emergence of the Public Relations Counsel.* Boston: Bellman Publishing Co., 1948.

Gras, N. S. B. "Shifts in Public Relations," *Bulletin of the Business Historical Society,* XIX, No. 4 (October, 1945), 97–148.

Greer, Thomas H. *What Roosevelt Thought: The Social and Political Ideas of Franklin D. Roosevelt.* East Lansing: Michigan State University Press, 1958.

Grimes, Alan P. *American Political Thought.* New York: Holt, 1955.

Heald, Morrell. "Management's Responsibility to Society: The Growth of an Idea," *Business History Review,* XXXI, No. 4 (Winter, 1957), 375–84.

Higham, John. *Strangers in the Land: Patterns of American Nativism, 1860–1925.* New Brunswick: Rutgers University Press, 1955.

Hofstadter, Richard. *The Age of Reform: From Bryan to F.D.R.* New York: Knopf, 1955.

—— *The American Political Tradition, and the Men Who Made It.* New York: Knopf, 1948.

Jenkin, Thomas P. "Reactions of Major Groups to Positive Government in the United States, 1930–1940: A Study in Contemporary Political Thought," *University of California Publications in Political Science,* I, No. 3 (1945), 243–408.

Kandel, I. L. *American Education in the Twentieth Century.* Cambridge: Harvard University Press, 1957.

Kandel, I. L., ed. *Twenty-five Years of American Education: Collected Essays.* New York: Macmillan, 1924.

Kaplan, Sidney. "Social Engineers as Saviors: Effects of World War I on Some American Liberals," *Journal of the History of Ideas,* XVII, No. 3 (June, 1956), 347–69.

Knight, Edgar W. *Fifty Years of American Education, 1900–1950: A Historical Review and Critical Appraisal.* New York: Ronald, 1952.

Knight, Edgar W. *Public Education in the South.* Boston: Ginn, 1922.

Lewis, Edward R. *A History of American Political Thought from the Civil War to the World War.* New York: Macmillan, 1937.

Lewis, Gordon K. "Twentieth-Century Capitalism and Socialism: The Present State of Anglo-American Debate," *Western Political Quarterly,* XII, No. 1 (March, 1959), 78–110.

Link, Arthur S. "What Happened to the Progressive Movement in the 1920's?" *American Historical Review,* LXIV, No. 4 (July, 1959), 833–51.

Mackenzie, W. J. M. "Pressure Groups: The 'Conceptual Framework,' " *Political Studies,* III, No. 3 (October, 1955), 247–55.

Maxwell, Robert S. *La Follette and the Rise of the Progressives in Wisconsin.* Madison: State Historical Society of Wisconsin, 1956.

May, Henry F. *The End of Innocence: A Study of the First Years of Our Own Time, 1912–1917.* New York: Knopf, 1959.

Merriam, Charles E. *American Political Ideas: Studies in the Development of American Political Thought, 1865–1917.* New York: Macmillan, 1929.

Mills, C. Wright. "The Contribution of Sociology to Studies of Industrial Relations," *Proceedings of the First Annual Meeting, Industrial Relations Research Association,* 1948, ed. Milton Derber, pp. 199–222. N.p., n.d.

Mowry, George E. *The California Progressives.* Berkeley: University of California Press, 1951.

—— *The Era of Theodore Roosevelt, 1900–1912.* The New American Nation Series. New York: Harper, 1958.

—— *Theodore Roosevelt and the Progressive Movement.* Madison: University of Wisconsin Press, 1946.

Noble, David W. *The Paradox of Progressive Thought.* Minneapolis: University of Minnesota Press, 1958.

Nye, Russel B. *Midwestern Progressive Politics: A Historical Study of Its Origins and Development, 1870–1950.* East Lansing: Michigan State College Press, 1951.

Persons, Stow. *American Minds: A History of Ideas.* New York: Holt, 1958.

Prothro, James W. *The Dollar Decade: Business Ideas in the 1920's.* Baton Rouge: Louisiana State University Press, 1954.

Regier, C. C. *The Era of the Muckrakers.* Chapel Hill: University of North Carolina Press, 1932.

Schlesinger, Arthur M., Jr. *The Coming of the New Deal.* Boston: Houghton Mifflin, 1958.

—— *The Crisis of the Old Order, 1919–1933.* Boston: Houghton Mifflin, 1957.

—— *The Politics of Upheaval*. Boston: Houghton Mifflin, 1960.

Scott, Andrew M. "The Progressive Era in Perspective," *Journal of Politics*, XX, No. 4 (November, 1959), 685–701.

Spitz, David. *Patterns of Anti-Democratic Thought: An Analysis and a Criticism, with Special Reference to the American Political Mind in Recent Times*. New York: Macmillan, 1949.

Stabley, Rhodes R. *Newspaper Editorials on American Education*. Philadelphia: The author? 1941.

Strout, Cushing. "The Twentieth-Century Enlightenment," *American Political Science Review*, XLIX, No. 2 (June, 1955), 321–39.

Sutton, Francis X., *et al. The American Business Creed*. Cambridge: Harvard University Press, 1956.

Taylor, Richard W. "Arthur F. Bentley's Political Science," *Western Political Quarterly*, V, No. 2 (June, 1952), 214–30.

UNESCO. *Contemporary Political Science: A Survey of Methods, Research and Teaching*. Publication No. 426. Paris: UNESCO, 1950.

Waldo, Dwight. *Political Science in the United States of America: A Trend Report*. Paris: UNESCO, 1956.

Walker, S. H., and Paul Sklar. "Business Finds Its Voice," *Harper's*, CLXXVI, Nos. 2–4 (January–March, 1938), 113–23, 317–29, 428–40.

Wesley, Edgar B. *NEA: The First Hundred Years. The Building of the Teaching Profession*. New York: Harper, 1957.

White, Morton. *Social Thought in America: The Revolt against Formalism*. New York: Viking, 1949.

Wilson, Francis G. *The American Political Mind: A Textbook in Political Theory*. New York: McGraw-Hill, 1949.

Younger, Edward. "Woodrow Wilson—the Making of a Leader," *Virginia Magazine of History and Biography*, LXIV, No. 4 (October, 1956), 387–401.

Index

Abbott, Lyman, 211, 214; quoted, 212-13

Academies: in republican era, 26, 27, 33; criticized by William Manning, 29; in Democratic thought, 65, 70; in conservative thought before 1861, 83, 86; obstacle to common schools, 104; in antebellum South, 128-29, 131

Adams, Charles Francis, Jr., quoted, 202, 203

Adams, John, 23, 28, 29

Advertising, 322; see also Public relations

Affluent Society, The (Galbraith), 331n

Agitation (concept), *see* Campaign of education

Agrarian democracy: in thought of workingmen, 46; in Democratic thought, 62; hailed in Virginia convention, 130; denied by proslavery theorists, 135

Agrarian radicalism: of working-class agitators, 52-53; of Orestes Brownson, 72; of workingmen, 116; target of proslavery theorists, 134; renounced by Ira Steward, 180

Agrarian unrest after 1865, 160-74; target of national leaders, 141, of professional educators, 158, 209, of middle-class liberals, 193, 198, 204; *see also* Farmers

Agricultural education, 175; *see also* Practical training

Agricultural experiment stations, 175

Agricultural Wheel: Declaration of Purposes, quoted, 168-69; committee report, quoted, 170

Alabama, educational legislation, 131

American Academy of Political and Social Science, *Annals, see Annals of the American Academy*

American Bar Association, committee report (1914), quoted, 287

American Capitalism: The Concept of Countervailing Power (Galbraith), 331n

American Economic Association, address by Ben W. Lewis, 294

American experiment, the, Robert Rantoul on, 66

American Federation of Labor, 208, 265; attitudes toward education, 178, 186-91, 366n20; compared with Grange, 178, 191-92; program, 186, 187, 191; compared with Knights of Labor, 186, 187, 191; compared with Farmers' Alliances, 187; report of committee, quoted, 188; compared with freedmen, 190

American Industries, editorial quoted, 291

American Institute of Instruction, addresses: by Robert Rantoul, 66; by Joseph Story, 75; by Theodore Parker, 96-97

Americanism: What It Is (Hill), 285

American Plutocracy, The (Howard), 172, 173

American Public Mind, The (Odegard), 318

American Social Science Association: address by A. D. Mayo, 147-48; memorial to Congress, quoted, 150

American Sunday School Union, 105-6, 351n4

American uniqueness, asserted: by Nicholas Biddle, 31; by Walt Whitman, 70; by conservatives before 1861, 79, 81; by Horace Mann, 99, 100

—— questioned: by workingmen, 45, 50; by Theodore Parker, 96, 97; by Horace Mann, 99, 100

Barnes, Harry Elmer, quoted, 307
Bascom, John, quoted, 212
Batchelor, Bronson, 297; quoted, 295, 296
Beard, Charles A., 254
Beecher, Lyman, 90, 94, 107, 108, 349n5; quoted, 107
Behaviorism, 308
Behavior of Crowds, The (Martin), 305
Belief in education: influence on thought of farmers after 1865, 167, 173-74, 175-76, on thought of labor movement after 1865, 178, 192, on democratic thought after 1865, 210, 242-43; criticized by Herbert Croly, 269; influence on contemporary thought, 328-29; obstacle to effective democracy, 334-35
Bellamy, Edward, 139, 169, 211, 218, 221-23, 224, 226, 234, 240, 264; quoted, 222, 223
Bentley, Arthur F., 317, 387n30
Bergson, Henri, 272
Berkeley, William, quoted, 16
Bernays, Edward L., 383n19; quoted, 305-6
Bible: used as school text, 105, 107-8; use advocated by Protestants, 107-8
Biddle, Nicholas, 30-31, 35, 39; quoted, 31
Bingham, Alfred M., 315
Bisbee, Horatio, 143, 151
Black, Jeremiah, 184
Blaine, James G., 184, 201
Blair, Henry W., 146, 152, 153, 155, 183; quoted, 143, 145, 151, 152-53, 155
Blair bills, 150, 151, 152, 156, 360n21
Boards of education, *see* Supervision of education
Bonaparte, Charles J., 205; quoted, 204, 205
Bosbyshell, William, 114
Boston, workingmen in, 344n14; quoted, 46-47
Boston Quarterly Review, articles by Orestes Brownson, 72
Boston Trades' Assembly, resolutions quoted, 180
Boston Trades' Union, 54
Bourne, Randolph, quoted, 279
Bowen, Thomas, quoted, 152

Brooks, John Graham, 226-27; quoted, 139
Brotherhood, *see* Fraternity
Brown, Joseph E., quoted, 132
Brown, Paul, 52-53; quoted, 52, 53
Brown, Rome G., quoted, 286
Brownson, Orestes, 95, 126-28, 136-37, 179; quoted, 72, 126, 127
Brownson's Quarterly Review, articles by Orestes Brownson, 126-27
Brown University, addresses at, 197, 198
Bryan, William Jennings, 168, 173-74
Bryant, William Cullen, 69, 70, 110
Building codes, 213
Bullock, Alexander H., quoted, 197, 198-99
Burke, Edmund, quoted by Joseph Story, 75
Bushnell, Horace, 78; quoted, 76, 108
Business leadership, *see* Business spokesmen; Leadership; Managerialism
Businessmen, after 1865: hailed by Andrew Carnegie, 235, 238, by N. P. Gilman, 238-39; *see also* Liberals, middle-class
Business spokesmen, after 1865: attitudes toward education, 210, 300; *see also* Liberals, middle-class
—— after 1900: theory of leadership, 283, 289-99; social theory, 290-91, 294, 297-99; political orientation, 290-91, 293-94, 295-96, 297-99; attitudes toward education, 291-92, 294-96, 299, 300; reaction to depression, 293-94, 295-96; adopt public relations, 295-96; adopt industrial relations, 297-99; aid formal education, 300; influence, 301, 302

Cabell, Joseph C., 32
California, University of, address by A. T. Hadley, 289-90
Call to Action, A (Weaver), 172
Calvinism, 93, 99, 104
Camp, George S., 119-21, 121-22, 123
Campaign of education (concept): advocated by PBK speakers, 76, 77; in Populist thought, 172, 173; in thought of labor movement after